ENGLISH LITERATURE ADVANCING THROUGH HISTORY 2
Renaissance Literature

Literature Series: 02

ENGLISH LITERATURE ADVANCING THROUGH HISTORY 2

Renaissance Literature

By Tatiana GOLBAN

Copyright © 2021 Transnational Press London

All rights reserved. This book or any portion thereof may not be reproduced or used in any manner whatsoever without the express written permission of the publisher except for the use of brief quotations in a book review or scholarly journal.

First Published in 2021 by TRANSNATIONAL PRESS LONDON in the United Kingdom, 13 Stamford Place, Sale, M33 3BT, UK.

www.tplondon.com

Transnational Press London® and the logo and its affiliated brands are registered trademarks.
Requests for permission to reproduce material from this work should be sent to: sales@tplondon.com

Paperback
ISBN: 978-1-80135-104-1
Digital
ISBN: 978-1-80135-105-8

Cover Design: Nihal Yazgan

Transnational Press London Ltd. is a company registered in England and Wales No. 8771684.

ENGLISH LITERATURE ADVANCING THROUGH HISTORY 2
Renaissance Literature

WITH THEORETICAL INTRODUCTION AND PRELIMINARIES

Tatiana GOLBAN

TRANSNATIONAL PRESS LONDON

2021

CONTENTS

Preface   1

Introduction   7
Approaching Literary Practice and Studying British Literature in History

Preliminaries   41
Learning Literary Heritage through Critical Tradition or Back to Tynyanov

Genre Theory for Drama   61

1. The Social and Cultural Scene   71
    1.1 The Intellectual Background
    1.1.1 Humanism
    1.1.2 Thomas More and *Utopia*
    1.2 The Idea of Literature as a Critical Concern in the Renaissance Period
    1.2.1 Philip Sidney and *The Defence of Poesie*: The Rise of the English Literary Criticism

2. The Period and Its Literary Practice   99
    2.1 Poetry
    2.1.1 Sonnet
    2.1.2 The Native Tradition
    2.1.2.1 John Skelton
    2.1.3 The Petrarchan Tradition
    2.1.3.1 Philip Sidney
    2.1.3.2 Edmund Spenser
    2.1.4 The Major Tradition
    2.1.4.1 William Shakespeare and the English Renaissance Sonnet
    2.2 Prose Fiction
    2.2.1 The Rise of the Picaresque Novel and Its Alternatives
    2.2.2 Thomas Nashe
    2.3 The Elizabethan and Jacobean Drama
    2.3.1 Origins, Features, and Typology
    2.3.2 The Pre-Shakespearean Dramatists
    2.3.2.1 Thomas Kyd
    2.3.2.2 Christopher Marlowe
    2.3.2.3 Robert Greene
    2.3.2.4 John Lyly
    2.3.3 William Shakespeare
    2.3.3.1 The Poet
    2.3.3.2 The Playwright
    2.3.3.2.1 *A Midsummer Night's Dream*
    2.3.3.2.2 *Macbeth*
    2.3.3.2.3 *Richard II*
    2.3.4 The Post-Shakespearean Dramatists
    2.3.4.1 John Fletcher

2.3.4.2 Francis Beaumont
2.3.4.3 Ben Jonson

Conclusion: The "Profitable Pleasure" of the Literature of English Renaissance — 203

References and Suggestions for Further Reading — 209

Index — 219

PREFACE

The present book is second in a series of works which aim to expose the complexity and essence, power and extent of the major periods, movements, trends, genres, authors, and literary texts in the history of English literature. Following this aim, the series will consist of monographs which cover the most important ages and experiences of English literary history, including Anglo-Saxon or Old English period, the Middle Ages, the Renaissance, the Restoration, neoclassicism, romanticism, Victorian Age, and the twentieth-century and contemporary literary backgrounds. The reader of these volumes will acquire the knowledge of literary terminology along with the theoretical and critical perspectives on certain texts and textual typology belonging to different periods, movements, trends, and genres. The reader will also learn about the characteristics and conventions of these literary periods and movements, trends and genres, main writers and major works, and the literary interaction and continuity of the given periods. Apart from an important amount of reference to literary practice, some chapters on these periods include information on their philosophy, criticism, worldview, values, or episteme, in the Foucauldian sense, which means that even though the condition of the creative writing remains as the main concern, it is balanced by a focus on the condition of thought as well as theoretical and critical writing during a particular period.

Articulating the literary phenomenon are literary voices and mediating its comprehension in the consciousness of the public are critical voices. Diachronically, they have different statuses. Homer, Euripides, Cervantes, Dante, Shakespeare, Donne, Austen, Dickens, Dostoyevsky, Proust, Joyce are among those literary voices whom the public has continuously perceived with an unchanged high intensity of interest and admiration. It is only natural that the "voice of an authentic author passes easier through time and possesses more longevity and resonance than that of the critics" (Munteanu, *Metamorfozele* 9). Indeed, Sarasin, Bayle, Lessing, Johnson, Herder, Taine, Sainte-Beuve, Gautier, Stephen, Lubbock are among those critical voices that can hardly be considered to be our contemporaries, and, in spite of the value of their critical discourse, time has eroded their ideas to such an extent that they do not constitute a viable presence in the contemporary literary theory and criticism any longer. Apart from these two groups, there is a third one represented by those poets, novelists and playwrights who manifested both as writers and critics. Here as well, with a few exceptions like T. S. Eliot, who is, to the present day, acclaimed as both writer and critic, or Pater, who is nowadays remembered mainly as critic not writer, the literary history has proven the assumption that in the case of the writer-critics, their literary voice attracts a wider audience and is more persistent in time than their critical one.

It also appears that literary work possesses eternal temporal validity due to its autonomous aesthetic value, whereas criticism provides points of view having temporary and transitory significance; in other words, criticism represents historical version of a particular type of approach to literature. Despite such claims, the vector of methodology in our series of books, dealing with the history of English literature, relies on Viktor Shklovsky, T. S. Eliot, Mikhail Bakhtin, and especially Yuri Tynyanov. In this issue of diachronicity, criticism, similar to literature, attempts to acquire longevity, but, contrary to literary work, whose system remains relatively stable in time, and because literary work necessitates a continuous actualization, critical endeavour requires a permanent renewal of its material. Hence literary criticism is in a continuous developmental process which, being influenced by different factors, involves constant and rapid transformation of its typology, methodology, concerns, and, especially, its attitudes and viewpoints.

What is the developmental process of English literary practice; and how it has come to constitute a particular system comprising various other systems representing different periods, genres, individual literary activities, and so on; along with its interrelatedness with the critical thinking having embarked on its own process of development, represent the main concerns of our books in the series.

As critical writing emerges with the appearance of creative writing, our emphasis on this interrelationship between literature and criticism sparks from the awareness that, particularly before the twentieth century, it is quite impossible to render literary history apart from literary criticism and theory, to separate the text from the context, as if trying to forget that literary criticism has roots in literary practice and vice-versa, and that most of the critics are actually practitioners of literature, rightly called "writer-critics" and situated between critical theory and imaginative writing as authors of two related discourses; only in English literature: Philip Sidney, Ben Jonson, John Dryden, Alexander Pope, Henry Fielding, Samuel Johnson, William Wordsworth, Samuel Taylor Coleridge, Percy Bysshe Shelley, Matthew Arnold, Walter Pater, Oscar Wilde, John Ruskin, Henry James, Virginia Woolf, T. S. Eliot, David Lodge, and many others. This awareness represents the starting point of the present books. Our main concern is to ensure that literary production is viewed in relation to literary criticism and the works of imaginative writing are examined in the light of the critical theory which inspires their creation and shapes their thematic and structural context, and vice-versa, the literary works shaping the critical thinking.

One of the most important writer-critics of all times and the exponent of English modernism, T. S. Eliot gave, towards the end of his life, his own definition of the type of criticism he had practiced, which is a highly revelatory statement, including for our own line of reasoning: "the best of my literary criticism", Eliot claims, is "a by-product of my private poetry-workshop; or a prolongation of the thinking that went into the formation of my own verse".

Other writers would use, or rather materialise, their own artistic credo and literary theory in their literary texts, such as Wordsworth reifying his theory of the origin of poetry from the Preface to *Lyrical Ballads* in his poems *The Prelude* and *Tintern Abbey*, or Pater exemplifying the principles of aestheticism in his novel *Marius the Epicurean*. For some, like for Sidney and Shelley, criticism was a means of defending the aesthetic value of literature; for others, criticism represented the instrument to be used in an attempt to found a new genre, as it did for Fielding and his "comic novel", or even to introduce into the contemporary culture and to validate a whole new literary movement, as it was for Wordsworth and Coleridge.

The interrelationship between literature and critical theory can be seen all the way through the periods, including the twentieth century, where the field of literary theory and criticism reveals a threefold perspective of development. First, one may argue that the development of literary criticism is dependent on literary genres and movements which are dominant in different periods. This is the case of literary criticism especially for the periods until the twentieth century. Douwe Fokkema and Elrud Ibsch (1-2) exemplify this aspect by the theory of classicism which "should be understood as a generalization of the drama and epic of the time"; similarly, the biographical method in criticism is viewed as "one of the effects of Romanticism, which drew largely on autobiographical material"; another example would be the psychological novel which "is responsible for the psychological approach in literary criticism"; also, "the view has been defended that Russian Formalism is indebted to the ideals and slogans of futurism". Second, which is mainly the case of literary scholarship in the nineteenth and twentieth centuries, trends and schools in literary criticism are related to or rather determined by the new developments in science, philosophy, and society. Fokkema and Ibsch again claim: "[t]here is an unmistakable influence of Freudian psychology in psychologically-oriented literary criticism" and "Marxist literary criticism has been intertwined with particular political and sociological views"; also, the "search for a literary system or structure has certainly been inspired by *Gestalt* psychology. Russian Formalism is not only indebted to futurism, but also to new developments in linguistics". Third, these critics argue, where some trends in literary criticism "are closer to new trends in creative literature, [and] others are directly related to current developments in scholarship and society", there are also trends which "are somewhere in between" or they rather emerge, in particular some of the twentieth-century trends in criticism, from within the interpretative perspectives of the discipline of literary theory and criticism itself (for instance, narratology developed by structuralism).

In most general terms, with focus on art and, in this respect, on literature as one of the arts, it is art criticism that provides the analysis, study, and evaluation of individual works of art, as well as the formulation of general principles for the examination of such works. Literary theory and literary criticism are particular manifestations of art criticism developed and applied for the understanding and evaluation of literature; they constitute two distinct but interrelated disciplines which co-exist and are interrelated with a third one, the discipline of literary history, all three representing actually our instruments of approach to English literature which is conceived and constructed by us in its historical movement following the formalist, or rather neo-formalist, assumption that literature is a system of various central and peripheral elements – just as periods, movements, trends, genres, subgenres, and so on, are – and the advancement of literature through history is the substitution of systems.

Focusing on literary practice, applying critical theory and emerging from within our own teaching experience, the books in the present series, dealing with the history of English literature, are theoretical and surveyistic, like a monograph, whereas their more practical and text-oriented aspect should appeal as a student handbook for didactic purposes, in which certain literary texts or fragments from texts belonging to various writers from different periods are analysed and compared with regard to their source, form, thematic arrangements, message, ideas, motifs, character representation strategies, intertextual perspectives, structural or narrative techniques, and other aspects. Theoretical component apart, it is equally important to focus on particular literary works dealing with various concerns and building up different thematic perspectives, such as the process of growing up of the protagonist, because a particular theoretical contribution has no validity and efficiency unless it is well-rooted in the reality of the literary discourse which would eventually provide its practical argumentation. Thematic consideration of the text is indispensable from its structural analysis, be it a lyrical poem stimulating discussions on the use of figurative language for musical and pictorial effects, or a narrative text involving elements of formal organization such as narrator, narrative, narration, point of view, voice, or the principle of chronotope.

Chronos and *topos*, time and place, play a significant role as counterparts of one single mechanism of literary approach to the development of literature, in general, and of the image of its persona rendered in the work, in particular, and specifically in fiction. For Bakhtin, the chronotope is of several types, and, concerning literature, in the "literary artistic chronotope, spatial and temporal indicators are fused into one carefully thought-out, concrete whole. Time, as it were, thickens, takes on flesh, becomes artistically visible; likewise, space becomes charged and responsive to the movements of time, plot and history. This intersection of axes and fusion of indicators characterizes the artistic chronotope" (Bakhtin, "Forms of Time" 84). In Bakhtin dealing with the novel, the "chronotope" – the name (literally, "time space") being given to "the intrinsic connectedness of temporal and spatial relationships that are artistically expressed in literature" – is a key-element in his theoretical framework on genre (an important organ of memory and no less important vehicle of historicity) and, in particular, in his theory of the novel.

We still consider that an attempt to provide the learners of literature with a comprehensive and analytically structured insight into the movement of the literature of a nation or that of the world, in general, through history can be better achieved by drawing on theories of genre, system, and literary development. And we still believe that some of the most congenial theorizations, still valid and viable nowadays – emerging in the most recent books of literary scholarship, such as in those by Linda Hutcheon with her "system" and "constant", and Bran Nicol with the "dominant" – belong to Yuri Tynyanov, whose main reasoning would be that literature is a system of dominant, central and peripheral, marginalized elements – to us, "tradition" (centre) versus "innovation" (margin) engaged in a "battle" for supremacy, demarginalization, and the right to form a new literary system – and the development or historical advancement of literature is the substitution of systems.

The rise and development of genres represent an important aspect of our discussion, but our main concern is the diachronic movement of English literature through its main periods, movements, and trends which succeed each other, and each has its origin in certain precursors by rejecting some previous literary manifestations and continuing others – where innovation would reject what was before tradition and continue what was before innovation, and vice-versa – as well as being influenced by various contemporary developments and socio-cultural conditions. For this, we rely primarily on more traditional but established and recognized approaches to national literature, particularly on Tynyanov elaborating on system and formalism, on the whole, chiefly its emphasis on internal factors in literary historical movement and change, which, given their applicability nowadays through some changed perspectives of theoretical and critical consideration, may be viewed and labelled as "neo-formalism".

In viewing the literature produced in Britain as a literary system, we follow Tynyanov; in adding the historical dimension to the rise and development of an English – and not only – literature, we follow Tynyanov and Bakhtin again, among others, but more importantly is that our approach to the movement of English literature through history is conceived to go cyclically from theory (the existing theoretical categories of literary analysis) to practice (the direct approach to a number of literary works following the appropriate conceptions and points of concern according to specific features of the chosen texts), and then again to theory, or rather new theoretical arrangements which we hope would emerge in order to be used again in one's endeavours at practical, text-oriented criticism. In both theoretical and practical cases, the main purpose is to disclose and investigate the development and advancement of literary practice in relation to literary theory and criticism, and in this respect, the books focus diachronically on English literature from its beginnings in the Anglo-Saxon period to the present. By their interdisciplinary perspectives involving literary history, literary theory, and literary criticism, the present volumes should be useful to experts in literary studies, professional scholars of literary history and criticism, or to a more general readership, or anyone concerned with theoretical and practical consideration and understanding of literature, in general, and of English literary phenomenon, in particular, and whose knowledge on certain aspects of literature and literary thought in Britain might be enriched by reading these books.

The works represent an attempt of academic research in the field of literature but also meet the requirements of a teaching aid. The main target is student audience and the intention of the books regards the needs of students in their literature classes, aiming at introducing them to the domain of literary history. To students new in the field, at least, the books would supply insight into the historical study of literature; for them, these works would become an accompaniment to a course on literary history; and, we believe, by reading these books, they would secure a reliable grounding in major authors, texts, genres, subgenres, literary movements, trends, and periods. From the incompleteness and disembodiment of bibliographical assistance with regard to certain matters of concern, we believe to have progressed to certain interpretative modalities of our own, which consider the wholeness and complexity of the British literary history. These interpretative arrangements receive ultimate practical argumentation through direct approach to certain authors and their major texts, and they have been also validated by our teaching experience at universities in Turkey, Romania, and Moldova.

Our books are basically a survey tracing the development of British literature and literature related critical and theoretical thinking both as a unique experience and within the larger context of British and Western cultural and literary tradition. The first book in the series focuses diachronically on English literary phenomenon from its Anglo-Saxon beginnings to the end of the Middle Ages and covers the first two periods and experiences of English literary history, which are the Old English (Anglo-Saxon) and medieval ones. This second book considers the movement of English literature from the 1480s to the 1620s and covers the next periods and experiences of English literary history, namely the Renaissance, in general, and, in particular, Humanism, Reformation, and the Elizabethan Age. The third book is about the seventeenth century and offers insight into its main literary manifestations, including metaphysical poetry, Puritanism, and the Restoration. The fourth book considers the eighteenth century and covers some of the most important periods and experiences of the history of English literature in this long, complex and creatively potent age, namely neoclassicism, the rise of the English novel, and pre-romanticism. The fifth book in the series focuses on the period from the 1780s to the 1830s and covers one of the most important periods and experiences of English literary history, which is that of romanticism. The sixth book discloses the essence of the literary development in Britain from the 1830s to 1900 and focuses on other important periods and manifestations of English literary history, which are assigned together as the literature of the Victorian Age, in general, and, in particular, are known as post- and neo-romantic literature, realism, naturalism, and the avant-garde encompassing aestheticism, symbolism, and Pre-Raphaelite Brotherhood. The seventh book in the series is about the development of English literature in the twentieth century and focuses on the first half of the century with its Edwardian literature, the rise of modernism and experimental fiction, its poetry and drama, as well as the traditional literature of the period. The eighth book covers the second half of the twentieth century and offers an insight also into the contemporary literary background; its direct reference is to the post-war new realism of the Angry Young Men and other manifestations of the traditional novel versus a more visionary and philosophical continuation of the modernist and experimental trends, but the emphasis is on the postmodern theory along with postmodernism in its literary expression in fiction, poetry and drama, as well as on more recent alternatives to the postmodern thought and literary practice.

Before actually entering into the period or century in order to discuss its authors, works, movements, trends, culture, philosophy, critical thinking, and so on, our books contain an introductory part aimed to assist the reader to form an opinion on what is literature, what are the approaches to literature, and what are the major periods, movements, trends, authors and texts in the history of British and European literature. Coming after Introduction, the Preliminaries, relying on Yuri Tynyanov and others, would strengthen the understanding of literature as a system and the diachronic movement of literature as the substitution of systems whose central and marginal elements, tradition and innovation are in perpetual interaction and fight, rejection and continuation in order to build up – also as influenced by contemporary socio-cultural stimuli – new systems which we see as periods, movements, trends, genres, subgenres, and so on. Also, in three books in the series dealing with those periods in which a particular genre emerged to dominate the literary scene, there are chapters dedicated to the theoretical, methodological, terminological, and practical consideration of the narrative, lyrical, and dramatic genres. Namely, the theory of drama is explicated in the book on the Renaissance; lyrical genre is theoretically introduced and explained in the book on the seventeenth-century English literature; and, given the rise of the English novel in the eighteenth century, the book on this period contains a theoretical part on the narrative genre, including fiction, narrative poetry, categories and elements of narrative organization, and so on.

Apart from this, in every book of the series, the special emphasis is on those authors who manifested as important writers in the history of British literature, those who developed a national literary discourse making it a part of international cultural heritage. Their names need to be known, their main literary texts understood, and the historical order of events properly grasped in order to comprehend systemically and coherently the rise and development of English literature as a process, a diachronic advancement which encompasses periods, literary movements and trends, genres and subgenres, major authors and texts. Whether or not and to what extent this desideratum is likely to be accomplished by our endeavours, we shall see in the following.

INTRODUCTION

APPROACHING LITERARY PRACTICE AND STUDYING BRITISH LITERATURE IN HISTORY

> *Keywords*: literacy, popularity, consumerism, literature, literary system, communication, aesthetic value, approach to literature, literary history, literary criticism, literary theory, diachronic versus synchronic, objective versus subjective, substitution of systems, innovation versus tradition, centre versus margin, to follow, to continue, to reject, contemporary stimuli, period, movement, trend, genre, author, literary work, text, ancient period, medieval period, modern period, postmodern period, post-postmodern period

In terms of a media-culture perspective, the decline of literacy and the indefinite future of the imaginative writing are nowadays matters of general lament, as it is the fact that literature might have lost its primary role to satisfy the aesthetic and intellectual needs of the post-postmodern man. Facing a complexity of new cultural alternatives, our contemporaries display exaggerated confidence in television, cinema, computers, and Internet; they often watch television or surf the net web-pages instead of reading books, use compact discs for learning languages or getting acquainted with Dickens's novels. The books, then, would apparently survive a limited time in the human cultural store, and many of them are in danger of being forgotten in a remote corner of an old library.

The concept of literacy is an essential principle for the survival of the books, yet, besides literature, literacy refers to many other types of mass communications and theories of mass culture, and literature is not the only reliable vehicle for cultural communication, or improvement of modern thought, or acquisition of information. In some of these respects, one may argue, television and computer are much more reliable, practical, and resourceful tools than the whole of imaginative writing.

On the other hand, the invention of television and the computer has not decreased the printing of books; moreover, the computer screen, Internet, and communication through e-mail display more alphabetic letters than images. Also, as every human being has a novel inside, critics metaphorically claim, "web-fiction" and other forms of online writing have allowed imaginative flight of the people to increase and their creativity to flourish.

The problem is not to oppose visual and written types of cultural communication. It is that, though the whole of image-oriented culture and media attempts to reify a new form of literacy, the problem consists in a general illiteracy caused by the open exposure to a form of visual illiteracy of the media and the insufficient exposure to important and mind-appealing books. In vindicating the role of imaginative literature, "do not fight against false enemies", argues Umberto Eco, because, first of all,

> we know that books are not ways of making somebody else think in our place; on the contrary they are machines which provoke further thoughts. Secondly, if once upon a time people needed to train their memory in order to remember things, after the invention of writing they had also to train their memory in order to

remember books. Books challenge and improve memory. They do not narcotize it. This old debate is worth reflecting on every time one meets a new communicational tool which pretends or appears to replace books. (Eco, *Apocalypse Postponed* 89-90)

Drama, poetry, and fiction have a long developmental history starting in ancient period; they have continuously developed types, forms, concerns, and for this, they are free from the danger of not surviving for years and centuries in the human cultural depository, or of becoming a handful of dust in a remote corner of an old forgotten library. They focus on those issues and tackle those thematic perspectives which reflect the period, its culture, answer to the aesthetic needs of the reader as a form of entertainment or didactic principles, and are imaginatively disclosed and theoretically and critically scrutinized.

Another criterion of their and literature, in general, survival is popularity which is provided and determined by consumerist, public and market demand, and another one is their literacy, or aesthetic validity, which is assessed and supported by academic and critical evaluation.

Today both concepts – popularity and literacy as essential principles of their survival – comprise many types of mass communication and theories of mass culture. According to this media-culture perspective, during the last decades a number of worrying reports have been produced in Western countries on the decline of literary value and the future of imaginative literature. One reason, perhaps, would be the overconfidence in and reliance on technology, internet, cinema, and other forms of communication, of which some have become alternative forms of art and which, apart from traditional arts, including literature, are simultaneously our contemporary forms of art and our contemporary sources of *utile et dulce*.

In order to keep literature at least on the same level with the newly emerged forms of art, strengthen its status, show and defend its aesthetic validity, a repeated insight into the historical advancement of the literary phenomenon is still a valid matter of scholarly concern, and, to us, also a matter of didactic interest aimed to assist the students in their literature classes. In this respect, the following issues are to be answered in this introductory part of the book:

---
1. **What is Literature?**
2. **Approaches to Literature**
3. **The History of British and European Literature: Periods, Movements, Trends, Authors, and Texts**

In relation to our attempts to provide a concise surveyistic perspective of **3. The History of British and European Literature** in order to assist students better comprehend its major periods, movements, trends, authors, and texts, prior to this, questions such as

---
What is a literary period?
What is a literary movement?
What is a literary trend?
Are there any differences between movement and trend?
---

would help our endeavour.

Another issue – **4. Literary Genres** – is equally important in literary studies; in our series of books, for didactic purposes, this theoretical aspect is the concern not in this introductory part but in certain chapters in books on specific literary periods and movements: theory of drama in the book on the Renaissance, poetry in the book on the seventeenth century, and fiction in the book on the eighteenth-century English literature.

1. What is Literature?

As for the definition, literature, a cultural phenomenon, one of the arts, the verbal art, is in the simplest way defined as imaginative writing. Apart from the long established opinion that literature is "imaginative writing", literature is also "creative writing" since it "employs a special form of language, more evocative and "conative" than that used in other forms of writing" (Castle 6).

Based on a strong critical tradition, having its roots in Saussurean declaration of language to be a system of signs as well as in the formal, including formalist and structuralist, critical theory, literature is understood as a system of elements framed within the boundaries of a communicative situation. The term "literature" is therefore used to designate "a certain body of repeatable or recoverable acts of communication" (Scholes 18).

It should be agreed, however, that in literature, like in art in general, the purpose is not only the communication of fact but also a kind of aesthetic communication involving "the telling of a story (either wholly invented or given new life through invention) or the giving of pleasure through some use of the inventive imagination in the employment of words" (Daiches 4-5).

Being a kind of "writing", literature uses language in "peculiar ways", "offending" language and deviating from its ordinary use; literature "transforms and intensifies ordinary language, deviates systematically from everyday speech" (Eagleton 2). It seems that this peculiarity of every artistic endeavour – be it literary or musical – to "deviate", "offend", "destroy" in order to create – was long ago acknowledged by the artist himself or herself, as to remember just *A Musical Instrument* by Elizabeth Barrett Browning.

Because its material is language, made of words expressed in relation to creative imagination, and besides its aspect of communication, the second important function of literature is the aesthetic one. Both functions are interrelated and of equal importance. The object of literature is the subjective and objective universe, the inner and outer world, and the verbal matter which materialises this object forms the beauty, which is established under the sign of joy and integrity and is in this condition communicated to the public.

In linguistic terms, the six elements in communication, in general, as identified by Roman Jakobson in *Linguistics and Poetics* (1963), drawing on Tynyanov's and formalist basic term "system" of elements, are the following (Jakobson 34):

Addresser	Context Message Contact Code	Addressee	- the addresser (usually but not necessarily the same as the sender) - the addressee (usually but not necessarily the same as the receiver) - the message (the particular linguistic form) - the context (the referent or information, or more precisely, the contextual information on the world in which the message takes place; the social and historical framework in which the utterance is made; also, it refers to the circumstances or conditions relevant to a fact – a setting in which events occur; more recently, as prompted by Bakhtin, it is part of a text which determines its meaning, since the meaning cannot be understood outside the context) - the contact (the medium or channel; the physical channel and psychological connection between addresser and addressee) - the code (the language common to both addresser and addressee, which permits communication to occur)

In the same study, Jakobson shows that corresponding to each element in this taxonomy is a particular function of language:

Emotive	Referential Poetic Phatic Metalingual	Conative	- the emotive (to communicate inner feelings and states) - the conative (to attempt to determine/affect the behavior of the receiver) - the referential (to carry information in order to describe a situation, object, state) - the poetic (to focus on linguistic form) - the phatic (to open the channel for practical or social reasons) - the metalingual (to focus on language or dialect in order to clarify it or change it)

Literature as a system, the literary system, constitutes a literary discourse to be communicated to the reader; in other words, it is involved in a literary communicative situation. The structure, simple but relevant to any learner of literature, is provided by Guy Cook. He shows that the six elements in communication, as identified by Jacobson in *Linguistics and Poetics*, each having a corresponding function of language, receive in literary communication their equivalent counterparts: "addresser" or "sender" is the "author" or "writer", "message" is the "text", "addressee" or "receiver" is the "reader", and so on. They constitute the elements of the literary system. Guy Cook identifies and places these elements in a simple but comprehensive structure of the literary communicative situation (128):

		Society	
Author	Text	(Performer)	Reader
	Texts	Language	

Every literary work represents a text, written or oral; it is a particular individual verbal expression, the product of an author, known to us or anonymous. The literary work addresses a reader. Even if no one has yet read a given text, the author is its reader. The material and means of expression of the text is language. It is produced in relation to a certain social background; it is the result of the literary production of an epoch, country, region; it is the expression of the social relations which occur at a certain historical moment. The literary work always exists in relation to other texts, which represent previous literary traditions or the period which is contemporary to the given literary work, by which disclosing intertextual relations on the structural and, above all, thematic level.

2. Approaches to Literature

The consumption of literature and the apprehension of its aesthetic values and effects go hand in hand with the approach to literature. The approach to literature has shown itself as a modality capable enough to reassure and strengthen the role of imaginative writing as an agent able to satisfy the intellectual needs of the humans by its permanent re-evaluation of the past national and international literary heritage as well as by its study and evaluation of the contemporary literary practice, in the context of what Matthew Arnold, during Victorian times, defined and described literary criticism as a disinterested effort or endeavour to learn and propagate the best which is known and thought in the world.

This endeavour, the nineteenth-century scholar believes, is the "real estimate", the real approach to literature leading to its true understanding and to "a sense for the best, the really excellent, and of the strength and joy". These ideas seem nowadays superfluous and obsolete, being long ago rejected and replaced by the more scientific and methodological critical perspectives of formalism, structuralism, psychoanalysis, deconstruction, and other approaches developed by the twentieth-century literary theory and criticism.

In the most general terms, the previous and subsequent to Matthew Arnold periods have developed in the field of literary studies three major perspectives of approach to literature, three directions offering theoretical and practical possibilities to study and understand literature, and which are commonly referred to as critical, theoretical and historical.

The three approaches to literature – literary theory (the theory of literature), literary criticism, and literary history (the history of literature) – despite the huge debates over their functions and even necessity, represent three distinct scientific disciplines with their own definitions, characteristics, terminology, objects of study, and methodologies. They are interconnected, having obvious points of identification and separation.

Prior to the discussion of these disciplines either from a historical perspective or as looking at their contemporary status, it is necessary to clarify their definitions, concerns, aims, relation to diachronic and synchronic elements, and to subjectivity and objectivity, as well as their interrelationship, interdependence and usefulness in the understanding of the literary phenomenon.

The standard dictionary definition regards history of literature or literary history as the diachronic approach to literature which focuses on literary periods, movements, trends, doctrines, and writing practice (authors and works), all that represents the "objective facts of literary history" (Jauss, *Toward an Aesthetic of Reception* 51). Although in the contemporary state of terminology, "literary history" and "history of literature" are considered synonymous, it is also claimed that "history of literature gathers and classifies literary works, whereas literary history places and tries to explain these works by relating them to a series of historic, social, political, ideological, and cultural determinants" (Gengembre 4).

The modern "literary history was created in the Romantic age" (Perkins 338), with Herder in Germany as its founder, Madame de Staël and Chateaubriand in France, and in England with Robert Lowth, Thomas Percy, and especially Thomas Warton's *History of English Poetry* (1774-1781), which came to replace the older history of learning (*historia litterarum*) as promoted by Francis Bacon.

Literary criticism is the study, analysis, investigation, or approach to particular literary texts on both thematic and structural levels. Criticism interprets the text, discloses its meaning, and mediates between the text and the reader. If there are debates whether the average reader needs or not any help from criticism, concerning professional readers, academics and students, criticism has definitely acquired a solid position in the field of literary education, in which "criticism is both an end and a means, the natural culmination of study of an author and the instrument of literary training" (Culler, *Structuralist Poetics* vii).

In the process of critical interpretation, the complete meaning emerges out of the investigation of both content and form, thematic and structural dimensions of the text which are organically fused, since it is impossible to separate "what" is said in a literary work, or "what" is the text about, from "how" it is said, or the "way" in which the text is written.

The task of criticism as interpretation has a long history, from the medieval Biblical interpretation to "self-consciousness about the problem of textual meaning introduced by the Biblical hermeneutics associated with Schleiermacher at the beginning of the nineteenth century" (Collini 3-4) and then throughout the entire text and texts oriented theories of formalism, New Criticism, structuralism, and poststructuralism.

The theory and practice of interpretation range from the attempt to establish the exact meaning to Saussure's insistence on the arbitrariness of the signifier, Derrida's claim about the instability of all meaning in writing, and a more recent method by Umberto Eco of "interpreting the world and texts based on the individuation of the relationships of sympathy that link microcosm and macrocosm to one another" (Eco, "Overinterpreting texts" 45).

Literary theory looks at the nature of literature itself; it develops and offers terms, concepts, rules, criteria, categories, general strategies, methodologies and principles of research of the literary phenomena, including the text and other elements of the literary system. Theory "may connote a poetics or aesthetics concerned not with interpretation of texts but with theorising discourse in general" (Selden, "Introduction" 2).

Furthermore, theorizing within the field of literary studies "may have various objectives", but "the main aim has been to answer the question "What is literature?" Discourses addressing this question have traditionally been called "poetics", more recently "theory of literature"" (Fowler 3). In short, literary theory is "the systemic account of the nature of literature and of the methods for analysing it" (Culler, *Literary*

Theory 1).

Concerning the concepts of "diachronic" versus "synchronic", if the first, historical approach or history of literature embarks on a diachronic perspective in literary studies and investigates the development of national and world literature, the second, literary criticism, is considered synchronic, and the third one, literary theory, is referred to as general and universal.

In matters of subjectivism and objectivism, literary history and, especially, literary theory are designated as sciences, requiring normative and methodological objectivism. Literary criticism is also required to be objective and to concentrate solely on text, not context: as seen by Stanley Fish in *Yet Once More*, the literary critic "is a specialist, defined and limited by the traditions of his craft, and it is a condition of his labours (...) that he remain distanced from any effort to work changes in the structure of society" (Machor and Goldstein 29). Literary criticism, however, "cannot avoid being partial and selective" (Lodge 63).

Literary criticism, indeed, allows subjectivism to intermingle with objective reasoning, art with science, fusing in one discourse the personal responses to literature and the scientific research, but what the critical discourse requires most is the accurate balance between the subjective and objective components.

The predominance of subjective element makes a certain type of criticism to be more "practical", "personal", or, as it is often called, "impressionistic criticism" in which, usually in the form of essay, "you wrote about your feelings, perhaps saying how moving you found a poem or how it reminded you of something in your own experience" (Peck and Coyle 177). The essay form is particularly popular among the Anglo-American critics and writer-critics, being the most "creative" critical writing. It is then only normal that the great writer-critics of the twentieth century T. S. Eliot and Virginia Woolf embraced this form, the latter, in particular, taking "full advantage of the liberties of the essay form, drawing her readers into playful digressions, allegorical fancies, unanswerable queries, and inconclusive reveries, inviting us through a collaborative "we" to join in an unchaperoned dance of impressions and ideas" (Baldick 257).

On the contrary, the reliance on theory rather than on personal impressions makes the critical text objective, neutral, at the same time "theoretical" or belonging to "academic criticism", which is "more analytic (...) commenting on the subject matter and method of the text" (Peck and Coyle 177). According to their methods and principles, in addition to practical, impressionistic, and theoretical, the critics are also categorized as formal, historical, moral, analytical, descriptive, affective, psychological, and so on.

The principle of separation within critical practice works on the more general level amid the three disciplines as well. There are many and influential voices that isolate literature and literary criticism from historical context and literary history, to mention just I. A. Richards and F. R. Leavis. There are even voices that separate criticism from theory, arguing that the theoretical account of literature "isn't useful in criticism, and will simplify, if attempted, encumber critics with "preconceived ideas" which will get between them and the text" (Barry 20).

> Where does the scientific/objective component in literary criticism come from? The answer is to be found in a more detailed presentation of the specificity of each of the three approaches to literature and in the explanation of the relationship of the three approaches to literature.

We have seen that literary history, or the history of literature, like literary theory and criticism, studies literature on the whole and the particular elements of the literary system.

> However, if the contemporary field of literary theory and criticism discusses the literary work as a synchronic phenomenon, removing the text from its temporal and spatial context, the history of literature performs a historical (diachronic) investigation of literature and studies the national and world literary development in relation to its periods, movements, trends, writers and works.

It is a critical, or rather metacritical, cliché in the Anglo-American academic world to start a book on literary theory and criticism by bringing into discussion Rene Wellek and his view (in *Concepts of Criticism*, 1963) of literary criticism as dealing with concrete works of art and that of literary theory as "the study of the principles of literature, its categories, criteria, and the like".

It is also a cliché to mention the name of Matthew Arnold and his definition of criticism as "a disinterested endeavour to learn and propagate the best that is known and thought in the world".

This definition is for many people a reason enough to claim that both literary theory and literary criticism should rely on science, objectivity, reason, method, and terminology, and reject creativity and imaginative flight. This opinion would contradict the claims by Raman Selden and Geoffrey Hartman that "critical and theoretical writing could assume a status equal to the literature it had once been thought to serve" (Stevenson 88-89). Likewise, in the twentieth century, Northrop Frye said that the "subject-matter of literary criticism is an art, and criticism is evidently something of an art too" (3).

Against Frye are those who consider literary criticism to be a science, among whom T. S. Eliot, who claims criticism to be scientific by focusing on technical analysis; also, Wellek and Warren, in the celebrated *Theory of Literature* (1949), call criticism "a species of knowledge or of learning"; and Roman Jakobson, who in *Linguistics and Poetics*, uses instead of "criticism" the term "poetics" or "literary study" and demands poetics to be an integral part of linguistics, since linguistics is the "global science of verbal structure".

Siding with Frye are those who view criticism as art, among whom Friedrich Schlegel and his famous statement on literary criticism: "Poetry can only be criticized by way of poetry. A critical judgement of an artistic production has no civil rights in the realm of art if it isn't itself a work of art". D. H. Lawrence, in *John Galsworthy*, calls criticism an art because it is too personal and based on emotion, not reason; Wilde, in *The Critic as Artist*, views criticism as full art emerging from the same imagination and creativity which are required by the literary work it criticises; whereas others see criticism "an art, although only a minor one" (Gardner 6). Theories are employed and methodologies and concepts are used, but most critics "have seen their profession not as a science but essentially an art, i.e., the art of commenting illuminatingly on literary works, of explaining and assessing them so as to increase our understanding and appreciation of literature" (Shusterman 213).

And it is the condition of the writer-critics to stand apart from other types of critics and be the first to promote criticism to the high sphere of creativity and imaginative flight, even against all threats of becoming subjective, defensive, combative, prescriptive, reflexive and slaves of literary practice.

The current critical theory, be it art or a scientific method of literary analysis, displays immense vitality and productivity, representing a complex phenomenon of theoretical diversity and intellectual collision, and being a true exponent of globalization and internationalization. This aspect is remarkably captured by the writer-critic David Lodge in his trilogy of campus novels; in his non-fictional works, Lodge also conceives highly of literary criticism, which is for him a "highly developed intellectual discipline" and "since its subject is human eloquence it has a responsibility to maintain as much continuity as possible with human discourse" (Lodge 41).

> Leaving aside the debates on scientific/objective versus creative/subjective binary opposition in literary studies, it is more important to assume that literary theory, literary criticism, and literary history (history of literature) are interrelated and interdependent, and co-exist in the field of literary studies as bound by their major and common object of study, which is literary work.

Their interrelationship and interdependence form a permanent circular movement from the historically placed literary practice to literary criticism, from literary criticism to literary theory and from literary theory back to criticism.

> The text – either produced recently or representing an earlier period in literary history – is subject to literary criticism whose concluding reflections (the necessary outcome of literary criticism), if generally accepted and proved valid in connection to other thematically and structurally similar literary texts, emerge into the domain of literary theory, become its general principles of approach to literature, and are applicable to the study of other particular texts and to the understanding of literature, in general.

This activity of the critic makes him or her expect to acquire a kind of eternal position in the critical discourse moving on "perpetually from one text to another": "the critic, having had a say about a particular text, hopes that later interpretations will assimilate that "say", incorporating it into an interpretative tradition" (Scholes 3).

Literary theory is fed and supported by the outcome of the practical action of criticism, but it often also "develops out of the application of a more general theory (of art, culture, language and linguistics, aesthetics, politics, history, psychology, economics, gender, and so on) to literary works in the interests of a specific critical aim", meaning that theory "grows out of this experimentation with concepts, terms, and paradigms taken from other spheres of intellectual activity" (Castle 9).

Literary criticism uses theory in practical matters of research whenever the study of particular literary works is required, adding to the objective theory the critic's individual response to the text. The expected result is, on one hand, the development of new or alternative theoretical perspectives, and, on the other hand, the change, promotion, discouragement, revival or, in some other ways, the influence upon the literary practice of its own historical period, and the influence upon the literary attitude of the reading audience concerning the contemporary and past literary tradition.

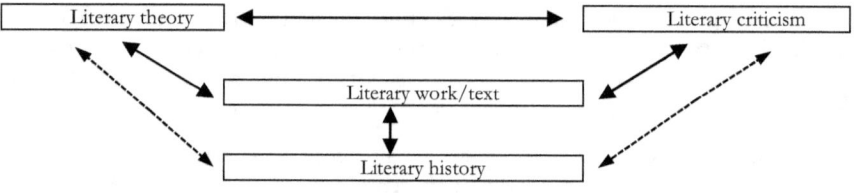

Literary criticism is thus not to be regarded as just the analysis or evaluation of particular literary works, but also as the formulation of general principles of approach to such works.

Co-existing in the field of literary studies with literary history and literary theory, literary criticism combines the theoretical/scientific and practical levels of literary analysis. Criticism as science follows and applies the general principles and methods of research from literary theory, but it also reveals an artistic/creative aspect when the critic personalizes the discourse by his or her own opinions.

The true literary critic uses literary theory to evaluate the literary text and out of the synthesis of the borrowed theory with his or her personal views, the critic develops other theoretical perspectives while keeping the proper balance between the objective and subjective component, between the use of theory and personal contribution. Otherwise, the criticism would be meaningless, "talking about literature in a way that cannot help to build up a systematic structure of knowledge" (Frye 18).

Since the balance is hardly possible, there is this often-made distinction between "theoretical criticism" (with its heavy reliance on existing theories and the attempt to develop new ones) and "practical criticism" (also known as "impressionistic", "interpretive", or "applied criticism", which applies theories but its main concern is individual text which is studied through observation, close reading, analysis, determination of thematic and formal qualities, intertextuality, and so on).

In the circular movement from criticism to theory and vice-versa, primarily the "theoretical criticism" both uses literary theory and proposes to develop "an explicit theory of literature, in the sense of general principles, together with a set of term, distinctions, and categories, to be applied to identifying and analysing works of literature, as well as the criteria (the standards, or norms) by which these works and their writers are to be evaluated" (Abrams and Harpham 61).

The "practical criticism" focuses on individual texts and expresses personal responses which the texts evoke. As such, this type of criticism is less concerned with developing theory or applying theory, and "the theoretical principles controlling the analysis, interpretation, and evaluation are often left implicit, or brought in only as the occasion demands" (Abrams and Harpham 62).

Whatever its typology, literary criticism focuses on individual texts and is connected to theory and history, but apart from these two fields, in the study of literature, the critical discussion cannot be separated from the domain of language in which a certain literature is produced. Literary criticism relies here on other domains, namely linguistics and stylistics. Literature and language are interrelated and interdependent, in that "the literature cannot be examined in any depth apart from the language, any more than the language can be studied apart from the literature", and the study of language can become "a complement and aid to the study of literature" (G. N. Leech 1). Furthermore, concerning the critical practice, Geoffrey N. Leech argues that

> The type of critical activity known as "practical criticism" or "explication de texte" relies more heavily on linguistic evidence than others. In addition, much of the basic vocabulary of literary criticism ("metaphor", "figurative", "antithesis", "irony", rhythm", etc.) cannot be explained without recourse to linguistic notions. As a meeting-ground of linguistic and literary studies, stylistics is the field within which these basic questions lie. (1-2)

Likewise, David Lodge considers that all good criticism

> is a response to language – that it is good insofar as it is a sensitive response – whether or not there is any explicit reference to language in the way of quotation and analysis. This applies not only to the "structural" approach, but to the moral, mythical, historical, psycho-analytical and thematic approaches too; and it explains, I believe, why we can profit from criticism using radically different approaches from our own. (63)

Umberto Eco, combining semiotics, cultural philosophy and literary criticism in one scholarly personality, extends the implication of language in critical interpretation of the literary works to the more general context of culture and literary history:

> a text is produced not for a single addressee but for a community of readers – the author knows that he or she will be interpreted not according to his or her intentions but according to a complex strategy of interactions which also involves the readers, along with their competence in language as a social treasury. I mean by social treasury not only a given language as a set of grammatical rules, but also the whole encyclopaedia that the performances of that language have implemented, namely, the cultural conventions that that language has produced and the very history of the previous interpretations of many texts, comprehending the text that the reader is in the course of reading. ("Between author and text" 67-68)

The relationship of the three approaches to literature – criticism, theory, and history – suggests that literary history is more of a distinct discipline, standing apart, whereas literary theory and literary criticism are stronger connected, which is also based on the assumption that there is no non-theoretical literary criticism. Theoretical principles and implications "lurk behind even the most "practical" forms of criticism, even the most text-oriented interpretations and evaluations" (Harland xi), and even the most personal opinions on literature.

Hence theory and criticism are being considered by certain scholars as one discipline under the generic name of "literary theory and criticism" or "critical theory".

Others provide a clear delimitation between literary theory and literary criticism, naming them "theoretical criticism" and "practical criticism" (also labelled "applied criticism"), respectively. But the former is just another label given to literary theory, since it "formulates the theories, principles, and tenets of the nature and value of art"; the latter, only sharing the same name with I. A. Richards's and F. R. Leavis's method, corresponds to literary criticism and "applies the theories and tenets of theoretical criticism [i.e. literary theory] to a particular work" (Bressler 7).

The names may differ, it is clear, but the essence concerning the object of study and aims does not change. The actual problem affecting the disciplines considers their outcome and utility.

There are strong voices recurrently providing apocalyptic declarations about the death of historicity, including the history of literature or literary history, as well as about the uselessness of any theory or critical study since there are doubts about the possibility to achieve originality, to construct and impose a meaning, and to employ language to represent or reflect whatever is the creative interest.

There have always been numerous and repeated efforts to revive and provide a scientific substratum to the historical study of literature. Yuri Tynyanov and the formalist school, on the whole, attempt to renovate literary history through the view of literature as a system, the theorization of literary evolution, and the discussions on genres. Hans Robert Jauss warns that history of literature is being reduced to a mere gallery of biographies and becomes an obsolete object of study, whose existence would be determined only by a didactic purpose and the necessity of being traditionally included as a part of cultural information. If literary history is to be rejuvenated, argues Jauss, "the prejudices of historical objectivism must be removed and the traditional approach to literature must be replaced by an aesthetics of reception and impact" ("Literary History as a Challenge" 13).

Earlier, Rene Wellek and Austin Warren (in *Theory of Literature*) claimed that "a history of a national literature as a whole, is harder to envisage (...) histories of groups of literatures are even more distant ideals (...) Finally, a general history of the art of literature is still a far-distant ideal". Strongly bound to their Russian formalist origins, namely Tynyanov's theory of literary system, Wellek and Warren claim that literary history must be the study of the systems of "literary norms, standards, and conventions", and must be "the tracing of the changing from one system of norms to another" (264-268).

Wellek and Warren believe that the separation of criticism from the diachronic dimension of the literary history and its subsequent consolidation as a distinct domain were caused by the distinction between the consideration of literature as a simultaneous order and the view on literature as a line of works arranged chronologically and regarded as constituent parts of the historical process. But the practice of historical approach to literature replied to Wellek and other challengers of literary history by such masterworks as Erich Auerbach's *Mimesis: The Representation of Reality in Western Literature* (1946) or Ernst Robert Curtius's *European Literature and the Latin Middle Ages* (1948).

Neither the research of the text as a synchronic phenomenon nor the historicism of the literary experience are to be neglected, but in order to achieve the adequate comprehension of the literary works of different writers and periods, it is necessary to overcome the gap between literary criticism and literary history by fusing the synchronic and diachronic dimensions in literary analysis, and by strengthening the relationship between text and context.

> It is the task of literary criticism – apart from the thematic perspectives of approach – to involve the diachronic perspective in the study of the text.

Otherwise, without understanding literature with what literary history provides, which is essentially a scrutiny of the literary phenomenon in its growth, the relationship between tradition and innovation, the origins of literary work, the author as artist possessing distinct psychology and sensibility, and the social and cultural circumstances which make the production of the work possible and which are reflected in the work, the critic would scarcely offer competent judgement on the value of the text. The "method of historical reception is indispensable for the understanding of literature from the distant past", claims Jauss, and how then the text can be properly understood if "the author of a work is unknown, his intent undeclared, and his relationship to sources and models only indirectly accessible"? (*Toward an Aesthetic of Reception* 29)

> The perspective is reciprocal: it is also the task of literary history to remain a scientific discipline by involving in the study on the rise and development of literature the synchronic dimension of the literary criticism and the scientific principles of research offered by literary theory. The history of literature, in order to claim the status of a science, must be a rigorous system equipped with scientific methodology.

Moreover, the

gap between literature and history, between aesthetic and historical knowledge, can be bridged if literary history does not simply describe the process of general history in the reflection of its works one more time, but rather when it discovers in the course of "literary evolution" that properly socially formative function that belongs to literature as it competes with other arts and social forces in the emancipation of mankind from its natural, religious, and social bonds. (Jauss, *Toward an Aesthetic of Reception* 45)

The literary work is undoubtedly a phenomenon dated in time, and represents, as Romul Munteanu clearly states it in *Metamorphoses of the Modern European Criticism* (1988), the product of a historical time in which a human community develops a particular view on existence, a view which comes to be expressed by exceptional individuals, the producers of literary works, themselves exponents of a particular historical background.

In this respect, as stated above, the discipline of the history of literature performs a historical investigation of literature, and studies the national and world literary development in relation to its periods, movements, trends, genres, types of text, writers, and works, which are inscribed in a process of becoming to reveal the victory of historicism in modernity – weakened but still alive nowadays – and strengthen George Calinescu's claim that literary history resembles an epic scenario on a vast cultural scene.

Like philosophy and history, criticism was conceived as part of a process, a becoming, a diachronic phenomenon, and even as part of history and philosophy, although the aesthetic legitimacy of the work to be judged by critical criteria would not be among the primary aims of the literary history.

Since the Renaissance through the nineteenth century, with empiricist, rationalist and positivist thinking at power, the literary work came to be conceived as a constituent part of a nation's spiritual existence more than it would be viewed as an act of artistic creation whose value emerges from its aesthetic indicators. Literary history would provide evidence about the life and specificity of a nation and become a means of understanding the national psychology as well as advance the literary work as the product and reflection of the milieu and history (Taine); earlier, the romantics already promoted the historical and national along with the individual significance in literary practice and literary studies through an anteriority and posteriority dualism, which later becomes the cause and effect dichotomy.

Literary history having embarked on diachronic research, the dominant opinion was that this discipline is nothing than history (Gervinus) and necessitates no insight into the specificity of the literary phenomenon. Earlier, Friedrich Schlegel negates both literary history and literary criticism by reasoning that if art should be science and the scientific research ought to acquire an artistic nature – since philosophy and poetry constitute a unitary phenomenon – than poetry can be criticised only through poetry, the aesthetic judgement having value only in so far as it is legitimized as an work of art (Munteanu, *Introducere in literatura europeana* 9).

Prior to the twentieth century, this separation of literary history from aesthetic judgement, including literary criticism, conferred low esteem to the historical approach to literature and discredited its status; Tynyanov, among the first, at the beginning of the last century, and later Jauss and others pointed at the systemic and methodological discrepancy in the field of literary history and attempted to provide it with scientific rigour and relate it to literary theory and criticism.

Apart from the debates on the status and usefulness of the historical approach to literature, there are still voices that argue for the uselessness of literary criticism too, which is summarised by Umberto Eco as follows: "Some contemporary theories of criticism assert that the only reliable reading of a text is a misreading, that the only existence of a text is given by the chain of responses it elicits, and that, as maliciously suggested by Todorov (...), a text is only a picnic where the author brings the words and the readers bring the sense" ("Interpretation and History" 24).

Critical text is a metatext, a second degree text, they say, a valueless imitation of the original literary text emerging in the process of reading. Northrop Frye speaks about the conception, popular among artists, of the critic as a parasite and consequently literary criticism as a

> parasite form of literary expression, an art based on pre-existing art, a second hand imitation of creative power. On this theory critics are intellectuals who have a taste for art but lack both the power to produce it and the money to patronize it, and thus form a class of cultural middlemen, distributing culture to society at a profit to themselves while exploiting the artist and increasing the strain on his public. (3)

Even the critics themselves may suddenly decide "that the true subject of criticism is ineffable, and criticism, as a consequence, unnecessary", whereas others may confess "that one is too stupid, too unenlightened to understand a book reputedly philosophical" (Barthes 34). Even if this were true, literary criticism has proved to be an important and necessary domain for centuries, providing, among other things, the establishment of literary traditions, advancement of literary practice, expression of literary value, and mediation between art and its audience. The question is not about the necessity of criticism but about the professional validity of such critics. Barthes again:

> But if one fears or despises so much the philosophical foundations of a book, and if one demands so insistently the right to understand nothing about them and to say nothing on the subject, why become a critic? To understand, to enlighten, that is your profession, isn't it? You can of course judge philosophy according to common sense; the trouble is that while "common sense" and "feeling" understand nothing about philosophy, philosophy, on the other hand, understands them perfectly. (35)

If literary history and literary criticism may be considered, unjustly, of course, by some as useless and helpless, then the sole surviving and necessary domain for literary comprehension is literary theory, still valued, developed and conceived as the only real science of literature. When not considered useless in defining literature, the role of literary criticism is minimized and perceived in the context of a mere reading experience. According to this first assumption, literary criticism is an alternative way of reading the literary text.

Criticism is a common practice helping readers to avoid discrepancies and misunderstandings, or it remains just a practical approach in universities explaining the text and improving the students' competence. In this respect, the critics "tend to minimize textual problems as reading problems. Their concern is usually with evaluating a poet's work or with arguing for a particular reading, rather than overtly demonstrating interpretive goals and reading strategies" (Fairley 311).

Contrary to this first convention, which regards criticism as being secondary to literature, there is another which argues that literary criticism "can be seen as a means of constructing the body of writing and knowledge which it appears to take as its object of study; in other words, literature can be seen as a product of and dependent on criticism rather than the other way round" (Webster 7).

Be theory of literature the most important discipline, yet the relationship of co-existence and interdependence of the three approaches to literature emphasises that literary theory, literary criticism, and literary history are parts of a single written discourse about literature. They are parts of a single science, the science of literature, having as its object of study an art, namely the art of literature, or, in other words, the work of literary art, which is the text, and all the elements which construct and condition the work of literature, where the literary work, or text, from a formalist perspective, would constitute the centre of the system of literature surrounded by and interrelated with all the other elements of the literary system.

The notion of "system" and its theoretical premises are congenial and applicable for the three approaches to literature – history, criticism, and theory, which build up the science of literature – as well: like every science, the science of literature "has as its final aim the truth, which is revealed through notions, and as such it is created as a system that is generally applicable. Being a science that focuses its system on an art, the literary science constitutes a meta-art and follows the disclosure, from a unique perspective, of the infinite individual patterns" (Bomher 11).

> In addition, the relationship of the three approaches to literature points out that literary theory, literary criticism, and literary history are parts of a single cognitive system, a single discourse that assists the pragmatic function by its aim to form or facilitate a particular type of communication which involves the producer of literature and its receiver.

Interesting, comprehensive, systemic, and, above all, didactically useful for the learners of literature are the identification and explanation of the critical theories as provided by M. H. Abrams in his celebrated *The Mirror and the Lamp: Romantic Theory and the Critical Tradition* (1953).

According to him, in art, in general, four critical theories emerge and are dominant in different periods: "mimetic theory", "rhetorical" or "pragmatic theory", "expressive theory", and "objective theory". Abrams points out that all critical theories, as different as they could be, concentrate around four constituents, or major elements, which represent "the total situation of a work of art": (1) the "work", meaning the artistic product, the thing made by the maker; (2) the "artist", or the creator of the work; (3) the "universe", which is the world or nature which is imitated, where, when art is viewed as imitation, the materials of the real world and of the world of ideas become the substance of the work, out of which the work may be thought to take its subjects; and (4) the "audience", which is the receiver or addressee, to whom the work is addressed.

According to Abrams, the concern with one of these four elements results in a special critical theory on art. The critic that focuses exclusively on the "work" of art and views it as a self-contained entity, approaching art basically in its own terms, follows the so-called "objective theory". If art is discussed in relation to the "artist", the work being understood as the expression of the maker's own psychological and emotional states, the approach is called the "expressive theory". To view art in terms of "universe", which is in terms of what is imitated in the work of art, is to follow the "mimetic theory". Finally, to regard art in relation to the "audience", studying the effects of the work of art on the receiver, is to follow the "rhetorical" or "pragmatic theory".

Elements of art as a system	Corresponding critical theory
work	objective theory
artist	expressive theory
universe	mimetic theory
audience	pragmatic theory

Furthermore, Abrams believes, when viewed diachronically, the development of art and art criticism in the Western world reveals these theories to be dominant in different historical periods. In ancient classical age, the most characteristic theory was the mimetic theory, with Plato and Aristotle as its promoters. However, with Aristotle's *catharsis* as the effect of drama on audience and Horace's idea of art as *utile et dulce*, instruction and pleasure, the pragmatic theory emerged in ancient period as another dominant perspective to view art in critical terms. From Antiquity through the most of the eighteenth century, these two theories remain dominant, in particular the pragmatic theory with its focus on art's usefulness and its effects on audience, although in the Renaissance and, especially, in neoclassicism, the principle of imitation was also central to the evaluation of art.

The linearity of the aesthetic attitude of the Western world governed by the view of art as a major source of instruction mingled with delight and pleasure – and thus subject to normative prescriptions – and by the confidence in the imitative nature of art was broken by the romantic rejection of tradition and rules, by its claim of the freedom of artistic expression, the revival of innovative principle in art, and, especially, the emphasis on the artist's own emotional and psychological states.

Aristotle developed a kind of "reader-oriented" approach to literature, but with romanticism, the artist became the centre of attention, his or her power of imagination, creative flight, sensibility, subjective and psychological experience expressed in the work of art.

Thus the expressive theory – also known as the "expressive theory of authorship" – emerges as the most characteristic of the romantic attitudes towards art. Also, dominant in the nineteenth century and later in the twentieth century was the objective theory on art, based on the idea of art for its own sake, art *per se*, the work being viewed as a separate entity, complex enough in its thematic spectrum, range of symbols and imagery, along with its patterns of structure and form, to be a matter of critical concern in itself, as for the late nineteenth-century avant-garde (symbolism, aestheticism, decadence, and so on) and the twentieth-century formal approach to literature (Russian formalism, Anglo-American New Criticism, and French structuralism). However, the present diversity of approaches to art keeps the contemporary critic aware of all the four major theories in his or her endeavour to evaluate art, in general, and literature, in particular.

A closer look at the rise of the critical tradition in Britain reveals a process of development during certain periods or stages generally corresponding to periods and movements in English art and literature. British literary criticism, in particular, reveals some concerns with literature in the medieval period, but its actual beginnings are found in the Renaissance, and its development and consolidation occurred during the subsequent periods of the Restoration, neoclassicism, romanticism, and the Victorian Age, as to establish itself in the twentieth century as a scientific discipline, an objective, methodological and terminological domain developing and consisting of its own schools and trends of literary theory and criticism.

In order to understand better the whole range and complexity of the contemporary trends and schools in the theoretical and critical approach to literature, we may rely again on Tynyanov, Jakobson, and Cook with their grounding of the idea of system consisting of various interrelated elements.

Like with Abrams's distinction between four elements of the system of art and their corresponding critical theories, the literary work in itself and the different relations between the text and other elements of the literary system gave birth to different theories, trends and schools in modern literary theory and criticism. As a result, the contemporary literary critic faces a multitude of schools and theories which correspond to the categories from the structure of the literary system.

The methods of these critical trends compete with each other or conflict over the evaluation and interpretation of particular works, but they also complement each other, being united by the aim to provide an as much as possible comprehensive account of the literary work and to expose the total range of its meanings. But "there is no satisfactory total account of a work of literature except the work itself. It is only the work itself that presents all its meanings in the most significant and assimilable form" (Lodge 63). A writer cannot be asked to reveal the whole truth about life and likewise a critic cannot be expected to disclose the whole truth about a particular literary work.

Criticism cannot offer all the meanings of the work, since it does not and cannot reproduce the work of literature it discusses. Instead, criticism "sets beside this work another work – the critical essay – which is a kind of hybrid formed by the collaboration of the critic with the artist, and which, in this juxtaposition, makes the original yield up some of its secrets" (Lodge 63). Facing a large amount of contemporary critical theories, the question which naturally arises is whether an approach is better than any other. Instead of asking this question, one should "admit that any given method is justified by the use made of it by a particular critic" (Lodge 63). Also, instead of heavily borrowing ideas and providing quotations from the existing critical and theoretical studies, the critic may relate and apply them to his or her particular matters of concern. A more skilled critic considers the essence of different theories, modifying it according to the specificity of the research, and, by providing personal points of view and ideas, the critic progresses to certain interpretative modalities of his or her own.

Concerning the most important critical theories, trends and schools, and according to Guy Cook's literary communicative situation, corresponding to each category in his scheme are various types of critical theory. Thus, in the field of literary theory and criticism, the "author" is the matter of concern of literary scholarship and biography; "text" is studied by formalism, linguistics, linguistic criticism, and stylistics; "performer" by acting theory; "reader" by phenomenology, hermeneutics, reception theory, reader-oriented and reader-response theory, as well as by psychoanalysis, feminism, and poststructuralism; "society" by Marxist theories, cultural materialism, new historicism, and feminism; "texts" by structuralism, poststructuralism, and deconstruction; and corresponding to "language" are the theories of linguistics and stylistics.

author	literary scholarship and biography
text	formalism, linguistics, linguistic criticism, and stylistics
performer	acting theory
reader	phenomenology, hermeneutics, reception theory, reader-oriented theory, reader-response theory, psychoanalysis, feminism, and poststructuralism
society	Marxist theories, cultural materialism, new historicism, and feminism
texts	structuralism, poststructuralism, and deconstruction
language	linguistics and stylistics

Concerning intertextualism, themes, motives, influence, reception, and, in general, the different relations between the literary works, the initiative is that of comparative literature. The particular elements of the literary system and literature, on the whole, are also the matters of critical and theoretical concern of other theories and principles of research, such as those prompted by rhetoric, semiotics, Bakhtinian criticism, archetypal and myth criticism, folklore studies, ethnic literary studies, racial studies, colonial, postcolonial and transnational studies, cultural studies, environmentalism and ecocriticism, posthumanism, transhumanism, and other contemporary trends and schools in humanities and in literary theory and criticism.

These theories, trends and schools represent the twentieth century and the contemporary objective, scientific, and methodological literary theory and criticism. They also offer the picture of the science of literature as a large and chaotic domain concerning both the methods and aims of these types of literary criticism. In the celebrated *Nouveau dictionnaire encyclopedique des sciences du langage*, Oswald Ducrot and Jean-Marie Schaeffer reduce this diversity to five main directions: a) the evaluative criticism of the works; b) the historical and institutional analysis of literature; c) the interpretative disciplines; d) the theories of reading and reception; and e) all types of formal analysis (62-63).

Roman Jakobson's article *Linguistics and Poetics* has become a founding text of contemporary poetics and a point of reference for those critics who follow the formalist school and consider the applicability of linguistic methods in literary studies. Similar to literature, which represents a process of communication, literary criticism is a process of aesthetic reception, production and communication which involves the critic, author, and reader.

Jakobson's structure can, therefore, be applied to individualize both literary communication and critical communicative situation. Robert Scholes, for instance, adjusts Jakobson's diagram to describe the "reading of a literary text" and to arrange the active schools of critical theory "by their emphasis of particular features of this diagram" (8):

	Contexts	
	Text	
Author		Reader
	Medium	
	Codes	

In his book on literary criticism, Raman Selden gives another interesting interpretation to Jakobson's view of communication, in general, as a system of elements and changes the structure according to the purpose of criticism (*A Reader's Guide* 3-4). Considering that "contact" can be omitted in discussing literature, "since contact is usually through the printed word (except in drama)", Selden rewrites the diagram as

	Context	
Writer	Writing	Reader
	Code	

and then places a number of critical theories according to their focus on a particular element in the diagram:

	Marxist	
Romantic	Formalistic	Reader-oriented
	Structuralist	

The long way of development of world literary theory and criticism has its origins in ancient period with its Greek and Latin critical theories, whereas concerning the rise and development of the theoretical and critical discourse on literature in Britain, one should consider the Renaissance and its subsequent periods until the rise of the formal approach to literature at the dawn of the last century.

In short, in the Western world, literary criticism starts its long developmental process in ancient Greece and Rome; it continues in the Middle Ages having a rather diminished status; the first modern methodological and analytical attempts at criticism based on the revived ancient tradition occurred at the beginning of the modern period in the Renaissance both in Britain and in Europe, in general.

Throughout the centuries, criticism developed within the context of the literary practice but gradually came to diversify its provenance, form, and category as to separate from the realm of literature in the nineteenth century and finally to flourish as an independent and scientific domain in the twentieth century and at the present time, which represent undoubtedly an age of criticism.

Throughout its history, criticism existed in a variety of forms, including dialogues, verse, essays, letters, prefaces, treaties, and books. Throughout its history, criticism belonged mainly to the domains of literature and philosophy.

Criticism has been continuously influenced by the literary process and has influenced in its turn this process. Criticism has been also continuously influenced by the new developments in thought as well as in natural and social sciences, art, culture, ideology, psychology, linguistics. As such, criticism has developed an impressive typology to which twentieth century and the present days have added a huge diversity of critical trends and schools.

Throughout its history, criticism has concerned first philosophers and later, to a much greater extent, artist-critics and writer-critics, especially poet-critics, as well as scholars from different fields (rhetoric, logic, mathematics, physics, sociology, psychology, linguistics, and so on), and finally reviewers, university academics, and just professional critics and theoreticians of literature, all those who are considered exponents of various contemporary schools and trends in literary theory and criticism representing a distinct scientific field of scholarly investigation into literature as a system with all its constituent elements.

3. The History of British and European Literature: Periods, Movements, Trends, Authors, and Texts

Before embarking on a surveyistic presentation of the historical advancement of literature, we should say a few words about a kind of rule of the development of literature, in general.

The place of literature in history is reified by the rise, development and consolidation of various literary periods, movements, trends, genres, writers, and literary works, which follow each other. Each of these is a particular literary system encompassing in its framework dominant (centre) and peripheral (margin) elements; the movement of these systems through history is their continuous development, change, or more precisely, substitution of systems.

Each of these is rooted in the previous ones, represents a continuation of the previous ones, and, at the same time, rejects the previous ones, attempting at suppressing them and taking their place in literary history. Also, each period, movement, trend, genre, etc., that is, every literary system, is determined by the contemporary developments in society, culture, philosophy, science, and so on.

Origins of the literary periods, movements, trends, genres, subgenres, and so on, each representing a literary system		
Relation to the past	1. **continuation**	of the previous periods, trends, etc., where innovation follows innovation, and tradition relies on tradition
	2. **rejection**	of the previous periods, trends, etc., where innovation reacts against tradition, and tradition marginalises innovation
Relation to the present	3. **contemporary**	socio-cultural stimuli

> Each period, movement, trend, genre, subgenre, writer, and text is followed by another; each has its own rise, development, consolidation and decline, but not complete disappearance, as each one influences the next, gives its origins or is rejected by the next one, or the elements of its system are acknowledged in the systems of the subsequent periods, movements, trends, and literary works under different forms and functions. Each period, movement, trend, writer, and text represents one to another tradition and innovation, is placed one against the other, where a continuous "battle" takes place between their elements which are either central or peripheral within the structure of the literary system.

> The place of literature in history is actually determined by the interrelationship, the "fight" between "**centre**" and "**margin**", "**tradition**" and "**innovation**", "**classical**" and "**modern**", "**conservative**" and "**experimental**", **dependence on rules** and the **freedom of artistic expression**. It is a correlation of two contrary factors whose interaction is the motor of change and development of literature, disclosing the **substitution of systems.**

In the history of literature, the concept of "**tradition**" is used to denote the ancient classical period, the revival of ancient classical tradition in the Renaissance, the eighteenth-century Age of Enlightenment (also referred to as classicism or neoclassicism), the nineteenth-century realism, and the twentieth-century and contemporary socially-concerned literature.

The term "**innovation**" denotes some literary experiences of the Renaissance period, metaphysical poetry, pre-romanticism, romanticism, the late nineteenth-century symbolism, aestheticism and other avant-garde trends, and the twentieth-century modernism in the first half of the century and postmodernism of the postmodern period, as well as other more recent experimental trends in literature.

> The scholars and students of literature are familiar with the fight between **tradition and innovation** as the opposition and juxtaposition of **center and margin**; they also know this conflict between tradition and innovation under the name of "**the battle of the books**" or "**la querelle des anciens et des modernes**". Whatever the terms, it points again to the war between **innovation and tradition**, between **originality and authority**, between **classicism and modernism.**

The war started in Antiquity, was reinforced in the Renaissance, peaked in France and then throughout Europe at the turn of the seventeenth century and is still going on. In English culture, this conflict was remarkably captured by the neoclassical man of letters Jonathan Swift (1667-1745) in his satire on the battle between ancients and moderns known as *The Battle of the Books* (1704).

> In English literature advancing through history, just like in literature in general, innovation rejects tradition and innovation continues innovation or, better saying, **innovation continues as well as innovates the previous innovation.**

An example of the continuation of innovation, paralleled by the innovation of innovation occurring as an indispensable part of the literary development, would be romanticism, as innovation, assuming and changing, in order to advance further on the path of originality and experimentation, the innovation of pre-romanticism; in its turn, romanticism would be innovated by the nineteenth-century avant-garde which assumes some and change or totally reject other aspects of romanticism; likewise, Joyce and Woolf would adopt and innovate Pater's "impressions" placing them within the larger context of the abstract manifestations of the mind thematized in their modernist novels which focus on the psychological experience of the individual rendered by the stream of consciousness technique in the form of interior monologue.

The literary history studies the rise and development of a national literature and the world literary phenomena from its beginnings to the present day, and divides the historical process into literary periods, which may or may not correspond to the social or political ones.

Literary periods consist of literary movements and trends, which are represented by authors and their literary works and/or literary doctrine. The distinction made between movement and trend relies actually on the fact that a movement groups those writers who produce both literary works (which share similar thematic and structural features) and literary doctrine (texts of literary theory and criticism which share common ideas about their own type of literature) – romanticism, for example; whereas a trend is formed of the producers of only literary texts having common characteristics – the nineteenth-century realism, for example.

Literary periods are considered to refer to different sequences of time conceived in the temporal boundaries of an age, century, centuries, or years, but such an understating of the period may thwart any attempts at tracing clear demarcation lines between literary periods, movements and trends, or at clearly asserting them terminologically. The Renaissance, for instance, is certainly neither a movement nor a trend but a distinct period in the literary history. Metaphysical poetry, however, is first of all a trend which manifested itself only on the level of literary practice, but it is also a part of the larger period of the English Renaissance.

Romanticism represents a period: "Romantic Period", or the "Age of Romanticism", dated between the years of 1798 and 1824, or, in more general terms, between the last decades of the eighteenth century and the first decades of the nineteenth century. At the same time, romanticism is a literary movement: "Romantic Movement", consisting of both imaginative writing and the doctrine, literary texts (such as *Tintern Abbey* by Wordsworth, or *Kubla Khan* by Coleridge) and the critical ideas (from Wordsworth's *Preface to Lyrical Ballads*, for example, or Coleridge's *Biographia Literaria*) about these texts.

In British literature, neoclassicism is a period in literary history covering the last part of the seventeenth century throughout the eighteenth century; neoclassicism is a movement in literature with its poetic works and a strongly normative and prescriptive doctrine; and also neoclassicism is the creator of a particular trend in poetry, philosophical and satirical. Likewise, in both English and world literature, modernism is a period in the first half of the twentieth century, a complex artistic manifestation consisting of a number of distinct movements (futurism, for example) and developing a number of trends in the production of literary texts (for instance, the "stream-of-consciousness novel" of Marcel Proust and James Joyce).

In general, concerning both world and English literature, a diachronic perspective on literature in Britain reveals a historical process which follows the general European pattern, yet in some moments having its particular manifestations. A special problem here is the consideration of some more or less exact periods in the development of both British and world literature.

In most general terms, literature is regarded as passing through three major periods: ancient, medieval and modern, whereas since the middle of the twentieth century, humanity is in the postmodern period, a period claimed to represent the transition to globalization. The first period in European literature is the classical period of the ancient Greece and Rome, rejected and replaced by the Middle Ages.

Concerning British literature in the Middle Ages, historians have noticed the discrepancy between English and general world/European conditions: first, English literature does not have an ancient period to be claimed in relation to a particular civilization and culture, like Greece, Rome, Egypt, China, or India, and, second, its actual medieval period starts much later than the European one, which is the eleventh/twelfth century, for the simple reason that there was no English nation at all until that period.

It is hypothesized that until the sixth century BC, the British islands were inhabited by Iberians and from sixth/seventh century BC by Celts. The year of 55 BC is that of the Roman invasion, and the years between 410 AD and 441 AD date the period of the Roman retreat.

It was the fifth century AD which saw the invasion of the British islands by the Anglo-Saxon tribes coming from the Continent, which lasted for more than a century (449-600), and then the formation, the "becoming" of these people as English for more than four centuries, which marked a period called in the history of English nation, language and literature as "Anglo-Saxon" or "Old English" (449/600-1100/1200). Conquered in their turn by the Normans in the eleventh century (the starting point being the Hastings Battle of 1066), the newly formed English nation enters now "officially" into the Middle Ages which lasted for centuries until around 1500.

The medieval period is in its turn rejected and replaced by the age of Renaissance, which is considered either as the first part of the modern period – a view based on artistic line – which lasted until the middle of the twentieth century, or as a period of transition from the Middle Ages to modern period, now conceived as lasting from the seventeenth-century Enlightenment – a view linked to philosophical line – to the middle of the twentieth century.

The art and literature of the Renaissance already reveal two contradictory but co-existing aspects of "innovation" (for instance, sonnet in poetry) and "tradition" (the revival of ancient models, as, for example, in Renaissance tragedy), and a more detailed consideration agrees that henceforth the growth of literature displays a rather complex picture.

The emergence of the innovative spirit in literature continues after the Renaissance as the Baroque period (metaphysical poetry in English literature, also considered by some critics as the last manifestation of the British Renaissance), but this cultural extravaganza is rejected and suppressed by the much stronger and dominant traditional element which, based on the revival of ancient classical artistic doctrine and practice, becomes itself a period and dominates as Enlightenment (or neoclassicism, in England) the entire social as well as cultural and literary background of Europe for more than one hundred years starting with the middle of the seventeenth century.

By the middle of the eighteenth century, the doctrine of Enlightenment or neoclassicism is put into practice by the more pragmatic British mind, giving rise to Industrialisation and thus determining the decline and end of neoclassicism as a distinct period. It is also the eighteenth century that saw the rise of the novel in English literature, and by the middle of the period, the rise of the pre-romantic poetry. As a rejection of neoclassicism and the continuation of pre-romanticism, the romantic movement emerges at the end of the eighteenth century as reviving the innovative spirit in literature and breaking the linearity of literary development dominated for a long period after the Renaissance by the traditional and normative principles of the revived ancient classical doctrine. Romanticism ends as a regular trend by the middle of the nineteenth century, and henceforth in literature, "tradition" and "innovation" co-exist again under different names and in the framework of different movements and trends.

In the simplest consideration of the facts, romanticism gave, in the second half of the nineteenth century, symbolism, aestheticism, impressionism, expressionism, and other manifestations of the artistic avant-garde, which, in the first half of the twentieth century, continue into a more complex range of experimental and innovative trends and movements (surrealism, dadaism, cubism, "stream-of-consciousness" novel, etc.) assembled and assigned together as modernism, which in its turn continues in the second half of the twentieth century as the innovation and experimentation of postmodernism – this is the component of "**innovation**" in literary history, a line of development having its origins in the Renaissance, which continued in the Baroque, was suppressed by classical tradition but revived by romanticism, was developed by the late nineteenth century avant-garde trends and diversified by the twentieth-century modernism and postmodernism.

Some elements of the main "enemy" of romanticism, which is neoclassicism, re-appear in the second half of the nineteenth century in the system of the likewise conventional, normative and socially concerned realism, which emerges almost unchanged in its thematic and structural perspectives in the twentieth century, opposing with its traditional realistic concern the innovatory and experimental art – this is the component of "**tradition**" in literary history, a line of development having its origins in ancient period, which revived in the Renaissance, changed, developed and was institutionalised in the seventeenth and eighteenth century neoclassicism, was rejected and replaced by romanticism, but became present again on the literary scene as nineteenth-century realism, and continued and was diversified by the twentieth-century writers of social concern and realist interest.

> To summarise, every new literary period, movement, trend results in and rejects the previous ones on the basis of the opposition between normative tradition and experimental innovation. Tradition and innovation are parts of a single process of literary change and development, contrary but interrelated, emerging in different periods under different names and in the system of different movements, trends and literary works, rejecting and succeeding each other, but from the second half of the nineteenth century to the present day co-existing as two distinct dimensions of literature. Apart from rejection and continuation, every new literary period, movement, and trend is determined by the contemporary developments in thought, science, and other domains.

Concerning the major periods in the history of British literature, the standard opinion, originated in the nineteenth century in relation to the development of English language, regards four periods: the period between 449/700 and 1100/1200 is called "Old English (Anglo-Saxon) Literature"; "Middle Literature" between 1100/1200 and 1500; and the period from around 1500 till the second half of the twentieth century is "Modern British Literature", followed by the "Postmodern Period". A more suitable consideration divides British literature into (a) "Old English (Anglo-Saxon) Literature", (b) "The Middle Ages", (c) "The Renaissance", (d) "The Seventeenth Century", (e) "The Eighteenth Century", (f) "The Romantic Movement", (g) "The Victorian Age", (h) "The First Half of the Twentieth Century", and (i) "The Second Half of the Twentieth Century". A more recent consideration of the major periods in the history of British literature is provided by Andrew Sanders in *A Short Oxford History of English Literature* (2004), who divides English literary history into "Old English Literature" (447-1066), "Medieval Literature" (1066-1510), "Renaissance and Reformation" (1510-1620), "Revolution and Restoration" (1620-1690), "Eighteenth-Century Literature" (1690-1780), "The Literature of the Romantic Period" (1780-1830), "High Victorian Literature" (1830-1880), "Late Victorian and Edwardian Literature" (1880-1920), "Modernism and Its Alternatives" (1920-1945), and "Post-War and Post-Modern Literature" (1945-present).

Each of these periods – except, perhaps, the Old English period and romanticism – has its own particular stages which correspond to specific sub-periods, or movements, or trends, or just some major authors. Thus, the medieval period of British literature, preceded by the Anglo-Saxon age, covers Anglo-Norman literature, Geoffrey Chaucer and his epoch, and the fifteenth century. The Renaissance is divided into the period of humanism and that of the Elizabethan Age. The seventeenth century includes metaphysical trend in poetry, the Puritan period, and the Restoration period. The eighteenth century consists of neoclassicism, the rise of the English novel, and pre-romanticism. Neoclassicism, actually, lasting from 1660 to 1780s, is divided into three periods: its rise during the Restoration period (1660-1700), its climax and dominance during the Augustan Age (1700-1750), and its decline during the Age of Johnson (1750-1780s). Following the period of the Romantic Movement, the Victorian Age covers the literature of realism, post-and neo-romantic writing, the Pre-Raphaelite Movement or Brotherhood, and aestheticism ("art for art's sake" doctrine). The twentieth century includes, in the first half of the century, Edwardian period, modernism, and the new realist writing, and, in the second half of the century, the Angry Generation and other manifestations of the traditional realistic writing, and the postmodern and postmodernist literature.

1. Old English (Anglo-Saxon) Period
- dated 447-1066, or between 449/600 (invasion of Britain by Angles, Saxons, and Jutes) and 1100/1200 (establishment of the Norman rule)
- no trends or movements, but some major authors (Caedmon, Cynewulf, the Venerable Bede) and texts (chronicles, the anonymous epic *Beowulf*, and a number of poems such as *The Seafarer* and *The Wanderer*)

2. Medieval English Literature
- dated 1100/1200-1500, or, more precisely, between 1066 (Battle of Hastings and the beginning of the Norman Conquest) and 1509 (death of Henry VII and accession of Henry VIII)
- the actual medieval period of British literature with no particular trends or movements
- covers three periods:
- the Anglo-Norman literature (1100/1200-1350s): includes chronicles, poetry, but the most important literary manifestation is the medieval romance (also referred to as chivalrous romance, Arthurian legend, metrical romance, or prose romance); for example, *Sir Gawain and the Green Knight*)
- Geoffrey Chaucer and his epoch (1340-1400): includes the poem entitled *The Land of Cockaygne*, the famous alliterative poem *The Vision of William Concerning Piers the Plowman* ascribed to William Langland, *Voyages and Travels of Sir John Mandeville* by Sir John Mandeville, the works of John Gower, but the period is entirely governed by Geoffrey Chaucer (1340-1400) and his writings, in particular *The Canterbury Tales*
- the fifteenth century: includes Sir Thomas Malory's prose romance *Morte d'Arthur*, the poetry of John Lydgate and Thomas Hoccleve, the popular ballads, but the most important literary manifestation is the rise of drama (with many forms, both religious and secular, of which the most important ones are "mystery play", "morality", and "interlude")

3. Renaissance Literature, or the period of "Renaissance and Reformation" in British literature
- very difficult to date precisely:
- the sixteenth century in general
- between 1510 and 1620
- between 1500 and the Commonwealth Interregnum (1649-1660)
- begins in 1485 (the accession of Henry VII and the establishment of the Tudor dynasty) or in 1509 (the accession of Henry VIII)
- ends in the early seventeenth century in Europe, in general, and the year of 1616 (the death of Shakespeare) in England, or by the middle of the seventeenth century in Europe, in general, and the year of 1649 (the execution of Charles I) or the year of 1660 (the restoration of monarchy) in England
- historically, it consists of "Early Tudor Age" (c.1500-1557) and "Elizabethan Age" (1558-1603); it may also include "Jacobean Age" (1603-1625) and "Caroline Age" (1625-1649), if one would consider that the Renaissance lasted until the middle of the seventeenth century
- concerning literature, Renaissance is divided into the periods of
- humanism (first half of the sixteenth century)
- Elizabethan Age (second half of the sixteenth century)
- baroque (metaphysical poetry) in the first part and middle of the seventeenth century, if one would consider that the Renaissance lasted until the 1650s
- no clearly defined literary trends or movements, except humanism and metaphysical poetry
- the former is considered within the fields of philosophy and politics, and the latter in the context of the baroque, which is said to have followed the Renaissance period as part of the seventeenth-century mannerism and cultural extravaganza
- major genres: sonnet and drama
- important writings: *Utopia* by Sir Thomas More; sonnets by Thomas Wyatt and Henry Howard; Edmund Spenser with *The Shepherd's Calendar*, *Amoretti* (88 sonnets), and *The Fairie Queene*; Sir Philip Sidney with 108 sonnets printed as *Astrophel and Stella*, a pastoral novel *Arcadia*, and *Apologie for Poetrie*; prose by Francis Bacon, John Lyly, Robert Greene, and Thomas Nashe
- the most important literary manifestation: the Elizabethan Drama
- Pre-Shakespearian drama: anonymous plays and various authors such as Thomas Kyd, John Lyly, Robert Greene, and Christopher Marlowe (famous for *The Tragical Historie of Doctor Faustus* and *Tamburlaine the Great*)

- William Shakespeare: poetry (sonnets) and drama (historical plays, comedies, and tragedies)

4. The Seventeenth Century, or the period of "Revolution and Restoration" in British Literature
- dated between 1620 and 1690, or between 1603 (the death of Elizabeth and the accession of James I) and 1714 (the inauguration of the Hanoverian Dynasty by George I)
- major historical events: the rise of Puritanism, the abolition of monarchy (the execution of Charles I) in 1649, the Commonwealth Interregnum led by Oliver Cromwell between 1649 and 1660, the restoration of monarchy (Charles II restored to throne) in 1660
- concerning literature, the period consists of
    - metaphysical poetry (or Baroque, 1620s to 1670s)
    - the Puritan period (1649-1660)
    - the Restoration period (1660-1700)
- includes already clearly defined literary trends, such as metaphysical trend in poetry and the "comedy of manners" in the Restoration drama
- major literary voices: metaphysical poets John Donne and Andrew Marvell, the great playwright Ben Jonson, the Puritan writer John Milton, and John Dryden as the most important representative of the Restoration literature

5. The Eighteenth-Century Literature (1700-1780s)
- the period of French Revolution, Agricultural Revolution, and Industrial Revolution
- in literature, the eighteenth century consists of
- neoclassicism (1660-1780s)
    - the rise of the English novel (throughout the century)
    - pre-romanticism (1750s-1780s)
- the neoclassical period is divided into three parts:
    - the "Restoration Age" (1660-1700), or the "Age of Dryden"
    - the "Augustan Age" (1700-1750s), or the "Age of Pope"
    - the "Age of Johnson" (1750s-1780s), or the decline of Neoclassicism
- major trends and movements include:
    - neoclassicism as a movement in literature with its poetic works (namely philosophical and satirical) and a strongly normative and prescriptive doctrine
    - pre-romantic trend in poetry
    - different trends in the genre of the novel, or rather types of the novel: picaresque novel, sentimental novel, epistolary novel, comic novel, moral novel, and others
- major literary voices representing:
    - neoclassicism: Alexander Pope and Dr Samuel Johnson
    - the rise of the English novel: Jonathan Swift, Daniel Defoe, Samuel Richardson, Henry Fielding, Laurence Sterne, Jane Austen
    - pre-romanticism: James Macpherson and Thomas Gray

6. Romantic Literature
- dated between 1780s-1830s, or between 1798 (the publication of *Lyrical Ballads*) and 1824 (the death of Byron)
    - romanticism represents a period: "Romantic Period", or the "Age of Romanticism"
    - romanticism is a literary movement: "Romantic Movement", consisting of both imaginative writing and critical ideas
    - important for breaking the linearity of literary development dominated for centuries by the traditional classical spirit and for reviving the innovative spirit in arts and the proclamation of the freedom of artistic expression, individualism, nationalism, authorship, emotional experience, imagination, nature and rustic life, dualism of existence, and so on
    - important for its literary doctrine: major critical texts include Wordsworth's *Preface to Lyrical Ballads*, Coleridge's *Biographia Literaria*, and Shelley's *Defence of Poetry*
    - the genres and representatives of Romanticism:
        - poetry: the most important genre, represented by William Blake, William Wordsworth, Samuel Taylor Coleridge, Robert Southey, Robert Burns, Percy Bysshe Shelley, George Gordon, Lord Byron, and John Keats

- prose: the historical novel of Sir Walter Scott and the gothic fiction by Horace Walpole, Clara Reeve, Ann Radcliffe, and others
- drama: Percy Bysshe Shelley and George Gordon, Lord Byron

7. The Victorian Literature
- dated 1830s-1900, or between 1837 (Victoria came to throne) and 1901 (the death of Queen Victoria)
- in ideology, politics, and society, the Victorian Age was a period of innovation, invention, progress, complexity, and change: democracy, feminism, unionization of workers, Newton's mechanics, Darwin's evolution, Comte's view of society, Marx's view of history, Taine's view of literature, Freud's view of human psyche, industrialization, steam power, railway, telephone, telegraph, photography, etc.
- in literature and other arts: the Victorians attempted to combine the romantic emphases upon self, emotion, and imagination with the neoclassical concern with the public role of art and responsibility of the artist
- hence the Victorian Age consisting of a great number of movements and trends co-existing during one period and as such revealing the co-existence of the traditional and innovative elements in literature
- "tradition" is represented by realism, a major literary trend which manifests in novel writing and which rejects romanticism and continues the neoclassical emphasis on rules and ethics, and the interest in the actual, immediate reality
- close to realism, but also different in many respects, is the trend called naturalism
- "innovation" is revived by the defiant spirit of the romantic writers, rejects tradition, rules and prescriptive doctrines, and manifests as a continuation of the romantic rebellious attitude in art
- the element of innovation represents the real source of literary complexity in Victorian period since it consists of a number of trends and movements
- the innovation in literature and arts growing out of romanticism has a twofold perspective:
    - first, innovation from romanticism, heavily influenced by the romantic attitude and comprising a great number of romantic characteristics
    - second, innovation out of romanticism, less influenced by the romantic attitude but still continuing a number of its features
- the first kind of innovation manifests as post- and neo-romantic trends, including most of the Victorian poetry as well as some of the fiction of the period, such as Emily Bronte's gothic novel and the later colonial prose of Kipling, Stevenson, Doyle, Wells, and Conrad
- the second type of innovation manifests as symbolism, aestheticism, impressionism, expressionism, Pre-Raphaelite Brotherhood, and other trends which represent the artistic avant-garde of the second half of the nineteenth century
- the dominant literary form is novel, then poetry, and to a lesser extent, drama
- the novel belongs mainly to realism and the realist novel is the main type of fiction
- there are some exceptions, like the gothic/post-romantic novel *Wuthering Heights* by Emily Bronte, or *The Picture of Dorian Gray* by Oscar Wilde which reflects aestheticism
- poetry in general continues the romantic tradition, but is also influenced by aestheticism and symbolism
- to summarise, the Victorian Age covers the literature of such literary trends and movements as realism, post-and neo-romantic writing, the Pre-Raphaelite Movement, aestheticism ("art for art's sake" doctrine), naturalism, and others
- main literary voices:
    - prose: Charles Dickens, William Makepeace Thackeray, Charlotte Bronte, Emily Bronte, George Eliot, Lewis Carroll, Oscar Wilde, Thomas Hardy
    - poetry: Alfred, Lord Tennyson, Robert Browning, Matthew Arnold, Gerald Manley Hopkins, Dante Gabriel Rossetti, William Morris, Charles Algernon Swinburne

8. English Literature in the First Half of the Twentieth Century, or the period of modernism and its alternatives (1900-1945)
- British literature in the first half of the twentieth-century consists of a wide range of movements and trends which can be grouped under two headings:
    - the first one includes the literary works which continue the nineteenth-century realistic texts, preserve unchanged the traditional and normative type of writing, and is referred to as realism, meaning realist, traditional, and conservative literature
    - the second one rejects the traditional and conservative type of literature and consists of innovative, original, experimental and avant-garde trends which represent the literary dimensions of

modernism
- the first half of the twentieth century includes
    - the Edwardian period (1900-1910)
    - modernism (1910s-1930s)
    - realistic writing (throughout the period, although dominant in the first decade   (the Edwardian period) and in the 1930s and 1940s)
- modernism is a period in the first half of the twentieth century, an artistic movement, or rather a complex artistic manifestation consisting of a number of distinct movements and trends
- in other words, it is more appropriate to use "modernism" as a generic term to be applied retrospectively to the wide range of experimental, avant-garde artistic and intellectual trends and movements of the first half of the twentieth century
- the trends and movements of Modernism manifested in art in general, including painting, music, architecture, and literature
- examples of modernist trends and movements: futurism, surrealism, cubism, dadaism, imagism, the stream-of-consciousness novel, and so on
- composers such as Stravinsky and Schoenberg represent Modernism in music
- the movements *les fauves*, cubism, and surrealism, and artists such as Picasso, Matisse, and Mondrian represent modernism in visual arts
- in architecture and design, modernism is represented by Le Corbusier, Walter Gropius, and Mies van der Rohe
- in literature, the leading figures of modernism are Guillaume Apollinaire, Louis Aragon, Jean Cocteau, Hilda Doolittle, William Faulkner, Ezra Pound, William Carlos Williams, Max Jacob, Federico Garcia Lorca, Franz Kafka, Marcel Proust, Gertrude Stein, Tristan Tzara, Paul Valery, and many others
- in Britain, the major literary voices of modernism are James Joyce and Virginia Woolf in fiction (including the "stream-of-consciousness novel"), and T. S. Eliot and W. B. Yeats in poetry
- other voice of Modernism in English fiction: D. H. Lawrence and Aldous Huxley
- the realist literature of the first half of the twentieth century is represented by John Galsworthy, William Somerset Maugham, Graham Greene, George Orwell, George Bernard Shaw, and others

9. English Literature in the Second Half of the Twentieth Century, or "Post-War and Postmodern Literature" (1945-present)
- the second half of the twentieth century includes
    - the post-war literature (1940s and 1950s)
    - the postmodern literature (1960s to the present)
- the post-war literature is traditional and realist rather than experimental; the main trend is the Angry Young Generation (or Angry Young Men), whose representatives are Alan Sillitoe, John Wain, Kingsley Amis, and John Braine; however, the period also includes the visionary and philosophical writing of the 1950s and 1960s, which made possible the transition from realism of the post-war period to later flourishing of postmodernism, and which was at best represented by William Golding and Iris Murdoch
- the postmodern literature consists of two main parts:
    - realism, or the traditional realist writing, at best represented by Graham Greene, Evelyn Waugh, Charles Percy Snow, Sir Angus Wilson, Muriel Spark, Margaret Drabble, and others
    - postmodernism, or experimentation in art and literature
- like with modernism, postmodernism is a generic term used to name the wide range of contemporary experimental, innovative and original artistic and intellectual trends and movements of the second half of the twentieth century and of the first decades of the new millennium
- postmodernism in British literature can be divided in several trends and movements, among which:
    - the campus novel/global campus novel, at best represented by David Lodge
    - magical realism, at best represented by Angela Carter
    - historiographic metafiction, at best represented by Murial Spark, John Fowles, Graham Swift, and Ian McEwan
    - postcolonial writing, at best represented by Salman Rushdie and Monica Ali
- other postmodern and postmodernist voices in British literature: Julian Barnes and Peter Ackroyd in fiction; Ted Hughes, Dylan Thomas, Seamus Heaney, and Philip Larkin in poetry; John Osborne, Samuel Beckett, Harold Pinter, Tom Stoppard, and Caryl Churchill in drama

To summarise, with regard to the major literary trends and movements in English and general European literature, the students may consider the following:

humanism (Renaissance)
metaphysical poetry (baroque, Renaissance, seventeenth century)
cavalier poets (seventeenth century)
comedy of manners (seventeenth century, Restoration period)
Enlightenment (seventeenth century, eighteenth century)
neoclassicism (seventeenth century, eighteenth century)
pre-romanticism (eighteenth century)
picaresque novel (eighteenth century)
sentimentalism/sentimental novel (eighteenth century)
epistolary novel (eighteenth century)
comic novel (eighteenth century)
moral novel (eighteenth century)
romanticism (eighteenth century, nineteenth century)
gothic novel (eighteenth century, nineteenth century)
historical novel (nineteenth century)
post-romantic literature (nineteenth century)
neo-romantic literature (nineteenth century)
Transcendentalism (nineteenth century)
colonial literature (nineteenth century)
impressionism (nineteenth century)
expressionism (nineteenth century)
symbolism (nineteenth century)
aestheticism / "art for art's sake" doctrine (nineteenth century)
Pre-Raphaelite Brotherhood (nineteenth century)
realism (nineteenth-century, twentieth century)
naturalism (nineteenth century)
modernism (twentieth century)
futurism (twentieth century)
surrealism (twentieth century)
cubism (twentieth century)
dadaism (twentieth century)
imagism (twentiethcentury)
Harlem Renaissance (twentieth century)
the Lost Generation (twentieth century)
stream-of-consciousness novel (twentieth century)
Angry Young Men (twentieth century)
postmodernism (twentieth century)
campus novel (twentieth century)
magical realism (twentieth century)
historiographic metafiction (twentieth century)
postcolonial literature (twentieth century)
minimalism (twentieth century)
Beat poets (twentieth century)
confessional literature (twentieth century)
spoken word (twentieth century)

Concerning the differences in the history of British and general European literary phenomena, it has been often brought into discussion the so-called "complex of insularity" of the British cultural background, its strong regional and conservative features in relation to the rest of Europe. Throughout its history, British culture seems reluctant to accept the Continental influences, new developments in literature and other arts, new movements, trends and styles, whose origins have been in France and Italy, and to a lesser extent in Spain and Germany.

Hence the fact that English literature is a late phenomenon, from the very beginning and throughout its entire literary history. It may take a century or more to speak about English Renaissance and about the rise and consolidation of a literary tradition in English fiction, or decades for romanticism or symbolism, as if British literary background must finally yield to the acceptance of what in contemporary Europe has been already established as a dominant literary tradition, movement, or trend.

Still, many English authors on the side of the freedom of artistic expression remained for centuries unknown or wrongly evaluated, such as Donne and Hopkins, or, like Byron, Lawrence and Joyce, had to escape from the conservatism and reluctance of the fellow-citizens and produce their works in some other countries. It is claimed, however, that English literary "complex of insularity" ends with the synchronization in the first half of the twentieth century of the British with European modernism, due to the contribution of, among others, Joyce and Eliot, though in the second half of the last century English literature turns again to realistic and social concerns rather than literary experimentation, being traditional rather than innovative.

It might be that British literature, in general, has been traditional rather than innovative, but it passes nowadays, as many national literatures do, through a process of decentralization due to globalization, the country's former membership in European Union, new developments in sociology, anthropology, women's studies, cultural studies, and postcolonial and transnational studies. Perhaps the most significant factor of decentralization of British literature is the advancement of English as a world language, spoken worldwide by millions who have no other connection with Britain.

English literature might have been traditional rather than innovative, but it is an aberration to assume that it represents weak literary phenomena, lacking aesthetic strength and significance, and that it is investigated and taught merely because of some political, economic, colonial, postcolonial or linguistic causes.

British literature is rich and complex, studied in almost every country of the world and acclaimed by Anglo-American as well as international scholarship, as to remember just Emile Legouis and Louis Cazamian who, almost a century ago, in their celebrated *A Short History of English Literature* (1929), already saw English literature possessing "a greater capacity than other literature for combining a love of concrete statement with a tendency to dream, a sense of reality with lyrical rapture", and English writers characterized by "loving observation of Nature, by a talent for depicting strongly-marked character, and by a humour that is the amused and sympathetic noting of the contradictions of human nature and the odd aspects of life".

British literature is an important part of the world literary heritage, answering and assuming during its history most of the innovation and development in arts and literature, and having its own contribution to world literary practice and literary doctrine, attributable to such major British literary voices as Chaucer and Gower in the Middle Ages, Shakespeare, Marlowe, Spenser and Sidney in the Renaissance, Donne, Marvell, Milton and Dryden in the seventeenth century, Pope, Swift, Defoe, Richardson, Fielding and Sterne in the eighteenth century, Blake, Wordsworth, Coleridge, Byron, Shelley and Keats in romanticism, Dickens, George Eliot, Emily Bronte, Charlotte Bronte, Tennyson, Robert Browning, Swinburne, Arnold, Ruskin, Pater, Wilde and Carlyle in Victorian Age, and, in the twentieth century, Joyce, Woolf, Lawrence, T. S. Eliot, Shaw, Hughes, Beckett, Pinter, Golding, Murdoch, Fowles,

Barnes, Mitchell, Spark, Lodge, Larkin, Ackroyd, McEwan, and many other writers of all these periods, whose works are landmarks in the history of English as well as European and world literature and thought.

Finally, a few terminological explanations may properly conclude our answering of the three questions, which we have focused upon in this Introduction, as well as strengthen the acquired knowledge.

With regard to literary criticism, the interconnected terms "criticism", "critic", "criticise", "critical", and "critique" entered English language at the beginning of the modern period, largely around 1600. The etymology of all these words starts in ancient Greek, namely from Greek *krites* ("judge, a person offering reasoned judgement or analysis") and its derivation *kritikos* ("skilled in making judgement"), as well as *krinein* ("to decide, to separate") and *krinô* ("I judge", or "to separate and distinguish in order to be able to judge"), which is also the root for the word "crisis". From Greek they passed into Latin, then French and finally English.

The term "critic", for instance, having in 1580s the meaning of "the one who passes judgement" and from c.1600 on that of "censurer, the one who judges quality of books", entered at that time English from medieval French *critique*, which comes from Latin *criticus* ("judge, critic of literature") which derives originally from Greek. "Criticism", from "critic" and "-ism", meant around 1600 "the act of criticising" and from 1670s on "art of estimating literary works". "Criticise", formed by "critic" and "-ise/-ize", meant in 1640s "to pass, usually unfavourable, judgement", then "to discuss critically" from 1660s and "to censure" from 1704. "Critical", from "critic" and suffix "-ial", meant "censorious" in 1580s, received its meaning of "pertaining to criticism" in 1740s, but also had a medical meanings from c.1600 and the meanings "of the nature of crisis" (1640s") and "crucial" (1840s). "Critique", around 1700, meaning "the art of criticism", is from French *critique* or *critick* and Latin *critica* as the feminine of *criticus*, but it also derives ultimately from the Greek *krites*, *krinô*, and *kritikē* ("the art of discerning").

Concerning imaginative writing, it is interesting and also necessary to point out that in place of the terms familiar nowadays "author" and "literature", the words "poet" and "poetry" were used for centuries until late into modern period to label all creative literature and the writer, in general. The etymology begins in ancient Greece and Rome, with the Greek word *poiëin*, meaning "to make, to do, to compose". It gave the Greek *poesis* ("a thing made, composition, poetry"), *poema* ("thing made or created, work of poetry"), and *poetes* ("maker, poet, author"); the Latin *poesis* ("poetry"), *poema* ("poetry, verse"), and *poeta* ("poet, author"); Vulgar Latin *poesia*; Old French *poesie*, *poetrie*, and *poete*; Old and Middle English (c.1300) "poesy"; Modern English (c.1500) "poetry", "poem", and "poet".

Thus, the terms "poetry" and "poet" signified literature and author, in general, and referred to all genres, which was mainly due to the fact that the greater part of imaginative literature produced until the rise of the novel was actually written in verse form. Philip Sidney in *The Defence of Poesie* insists that "it is not rhyming and versing that maketh poesy. One may be a poet without versing, and a versifier without poetry". Literature was, therefore, named as "poetry", a text of literature of whatever genre as "poem", and the author as "poet". Drama was labelled "poetry", as in Dryden, for whom plays are "dramatic poesie" and Shakespeare and Jonson are "poets". Even novel was included in poetry, as in Fielding, who calls his novel *Joseph Andrews* a "comic epic poem written in prose". Gradually, in the course of literary history, the words "poetry" and "poet" were limited to the meaning of literature written in verse form.

The term "literature" originates from the Latin *littera*, meaning letter of alphabet, and its form *litterarum*, referring to books, manuscripts, letters, acts, memories, and literary and scientific works. Terry Eagleton points to the fact that throughout the periods of literary development in England, and especially in the eighteenth century, "the concept of literature was not confined as it sometimes is today to "creative" or "imaginative" writing", that it "meant the whole body of valued writing in society: philosophy, history, essays and letters as well as poems", "conformed to certain standards of "polite letters"", and that it was only in the romantic period that the modern definition of "literature" began to develop, "the privilege accorded by the Romantics to the "creative imagination"" leading to "a narrowing of the category of literature to so-called "creative" or "imaginative" work" and literature became "virtually synonymous with the "imaginative"" (Eagleton 15-17).

Today, the term "literature" denotes the entire imaginative writing and all the works which belong to all literary genres and forms, including narrative, lyrical, dramatic, or fictional prose, poetry, drama, or, to be more specific, novel, short story, poem, play, epic, tragedy, ode, satire, dramatic monologue, etc. Also, the term "literature" has another meaning: "if we describe something as "literature", as opposed to anything else, the term carries with it qualitative connotations which imply that the work in question has superior qualities; that it is well above the ordinary run of written works" (Cuddon 505-506).

This is the reason why anyone concerned with the history of literature and that of literary criticism should pay attention to the ways in which certain terms derive etymologically from others and the ways in which they change their meanings, as one should bear in mind that the criticism of "poetry" and "poets" produced before the nineteenth century actually means criticism of imaginative literature, in general.

To conclude this rather long but necessary part of our book, the argument to be considered in the field of literary studies dealing with the history of English literature is that the literary texts produced by different writers in different periods of British history and civilization are not merely a category which needs to be included in an overall literary system of English or international cultural heritage for the sake of rendering its completeness and aesthetic validity.

It is rather that they are different in kind, unique and representative of a type of literary discourse which should be studied as a system in itself, and which, if properly comprehended, may perform the function of breaking down the existing views and theories about English literature, in general, or a particular literary manifestation in Britain, reorganizing them and suggesting new ones.

In our series of books, we attempt to argue that, following the principles announced by Yuri Tynyanov, the investigation of literary history is possible in relation to the view of literature as a system, interrelated with other systems and conditioned by them and by assuming that the movement of literature through history represents substitution of systems.

A more detailed and comprehensive presentation of Tynyanov's principles and opinions on historical investigation of the literary phenomenon may provide a vector methodology to those concerned with the diachronic movement of literature, as we shall see in the Preliminaries to this book.

PRELIMINARIES

LEARNING LITERARY HERITAGE THROUGH CRITICAL TRADITION OR BACK TO TYNYANOV

> The point is that most people don't want what you and your colleagues think of as history – the sort you get in books – because they don't know how to deal with it. Personally, I've every sympathy. With them, that is. I've tried to read a few history books myself, and while I may not be clever enough to enrol in your classes, it seems to me that the main problem with them is this: they all assume you've read most of the other history books already. It's a closed system. There's nowhere to start. (A character in *England, England* by Julian Barnes, London: Jonathan Cape, 1998, pp. 70-71)

Keywords: Tynyanov, Shklovsky, Eliot, Bakhtin, system, literary system, system of elements, substitution of systems, centre versus margin, innovation versus tradition, internal change, function, order, depersonalization, *ostranenie* (defamiliarization), literariness, intertextuality, dialogism, chronotope

It is a remarkable coincidence that the *fin de siècle* of all centuries before and during modernity represents an important breakthrough in the literary advancement: around 1370, *Sir Gawain and the Green Knight* is said to have emerged on the literary scene; around 1387, *The Canterbury Tales* came to claim the rise of Englishness in the literary art; 1470 saw the publication of *Morte d'Arthur*; the end of the sixteenth century saw Elizabethan drama and Shakespeare; the end of the seventeenth century proclaimed the age of reason and, particularly in English literature, neoclassicism; the eighteenth century ended in romanticism and the dominance of poetry (in English literature, with Blake, Wordsworth, and Coleridge), and, also in English literature, the novel is founded; the nineteenth century ended with the innovation of symbolism and aestheticism as origins and precursors of modernism; and the last decades of the twentieth century, as postmodern, also revealed the flourishing of literary innovation and experimentation under the auspices of postmodernism, which mainly manifest themselves in imaginative prose.

The movement of English literature (or any other national literature, or the world literature, in general) through history is the main concern of the history of literature (literary history), a distinct discipline of literary evaluation which is nowadays alive and applied – and still developed and attempted to be conferred with scientific and methodological apparatus – despite the postmodern laments over the death of history, originality, meaning, reality, and authorship, along with the mourning of the end of reflexiveness, reflexivity, reflection, and the impossibility of language to truthfully represent whatever an artist would endeavour to reflect.

In its diachronic perspective focused on literary periods, movements, trends, authors, and texts, the historical investigation of literature is interrelated with literary theory (offering terminology and general principles of research) and literary criticism (providing the way of approach to particular texts), which, in turn, are indispensable from literary history (history of literature), as we have seen in the Introduction to this book.

In the discussion of the rise and consolidation of an English literary tradition, one should focus on the elements of the literary system in order to conduct a general, surveyistic as well as coherent approach to the complexity of the literary phenomenon considered diachronically from its Anglo-Saxon beginnings to the present day.

Rewriting Jakobson's structure of communication, Guy Cook identifies author, reader, text, performer, society, texts and language to be the main elements of the literary communicative situation, or the elements of the literary system. Among these elements is language; the formal, particularly structuralist and post-structuralist, interpretative arrangements of Shklovsky (*O teorii prozy*, 1929) and Lotman ("Lektsii po strukturalinoi poetike", 1994) – concerning art as language and system of signs, and the written language of the novel, poem and other literary works as their instrument and material – argue that language influences diachronically the essence of every cultural system, including literature and fiction. In turn, written language is indispensable from the instability and dynamics of various historical and cultural circumstances.

In order to be closer to the objective theory of art, from a formalist perspective, the aestheticization of written language, as a central aspect or element in the literary act of communication, prompts literariness and becomes possible by means of a set of literary devices, figures of speech, verbal nuances, and so on. Shklovsky, over a century ago, already showed that these devices would eventually make things unique and complicate the form of a work of art in order to increase the difficulty and time of perception since this process in art is an end in itself and must be prolonged.

This principle working in art and literature, called *ostranenie* ("defamiliarization"), has become the fundamental credo of modernism and is still successfully applied nowadays in literary practice, such as in the works of magical realism.

Adding Bakhtin to Cook, Shklovsky, and Lotman, other canonical principles, underpinning the development of literature and representing elements of its consolidated pattern, include chronotope, *raznorechie* (heteroglossia), polyphony, carnivalesque, and, especially, dialogism.

Adding Tynyanov to Bakhtin, Cook, Shklovsky, and Lotman, literature is to be viewed as a system of elements with centre and margin, with dominant and peripheral elements which fight to move into centre, to resist what denies them.

These elements do not disappear; they always are; they just exist; they are "Lord's", as Shklovsky says about his "images", just as T. S. Eliot speaks about impressions and experiences which do not change but are continuously recombined and rearranged.

Based on Tynyanov, a "rule" of literary development would declare periods, movements, trends, genres, subgenres, even texts, and so on, to be literary systems placed in a diachronic relationship of substituting, following or succeeding each other by continuing and rejecting each other, as well as by being influenced by contemporary socio-cultural stimuli and developments in philosophy and science.

In the light of Tynyanov's ideas on literary work and literature conceived as systems, speaking solely about literary practice, its development in the context of literary history is based on the "fight" between the aspect of "innovation" and that of "tradition". These two aspects are represented diachronically by different periods, movements, trends, types of text, and so on, which either continue or reject and either follow or replace one another.

> These aspects, therefore, constitute the central (tradition) and marginal (innovation) elements within a literary system, which are engaged in a battle for dominance and to be central, to achieve defamiliarization, by which allowing development, change, and advancement of literature through history.

> The movement through history of a national literature can be better explained by drawing on theories of genre and literary development, of which one of the most congenial theorization, still valid and viable nowadays, belongs to Yuri Tynyanov, whose main reasoning would be that **literature is a system of central and peripheral elements** – in other words, tradition (centre) versus innovation (margin) in the fight over supremacy, which means for tradition to stay in the centre, whereas for innovation, it implies to proclaim demarginalization, to move into centre, and by this, to claim the right to build up a new system – **and the development or historical advancement of literature is the substitution of systems**, in other words, the substitution of various periods, movements, trends, genres, subgenres, styles, textual typologies, and so on.

Amid the huge amount of critical attention given to English literature, in general, and amid the multiplicity of theoretical perspectives to be applied to its analysis, Tynyanov's theories are appropriate and applicable also because they characterize national types of literature with their own characteristic features and peculiarities of historical development.

Drawing on the assumption that a literary work, like literature in general, is a system of interrelated and interdependent elements, the Russian formalist scholar discusses the genre in his essay entitled "Literaturnyi fakt" ("Literary Fact") and the development (history) of literature in "O literaturnoi evolutii" ("On Literary Evolution"), both written in 1927. Both works postulate the formalist theory of system and that of internal change in literary history.

In "Literary Fact", in matters of its principles, rise, development, sources, death and rebirth, these aspects of the genre, along with the migration and transformation of the genre, co-exist with and depend on the larger literary process, namely, the emergence of new literary trends, movements, forms, as well as views and conceptions in literary history.

The genre represents, in this respect, Tynyanov argues, not "a fall from the system", "not a planned evolution", not a "development", but "a jump or leap" and a shift, "a substitution of systems", and is therefore innovative and "unrecognizable" ("Literaturnyi fakt" 255-256). Like a literary work or movement, or literature in general, a genre is a system, but not a static, motionless system; it is a structure that may fluctuate, emerge from other systems, and weaken to become vestiges of subsequent systems.

A new genre replaces an old one, or becomes its successor, and the decline and rebirth of a genre are to be understood, as Tynyanov shows, in relation to the concentric model of literature, which is organized by the principles of "centre" and "margin": moving within this structure, a genre degenerates or dies out when it departs from the centre towards the periphery, but revives its literary potential when it approaches the centre, or "in its place from the trifles of literature, from the backyards and bottoms of literature, a new phenomenon emerges in the centre" (Tynyanov, "Literaturnyi fakt" 257-258).

Tynyanov emphasizes the diachronically inconstant feature of the literary periods, movements, and genres, which are viewed as literary systems, their dynamic, not static, essence, which is based on the perpetual clash between tradition and innovation, the permanent conflict over hierarchy, which involves various elements in their position within the system as centre and margin, in other words, as central or peripheral, dominant or marginal elements. An element or a form originally not considered literary is placed into a literary system, or it diverges from another element or form, and thereby it may give birth to a new trend or genre as a new system. Once established, a literary genre or trend never goes out of existence since its elements may emerge in either dominant or marginal positions in various other systems, namely newly emerging periods, movements, trends, genres, subgenres, and so on.

The medieval ballad, for instance, receives a new expression in romanticism by Coleridge. Also, in this period, the historical element becomes dominant in the system of what is established as the historical novel by Scott. In Wieland and especially Goethe, the element of ordeal from medieval romances re-emerges as an important element in the Bildungsroman literary system to determine the inner change of the character and prompt his or her identity formation.

Focusing primarily on literary genres, Tynyanov develops the formalist theory of internal change in literary development. After providing a concentric model of literature, he postulates the principle of the conflict between centre and margin, theorizes the obliteration and rebirth of genres, and insists on the migration and transformation of genres, according to which, moving within the literary system, a genre is forgotten or silenced if it moves away from the centre, and is renewed when it comes closer to the centre.

A particular genre becomes dominant in a certain period and develops its system of elements: it attracts writers, who become more imitative than creative, expands temporally and territorially, and, in this way, a literary tradition or convention is established. Confronted by innovation and originality, the genre may lose its dominant position and be replaced by a new one which becomes dominant.

The way in which Tynyanov discusses the genre is true for literary periods, movements, trends, species, and works, i.e., all literary phenomena which constitute, in the formalist view, literary systems with distinct characteristics.

We also follow in our study the theory of internal change, and start from the premise of literature to be a system of elements which denote either centre or margin prompting a battleground for innovation and tradition.

In order to explain this practically with direct reference to a literary tradition established as literary system, a good example would be the subgenre of the novel known as the Bildungsroman. Just like with various genres, in Tynyanov's opinion, the thematic and, to a lesser extent, structural elements of various literary systems –

literary systems are represented diachronically from ancient times to the end of the eighteenth century by different periods, movements, trends, genres, subgenres and text categories – perform individual breakthroughs and survive, or are modified, receive new positions, and interrelate anew around the central element of identity formation as established by Goethe in his canonical novel of formation *Wilhelm Meisters Lehrjahre*. In doing so, these elements, primarily thematic, are placed into and become elements of the new Bildungsroman literary system; among them, pseudo-biographical material, childhood experience, education, ordeal, chronotope of road, epiphany, and others become central and peripheral elements of the literary system of the Bildungsroman, whose dominant and central element is formation.

The Bildungsroman, being currently perpetuated by various writers around the world, reveals that changes still occur within its literary system. These changes have occurred and occur for both internal and external reasons, such as the newly emerging trends (magical realism, for instance), the audience, the publisher, or various social, cultural and political developments.

Unlike the romance, or the picaresque novel, or the gothic narrative, the Bildungsroman stays to the present day one of the few "strong" genres, or rather subgenre of the novelistic genre, as to be more correct terminologically in accordance to the categorisation by literary theory and criticism. The Bildungsroman proves, historically, literary vitality and multifaceted creative consistency, since, in its depiction of the life of a particular individual, this fictional subgenre relies on and confirms the view that literature has always been and will always be, to a lesser or greater extent, a reflection of the personal experience of the author.

The formalist theory of internal change covers the domain of genres, and also those of literary periods, movements, trends, types of texts, including the Bildungsroman, and so on; nowadays it is also applied in feminist, minority and cultural studies and in postcolonial theory. In postulating intertextuality – new texts emerge as imitating, completing, competing, negating, or parodying other texts – the formalist theory of internal change alludes to Bakhtin's dialogism, Shklovsky's *ostranenie*, and Eliot's new combinations of elements.

"A new art emotion" is what T. S. Eliot declares, in "Tradition and the Individual Talent" (1919), to be novelty in literature, its significance and the real artistic and poetic achievement. Tradition is for him an "order", which is a term identical to that used by Tynyanov; for Eliot, likewise, order is not static or ideal but is continuously modified by new works which attempt to acquire their place in literary history, making order simultaneous, bringing it into the present of literary activity when intertextuality is at work.

The poet is not an individual separated from history, and the significance of his poetry stands in its relation to the past: "No poet, no artist of any art, has his complete meaning alone. His significance, his appreciation is the appreciation of his relation to the dead poets and artists" (Eliot 44).

The ideal order established by tradition becomes a simultaneous order when the past and present are united and expressed concomitantly: the simultaneous order is a kind of archive. Accordingly, the individual talent does not need to invent something or attempt to produce originality, since everything has been already written, but to recombine, rearrange the elements of order, keeping in mind – and here Eliot is not far removed from "dialogism" in Bakhtin and "intertextuality" in Kristeva – that "the past should be altered by the present as much as the present is directed by the past" (Eliot 45).

Another important aspect in the act of artistic creation is, for Eliot, the "process of depersonalization" based on the continuous surrender to tradition and "self-sacrifice": the poet does not express a personality, but "a particular medium"; poetry, in Eliot's famous anti-Wordsworthian declaration, "is not a turning loose of emotion, but an escape from emotion; it is not the expression of personality, but an escape from personality" (Eliot 52-53).

Actually, the process leading to novelty or "new art emotion", as articulated by Eliot, is not far removed from a formalist perspectives: it begins with (1) learning, acquiring the knowledge of canonical works as standards of greatness (as later Harold Bloom would insist), in other words, evolving an awareness of the past tradition, order and the world, the human condition; it continues with (2) self-sacrifice or surrender to past tradition; which leads to (3) poet losing personality and acquiring "depersonalization" or impersonality; so that (4) the poet becomes a medium for the expression of existing elements, "impressions and experiences"; (5) the poet thereby produces new, original combinations of impressions, experiences, images, feelings, phrases, etc.; which results in (6) the ideal order becoming simultaneous; which means, finally, that (7) a "new art emotion" emerges to take its place in the order or, in Tynyanov's terms, in the literary system.

The modernist author T. S. Eliot is viewed, as a critic, in relation to Anglo-American "New Criticism", whereas Yuri Tynyanov represents Russian "Formalism"; they are united in their pursuit of a formal approach to literature, hence certain similarities of their critical thinking.

Examples of a common pursuit and similar concepts and perspectives of literary investigation are to be found in the work of the formal and formalist Viktor Shklovsky, namely in his "Art as Technique" (1917), in which self-sacrifice and depersonalization become *ostranenie* ("defamiliarization") and the key concepts are again "rearrangement", "recombination" of elements and images so as to pursue the technique of art which is "to make objects "unfamiliar", to make forms difficult, to increase the difficulty and length of perception because the process of perception is an aesthetic end in itself and must be prolonged" (Shklovsky 778). "Art is thinking in images", and poetry is a special way of thinking, namely, thinking by means of images, where thinking in images allows for "economy of mental effort" (Shklovsky 775).

"Images", in Shklovsky (or "elements", in Tynyanov, and "impressions and experiences", in Eliot), change little diachronically, or, actually they are the same; they pass or are taken unchanged from poet to poet: "from century to century, from nation to nation, from poet to poet, they flow on without changing" (Shklovsky 776); they belong to no one but the Lord, and they are identical in the works of various poets.

Like Tynyanov and Eliot, Shklovsky draws attention to the fact that a certain poet would never invent or produce new images. Like Tynyanov, for whom elements are linked to co-exist in the system in correlation and interrelationship, and, like Eliot, for whom impressions and experiences are combined in new and original ways to produce a new art emotion, Shklovsky contends that the poets should remember images rather than create them – since images are given to poets – in order to rearrange and combine them in new and original ways.

As in Tynyanov and Eliot, elements, images, experiences, feelings, themes, concerns, motifs, ideas, etc. are static; what is continually changing is their relation, or combination, or arrangement. The motivation for such arrangements and combinations focuses on impression, in that poetic imagery "is a means of creating the strongest possible impression" (Shklovsky 776). Shklovsky's "impression", like that of Henry James and especially Walter Pater, concerns the process of artistic perception; as in Pater, personal impression is a means of fighting stereotype or unconscious existence, or, as Shklovsky calls it, fighting "habitualization", the process of "algebrization", "the over-automatization of an object" (Shklovsky 778).

Hence, the requirement for successful and accomplished artistic endeavour is "ostranenie" or "defamiliarization", by which the sensation of life is recovered, things are felt, the stone is made "stony", and the purpose of art is achieved, namely, "to impart the sensation of things as they are perceived and not as they are known", since "Art is a way of experiencing the artfulness of an object; the object is not important" (Shklovsky 778). One should remember here that the romantic critical theory already pointed at this feature of literature – Wordsworth and Shelley stipulating the ability of poetry to achieve unusual, unfamiliar expression – as later the nineteenth-century avant-garde did.

Shklovsky's view of the arrangement of images in various new ways – just like Tynyanov's view of elements and Eliot's of impressions which are arranged and combined in new, original ways – represents one way to understand the historical movement of literature through periods, movements, and trends.

Poets and their works are classified or grouped according to the arrangement of images, the "development of the resources of language", and "the new techniques that poets discover and share" (Shklovsky 776), where this "grouping" would allow the foundation of new trends and movements.

To us, such ideas represent a congenial way to understand the movement of literature as a system diachronically, including the rise, consolidation, fall, further development, and change of various periods, movements and trends.

In matters of literary genre, Viktor Shklovsky talks about "the canonization of minor genres", such as the romance, the picaresque novel, or the gothic narrative. The Bildungsroman is also such a historically emergent literary fact, first in German pre-romanticism with Goethe, to become aesthetically strengthened by the realists and modified and diversified by the modernist and postmodern writers.

To revert to Tynyanov, a literary system, as a particular period, movement, trend, literary species, category, type, genre, or subgenre, demonstrates in the system of literature, in general, that "the literary fact is multi-structured and in this respect literature is a continuously evolving order" ("Literaturnyi fakt" 270) consisting of a myriad of diverse forms within which occur a myriad of "merging episodes of the constructional principle with the material" ("Literaturnyi fakt" 269).

Tynyanov further applies his conception of literature as a system to the discussion of literary development, or, in his words, "literary evolution", whose principles are, also in his terms, "fight" and "substitution". In his study "O literaturnoi evolutii", Tynyanov compares the domain of the history of literature to a colonial state driven by an "individualistic psychologism" and "a schematically causal approach to the literary order" (270). The divergence between them leads to a methodological discrepancy in the field of the historical investigation of literature. The former type replaces the problem of literature with the question of the author's psychology and the issue of literary evolution with that of the genesis of literary phenomena. The latter leads to the disagreement between the literary order and the standpoint from which the observation of this literary order takes place.

This place of observation constitutes social orders, and the construction of a closed literary order and the approach to evolution inside it (that is, to literary variability) would frequently come up against neighbouring cultural, domestic and, in the broad sense, social orders, and as such are doomed to incompleteness. Moreover, the theory of value in literary science has brought about the danger of studying major but isolated works and has changed the history of literature into what Tynyanov calls "the history of generals", meaning "great works" or masterpieces of literature (the literary canon), to the detriment of the study of mass literature.

The very term "history of literature" is a problem as well, continues Tynyanov, as it seems to be extremely broad and pretentious, suggesting the study of the history of *belles lettres*, the history of verbal art, and the history of writing, in general. Meanwhile, the historical investigation of literature has forked into the investigation of the genesis of literary phenomena and the investigation of the "evolution" of the literary order, or literary mutability.

The problem plaguing the historical approach to literature is the lack of theoretical methodology and the lack of an awareness of the character of research. The solution for making the history of literature a science, conferring on it the necessary methodological rigour, must be its striving for "reliability" and veracity ("O literaturnoi evolutii" 271). The study of literary development must avoid the theory of "naïve evaluation" and the subjective response; it is also necessary to reconsider the notion of "tradition", which is the abstractzation of one or more literary elements in a system.

The central concept in literary evolution, which is responsible for literary change and development, is the **"substitution of systems"** ("O literaturnoi evolutii" 272). In order to analyse this essential issue in the context of studies on literary history, Tynyanov starts from the fundamental assumption that a literary work is a system, as is literature itself. In his opinion, the foundation of a science of literature and the investigation of the historical progress of literature are possible only in the view of literature as a system interrelated with other systems and conditioned by them.

All the elements of a literary work are the elements of a system, in the sense of a literary system which is a system of functions of literary order which are in continual interrelationship with other orders. All the elements of the system of a literary work are interrelated, interdependent and interacting. Some elements of a work in prose, such as rhythm, are also elements of the system of a work in poetry, and their study shows that the role of such elements is different in different systems.

The interrelationship of each element with every other in a literary work as a system, and, therefore, with the whole, is what Tynyanov calls the "constructional function of the given element" ("O literaturnoi evolutii" 272). This function is a complex entity: it shows that a distinct element is, on the one hand, interrelated in the order with similar elements of other works-systems and even of other orders, and, on the other hand, interrelated with other elements within the same system. Tynyanov names the former "auto-function" and the latter "syn-function". Both operate simultaneously but are of different relevance. The lexis of a given literary work, for instance, is related at once to the literary lexis and the general verbal lexis, and to other elements of this work.

Tynyanov points to the mistake of extracting certain elements from a system and, without their constructional function, of correlating them outside the system with a similar order of other systems. It is also impossible to study synchronically a literary work as a system outside its relation to the general system of literature; otherwise, such a study is another abstractization. The isolated study of the literary works is applied, successfully enough, to the evaluation of contemporary works, since the interrelationship of a contemporary work to contemporary literature is involuntarily taken as an established fact.

However, Tynyanov argues, even in contemporary literature, isolated study is impossible because the very existence of a text as literary depends on its differential quality, which is on its interrelationship with either literary or extra-literary order. In other words, its existence depends on its function: what in one period would be a matter of casual social communication, in another would be a literary fact, or vice versa, depending on the whole of the literary system in which the given text appears.

Therefore, "studying the work in isolation, we cannot be sure that we speak in correct terms about its construction" ("O literaturnoi evolutii" 273). The auto-function (the interrelationship of an element to the order of similar elements in other systems and other orders) is a condition for the syn-function (the constructional function of the element).

To summarize, according to Tynyanov, the constructional function is the correlation of each element of the literary work with other elements of the system, and thus with the whole system. It is a mistake to separate the elements from the system and to correlate them outside the system, which is to neglect their constructional function. The existence of a literary fact depends on its differential quality, meaning its function.

Next, Tynyanov offers examples of poetry and prose, and focuses on the novel and its adjustment genres of story and novella to insist again that "the evaluation of literary phenomena does not occur outside their interrelationship" ("O literaturnoi evolutii" 276) and that, unfortunately, the evolutionary relation between the function and the formal element has not been studied. There are examples in literature of how the evolution of literary form determines the change of function; examples of how a form with indefinite function calls and builds up a new one; and examples of how function searches for its form.

The variability of functions of a formal element of the system, the appearance of a new function of the formal element, and its association with the function are important issues of literary evolution. Again, the whole research depends on the consideration of literature as an order, a system, where "the system of literary order is first of all the system of functions of literary order in continuous interrelationship with other orders" ("O literaturnoi evolutii" 277). Each literary work is correlated with a particular literary system depending on its deviation, its difference, as compared to the literary system with which it is confronted. Moreover, since a literary system is a system of the functions of the literary order which is in continual interrelationship with other orders, such as social and cultural, orders or systems change in their composition, but the differentiation of human activities remains.

Due to the specificity of its material, the growth of literature, like that of other cultural orders, coincides neither in rate nor in character with those systems or orders, such as social, with which it is interrelated. The evolution of the constructional function occurs rapidly; that of the literary function occurs over epochs, and the one concerning the functions of the whole literary system in relation to the neighbouring systems occurs over centuries.

To follow Tynyanov's line of argumentation, to understand the development of literature as the "substitution of systems" is to perceive it as the change in the interrelationship of the elements of a system, which is the change of functions and formal elements.

A system does not represent an equal interrelationship of all elements, promoting instead the differential interaction of its elements, where through a group of dominant elements producing the deformation of other elements, a new literary work emerges in literature and acquires its literary function by means of these dominant elements.

Drawing especially on these theoretical assumptions by Tynyanov, as well as on those by Shklovsky and Bakhtin, the books of our project focusing on English literature aim to demonstrate the diachronicity of the literary phenomenon as an order or system of elements. We argue that English literature is a literary system which has passed through development and change of its thematic and formal elements and functions in order to establish itself as a continuous movement of periods, trends, genres, subgenres, authors, texts, and so on, each a literary tradition or system with preceding systems as cornerstones.

The substitutions of literary systems leading to new ones vary from epoch to epoch; they may occur rapidly or slowly; they do not necessarily require the complete renewal or replacement of the formal elements of the systems, but rather "a new function of these formal elements" (Tynyanov, "O literaturnoi evolutii" 281). A potential collation of certain literary phenomena must consider functions in addition to forms.

Tynyanov concludes his study by summarizing his ideas: the study of literary evolution is possible only by viewing literature as an order, a system which is interrelated with other orders, systems, and is conditioned by them. The study must move from the constructional function (the interrelationship of each element with other elements of the system, and thus with the whole system of the literary work) to the literary function (the interrelationship of a literary work with the literary order), and from the literary function to the verbal function (the interrelationship of a literary work with the social conventions), while clarifying the issue of developmental interaction of functions and forms. Also, the investigation of literature in its development "must go from the literary order to the nearest correlated systems, not some distant ones, although these could be important" ("O literaturnoi evolutii" 281), such as social conventions, cultural doctrines, historical background, the author's psychology, daily life and personal experience, and the tastes and interests of the reading audience.

Concerning the two components – social or historical, on the one hand, and biographical or psychological, on the other – that is, the author's times and life, from a formalist perspective, literature is above all interrelated with social conventions, and as such the correlation takes place first of all through its verbal aspect. In other words, the interrelation between literature and society is realized through language, and in relation to the social background the prime function of literature is its verbal function. Using the term "orientation" to denote the author's creative intention, Tynyanov and the formalists suggest that the intention is changed by the structural function (the interrelationship of elements within a work) into a catalyst, that "creative freedom" yields to "creative necessity", and that the literary function (the interrelationship of a work with the literary order) completes the process.

Simply stated, the "orientation" of a literary work proves to be its "verbal function", its interrelationship with social conventions. It would be futile to study the verbal function of literature in relation to some distant conditions, such as economic, as it is useless to study the author's psychology, environment, daily life, and class directly in order to establish the origins of the literary phenomena. Clearly, Tynyanov and the formalists believe, the problem here is not one of individual psychological conditions, but of objective, evolving functions of the literary order in relation to the adjacent social order.

Likewise, in discussing practical criticism, David Daiches states that the approach to the literary work should be different from going to biography or psychology to discover the author's intention, for "it is less personal intention than artistic tradition that is the real question" (265), where literary tradition is the object of study of the history of literature. Earlier, W. K. Wimsatt together with Monroe C. Beardsley condemned both "affective fallacy", which leads to a confusion between ends and means in judging the literary work in terms of its results in the mind of the audience, and "intentional fallacy", which is an error of evaluating a literary work by trying to assess what the author's intention was and whether it has or not been fulfilled.

In the historical studies of British literature, or any national literature, or the history of world literature, on the whole, it is clear that literary history, which provides a chronological vision on literature, is confronted with repeated methodological crises, as this discipline is unable to fully synchronise itself with the innovations which constantly take place in modern literary theory and criticism. As Tynyanov has already warned on this matter in his formalist attempts to renovate the history of literature through the theories of literature as a system, literary evolution, and the genre, the historical investigation of literature might still have no clear theoretical awareness of how to study a literary work or what the nature of its significance is. Rene Wellek and Austin Warren, in their celebrated *Theory of Literature*, also claim that the history of a national literature is hard to envisage and remains a distant ideal; strongly bound to their Russian formalist origins, they assume the theory of the literary system and claim that literary history must be the study of systems of "literary norms, standards, and conventions" and must be "the tracing of the changing from one system of norms to another" (264-268).

Wellek and Warren believe that the separation of criticism from the diachronic dimension of the literary history and its subsequent consolidation as a distinct domain were caused by the distinction between the consideration of literature as a simultaneous order and the view on literature as diachronic order, a line of works arranged chronologically and regarded as constituent parts of the historical process. Our study attempts to balance the levels on the assumption that neither the research of the text as a synchronic phenomenon nor the historicization of literary experience are to be neglected. To achieve an adequate comprehension of the literary works of different writers and periods, it is necessary to overcome the gap between literary criticism and literary history by fusing the synchronic and diachronic dimensions in literary analysis, and by strengthening the relationship between text and context.

To revert to Tynyanov, the two main types of the historical investigation of literature – the investigation of the genesis of literary phenomena and the investigation of the growth of a literary order or system – are both problematic, as problematic is to re-examine the problem of "influence", one of the most complex issues of literary history, in relation to the existence of specific literary conditions. Also, coming back to the concept of "tradition" in literature, it is to be remembered that what may be called "traditionalism" is, as to give an example from Tynyanov, the fact that each literary movement in a given period seeks its supporting point in the preceding systems, as each new genre, or form, or type of literary text does.

In the process of literary development, tradition continues tradition and rejects innovation, just as innovation continues innovation and rejects tradition, making literary systems – which we view as literary periods, movements, trends, genres, subgenres, texts, and so on – follow, replace, substitute each other. This process implies the struggle between tradition and innovation in terms of a binary opposition involving centre and margin, or central and peripheral elements, where the differential interaction of the elements of a system, the existence of some "dominant" elements which produce as such the "deformation" or marginalization of other elements, mean actually, in Tynyanov's opinion, literary evolution as substitution of systems.

Yuri Tynyanov's views on the literary work and literature conceived as systems and on the development of literature as substitution of systems are applicable in other domains of the humanities, such as linguistics (since language itself is a system), translation studies, and cultural studies, and in different literary disciplines, such as comparative literature, where, in particular, the issue of "reception" – the study of the process of reception of a literature (as a system) in another literature or another cultural background (also conceived as systems) – receives a strong theoretical and practical basis. Although highly important for the elucidation of the status and role of literary history as a scientific discipline, Tynyanov's theory of the literary system, due to its normative principles and methodological rigour, may not always be appropriate to the study of literature. This is especially the case when we face some national peculiarities of literary history, or when the individual creative imagination is both ready to assume an established tradition, model or pattern of writing and to pursue unexpected innovation, literary experimentation, and modernization of the literary discourse.

However, like many other concepts and principles of the formalists, and from the Russians' ranks also those of M. M. Bakhtin, Tynyanov's idea of literature as a system of dominant and peripheral elements turns out to be an important issue for postmodern theoretical and ideological debate regarding the "centre and margin" dichotomy. Bakhtin himself focuses on the concepts of "self and other"; he also coins the terms and discusses chronotope, polyphony, *raznorechie*, carnivalesque, dialogism, unfinalizability, *roman vospitaniya* ("the novel of education" or Bildungsroman), where these and other principles and ideas on literature are the most congenial to our approach to the rise and development of a national literature, English, and world literature, in general.

To return to the idea of system and the "centre and margin" dualism, this binary opposition is nowadays discussed in cultural, postcolonial, social, feminist, and literary studies. The postmodern attitude towards dominant elements, and, in particular discourses, is twofold: (1) to come within dominant discourses and try to modify them from within, and (2) to accept and proclaim marginalization and try to make fringe move into centre.

The relationship of centre and margin, or dominant and peripheral elements, can be applied to literature both diachronically and synchronically. From a diachronic perspective, we would link two explanations in the discussion of the development of literature, in general, one late modern by Tynyanov, based on his theory of system, and another postmodern, based on the concepts of margin and centre. In its shift from centre or a dominant position to margin or periphery, literature becomes ex-centric (outside the centre), and "ex-centric" means "eccentric", in the sense of being unconventional, original, new. Thus, innovation emerges by rejecting tradition as centre within tradition, and moves towards the margin to become a peripheral phenomenon; if strong enough, innovation may eventually become a centre and establish itself as tradition, as it happened with baroque, romanticism, symbolism, modernism, and, more recently, with magical realism.

Innovation and tradition in literature are reified by various following each other periods, movements, and trends as literary orders or systems; their rise is based doubly on rejection of some prior literary systems and continuation of other previous literary systems, and is influenced by contemporary developments in other more or less distant systems, such as cultural, linguistic, scientific, sociologic, and so on.

Although postmodernism rejects the notion of system, we should still pay attention to Tynyanov pointing to literature as a system containing dominant and peripheral elements when we speak about centre and margin from a postmodern standpoint to explain the development of literature by recourse to such concepts as innovation and tradition. We ought especially to recall Tynyanov's theorization of literature as a system, the evolution of literature as substitution of systems, and the elements of the literary system as interrelating and interacting both (1) among themselves and (2) with the elements of other literary and non-literary (social, cultural, political, ideological, artistic, etc.) systems.

From a synchronic perspective and within national boundaries, a literary system may be described in terms of three criteria of development with regard to the interrelationship of its elements: (1) concerning individual authors, for example Alexander Pope as centre and Thomas Gray as margin, or Shakespeare as centre and Ben Jonson as margin; (2) the substitution of periods and movements, for instance neoclassicism as centre and romanticism as margin at the end of the eighteenth century, where subsequently romanticism becomes itself a centre and replaces neoclassicism; and (3) the shift of periods and movements, for example realism as centre and modernism as margin changes to modernism as centre and realism as margin in the first half of the twentieth century.

The centre and margin dichotomy in feminism and in social studies is actualized as male/man as centre and female/woman as margin, heterosexual versus sexual minorities, dominant nationality or race versus national or racial minorities, and so on. In postcolonial studies: white versus non-white, colonizer/West/Europe as centre and the colonized/Non-West as margin. The opposition emerges also within each of the two elements taken separately. In Europe as centre, for example, Western Europe is centre and Eastern Europe is margin, which can be seen in literature as well: in anthologies of literature you would barely find Alexe Rudeanu in the company of Ian McEwan. The margin may move into the centre, along with the emerging issue of identity, when an author is translated but especially when he or she assumes the language of the centre, its values, mentality and attitudes, but, above all, enhances the centre, just as Eliade, Ionesco, Kundera, Kis, Safak, and others have done. Another example would be Latin America as margin which, in its relation to the West as centre, nevertheless produced a type of reversal of the binary opposition: after producing outstanding literature (Marquez and Coelho, among others), the erstwhile margin becomes centre when it is imitated by the already existing centre, as is the case, in English literature, of Angela Carter and her novels of magical realism.

The basic term "system" in Tynyanov and formalism receives a new life through Linda Hutcheon's "constant" and "system" as well as Bran Nicol's "dominant" in their explanation and evaluation of the postmodernist literature. Hutcheon, in *A Poetics of Postmodernism* (1988), speaks about a constant, meaning a central, dominant element, in postmodern fiction, namely that "the assertion of identity through difference and specificity is a constant in postmodern thought" (59). Furthermore, Hutcheon views modernism and postmodernism as two incompatible ideological "systems", where postmodern fiction rejects from the system of modernism such elements or features as the modernist ideology of artistic autonomy, individual expression, and the deliberate separation of art from mass culture and everyday life.

Nicol, likewise, considers "postmodern" as adjective to refer to "a particular period in literary and perhaps cultural history" and, at the same time, to a system or "set of aesthetic styles and principles", whereas, postmodernism, as an aesthetic phenomenon and the reflexive or reflecting mentality and artistic practice of postmodernity, refers to a system or "set of ideas developed from philosophy and theory and related to aesthetic production" (2). Furthermore, Bran Nicol introduces the notion "dominant" in his consideration of three main features or elements, which are mostly important, or dominants, in the postmodern novel (xvi), itself conceived as a literary system. They are identified by Nicol in his book as (1) a self-reflexive acknowledgement of a text's own status as constructed, aesthetic artefact; (2) an implicit (or sometimes explicit) critique of realist approaches both to narrative and to representing a fictional "world"; and (3) a tendency to draw the reader's attention to his or her own process of interpretation as s/he reads the text (6).

In conceiving the postmodern fiction as a system with certain dominant or central elements, Nicol relies on Jakobson's formalist concept of "dominant" which determines and rules the other components or elements of the system or structure, stays in the centre of the system and guarantees its integrity, and changes over literary history.

It is certain and there is no further need to argue that Jakobson with his theory of communication relies entirely on the formalist conception of the system containing various elements possessing specific functions and, to the present, his theory has remained highly influential in both linguistics and literary studies. It is also worth mentioning here another approach which, drawing on the assumption that a particular literary work is a literary system within the larger system of a genre within the general system of literature and interrelated with other socio-cultural systems, is based on Itamar Even-Zohar's theory of polysystem. Even-Zohar views literature as a polysystem, a system of systems, a complex and heterogeneous structure, coherent yet dynamic, in that its elements are in a constant agonistic relation among themselves. Applicable along with formalism to the study of literary history and genre, this view of literature as a kind of system widens the approach to literature, whose system is regarded in relation to other systems and domains such as culture and cultural studies, translation, anthropology, and so on.

Jakobson and French structuralism, on the whole, later Hutcheon and Nicol, to say nothing about Itamar Even-Zohar, to a certain extent Julia Kristeva, and even Homi Bhabha – as well as our humble contribution, we would like to believe – maintain Yuri Tynyanov's line of thinking and concepts alive, which have developed and emerged nowadays more like a kind of "neo-formalism".

> Within this neo-formalist framework of reasoning, in order to strengthen the understanding by the students of the mechanisms working to make possible the movement of literature through history, it is to comprehend again that speaking solely about literary practice in the light of Tynyanov's ideas, its development in the context of literary history is based on the "clash" between "innovation" and "tradition". They stand to each other as centre and margin, the dominant element versus marginal element in the system of literature, each striving against marginalization and for the supremacy of its aesthetic validity, longevity and potency. They are represented diachronically by different periods, movements, and trends which follow and replace one another. Just like the literary genres, they are systems whose elements are correlated as depending again on their central and peripheral nature. Literature on the whole is a system with an on-going battle between central and marginal elements, where mutations happening on the level of any element generate and determine mutations on the general level of the system.

> If we conceive of the **literary work and literature, on the whole, as systems**, the interrelationship between "tradition" and "innovation" in the historical advancement of literature acts upon a literary system, which, by placing a group of its elements in the "dominant" position, makes the marginalization and deformation of other elements possible. A new work, or writing style, or subgenre, or genre, or trend, or

> movement emerges in literature and takes on its own literary function through this "dominant": this is the factor which stipulates the **substitution of systems** and determines the change and development of literary phenomena in the course of succeeding periods.

This is true as much of genres as of periods and movements. For instance, the literary system of the medieval romance changes in the Renaissance into the system termed by the noun *roman* ("novel") when elements of extended narration, setting, character representation and others become "dominant", whereas others, like verse form and the supernatural element, are extinguished.

On the contrary, when other elements, such as love intrigue, subjective and psychological experience, the fantastic and the irrational involved in action, are placed in the "dominant" position, the literary system of the romance is substituted in the second half of the eighteenth century by the system of a particular type of poetry called by the adjective "romantic". Another example: the element of "the revival of ancient classical tradition" in the literary system of the Renaissance becomes "dominant" in relation to the social and cultural orders (systems) of the seventeenth and eighteenth centuries, making possible the substitution of the system of the Renaissance literature by that of Enlightenment and neoclassicism.

This is also true about any particular literary tradition, or type of literary text. The "dominance" of such elements as adventure, ordeal, trial, the road chronotope, moral issues of personal conduct, love experience, autobiography, change of condition with respect to the social background, representing the system of the picaresque novel, to which the "dominant" element of *Bildung* or character formation (emergence or becoming, as in Bakhtin), implying inner change, is added in Goethe's *Wilhelm Meisters Lehrjahre*, makes possible the rise of the fictional system of the Bildungsroman in the nineteenth century. This type of novel, now a literary tradition, seeks its support in the previous systems, especially in the ancient and picaresque narratives and the romantic tradition, but places, in turn, a group of its elements in the "dominant" position, which makes possible the deformation of other elements, and as a result the related fictional types of *Entwicklungsroman*, *Erziehungsroman*, and *Künstlerroman* emerge in world literature.

A literary system can, therefore, be a literary period, such as the Renaissance, whose main elements are humanism, individualism, observation, rationalism, deduction, revival of the ancient classical tradition, etc.; it can be a literary movement, such as romanticism, whose central elements are imagination, subjective experience, dualism of existence, escapism, rebelliousness, and so on. A literary system can be also a genre, such as the novel, or a subgenre, for instance, the Bildungsroman.

Concerning this novelistic tradition, as to further exemplify our line of reasoning, we regard the literary discourse of the Bildungsroman as a well-structured literary pattern and likewise as an ordered system of elements whose aesthetic values stand within the larger system of the novel. The novel, as a self-standing system, belongs, along with other literary genres and types of text, to the system of literature. Literature, in turn, is a system framed within the general system of culture and should be approached in relation to other cultural systems. Such an analysis takes into consideration the national peculiarities of a literary system (here English), its relation to world literature, as well as the interrelationship between national culture and the world cultural phenomenon in general.

The peculiarity of the Bildungsroman as a literary work centred on the process of character formation – as both self-formation and guided formation – implies certain interpretative considerations. A critic should examine such elements of its system as (1) the author, particularly in his or her relation to the character, and the degree of their identification and separation, as well as the character as an autodiegetic narrator, since the Bildungsroman is an autobiographical type of fiction; (2) the reader, since the Bildungsroman is intended to be representative of the human condition; but, especially, (3) the content, or the thematic level, and (4) the form, or the narrative level, with their distinct but interrelated arrangements within the text of the whole process of an individual's development and formation.

In matters of (3) the content, or the thematic perspectives, particular concerns represent the milieu or society, the family background, parental figures, education, professional career, sentimental experience, ordeal, the philosophy of living, epiphany, moral didacticism, and others. In matters of (4) the form, meaning the structural perspectives, the focus is on the type of narration, point of view, narrator, narratee, mode, voice, and especially chronotope and its typology, and language as a means of both textualization of the process of growth and maturation and expression of the authorial point of view on this process. These elements are at the same time the main thematic and narrative aspects of the Bildungsroman literary system.

The elements to be focused upon in the study of such a particular type of text as the Bildungsroman may recall the elements of Roman Jacobson's structure of communication in general (sender, receiver, message, context, contact, and code) and those of literary communication as stated by Guy Cook: author, reader, text, performer, society, texts, and language. Such elements emerge from the condition of the Bildungsroman as a literary phenomenon which represents a specific type of fictional discourse framed within a specific type of communicative situation, a literary discourse intended to be communicated to the reader; in other words, the text of the novel of formation is involved in a literary communicative situation, it is the central element of a particular type of literary communication involving its author and reader and being organized as a literary system.

The Bildungsroman is to be considered a particular novelistic subgenre structured as a literary system in the line of such established literary and non-literary traditions as picaresque fiction and biography. Romanticism is a literary system in the line of such movements and trends in literature as metaphysical poetry, neoclassicism, aestheticism, or realism. The Renaissance is a literary system similar to such periods in the history of literature as medieval period, Victorian Age, the period of modernism, or the postmodern one.

They are phases and aspects of the diachronic movement of English literature and, as such, they are matters of concern of literary history, theory, and criticism. However, one should avoid making his or her study of English literature a compilation of unverified critical and theoretical categories simply due to their wide dissemination. In our case as well, instead of heavily borrowing ideas and providing quotations from historical, critical and theoretical studies in an attempt to relate and apply them to the analysis of English literature, it is necessary to consider the essence of different opinions and ideas, to adapt them according to the vector of research, and, especially, to follow the interpretative perspectives emerging from the direct, textual, contextual and comparative approach to English literature.

> We suggest to our students that a particular subgenre, such as the Bildungsroman, as well as the novel or fiction, generally, together with a poetic or dramatic text, or poetry and drama, or a particular literary period, movement, and trend, along with literature, in general, can be studied as systems of elements which would become concerns and objects of study of various trends and schools of the large domain of literary theory and criticism.

Literature, on the whole, and the particular elements of the literary system represent the main concern of the history of literature as well, especially in the light of Paul Ricoeur's hermeneutic perspectives of the textual arrangement and text analysis with regard to the human experience considered diachronically: (1) the implication of language as discourse, (2) the implication of discourse as a structured literary work, (3) the relation between verbal and written forms in the discourse and the structured literary work, (4) the structured literary work/discourse as the projection of another world, (5) the structured literary work as the projection of the authorial life which is transfigured through the discourse, and (6) the structured literary work as the self-comprehension of the reader (94).

In our books, the "world" of the literary system of English literature receives evaluative attention from three perspectives, which are the long-established domains of literary theory, literary criticism, and the history of literature. An accurate approach to English literary phenomenon would require the symbiosis of the three directions of research; unfortunately, much of the modern literary theory and criticism addresses the literary work as a synchronic phenomenon, removing the text from its temporal and spatial context.

The study of literature may avoid references to some distant systems, such as science and economy, but it should not ignore the importance of the private, social and/or historical factors, and especially cultural, philosophical and theoretical ones, since it is within these contexts that the literary significance of the work can be better clarified.

We agree with those who, like Brian Vickers, attempt to balance the impact of the internal and external factors acting upon the historical movement of literature in that a particular period, movement, trend, or genre is punctuated by social events, such as changes of governments or industrialisation, but it also necessarily obeys its own internal logic and is subjected to the organization and interrelationship among the elements of its system.

In his presentation of the seventeenth century, Vickers states that "[p]olitical events do impinge on literature, nowhere more dramatically than in the closing of the theatres in 1642, but the introduction, development, and ultimate decline of literary modes or genres follow their own laws, depending on the innate vitality of a form of the inventiveness of the writers using it" (160).

The emphasis on cultural, theoretical, philosophical, scientific, and historical dimensions and the consideration of various social and biographical influences on literary work must not, of course, exclude the synchronic dimension, methodological principles and the scientific rigour of literary theory and criticism to which literary history has access. Especially in the case of the diachronic advancement of English imaginative writing – which has a long developmental history – without understanding literature in its movement through history, the dualism of tradition and innovation, the origins of the literary work, the author's artistic sensibility and especially his or her theoretical and philosophical views, and the social and cultural circumstances and context of the act of literary creation, the critic would scarcely offer competent judgement on the value of the text, its author, period, movement, trend, or genre.

Despite the apocalyptic death verdict announced by so many concerning the future of literary history, the fact that any literary work is not historically determined, or that no literary text is an expression of an epoch, or that its production has no connection with the individual experience of the author, would never be proved. It is counterintuitive to think that a literary work can be properly understood by some criteria lacking temporal significance.

Therefore, it is crucial to shoulder the effort of joining the synchronic and diachronic research, and to examine the literary work as projected on a diachronic scale, in relation to both its past and its contemporary perspective. In this case, the history of literature should endeavour to find ways to innovate its discourse by getting support from other disciplines of the humanities, such as cultural anthropology, social history, sociology, linguistics, and cultural studies, but especially from the most recent and world-wide acknowledged theoretical and critical modalities advanced by literary theory and literary criticism.

Possessing scientific consistency, the history of literature is expected to form together with literary theory and criticism a distinct unified discourse of aesthetic evaluation of the literary phenomena. If continuously and adequately modernized, this discourse would be efficient enough to sustain the proper study of national and international literary heritage, and even eliminate the general illiteracy caused by the deformed vision of the literary truths from the past.

The books of imaginative writing might then remain an important stimulus for the aesthetic and intellectual needs of the human race, despite the complexity of new cultural alternatives and the changing rhythm of human existence at the beginning of a new millennium.

Likewise, the books of literary history or history of literature might remain important guides into the cultural heritage, which needs to survive and stay known, despite the claims, which are still heard nowadays, in the aftermath the postmodernity, that history and historicism are dead or writing history is an equivalent to writing stories which encompass, like fiction, events and characters specific to the narrative. A character, in Julian Barnes's *England, England*, states that concerning the reception by readers of the historical books, it occurs in view of history as a system which is closed and the reader is expected to have already read other books of history. The statement is given at the start of these Preliminaries.

To justify our own series of books on the movement through history of English literature, and contrary to what is stated in Barnes's novel, we do not expect readers to have read books about English literature since we aim our work to be their starting point in learning or strengthening the knowledge about a remarkable share of the international cultural depository, a part of which – focused on particular periods, or movements, or trends, certainly on genres and unavoidably on various authors and their works – our readers will discover in the following.

GENRE THEORY FOR DRAMA

The modern critical thinking got accustomed to make divisions and categorizations in its approach to literature. Literary theory and literary criticism, and especially literary history divide the literary phenomenon into periods, movements, and trends following the temporal principle and grouping authors of imaginative writing through identifying their shared artistic credo and common literary doctrine as well as similar thematic concerns and, to a lesser extent, structural similarities of method and means of artistic expression.

The literary science also categorises literature into types called "**literary genres**" with a special focus on literary practice, having text in the centre of attention and chiefly with regard to its formal typology.

The separation of literature into genres is indeed done chiefly according to the form of the literary work, the most general naming of genres in this respect being prose, poetry, and drama or fiction, poetry, and drama, where "fiction" is used to designate imaginative prose, the product of the art of literature, which is to be differentiated from other types of written prose, such as scientific or journalistic ones.

Each genre is a distinct system of elements which are termed and categorised – apart from form – also according to its producer (writer or author), subgenres or species, work of literature or text and textual typology, the organization of language as a literary discourse, as well as the act or action performed by each genre.

The author of prose or fiction is open to rich labelling: he or she is often called prose writer or fiction writer; in case he or she writes only short fiction, such a writer can be also called short fiction writer or short-story writer; the producer of novels is commonly termed novelist; the author of fiction or author of imaginative prose are other terms often used along others alike. The persona speaking in a text of fiction representing the author's voice and delivering his or her point of view is called narrator. In the case of poetry, the writer is named poet, while his or her textual self is either called lyric I (in lyric poetry) or narrator (in narrative poetry). The author of drama is dramatist or playwright.

Each genre is made of literary works whose generic name is text. The text of prose or fiction is simply called prose text or text of fiction, but it displays a distinct typology which includes novel, short story, novella, and so on. In poetry, the text is called poem, whose typology is large, perhaps the largest of all genres: a poetic text can be simply lyric poem or narrative poem, but more often it bears various names such as epic, romance, sonnet, elegy, ode, hymn, dramatic monologue, and others. The text of drama is called play and its typology is likewise complex: tragedy, comedy, tragicomedy, history play, interlude, masque, etc. Unlike in fiction and poetry, the text of drama can be also performed, the relationship between text and performance being actually the most discussed topic of critical theory focused on drama.

Every literary work or text of each genre has its specific form, where the form of prose or fiction is called prose, the form of poetry is verse, and dialogue is used to give form to a dramatic text.

Each genre is involved in a particular act of communication between the producer and receiver of literature performing in the course of delivering the message a particular action or activity: prose or fiction narrates; poetry expresses and narrates; and drama shows.

Literary Genres	prose / fiction	poetry	drama
Author	novelist, fiction writer, author of short fiction, and so on	poet	playwright, dramatist
Text	novel, short-story, novella, and so on	poem	play
Form	prose	verse	dialogue
Action	narrate	express, narrate	show
Speaking persona	narrator	lyric I, narrator	character

The problem with the division of literature into genres – or, in other words, with grouping the literary works into genres – according to the form of the text is, first, that novels and other types of fiction narrate just as some works in verse, such as epic, metrical romance, or various narrative poems do; second, the speaker in lyric poetry is called "lyric I", whereas in narrative poetry, likewise written in verse, the speaker is "narrator", is a structural device in the text which is also responsible for the telling of the story in the works of fiction written in prose.

If one considers action rather than form of each genre to be more appropriate for the categorization, then a more correct consideration of the literary genres would state **narrative genre, lyric genre, and dramatic genre**.

In this case, the narrative genre would include texts written in both verse and prose and belonging to both narrative poetry and fiction or imaginative prose, namely novel, short story, novella, epic, romance, or a narrative poem such as *The Canterbury Tales*, meaning all literary works which narrate stories through the voice of a narrator and contain narrative or story as the central element of their system regardless of the form (prose or verse) of the literary work. The lyric genre would then include only lyric poetry meaning literary texts written in verse form and expressing feelings and states of mind through the voice of a lyric I, among which ode, sonnet, hymn, elegy, dramatic monologue, and other textual types of lyrical expression. The dramatic genre or drama remains the most fixed and normative type in matters of form, action, and typology, and is formed of plays such as tragedy, comedy, morality, mystery, interlude, and so on. Also, the specificity of drama and what makes it stand apart from the other two genres is its stepping beyond its status as literary production in literary field into the larger artistic and cultural sphere acquiring there the status of theatrical performance, and the relationship of text and performance has become one of the most discussed issues in drama and theatre studies.

Literary Genres	Narrative genre	Lyric genre	Dramatic genre
Type of literature	fiction (imaginative prose) and narrative poetry	lyric poetry	drama
Author	novelist, fiction writer, author of short fiction, poet, and so on	poet	playwright, dramatist
Text	novel, short-story, novella and other types of fiction plus narrative poem	poem	play
Subgenre / species	picaresque novel, gothic tale, realist novel, Bildungsroman,	ode, elegy, hymn, sonnet, dramatic	tragedy, comedy, morality, tragicomedy,

	stream of consciousness novel, epic, romance, and so on	monologue, and so on	interlude, history play, masque, and so on
Form	prose, verse	verse	dialogue, performance
Action	narrate	express	show
Speaking persona	narrator	lyric I	character

Despite an apparent complexity and confusion, in the strictest sense of terminology a competent scholar would tend to be more precise in all classifications and terminological acceptations. For instance, narrative is genre; novel is subgenre (also referred to as species or type); and picaresque novel, gothic tale, realist fiction, psychological novel, Bildungsroman, stream of consciousness novel, postcolonial novel, historiographic metafiction, or novel of magical realism are sub-subgenres (also referred to as subspecies, or subtypes, or subcategories).

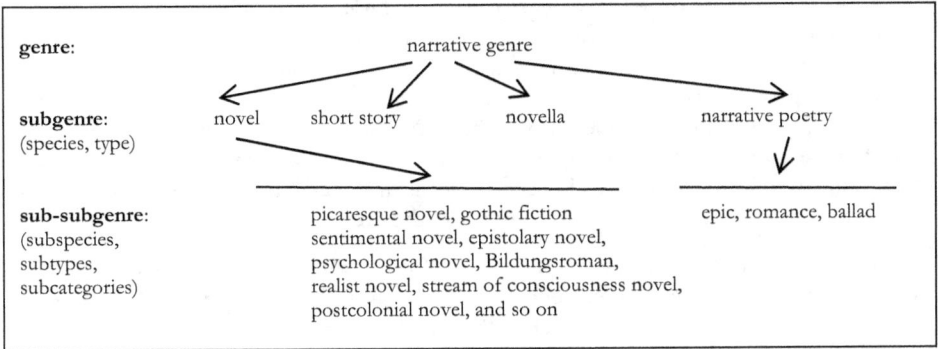

Even more accurate classifications may be attempted, beginning again from the general to particular. For example,

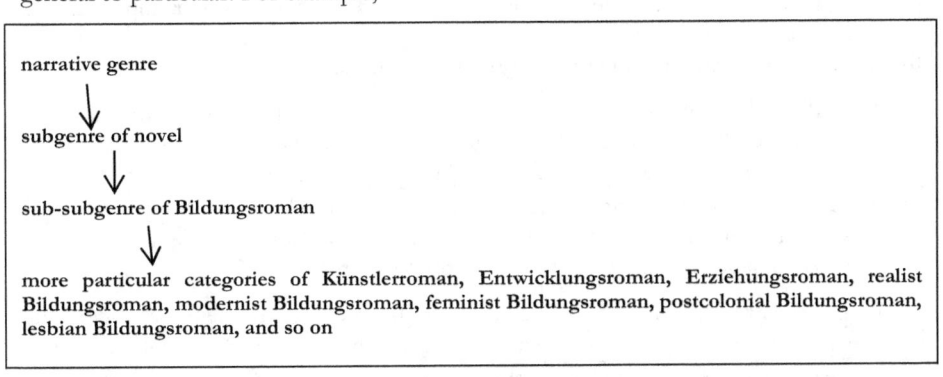

Genre terminology, however, blurs nowadays and many terms have become terms of abuse used randomly: lyric genre would be the more correct label but one can find statements such as poetic genre or that sonnet is a genre specific to Renaissance; likewise, one can say that tragedy is among the most important dramatic genres; also, Bildungsroman is called a novelistic genre or a type of novel, and so on.

Genre classifications also blur, especially in contemporary period when no writer would follow and no critic would impose strict parameters of writing. Authors of imaginative writing, in particular, in their attempt to experiment and innovate the literary discourse, striving for originality, would often mix genres and break the established rules. This common practice has emerged diachronically since long ago, where Shakespeare, for example, introduces tragicomedy (critically defended by Dryden during Restoration in his treatise *An Essay of Dramatic Poetry*); Sterne, Carlyle, Joyce, and Lodge subvert many novelistic conventions; T. S. Eliot remodels dramatic monologue, in *The Love Song of J. Alfred Prufrock*, and, in *The Waste Land*, achieves a pastiche and collage of genres and subgenres.

...

Drama is one of the oldest literary forms having its origins, like many other genres and subgenres, in Greek antiquity.

By its very nature, drama, or dramatic art, or the literature of theatre, is related to a space and personages in action more than any other literary forms. Particularly, it differs from fiction in which the narrated action about some characters and events already happened in the past, whereas drama delivers a perpetual present, a possible *illud tempus*, to use Mircea Eliade's words, an ultimate time which is always happening, carrying the potentiality of eternal recurrence among us. The perpetual present created by drama requires a place to be seen and heard, and this frequently generates confusion between the meanings of drama and theatre.

The word theatre comes from the Greek *theatron*, which signifies a "seeing place", a viewed place denoting the existence of a watcher and a watched, a listener and a speaker. The origins of theatre are related to some sacred rituals, and the etymology of the word discloses the obligatory presence of spectators during the action. This seeing place is primarily a social space in which the action taking place is significant for all people gathered together. At the beginning, this action implied the worshiping rituals and sacrifices; later, this action reflected the ways in which humans perceive themselves or the ways in which they contemplate humanness.

Nowadays, the term "theatre" is mostly used to refer to the building, the stage, an epoch or the totality of works of a dramatist (for example, Restoration theatre or Shakespeare's theatre), and especially to the living art form which unfolds in front of spectators in present time until the built illusion is over. The immediacy is a quality which separates theatre from other forms of art. David Cole considers theatre "an opportunity to experience imaginative life as physical presence" (5).

In the theatre, imaginative events occur in the present moment producing the nowness of the physical events. In the space of the theatre, the actor or actress conveys imagination and presence, and when both are juxtaposed, the spectator becomes capable of judging the strengths of the imaginative text versus the art of the actors.

Anne Ubersfeld points out that theatre is "a paradoxical art [...] we might see in theatre the very art of paradox; it is literary production and concrete performance at the same time. Theatre is both eternal (indefinitely reproducible and renewable) and of the instant (never reproduced identically)" (3). Concomitantly, the paradoxes intensify when the art of textual creation is considered. The complexity of the poetic language, the wit of the writer, the depth of the playwright, and so on, produce an infinite variety of the poetic reading.

These paradoxes strengthen the distinction between the written text (drama) and performance (theatre), a distinction which increased considerably with the passage of time.

The word drama is a transliteration of the Greek word *dran*, which means "a thing done", and the etymology of this word suggests its representability only in performance. Indeed, at its origins, theatre was primarily associated with doings, with manifestations, and the interrelatedness of the action and space was inseparable; however, after the increase of literacy, drama becomes primarily associated with the written text, an encoded paradigm of written words. Even though the Ancient Greek theatre carried the task of transmitting the codes of action, in time, the written text assumed greater significance, and the possibility of preserving the words intact became a priority in many communities. Richard Schechner explains that "historically speaking, in the West, drama detached itself from doing. Communication replaced manifestation" (7).

Origins of Drama

Drama represents a communal art which involves performers and spectators. This communal aspect of drama originates in the primitive fertility rites and religious ceremonies in some early stages of societal development, when a larger group of people becomes aware of forces which appear to influence or control their harvest and well-being. Ignorant of natural causes, the members of the primeval community attribute both desirable and undesirable occurrences to supernatural beings and forces. When certain actions performed by a group result in the desired outcome, the connection to divinity is perceived, and those actions, which are performed by shamans or group members, become more refined and formalized into fixed ceremonies or rituals. The growing sophistication of a community produces a change in its conception of supernatural forces and causal relationship, abandoning or modifying some of the rites.

However, the myths which emerge out of these rites continue to circulate as a part of communal oral tradition, or they can be acted under circumstances different from ritualistic concerns. This moment represents the first step towards the autonomous activity of theatre, where aesthetic values and perception of entertainment gradually replace the former mystical concern.

In Ancient Greece, the dramatic performance originates in religious ceremonials and festivals dedicated to god Dionysus, the fertility deity being worshiped in dithyrambs, which are hymns sung and danced by a large chorus. In Athens, a citywide religious festival called City Dionysia would take place, representing an event which celebrated the fertility god and organized a dramatic contest, where the playwrights, actors, and choruses presented their plays and competed for prizes and prominence among their fellow citizens.

The connection between early drama and religious ceremonial was preserved for a long time, and this essential nature of Greek drama remained obvious in the space of the amphitheatre, as the performance held a powerful link to the sacred temple of god

Dionysus and the ritual of sacrifice, apparent in the significance of the *tragoidia*, originally meaning "goat song", which indicates the ritual of sacrifice. Especially in the case of tragedy, there is a strong connection with religious worship, and even though it became secularised gradually, it still preserves some powerful ritualized effects.

The Essence of Drama

Action and Imitation

The term "drama" originates in a Greek word which signifies "act" or "deed"; consequently, action became a fundamental part of the dramatic art, especially after the ancient Greek philosopher Aristotle gave the definition of tragedy in his *Poetics* as "imitation of an action". Aristotle views drama as an imitation, which is achieved through representation, or re-presentation, or re-creation, be it realistic or highly stylized, by impersonators of an action.

Patris Pavis views action as a "series of stage events produced mainly through the behaviour of the characters, the action is both the entire *process* (*theatrical process*) of visible transformations on stage on a concrete level and, at the level of the *characters*, that which characterizes their psychological or moral progression" (9). Rather than seeing action as a series of deeds, the transformative process of doing is emphasized; instead of focusing on the arrangement of the events, the progressive transformation of the action in a dramatic text is observed. In other words, action does not result necessarily from a physical movement but rather from the progression which emerges with the intensification of the conflict, from the inner and outer forces which push forward the confrontation and, eventually, the ultimate resolution.

Dialogue

Drama is primarily conceived as a representation of characters in action, where the dialogue becomes the playwright's essential tool representing the main literary device of the dramatic art. Dialogue is the verbal exchange between the characters involved in the action and it may be perceived as the best way of communication of the action, since the spectators are mostly accustomed to it. However, the imitation of an action does not necessarily require dialogue, since, in order to communicate a message, a monologue or silence can be used by the dramatist to convey a meaning. From Chekhov to Pinter, spectators frequently witness how communicative silence can be.

Dramatic Conflict

Since Aristotelian view of action was not very clear, most definitions of the dramatic action got quite ambiguous until Ferdinand Brunetière coined the term "law of conflict" in 1894. This concept echoes Hegel's concept of "the tragic conflict", which sees dramatic actions not in mere terms of simple and undisturbed accomplishment of a certain purpose, but in terms of a collision of circumstances, desires, and characters, which leads the action to the resolution of the conflict.

In classical drama, the conflict is related primarily to the protagonist of the pay, as the hero is mostly viewed in terms of progression to self-awareness; therefore, the "collision" between hero and an opposing force is inevitable. There are various types of conflict, each of which arising from a struggle of divergent forces. The most common types of conflict are (1) Character versus Himself: an emotional or moral struggle which is internalized by the protagonist by reasoning some opposing or contradictory ideas; (2) Character versus other Character(s): an externalized form of conflict which is made visible through the opposition between protagonist and antagonist, hero against villain; (3) Character versus Society: an externalized form of conflict which reflects some irreconcilable moral or political values which are represented by the opposition between the protagonist and the community.

Regardless of the type of conflict, which is reflected in the action of a play, the force which keeps the attention and entertains the spectators is struggle. The impact and effect of drama rely not only on the reflection on the ways in which human conscious operates while engaged in a struggle but also on the quantity and quality of will or volition which are exhibited during the struggle. Therefore, in order to have a truly an intense situation, which would reflect a struggle which is really meaningful, the volition of the character must be challenged with obstacles and opposition formidable enough to create a sustainable conflict. The most fascinating and memorable characters in drama are those with insurmountable volition, those with clear but difficult to attain aims, those driven by strong desires, and those mostly determined to change a situation regardless of the necessary sacrifice.

Dramatic Structure

The ancients viewed the plot of drama in terms of tying and untying of a knot. This principle of dramatic structure is implied in Aristotle's suggestion that a play must have "a beginning, middle, and an end" and that the action in a play must be "complete". Dramatic structure is necessary because, upon it, the dramatic conflict develops. A well-built play follows some certain divisions which correspond to different phases of the dramatic conflict: **exposition, complication, crisis, climax, and catastrophe**. These divisions are frequently represented graphically in the form of a pyramid, called frequently Freytag's pyramid, in which the rising slope of the pyramid reveals the rising action, or the "tying of the knot", the apex represents the climax, whereas the falling slope discloses the falling action which leads to the denouement, or to the "untying of the knot".

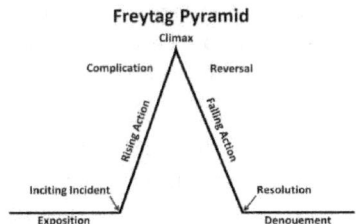

The **exposition** (or introduction) is the opening section of a play which sets the scene, creates the tone, introduces the main characters, and supplies the background information necessary to the understanding of the action of the play. It is a very important division in the play's structure since many plays begin in medias res, in the middle of things, and the exposition clarifies the situation which happened prior to the action in the play.

The **complication** (or rising action) is stimulated by an **exciting force** and is continued through some consecutive phases of conflict between the protagonist and other opposing characters. The increase in the tempo of the events leads to the **crisis**, a moment of high tension, which is resolved, but is followed by another even more intense moment, which brings inevitably to the **climax** (or turning point). Climax is the phase of the highest intensity in the action of the play; it is the point which determines the outcome of the action.

The falling action emphasizes the strength of forces opposing the protagonist, and, although there is still some suspense maintained, some slackening of the tension is felt and it leads finally to the **catastrophe** (denouement). This is the moment of final suspense and it provides an opportunity for the protagonist's rehabilitation in front of spectators. Except emotional sympathy, the audience experiences the impression of a restored order, which is extremely important in a play. The dramatists respected this formula of the dramatic structure but many of them enjoyed the satisfaction to create variations on the basic structure of action.

Dramatic Conventions

Convention is the tacit agreement between the dramatist and the audience to suspend the disbelief and accept a substitution for reality on stage as real, even though they are aware that it is not. It is an unwritten pact between the playwright and spectator in which the former writes and stages the play conforming to some norms, whereas the latter recognizes and accepts them. In order to grasp the pleasure of playacting, the spectators must transcend beyond some limits of representation and embrace the theatrical conventions.

There are some **permanent and universal conventions**, valid to all theatrical representations of all times. Since drama delivers the portrayal of an action, the audience of all times accepts **actors on the stage** as the **personages in the action**, and that they belong to the geographical and historical background which they pretend to belong to. The **stage** should be viewed as the **place of the actual action** of the play. Then, the **selection** and **condensation** of events should be considered. Drama, par excellence, employs great economy in the mode of delivering the events of action. The dramatist removes all non-essential events, focusing instead on the most indispensable and vital moments of the story. Time is often condensed in theatre, especially necessary in the shift of scenery or to indicate the passage of time.

On stage, this condensation is arranged with the lowering of curtain and an interval which is taken to accommodate the spectators with the time and setting change. Moreover, the **language** used on the stage or in the play is expected to be taken as the language of the characters, regardless of their nationality. In the majority of cases, on stage, the characters speak the language of the audience, without being questioned. Furthermore, there are multiple examples of plays written in verse form and even though nobody speaks in verse in real life, the audience is expected to accept the versified and stylized language on the stage as the medium of communication of the characters.

Some other theatrical conventions have **temporary** validity and they are used by particular ages, though some of the temporary conventions may be reintroduced on stage in different periods of time. Some of the most influential conventions are the ones employed by the Ancient Greek Theatre and Elizabethan Theatre.

In Greek tragedy, apart from chorus, only three characters appeared on the stage. Regardless of the character's gender, the actors were all male, they wore stylized masks which would make visible from a long distance the emotion transmitted by the character. The footgear and the headgear also contributed to the visibility and audibility of the character on the stage, which was of essential importance when the enormous space of amphitheater is considered. The appearance of the characters was intensified by the conventionalized costumes worn by actors to reveal the gender and the social rank of the represented characters.

The performance almost equaled a ceremony, so that the solemn background justified the characters speaking in verse form. Paradoxically, even though originating in a sacrificial ritual, tragedy never employed onstage violence, all brutal acts unfolding offstage and the news of any violent acts would be delivered indirectly by a messenger.

Elizabethan stage conventions continue some of the conventions of the Greeks, like the use of verse dialogue, the outdoor performances which took place during daytime, the lack of scenic illusion, and only male actors engaged in performance. However, there were many differences as well. First of all, the costumes used by the Elizabethan actors were never historically accurate. Regardless of the geographical or historical background of the action, the Elizabethans used the outfits of their own day. There was no restriction in the number of characters on the stage.

Unlike the Greek tragedies, which focus on a single plot in action, the Elizabethan plays employ twisted plots, main plots and subplots, which complicate and intensify the action in plays, and they are also fascinated by the onstage violence. The Elizabethans frequently employ the soliloquy and the aside, two conventions of the stage language which became an integral part of Elizabethan theatre.

The aside is spoken by a character as if it was a slip of tongue and is overheard by the spectators "by chance". The aside reveals the character's true intentions and feelings, and the spectators know that the things are not as they seem to be.

The soliloquy is a speech delivered by a character to himself or herself while presumed to be alone. In the soliloquy, the character reflects upon some moral or psychological concerns. This device allows the audience to have glimpse of the character's true feelings, beliefs, his or her psyche, representing a moment which divulges characters desires, temptations, or aspirations. Both these devices are untrue to life, but they conferred complexity and intensity to the representation of the characters.

With the passage of time, the aesthetical tastes in theatre change and the theatrical conventions change respectively. Some old conventions are rejected, making way to some new ones which would most probably be abandoned in time. But it is important to understand that by employing conventions, the dramatists conceive and use a manner of shaping the play for his audience and counts on the acceptance of some arrangements which would sustain the joy of watching a play.

Types of drama

Throughout the history of drama, a variety of dramatic types or subgenres develop. This variety is prompted by the cultural and aesthetic peculiarities of place and time of their origin. Antiquity is dominated by **tragedy** and **comedy**, which continue to the present to satisfy our aesthetic needs despite having made way to the emergence of other species of drama, such as tragicomedy, history play, farce, masque, melodrama, and others.

Some of these, along tragedy and comedy, represent the power and extent of dramatic production of English Renaissance literature, as we shall see in the following.

1.

THE SOCIAL AND CULTURAL SCENE

Following the Middle Ages, Renaissance is the next major stage in the historical advancement of British literature, rejecting and replacing the medieval period in the fifteenth century firstly in Italy and soon spreading all over the Europe, and reaching England around 1500.

The term "Renaissance" derives from the Italian word *rinascimento*, which means "rebirth" or "revival", and "was used in contemporary Italian to describe what was seen as a revitalization of the arts under the influence of classical letters" (Hadfield 3). Considering England, the word did not enter the English language until the nineteenth century as advanced by Ruskin, Pater, and others.

Renaissance is commonly considered as the first part of the modern period which lasted until the middle of the twentieth century; for others, Renaissance is a period of transition from medievalism to the modern period now conceived as lasting from the rise of the seventeenth-century Enlightenment/Neoclassicism to the middle of the twentieth century. The break from the Middle Ages was gradual and to date precisely the period of Renaissance in Europe is difficult, though it suggests the fourteenth, fifteenth, sixteenth, and early seventeenth centuries.

The dates are also different for different countries, as the beginning of English Renaissance, for example, was a full century behind the Italian Renaissance. It is usually considered that the period of English Renaissance began around 1500 and lasted until the Commonwealth Interregnum (1649-1660), and that it consisted of the "Early Tudor Age" (c.1500-1557), the "Elizabethan Age" (1558-1603), the "Jacobean Age" (1603-1625), and the "Caroline Age" (1625-1649). Historians are inclined to trace the exact beginning of British Renaissance going as back as 1485 (the accession of Henry VII and the establishment of the Tudor dynasty) or 1509 (the accession of Henry VIII).

Opinions also differ concerning the end of the period: it is either the early seventeenth century in Europe, in general, and the year of 1616 (the death of Shakespeare) in England, or by the middle of the seventeenth century in Europe, in general, and the year of 1660 (the restoration of monarchy) in England, which is the year that followed the rise of Puritanism in the first half of the seventeenth century, the execution of Charles I in 1649, and the Commonwealth Interregnum led by Oliver Cromwell between 1649 and 1660. In accordance with the first opinion, the history of literature excludes Baroque and mannerist literature of Europe from the period of Renaissance, and, in particular in British literature, the metaphysical poets and John Milton are no longer representatives of English Renaissance. In accordance with the second opinion, the European Baroque and English metaphysical trend in poetry from the first half of the seventeenth century are the last artistic and literary manifestations of Renaissance, and John Milton is the last great figure of English Renaissance.

Be it one or another way, yet in a more convenient way, it is accepted that English Renaissance literature covers the whole of the sixteenth century and is synonymous with the term "Tudor literature" between 1485 and 1603, which is between the first of the Tudors – Henry Tudor, who on 22 August 1485, at Bosworth Field, defeated Richard III and took the throne as Henry VII, claiming the crown of Arthur – and Queen Elizabeth, the last of the Tudors.

Significantly, the literary practice reveals the end of the medieval period and the climax of Renaissance through two literary works with characters and events of the Arthurian story: in July 1485, the publisher William Caxton finished printing *Le Morte Darthur* by Sir Thomas Malory, who died earlier in 1471, a text representing medieval literature, whereas the year of 1590 saw Edmund Spenser's *Fairie Queene* which represents Renaissance.

Malory's romance synthesises various tales in English and French, in prose and verse, and in alliterative and non-alliterative poetry in a literary attempt to create a new Arthurian cycle, but the text lacks narrative unity, while the narrative tone is rooted in the destructive outcomes of the Wars of the Roses; it displays a sense of the inescapable past and remains essentially pessimistic with regard to the continuity of kingship as well as nation on the whole. The work is symbolical for the end of the medieval cultural and social systems which break up once and for all amid morbidity, death, immorality, betrayal, and incest which apparently opens and closes a cyclical condition: Arthur is an incestuous son of his father disguised as his mother's husband and he will be eventually slayed by an illegitimate son (likewise incestuously begotten) in the Battle of Salisbury, by which ending the Round Table.

Malory's king Arthur is an old man, killed in battle although claimed by many not to be dead; his death is uncertain just like his return is despite Malory declaring that "he shall come again, and he shall win the holy cross". Some fifteen years later, Caxton, working with the discorded text, attempted to provide a unity of stories suggesting artistically the unity of England and Wales as achieved by Henry VII who claimed the throne of both nations: for this, arriving in Wales, Henry Tudor unfurled above the Welsh aristocratic families the red dragon of King Arthur as if announcing the return of the sleeping lord. Rendering another image of the mythical Arthur, this time a young man seeking Gloriana (Queen Elizabeth), Spenser proclaims a Renaissance spirit of youth and vitality, joy and optimism, and positive expectations of the future of the country ruled by the Tudors.

This contrast, a type of literary binary opposition, between Malory's and Spenser's works, which is between medieval mind-set and Renaissance reinvigoration of thought and artistic creativity, saw its counterparts, in the first decades of the seventeenth century, in the conflict between Cavalier and Puritan growing in intensity, as also grew in intensity the conflict between the extravagance of Baroque (innovation) and the authority of classical culture (tradition), which is known as the dichotomy "school of Donne" versus "sons of Ben".

The elements of the latter came to suppress those of the former by the middle of the seventeenth century, which determined the end of Renaissance in England and thus instituted the next period in the historical advancement of British literature, which is that of neoclassicism – the English version of classicism – which lasted until the end of the eighteenth century.

1.1 The Intellectual Background

Regarding the origins of Renaissance, the emphasis is placed on issues concerning the new intellectual and artistic forces that were intended to adjust and harmonize the newly interpreted Christian tradition, the newly discovered, or rather revived, ancient classical tradition, and the demands of the newly emerging modern world. Apart from this, one should not disregard the economic premises of Renaissance, wealth being one of the major factors which made Renaissance possible. Wealth was a consequence of trade, in the fifteenth-century Italy the city of Florence being the most important manufactory centre and Venice the most important commercial centre of Europe. Likewise, during the reign of Elizabeth, England became an important trading nation due to its colonial expansion in the New World.

The establishment of the Tudor dynasty in 1485 with Richard III defeated at the Battle of Bosworth and accession of Henry VII offered to England a period of internal peace, and the last decades of the fifteenth century already showed traces of Humanism and early Renaissance.

The background information may start with 1484, when Richard III was defeated in battle by Henry Tudor, and the Tudors dynasty began. The reign of Henry VII diminished the authority of the Pope in favour of the Crown, which marked the first step away from primitive feudalism.

King Henry VIII reigned between 1509 and 1547, and in the first year of his reign, he married Catherine of Aragon. Between 1512 and 1513, Henry and Wolsey began their first war against France. In 1517, Martin Luther began his revolt against the Church of Rome at Wittenburg. In 1521, Henry VIII wrote *Aseptio Septem Sacramentorum* against Luther and Pope Leo X gave him the title "Fidei Defensor". In 1531, Henry was proclaimed the Supreme Head of the Church of England. In 1535, his first wife died and Henry married Jane Seymorer who died a year later. In 1540, Henry married Ann of Cleves, but a Church meeting annulled the marriage. Thomas Cromwell was executed the same year later and Henry married Catherine Howard, niece of the Duke of Norfolk, who, two years later, was executed for immorality. In 1543, Henry VIII married Catherine Parr who survived him.

After his death, the reign of Edward VI (1547-1553), the reign of Mary (1553-1558), and the reign of Elizabeth, the Virgin Queen (1558-1603) followed.

Many nineteenth-century historians coined the phrase "discovery of man and of the world" to describe Renaissance as a sudden explosion of individualism against the medieval unanimity of the mass, realistic observation of the world and men, less the medieval preoccupation with the world of spirit, and the assertion of democratic liberalism over the medieval authority and hierarchy.

Renaissance, however, was not a sudden but a gradual upfolding: the emergency of individualism and realism in English life and literature is shown in Chaucer's fourteenth century and, perhaps, even earlier, long before Renaissance, when there can be found hostility to medieval authority.

The first phase of Renaissance in England is the "New Learning"; the term defines a trend of education set by scholars returned from the Continent, especially Italy. The second phase of Renaissance is one of translation and scholarship; it brought English, instead of Latin, Greek, and other foreign languages, into the culture and prepared the literary creation in English. The third phase is the phase of the new poetry of Thomas Wyatt, Henry Howard, Edmund Spenser, Sir Philip Sidney, and others. The fourth phase might be considered that of prose, both fiction and non-fiction, imaginative writing and non-imaginative. The fifth aspect, governing the whole Renaissance age to be prolonged into the Jacobean period, is drama.

Concerning first the level of thought, historians seem in agreement that Renaissance philosophical and intellectual attitude, complex and multi-faced as it was, manifested especially in Humanism.

1.1.1 Humanism

The Humanism of Renaissance, as distinguished from many other uses of the term "humanism", is a half-way between Theology (the medieval mind-set) and Rationalism (of the Age of Reason following the Renaissance).

The humanist (*humanitas*) is a great individualist of the physical world; he or she wants to cultivate the human experience of this world and his or her life, and the art of living; he or she is not anti-religious but secular-minded; he or she is curious about human view-points and always fascinated by the effects of the external world on his or her physical and psychological self. The humanist spreads optimism and moral values; the artist as well, including the poet, for instance, is a good man, a guide and guardian of morality.

Humanism is the starting philosophy of modernity asserting ideas which are both original and, at the same time, based on the revival of ancient classical tradition. The humanist philosophy develops and promotes principles which would come to establish the pattern of modern thought on the whole from its beginnings in Renaissance to the mid-twentieth century, which is a type of thinking emphasizing learning, progress, reality, foundation, essence, and so on, and which is reified, following humanism, by the new method of Francis Bacon, rationalism of Descartes, empiricism of Locke, idealism of Hegel, and Kantian method as to culminate in the supremacy of Enlightenment whose essence is kept alive in the next phases of the modern period by positivism and phenomenology.

Humanism, the foundational philosophy of modernity, contributes to the rise and consolidation of the western, modern though by establishing principles and concerns such as (1) the importance given to the world of man and to man in the physical world; (2) emphasis on the individual being, his or her intellectual capacity, self-analysis, and personal potential; (3) human being as an integrated consciousness, unified self; (4) search for knowledge and the discovery of the hidden mysteries of the outer world and human existence; (5) exploration of the world and acquiring of knowledge through observation, experiment, intellectual curiosity, actions of the mind; (6) discovery, invention, knowledge, emancipation as granted by Divine Power; (7) the reconsideration of the ancient notions of *anima vegetativa*, *anima sensitiva*, and *anima intellettiva*, and the reinforcement of the dichotomy *vita contemplativa* and *vita activa* (predominant later in Francis Bacon); and (8) positive and optimistic outlook grounded in a sense of ethical didacticism.

The greatest humanists of the age were William Grocyn, John Colet, Erasmus, and Thomas More. Most of them represent a new type of Renaissance man, not aristocrat or knight, but cleric or civil servant, an exponent of the rising urban bourgeoisie, like More, who was a citizen Londoner, conversant in Latin and possessor of classical learning.

Desiderius Erasmus (1466-1536), a Dutch by birth, resided in England for a number of years. His significance for English literature is to be understood in view of the fact that, up to this time, Western Europe still possessed a common language, Latin, and a common religion, Roman Catholicism. This led, especially in the intellectual class, to a feeling of unity throughout Europe, which made for easy movement of people and ideals from one country to another. Erasmus's most famous book, *Moriae Encomium* (*The Praise of Folly*), was written in 1510 in the London home of Sir Thomas More.

Terminological nuances

The term "Renaissance humanism" should be approached with care, since, during Renaissance period, the word "humanism" was not established yet, and the only word celebrated and embraced at the time was "humanist". In English, the word "humanist" derives from the Italian *umanista*, signifying a Latin teacher, which is a meaning evolving from the way Cicero approached the word *humanitas* with both educational and political purposes. In Latin, the word *humanitas* has a dual significance: the first refers to humankind (hence the word "humanity"), whereas the second meaning relies on the translation of the Greek word *paideia*, implying culture and liberal education which contribute to the development of man (a connotation still preserved in the term "humanities"). The Humanism of Renaissance was first and foremost an educational movement which originated in the early fourteenth century and spread later throughout the entire Europe, reaching England only by the end of the fifteenth century and the beginning of the sixteenth century.

The humanist (*humanitas*) is a classical scholar who assumes the task of recovering the moral values of the classical life, and, concomitantly, of imitating the classics both in language and style, and in a manner of fusing wisdom (*sapientia*) and eloquence (*eloquentia*). For humanists, Cicero becomes the epitome of a complete man, since, in his hypostases as politician, orator and moralist, he provided a model for combining action and contemplation, by which being efficient in both public and private life.

As a result of material advances and the revival of the classical learning, the humanists abandon gradually the preoccupations with afterlife, shifting their interests in order to cultivate the human experience in this world, aspiring for the art of living, which is not anti-religious but secular-minded. The fascination with human viewpoints and the impact of the external world on physical and psychological self brought to the development of a code of conduct by the Renaissance Humanists, which emphasize the earthly, the moral, and the aesthetic. The Renaissance Humanists place great emphasis on the dignity of man, in the sense infused by Pico della Mirandola's work *On the Dignity of Man*, and on the broad possibilities of the human life in this world. Mostly, the humanists regard human beings as social creatures who would create meaningful lives only in association with other social beings.

Humanism may be considered as the starting philosophy of modernity, asserting ideas which are both original and, at the same time, are based on the revival of ancient classical tradition. The humanist philosophy and ethics develop and promote certain key concepts which would hold validity from the beginning of Renaissance to the first decades of the twentieth century.

Among these concepts, the first in line is *mimesis*, which derives from the classical past but is explored extensively in Renaissance. Of the two meanings of the term "imitation", Renaissance scholars mostly focused on the "following predecessors" significance rather than on "mirroring life". In this respect, Isabel Rivers explains that humanists taught their followers to imitate the style and language of the classical predecessors, an emphasis which "[at] its worst was an absurd and stultifying exercise (satirised in Erasmus's *Ciceronianus*), divorcing style and content; at its best imitation meant taking as a pattern not only the style but also the attitudes and conduct of the chosen model" (129). The stress was not on originality, as one would expect, because the Renaissance scholars believed that the greatest works which represent definitive moral values had already been created by the classical authors. The main task of a Renaissance writer was to translate for the contemporary readers the moral vision of the past and adapt it to a Christian mind-set. While the principle of imitation led writers to capture the spirit of the original models, learning from them and using them to fit their agenda, it also led concomitantly to the imitation of the classical genres, which brought the revival of important literary forms. Initially, epic and satire were the most imitated forms of antiquity, being followed by dramatic genres of tragedy and comedy.

The second concept extensively embraced by the humanists is pragmatism. Revealing a growing disapproval towards the abstract theoretical knowledge, the humanists appreciated mostly that type of knowledge which would serve their aspirations for a good life. The humanists' belief in education to improve the worth of man was adamant, as well as their emphasis on knowledge attained through constant education which would annihilate the consequences of the fall and would eventually restore and redeem man – a rational and moral being – in the face of the God. The classical ethical works of antiquity, such as Aristotle's *Nicomachean Ethics* and Cicero's *Of Duties* were highly esteemed by the humanists, especially due to the ways in which these works reveal man as a political being who constantly evolves in society. For humanists, the concept of the "Renaissance Man" exposes an individual who possesses vast knowledge and skills in many subject areas and uses them actively in the affairs of public life. Such figures include Leonardo da Vinci, John Milton, as well as Francis Bacon, who has declared, "I have taken all knowledge to be my province". Yet, the major preoccupation of the Renaissance Humanists was not the individual aspiration but the teaching of people to participate in and rule a society. Ironically, though beautiful and optimistic, this ideal included only the nobility and few members of the middle class. Perhaps, in the conscious attempt of the Renaissance Humanists to revive the thought and culture of the classical antiquity, they have gained the important knowledge of the social nature of humanity.

The third concept vastly explored by the humanists is duty. The humanists were fascinated by Plato's depiction of the education of the philosopher-king in his *Republic*, and, regardless of their awareness of the unreachable ideal, they still revealed their desire to attain it, which is expressed in the encouragement of the relationship between men of letters/philosophers and rulers. The model established in the past by Plato and Dionysus or Aristotle and Alexander inspired the collaboration between Desiderius Erasmus and Charles V, and Thomas More and Henry VIII. The humanist shift from the "contemplative life" to the "active life" revealed their aspirations for the highest cultural values, which were usually associated with the active involvement in public service, in ethical, political, and military counsel, and in the service to the state. The humanist contribution to public life implied their guidance of the rulers throughout their moral education; however, the princes' inflexible attitudes towards ethics inherent in humanism brought an unresolvable conflict, which ended up at times like in the execution of Thomas More by Henry VIII in 1535, where More's final words from the scaffold – "The King's good servant, but God's First" – epitomize it. Due to "this tension the humanists felt strongly the temptation of the retired, contemplative life, of Horace's *otium* (leisure) as against Cicero's *negotium* (business); the garden often seemed a more fitting symbolic setting for the pursuit of wisdom than the court" (Rivers 129).

1.1.2 Thomas More and *Utopia*

Sir Thomas More or Morus (c. 1477-1535), later St Thomas More, began the writing of *Utopia* in 1515, and many scholars consider it to be the beginning of English Renaissance. This famous work was published in 1516 at Louvain, Erasmus supervising the printing. An English translation by Ralph Robinson of *Utopia* was published in 1551. In collaboration with Erasmus, actually, More produced in 1506 his first published work, which is the Lucian translations. More's English translation from Latin of the life of Giovanni Pico della Mirandola, an Italian humanist, followed in 1510.

His unfinished *History of Richard III*, written c. 1513 – 1518 and existing in both Latin and English versions, was used by various contemporary authors who consequently transmitted its material to Shakespeare for his *Richard III*. The late 1520s and early 1530s saw various written defences of Catholicism, and, while in the Tower, to which More was committed in April 1534 for finding himself unable to swear to the Act of Succession, he wrote *A Dialogue of Comfort against Tribulation*.

The son of a judge, Thomas More himself studied common law to be admitted to Lincoln's Inn in 1496 and become a barrister in 1501. In 1504, More entered Parliament; from 1510 to 1518, he was one of the two undersheriffs of London; in 1521, he was knighted. His career prospered rapidly – Speaker of the Commons in 1523, Chancellor of the Duchy of Lancaster in 1525 and lord Chancellor in 1529 – just as his fall occurred rapidly: refusing to attend the coronation of Anne Boleyn, in 1534, More was accused of complicity with Elizabethan Barton; on 17 April 1534 followed the Temple, sentence as a traitor, and execution on 6 July 1535. Claiming that he was dying for his faith, and indeed considered a martyr by many, More was beatified in 1886 and canonized in 1935. His entrance into religious life occurred earlier while at Lincoln's Inn, when he lived at a nearby monastery and, although he did not follow a vocation for priesthood, the monastic life provided him for the rest of his life with the values and habits of penance, redemption, fasting and prayer.

Three important people marked and influenced his whole life. First was Cardinal Morton, his patron at whose house More spent his youth and who facilitated his studies at Oxford predicting that More would become a "marvellous man". Second was Henry VIII, who favoured and prompted his political career. Regarding his writing, the most important person in his life was Erasmus, whom More met in 1499, and whose friendship, collaboration and correspondence helped shape More's literary personality.

Despite a hectic and turbulent political career and a number of various writings, More is chiefly viewed as England's leading Christian humanist, a martyr to Catholics and a traitor and enemy to Protestants, as well as the author of *Utopia*.

Utopia is written in Latin, the language of Europe, but its title is of Greek origin: "u topos" meaning "no place" or "nowhere land". The reader will find such word-plays throughout the whole work, for example, Hythlodaeus meaning "nonsense-pedlar" and Anydeus, a mariner, standing for "waterless".

More's work is considered the first great humanistic text by an Englishman. It can be called a speculative political essay combining literature and philosophy, art and theory, and written in the realistic fashion of many Renaissance writings, derived, most likely, from Plato's dialogues.

The world described and presented is an irrational one striving for reason and order, as to become a world governed by truly humanistic principles in an age when Christendom apparently failed to produce a good society, and More suggests a new approach of the humanists to create the right world for men.

The subject of *Utopia* is the search for the best possible form of government, a search build up on bourgeois values and classical heritage, particularly Greek. It can be said that More is responsible for the first entry of Greek philosophical and rhetorical systems into English culture.

More's work is divided into two Books, quite different, yet each interesting in its own way, and both revealing a juxtaposition of two main types of Greek thinking, namely, the private identity of Socrates in the first Book and the social identity of Plato in the second Book.

Book I is indeed Socratic since justice and truth are viewed as inner values and the inward is a private individual matter concealed by the individual and unclaimed by others. More and his friend Peter Giles leave the church service and meet at Antwerp a traveller, Raphael Hythloday, a Portuguese seaman, who has discovered Utopia, and who accompanied Amerigo Vespucci on his third voyage to the New World. The mariner found in Utopia a far different world from European corruption, war and waste, national and international bad faith, poverty and crime, cruelty and immoral conduct at every social level; in this, the first part constitutes a true historical document of contemporary conditions.

Book II renders everything as public and outward, including virtues and vices, which are not concealed by anyone; for instance, ruthless war tactics permit to bribe the enemy to kill their leaders or mercenaries are used because they are inferior beings that do not deserve to live.

This second Book about Utopians is actually the part which the readers general think of when considering *Utopia*. Hythloday talks about the ideal state, where communism is the general law, where there is no poverty since there is no private wealth, where a national system of education is extended to men and women alike, and the freest toleration of religion is recognized. Gender equality allows prospective husband and wife to see each other naked before marriage, and men as well as women receive as much education as their capabilities permit. Utopian houses are of equal comfort and are exchanged regularly by people; each house has a garden and stands on a street twenty feet wide. A six-hour day is all the work required of a man. The complete religious toleration implies that the Utopians have many religions; they thank God for their present government and religion, and pray that if there should be superior systems of government and religion, God might reveal the new truth to them.

These characteristics and others alike may stand against the principle of the rise of individualism in an age governed by humanistic principles, where, in More, happiness is the highest good for the humans, but the welfare of the state is always placed above that of the individual.

In *Utopia*, Thomas More does not celebrate individualism, but, more importantly, he expels the idea of a perfect state; the state is not perfects since his Utopians are not perfect because their moral goodness is relative and they are vulnerable and subjected to concealed passions. Consequently, the law reveals desires instead of hiding them, by which human virtues and vices, innocence and guilt are driven out into open. In Utopia, idleness and privacy are forbidden and when a person is lead into anger, or fear, or envy, which is into the private, he or she is made a slave whose soul is lost and whose body is to be used.

The possibility of the state and human condition not to be perfect and allowing for change and improvement suggest the almost startling difference between More's work and the multitude of subsequent imaginary ideal states termed "utopian" in reference to More's work: while most ideal states are conceived of as perfect and changeless, More sees the ideal state as dynamic, recognizing the necessity of change and improvement, and adding to it a distinctly fertile imagination and a confident idealism.

Probably More was influenced by Portuguese reports of the Inca Empire of Peru, St Augustine's *De Civitate Dei (City of God)*, upon which More had lectured, *Institutio Principis Christiani (Establishment of Christian Principles)* by Erasmus, and *Civita Soli* by Tomaso Campanela, but Plato's *Republic* is the strongest source.

The work was highly influential and at once became popular, being translated by Ralph Robinson into English in 1551, and into French (1550), German, Italian, and Spanish (the rapid fame of the book is shown by the reference to Utopians by Rabelais). Its contemporary connections represent what is usually called "Black Utopia" or "Dark Utopia", as in G. Orwell's *Nineteen Eighty-Four* and *Animal Farm*, A. Huxley's *Brave New World*, and Kurt Vonnegut's *Slaughterhouse-Five*.

More's English writings are often too Latinical in style, prosaic and lacking imagination. Yet he is a great writer if he is the author of the *Historie of Richard the Third*, published in 1557, a great work, used by later chroniclers and influenced Shakespeare's interpretation of Richard III. His another work, *A Dialog of Comfort against Tribulations*, was written in prison in 1553, as the author faced death, and More argues that all people are prisoners under condemnation, and consequently his fate is similar to that of the others.

"Utopia": the significance of the concept and the origins of utopianism

The concept of "utopia", though coined by Thomas More in 1516, cannot be limited to More's reference to the name of the island which is presented in his work *Utopia*. A careful deliberation over the emergence of the word "utopia" can clarify primarily what Thomas More implied by it and also reveal the acquisition of new meanings which were attained after the invention of the term.

In should not be ignored that in 1516, the word "utopia" was created in order to name something new; it was a neologism which exposed the shifting values and expectations of a community. Even though this word emerged as a lexical neologism to name a new concept, with the passage of time, curiously enough, it faced what Fatima Vieira calls "the process of deneologization" (3). The meaning of the word changed considerably, as with each adoption of the term, various researchers from a range of fields of study and having diverging agendas allowed a continuous semantic renewal of this word. Moreover, the word "utopia" started being utilized frequently as the root for the formation of some new words, like dystopia, eutopia, anti-utopia, alotopia, heterotopia, hyperutopia, and ecotopia, all these being derivation neologisms, as they represent variations of the earlier produced word, but in the process of transformation, the emerged mutations also become semantic neologisms, as they use the pre-existing word to designate new cultural contexts. Since with each variation of the word the concept of utopia gained more precise significance, it becomes important to differentiate between the meaning conferred to this word by Thomas More, when it was invented, and the connotations attributed to later metamorphoses of the word.

The attempts to disclose the initial meaning of the word "utopia" reveal an ambiguity, since More used the word with a double purpose, as a title for his book and as a name for the mysterious island described by the explorer Raphael Hythloday. The uncertainty concerning the purpose of the word led to the rise of two distinct meanings of "utopia" which were shaped in the process of deneologisation: though the word "utopia" emerged to refer to an imaginary edenic space, its usage was extended to designate a new literary form which was later recognized as utopian literature, so the newly risen genre validated the necessity for the created neologism.

Prior to the invention of the term "utopia", More employed the word "Nusquama" to refer to his imaginary island, a word which in Latin signified "nowhere", "in no place" and "on no occasion". But since Thomas More had the intention of transmitting the newly rising spirit of Renaissance, which is reflected in the state of awe for the ancient world and the consideration of their products as the superlative of the intellectual achievement, combined with the humanistic attitude which welcomed ingenuity, playfulness and the ability to confront paradoxes and even contradictions in an attempt to reveal human perfection, his term "utopia" tried to convey it all. The extension of the boundaries of the intellectual horizon was strongly inspired by the broadening of geographical horizons, and with the geographical expansion achieved by such explorers as Amerigo Vespucci, Christopher Columbus, and Angelo Poliziano, came out the awareness of otherness, which justified the exploration of new spaces, with people living in different communal organizations. This new experience also required the creation of a new word. In his quest for a neologism, More first took into consideration the Greek word *eutopia*, which signifies the place where things are good, but in his intention to create something new, he goes further and blends two Greek words – *ouk*, meaning "not", a negation which was reduced to *u*, and *topos*, signifying "place", and, by adding the suffix *ia*, the newly emerged word "utopia" assumes a life of its own, indicating a non-place, which simultaneously affirms and rejects its existence. This joke, inherent in the meaning of the word, transmits the Renaissance fascination with contradictions, but also the spirit of ingenuity and ambiguity which characterises More's entire work. By resurging the meaning of *eutopia* (a good place) and by creating the new word *utopia* (non-place), More created a tension which increased over time and strengthened the ambiguity related to the term.

Although More coined the word "utopia", he most certainly did not invent "utopianism", which emerged in fictional works preceding *Utopia*, which attempted to describe truthfully some ideal communities. The fictional representation of an ideal world was a known literary practice by Renaissance. This tradition of thought – nourished by the myth of the Golden Age, the myth of the "Lands of Cockaygne", which deliver the fantasies of the lands of plenty, along with other mythical and religious archetypes such as the Biblical story of Moses's journey to the promised land, the edenic state of Adam and Eve, as well as the prophesies of the second coming – gave rise to some works of "high" culture, like Plato's *Republic*, Lucian's *Menippus*, and St Augustine's *The City of God*. All these myths and fictional works can be loosely presented as "utopian" since they express various alternatives for a better world.

Undoubtedly, Thomas More is inspired by the classical and Christian traditions. However, even though More shares with the earlier representations the aspiration for a better life in an ideal commonwealth, his utopia differs greatly from the preceding hypostasis of the utopian desire, "as they lack the tension between the affirmation of a possibility and the negation of its fulfilment" (Vieira 6). In his *Republic*, Plato only speculates about the possibilities for a better organization of a city, whereas St Augustine envisages his ideal only in the form of afterlife. More, in his representation of the desire for a better life, added a new dimension, a very modern one, precisely the role played by the individuals during their lifetime and, without idealising human being, he seeks human solutions to human problems.

Originating in a paradox which never seeks to be solved completely, the concept of "utopia" is the result of a modern thought and it renews its significance each time, while serving new interests and assuming new formats. Regardless of its usage, as an imagined society, as a literary genre, or as an expression of a desire for a better life which stems from the discontent in the societal organization, utopia is regarded mostly as an attitude, a revolt against an undesirable present and as a yearning to surpass the present societal difficulties by the creation of alternatives.

Thomas More's *Utopia*

Sir Thomas More began the writing of *Utopia* in 1515, and many scholars consider this year to be the beginning of English Renaissance. This famous work was published in 1516 at Louvian, with Erasmus supervising the printing. It was a collaborative product of the European intellectual elite, which included More, Erasmus, Giles, Budé, and Busleyden. The result of this collaborative work is mostly reflected in the plurality of the expressed sides of conversations, which contributed to the interpretative openness which continues to fascinate the readers to the present day.

Emerging from the European intellectual milieu, More's work can be considered a speculative political essay which fuses literature and philosophy, art and theory, and, being written in the fashion of many Renaissance writings, it overlaps fiction and reality, blurs the illusion, the self-delusion and the dissimulation of the displayed aspects of social, political and cultural life. The title of More's work is suggestive in this respect, signalling from the very beginning the interplay between real and fictional, credible and incredible.

Focusing from the beginning of his work on the principle *dulce et utile*, used by Horace, Lucian, and later Erasmus, More indeed delivers a combination of profit and delight, producing a work which entertains as much as it teaches its readers. Setting the scope of telling the truth and truth only from the beginning of the narrative, this purpose wittily introduces some very serious Renaissance uncertainties concerning the distinction between fact and fiction, true lives and romance, history and literature. Michael McKeon speaks of a major cultural shift regarding the ambiguities of "how to tell the truth in narrative" in the early Renaissance (20). More reveals these problems, which are central to the early modern experience, in his typically playful manner, creating one of the most slippery texts, which prompts an extraordinary interpretative complexity regarding the authorial intention.

The narrative begins with Thomas More (a real person and author), who performs a journey to Flanders as a part of a diplomatic mission on the behalf of King Henry VIII (a historical fact) and, while being outside the church of Notre Dame in Antwerp (a real place), he meets Peter Giles (a real person and friend) in a possibly real encounter. The ambiguity concerning the intention of telling of truth emerges when Peter Giles introduces Thomas More to Raphael Hythloday, a Portuguese explorer and intellectual (a fictional character), blurring the boundaries between fact and fiction, truth and imaginary. This subversion of boundaries is also sustained by the contradiction suggested by the names of the characters, most probably immediately detected by More's readers: "Raphael" is the name of an angelic messenger, God's healer, whereas "Hythloday" signifies the speaker of nonsense or an expert in trifles. The same word-play is easily depicted in the case of "Thomas More", where "Thomas" refers to the sceptical apostle, and "Morus" (the Latin form for More) signifying the "fool", gaining more relevance especially after the publication of Erasmus's work *Moriae Economium* (*The Praise of Folly*) in 1511. J. C. Davis mentions that following this recognition, "the readers were immediately asked to decide whether to attach credibility to an account by the most disinterested and experienced of travellers, or to the reaction of a sceptic who might also be a fool" (30). It should be mentioned that the interpretative ambiguities remain present throughout the entire text.

Thomas More's work is divided into two Books, quite different, yet each interesting in its own way. More sets a perpetual intertextual relationship with Plato's *Republic* when he creates a dialogue inspired by Socrates, which produces several distinct perspectives on stringent political and social issues, delivered through different views and expressed by his characters Hythloday, More, and Giles.

Considering the idea of the best state presented by Plato, More introduces a platform for the diverging views on true nobility: as a part of one's merit (Plato) or lineage and wealth (Aristotle). Moreover, he continues to increase the tension in the Book I by presenting the opposition between *vita activa* (active political engagement) and *vita contemplativa* (political detachment), which is a hotly debated issue among More's contemporaries. The Platonic idea of the collaboration between philosophers and kings for the establishment of a good life is conveyed by More when he points out the problem of the necessity and usefulness of the political counsel.

More-the-author carefully introduces Raphael Hythloday through Giles-the-character to More-the-character, the three of them exhibiting different personalities, experiences and ideas about the value of counsel to kings, each having distinct opinions of what constitutes the best state of commonwealth. The approaches of the three men to these subjects are also very distinct. Giles-the-character is a stalwart, unmovable man, who, although apparently interested in Hythloday's tales, is not interested in any reforms which would lead to the best commonwealth. His enjoyment in listening to the stories of faraway lands is only a form of entertainment, their delight never stirring a desire to change anything in his society. The attitude of Giles-the-character, namely that nothing needs to change in England, differs greatly from the attitude of Giles-the-real man, a humanist who strongly believes in the necessity of social reforms, this stark discrepancy being easily noticed by the Renaissance reader.

Hythloday is an explorer and an intellectual who finds delight in travel and philosophy; he is also a perfectly equipped counsellor who could truly make a difference in politics if he takes a place by a king. However, Hythloday quickly expresses his reluctance of becoming the counsellor to a king, insisting on the value of his freedom of action and thought which stands above any desire of acquiring power and influence. His lack of political or social ambition is obvious, as he has dispersed all his possessions to his relatives, setting himself free to explore the world in his quest for knowledge and meaning.

Seneca's advocacy of *vita contemplativa* is recognized in Raphael's choice of personal happiness over glory and contemplation over participation. More-the-character, though admitting the appealing side of isolation, encourages Hythloday towards a Ciceronian outlook, of *vita activa*, to abandon his personal distaste for power in order to inspire a good ruler to do good things, his broad knowledge and vast experience being extremely useful for a leader in a state.

The shift in their debate is made by Hythloday's questioning the effectiveness over ability. Raphael insists that rulers find more delight in *gloria*, and, instead of trying to improve the governmental policies in the territories they already possess, they choose war over peace, because this is the way to experience triumph over their rivals. Moreover, since the kings do not live in a community of friends (Sallust) where everything is based on *concordia* (friendship between equals), but in a society of enemies, where everything is based on rivalry, how then effective could be the voice of a counsellor who lacks completely any territorial ambition and is not a part of dynastic competition? In the same manner, when confronted with the fiscal rapacity of the state builders, the recommendation of the counsellor to decrease the royal treasuries would be met by the same rejection, as flattery and false interests prevail over justice. For Raphael, the choice of political engagement leads inevitably to the corruption of the attendant of political involvement, and, in order to preserve his moral integrity, he prefers the retreat from any duties, isolating himself from ambition and corruption in his own thoughts and opinions.

Though Raphael's attitude seems rigid and lacking plasticity, one acknowledges the challenge, which is stated explicitly in *Utopia*, regarding political attendant's ability to find a balance between integrity and accommodation to circumstances, nobility and its perversion through opportunism. The Book I presents a devastating image of the early sixteenth-century government and society, where "the pursuit of false pleasure and false interests is the norm. Friendship is negated in favour of competitive emulation, community eroded by gross inequality. Folly shuts out wisdom along with Christian precept in all areas of policy – fiscal, military, economic and penal" (Davis 38). When such prejudice is brought to wisdom and justice, little can be said to Raphael's decision of detachment from public life, and even though More-the-character is still full of questions, he abandons the confrontation, possibly from the fear of appearing an idealistic fool.

The prolonged debate on social and political evils represents a serious critique of the sixteenth-century England, and Hythloday thinks that the only way to overcome the ills of the community is through the eradication of the reason for the competitive emulation by abolishing the private property. This is his answer to the establishment of a community of equality and friendship. More-the-character, who plays the role of an overly cautious realist, though finding delight in the thought of a just and equal society, is sceptical regarding any real and substantial change. He acknowledges the problem in the society, but he believes that the solutions to this problem can only be minimal, the ideal state being impossible to achieve.

This is the opportunity for Hythloday to introduce the land of Utopia, which covers Book II of More's text. This second Book about Utopians is actually the part which the readers generally think of when considering *Utopia*. Hythloday enthusiastically talks about the ideal state, where communism is the general law, where there is no poverty since there is no private wealth, where a national system of education is extended to men and women alike, equal access to healthcare is provided for everyone and the freest toleration of religion is recognized. Gender equality allows prospective husband and wife to see each other naked before marriage, and men as well as women receive as much education as their capabilities permit. Utopian houses are of equal comfort and design, and are exchanged regularly by people; each house has a garden and stands on a street twenty feet wide. A six-hour day is all the work required of a man. In Utopia, the clothes are almost like uniforms and jewels, gold and silver are despised; moreover, no markers associated with elite culture and aristocratic prestige are allowed.

At first glance, it seems that Utopia represents the opposite of the earlier criticized England, since the injustice in England stands diametrically opposed to the impartiality in Utopia, and the existence of extremely rich and poor in England creates a stark contrast to Utopian equality, in which nobody lacks anything and all things are common to every man. However, Hythloday's enthusiastic description of Utopia should be approached with caution, as More-the-character keeps his silence while conducting Hythloday for supper, his lack of agreement with Hythloday raises doubts about More-the-author's intention about the writing of *Utopia*.

Though many could be captured by the enthusiasm displayed by the description of Utopia and take this mode of life seriously, there are several warnings which are scattered throughout the entire text in order to prevent such a naive reading. To begin with, the cunning use of names of characters and the word "utopia" itself play some jokes on the readers. A similar warning is there to those who intend to read More's text as a serious suggestion for an alternative communal organization, as there are multiple traps into which an eager reader may fall. The most obvious warning is in the questioning of the good place's goodness. In Utopia, capital punishment is practiced and their colonial policies leave much to be desired. In Book I, the social injustice of European society is vehemently criticized, but such injustices are questionably cured in such a regimented and faceless society. The citizens of Utopia are robotically obliged to work for some uniformly restricted hours, the hours for communal dining are controlled, and strict conformity to rules of travel, occupations, and relocation are expected. The separation of children from their family and friends for the sake of demographic stability does not confer any feeling of the real happiness of life either. These issues raise some serious questions concerning the delight and true happiness of Utopians and also about More-the-author's consideration of this state as an alternative model of government.

Definitely, *Utopia* ends with some challenges. It asks the question of the possibility of conceiving a better world, where true nobility and the pursue of true happiness in a community based on justice for all are possible. The final silence of More-the-character regarding the customs and laws of Utopians reveals an attitude of hesitation, or even scepticism concerning the prospect of creating a community where all humans are capable of relation to others as equal friends rather than enemies when the real and the ideal worlds collide. The pursuit of happiness to the good of the community is a serious concern for More-the-author and his contemporaries, but equally serious for the humanists is the subordination of individual choice and happiness in order to achieve homogeneity with no exceptions, with no one ever revolting against the universal system, with never a refusal to conform. Between *Utopia*'s playfulness and social critique, "More seems to be saying that we need fiction to see reality afresh: in particular, we need utopian fiction to see the reality of our own society and the costs of putting it right" (Davis 47). With humour and delight, Thomas More brings in his work the unresolved dilemma which continues to intrigue the readers to present day.

1.2 The Idea of Literature as a Critical Concern in the Renaissance Period

It is an established formula to see the Renaissance as "a rebirth of classical art", "a conscious return to the culture of classical Antiquity" (Christensen 162), including ancient philosophy, mythology, and literature. The Renaissance, also referred to as "early modern period", is seen as a rejection of the entire medieval spirit in all its socio-cultural ramifications. But there are scholars, among whom Martin Heidegger asking the question of matter and form, who could see continuity between the two apparently dissimilar periods in the history of humanity:

The idea of creation, grounded in faith, can lose its guiding power of knowledge of beings as a whole. But the theological interpretation of all beings, the view of the world in terms of matter and form borrowed from an alien philosophy, having once being instituted, can still remain a force. This happens in the transition from the Middle Ages to modern times. The metaphysics of the modern period rests on the form-matter structure devised in the medieval period, which itself merely recalls in its words the buried natures of eidos and hule. Thus the interpretation of "thing" by means of matter and form, whether it remains medieval or becomes Kantian-transcendental, has become current and self-evident. (Heidegger 30)

However, without entering into all the details of the philosophical thinking about the transition from the Middle Ages to modern times, it is, in general, accepted that the medieval period is rejected and replaced by the age of Renaissance. The new period in the course of history is considered either as the first part of the modern era that lasted until the middle of the twentieth century, or as a period of transition from the Middle Ages to modern age, which would be then conceived as lasting from the seventeenth-century Rationalism and Empiricism – placing Enlightenment on the throne of the modern thinking – to the middle of the twentieth century and as followed, in turn, until nowadays, by the postmodern period.

The Renaissance as a period of history or a historical development is first a new mind-set based on "the rediscovery of the ancient classics of Greece and Rome which scholars edited, translated, and wrote commentaries on" (Blamires 44). There were certainly some political and economic conditions determining the beginning of Renaissance, but there were also some theoretical impulses whose work was accelerated, among other things, by the input of scholarship from Byzantium after the capture of Constantinople by the Turks in 1453. After the medieval mind had placed God in the centre of universe and the ancients had placed man, it was a new movement in the thinking of the period which shaped "Humanism" as the theory of an individual rational man and which had direct repercussions on contemporary literature.

The art and literature of the Renaissance already reveal the two contradictory but co-existing aspects of "innovation" (for instance, sonnet in poetry) and "tradition" (the revival of ancient models, as, for example, in Renaissance tragedy). Concerning the latter aspect, one of the first manifestations of the revived Greek and Roman antecedents was actually the philosophical thought of Humanism. Desiderius Erasmus and Thomas More were among the most renowned humanist intellectuals of Europe, applying the ancient heritage to the solution of the contemporary, especially political, issues. Their contribution reflects a twofold perspective: "for Erasmus the world was best improved by writing, by education, and by a scholar's freedom of action, not by a direct involvement in state politics; for More, however, the highest duty of a man learned in the theory and practice of ancient government was to serve the king" (Sanders 92). On the more general cultural level, the admiration for Aristotle led to a certain formula regarding the literary phenomena, the emphasis being placed on the conscious activity and on rules based on authority, common sense, and reason. Imagination, inspiration, and invention are accepted but are placed under control, the main role being played by mind and thought. *Mimesis* is conceived as the imagination of nature, which is the duplicate of reality, and art must reflect beautiful nature. As Aristotle distinguished between real, possible and verisimilar actions, preferring the impossible verisimilitude, in the Renaissance, the emphasis is on fiction as against reality. Emotion and idealization are left aside, except a type of moral ideal. The ancients required the combination of all parts of the literary work, whereas the rising in the Renaissance neoclassicism developed the dichotomy of form and content and discussed separately their constituent parts. The new theoreticians followed primarily the principles of Aristotle and Horace, combining the former's theory of *catharsis* with the latter's *miscere utile et dulce* and *aut prodesse, aut delectari*. The poet must present a universe of order and assume social responsibility and literature must possess social utility. Only later, with the rising Romantic spirit, the literary creation would be considered as a personal expression of inner states and discussed in the unity of content and form.

Concerning literary practice, the crown of Renaissance art was tragedy, whose development took place within the larger experience of the revival of ancient classical tradition, the rediscovery of Aristotle and Horace, and the imitation of ancient models. In thought and writing, Renaissance authors "modelled their styles on Seneca and Tacitus. Writing should be economical, pithy and sententious, although we still find balance and parallelism, as in the opening of Francis Bacon's essay "Of Revenge"" (Hattaway 37).

The classical tragedy was revived and imitated in all its formal and thematic components and the total adherence to models and rules excluded whatever change and originality. At the beginning of the Renaissance, especially in Italian drama, the main model was Seneca, but what was borrowed from him

were his defects rather than qualities. The Italian tragedy is characterised by the same low theatricality, action and conflict are replaced by dissertations, characters make pathetic discourses. The topics belong to ancient mythology, but also to contemporary period. This is actually the only innovation. As in Seneca, there are scenes of violence and cruelty, beheading, revenge, assassination, rape, incest. (Ceuca 101)

Gradually, however, drama, in general, and tragedy, in particular – due to Shakespeare, Lope de Vega, and in the seventeenth century to Calderon de la Barca, Racine, Corneille and others – receive freedom of expression, negates the strict rules (especially the three unities), becomes an open form, rediscovers Euripides, and "keeps from Aristotle only the general construction, exposition, development, etc." (Ceuca 102) Among the representatives of the aspect of innovation, Francesco Petrarca (or Petrarch, in English, 1304-1374) is one of the first to become aware of the conflict between old and new, tradition and originality, and solves this conflict in favour of the new, which is the humanistic ideal, as opposed to the old, medieval conception, and, to a certain degree, to the classical values as well. In this respect, Petrarch produces the sonnet and "turns to lyric poetry to express the thoughts, emotions, and inner states of the human personality being in the process of emancipation" (Pavlicencu 40). On the other hand, while medieval scholars ranked poetry "among the natural and moral sciences, as did the Chartrian academician John of Salisbury in his *Metalogicon*", and in the spirit of the classical scholarship, the humanists "associated poetry with rhetoric, serving as a practical means to stimulate the intelligence, inspire learning, and persuade to civic virtue" (Kennedy 91).

The emergence of the innovative spirit in literature continues after the Renaissance as Baroque art (metaphysical poetry, in English literature, also considered by critics as the last manifestation of the British Renaissance). This cultural extravaganza is rejected and suppressed by the much stronger and dominant traditional element. The tradition, based on the revival of ancient classical artistic doctrine and practice, becomes itself a period and dominates as the Enlightenment and classicism (or neoclassicism, in England) the entire social as well as cultural and literary background of Europe for more than one hundred years. The period starts with the middle of the seventeenth century to the last decades of the eighteenth century which witnessed the rise of a new, romantic literary sensibility.

> Concerning the general development of literary practice and critical thought, the element of innovation in literary history has its origins in the Renaissance, persists in the Baroque, is replaced by classical tradition, but is reborn in romanticism, diversified by the nineteenth century avant-garde trends and flourishes by the twentieth century modernism and postmodernism. The element of tradition in literary development originates in classical antiquity, is suppressed in the Middle Ages but revived in the Renaissance and institutionalised as the dominant doctrine by the seventeenth and eighteenth centuries Enlightenment and neoclassicism. Romanticism rejects it but it is important again as the nineteenth century realism, being to the present day kept alive by the realistic and socially concerned writers.

Renaissance is thus the first period of the modern literary history in which both elements of innovation and tradition co-exist and initiate their ever-lasting reciprocal struggle. Based on the humanistic views, Renaissance period revived ancient classical tradition, attempting to produce art following the ancient models, on one hand, and, on the other hand, to develop theories and doctrines reminiscent of classical ideals, and to judge literature by literary, not religious, values. The literary practice consisted mainly of drama, whose primary model was Seneca, and of poetry modelled on Horace's and Pindar's grave, noble and serious spirit, and their ornamented and decorated style. The *ars poetica* of the Renaissance "was that of Aristotle and Horace, that is to say, similar to the one which existed in classical Antiquity" (Cioranescu 11). In addition, the interest in and the understanding of classical tradition were deepened by Greek scholars who fled to the West after the fall of Constantinople in 1453.

There was the theory of epic poem, as in Torquato Tasso's (1544-1595) *Discourses on the Heroic Poem* (1594), which asserts the four major elements in epic poetry: the story or fable, the morality of the characters, the purpose behind the story, and the language. The purpose of epic is to delight the reader as a source of intellectual and moral improvement, since for Tasso "delight is the cause why no one fails to obtain benefit, because delight induces him to read more gladly".

At odds with ancient principles of epic writing tradition were romances as proto-novel inventions of the period, such as Ariosto's *Orlando Furioso* (1516) and Spenser's *Faerie Queene* (1596), and the literary criticism of the period that focused on such texts attempted to justify their literary validity. For instance, as Ariosto introduces fantastic and marvellous elements in his romance, so Giovambattista Giraldi (1504-1573, better known as Cinthio), in *On the Composition of Romances* (1554), explains and defends the use of the supernatural beings and action in romances, as well as a great variety of characters and events, as to prove that romance is a genre totally different from both epic and tragedy and should be judged as such.

The most discussed genre in Renaissance criticism was drama, where modern standards of dramatic criticism were being built up through the Renaissance, partly by experiments in new forms, and partly by study and discussion of Greco-Roman literary theory – represented chiefly by Aristotle's *Poetics*, Horace's *Art of Poetry*, and, much less influentially, by Longinus's essay *On the Sublime*. Much of Renaissance drama was created by the lofty standards of Renaissance critics, who, in spite of their frequent pedantry, would not tolerate slovenly work. (Highet 142)

The most discussed issues in relation to drama were the nature of tragedy and the concept of the tragic hero, as well as the doctrine of the "three unities" in the dramatic structure involving the principles of time, place, and action. The theory of the "unity of action" in the play was developed by Aristotle, and Gilbert Highet argues that the unities of time and place (the former just mentioned by Aristotle and the latter not mentioned at all) were largely the creation of Renaissance scholars Cinthio, Robortelli, Segni, Castelvetro, and others in the sixteenth century.

All three unities were very useful in the period as "an attempt to strengthen and discipline the haphazard and amateurish methods of contemporary dramatists – not simply in order to copy the ancients, but in order to make drama more intense, more realistic, and more truly dramatic" (Highet 142). The unities of time and place developed out of the presence of the chorus in the play and, although the modern tragedy does no longer believe in them as rules, they still possess certain roles: if the unities are observed through the play, "we feel more easily that the characters presented in the drama cannot get away from each other: they have to fight (and die sometimes); there is no room for anything but elegance or at least economy, no room to sprawl" (Leech 75).

The extensive approach to drama in Renaissance criticism is undoubtedly the result of drama being the most important literary genre. Only in English literature, its significance owes much to Marlowe, Jonson, and especially Shakespeare. Unfortunately, the development of English literature during the periods subsequent to Renaissance saw a decline of the genre, although there were some attempts, but unsuccessful, at its revival in Restoration.

There were few authors in eighteenth century (Oliver Goldsmith and Richard Brinsley Sheridan), few romantic works (by Shelley and Byron), and its status was even worse in the nineteenth century, except Oscar Wilde and George Bernard Shaw. The latter is also accredited with the revival of British drama in the first half of the twentieth century, but it flourished again in English literature especially starting with the mid-1950s.

Apart from drama and tragedy, in Renaissance criticism, there was also much debate on poetry as philosophy and imitation, the doctrine of verisimilitude in poetry, the poetic diction and decorum, and the twofold purpose of poetry to please and instruct. There was also the debate on the language of poetry, in particular, and of literature, in general: as Renaissance was the period of the revival of ancient classical tradition, there was no question about imitating the classical models but about the language used in writing, whether it should be Latin, the "universal" language of the classics, or the vernacular ones (French, Italian, English). The use of vernacular language was earlier defended by Dante (in the unfinished *De Vulgari Eloquentia*) and, in Renaissance, by, among others, Joachim du Bellay (in *Defence and Illustration of the*

French Language, 1549). The question of language emerged by the side of the growing national consciousness corresponding to the rise of new European nation-states, for which a common national language, among other factors, would provide grounds for a national identity.

During Renaissance, the major European critical voices were Italian (Vida, Robortelli, Daniello, Minturno, Scaliger, Castelvetro), whereas the mid-sixteenth century throughout the seventeenth century saw the dominance of French critical works, which, like those of the late medieval and Renaissance periods, were first rhetorical and metrical, guiding the growth of classicism already supported by Humanism, Aristotelianism, and rationalism. Minturno in *De Poetica* (1559), Scaliger in *Poetices libri septem* (1561), and Castelvetro in *Poetica d'Aristotele vulgarizzata et sposta* (1570) are credited for having rediscovered and revived in the Renaissance the *Poetics* of Aristotle, which became very influential after being translated into Italian in 1549.

Richard Harland calls them "the Italian Aristotelians" and praises them for having developed the theory of the "unity of time" (Minturno and Scaliger) and that of the "unity of place" (Castelvetro), and for having developed the principle of verisimilitude, deriving it from Aristotle's concept of *mimesis*. With the principle of verisimilitude, the Italian Aristotelians pointed to the achieving of likeness to reality in literature and, unlike Aristotle, "gave more weight to believability, less to emotional effect", thus prefiguring the later, "modern notions of realism and the realistic" (Harland 36-39).

Concerning French Renaissance criticism, mention should be made of *Art of Poetry* (1548) by Sibilet, and the writings of Pierre de Ronsard and Joachim du Bellay as representatives of the group called "Pleiade", which attempted to refine French literature, as well as language, by following the classical models. Pierre de Ronsard, in particular, attempts in this respect to combine classical poetics with Christian beliefs, invention with imitation, and to adjudicate the claims of competing languages and dialects.

In English Renaissance, criticism was first concerned with rhetoric and diction (Caxton, Leonard Cox, and Thomas Wilson), and then moved to issue of the development of a national literature in native language (for instance, Elyot in *Book Named the Governour*, 1531), which received a strong opposition from the humanists and inkhornists who searched to adopt Latin words instead of developing a native lexicon. Sir Thomas Elyot (1490-1546) insists on and recommends the classical models, namely Homer and Virgil, and prefers that literature which delights but also improves morally the human condition. Elyot's book is "really the first English book on education and what Elyot has to say about the place of literature in education certainly expresses the Renaissance spirit" (Blamires 46). A seventeenth century version of *The Governour* will be Henry Peacham's *The Complete Gentleman* (1622).

Also concerning the use of English in writing, it required the building up of the English vocabulary and the development of different technical devices in versification, such as rhyme and meter, the first work on versification in English being Gascoigne's *Certain Notes of Instruction* (1575). The development of the verse devices which would urge the use of English in poetic composition followed two directions.

One was theoretical, insisting on the imitation of the classical forms, such as the unrhymed hexameter, and on decorum and *mimesis*, and often condemning the rhyme (as in Thomas Campion's *Observations in the Art of English Poesie*, 1602, promptly answered by Samuel Daniel in *A Defence of Rime*). Another, the practical direction, aimed to perfect English versification by means of the creative activity of the poets, where the same Campion and other poets, like Pierre Corneille some decades later in relation to drama, would often attempt at originality against the prevailing insistence on classical forms.

Perhaps the main advocate of the classical tradition was Ben Jonson, who turned a critic in *Timber: Or Discoveries*, representing, together with Dryden some twenty years later, the attempt to promote neoclassicism in English literature and criticism. Some noteworthy critical ideas are also to be found in Francis Bacon's *Advancement of Learning* (1605). Although this work, together with the *Novum Organum* (1620), was published at the beginning of the seventeenth century,

> in spirit and outlook he [Bacon] belongs rather to the sixteenth century than to the age of the new mathematical physics and of rationalism in philosophy. Unlike Descartes, he had no vision of the application of mathematics in the study of nature and he made no lasting contribution to the analysis of concepts or of the different categories of thought. (Hampshire 19)

Bacon's views concern philosophy and science, politics as well as ethics, and many other topics. His works influenced immensely the thought of the periods to come, in particular by what is called his "inductive method", meaning the ascent from observation of facts to generalisations which are mere probable:

Bacon, like Descartes, proclaimed a new method in the sciences; but his method, unlike Descartes's, was not to involve a priori reasoning to indubitable truths. He advocated a purely empirical, experimental method which, starting from observations of particular things and events, would move towards wider and wider generalization. These general statements, unlike those of mathematics, would be capable of being proved false by experiment. (Hampshire 20)

1.2.1 Philip Sidney and *The Defence of Poesie*: The Rise of the English Literary Criticism

With regard to the literary filed, the spokesperson and master critic of English Renaissance was Philip Sidney (1554-1586). Scholar, poet, courtier, and soldier, Sidney is the author of the most significant critical treatise of the period, the essay *The Defence of Poesie* (also entitled *Apologie for Poetrie*). It was published in 1595, but was written much earlier as an answer to the Puritan minister Stephen Gosson's *The School of Abuse* (1579), a Puritan moralistic attack on imaginative writing of the period, dedicated to Sidney himself. Owing it to his *The Defence of Poesie*, the Renaissance marks the actual beginnings of literary criticism in Britain. "Well documented and skilfully written" and being "the most important work of literary theory in English Renaissance" (Cartianu and Preda 324), Sidney's critical text is to be considered in relation to co-existing in the period innovative element in literature, represented, among others, by Sidney himself as the writer of sonnets and pastoral poetry, and the traditional element in literature, standing for the revival of ancient classical tradition.

The text is also to be considered in relation to the fact that the poetry of the period, both pastoral and sonnet writing tradition, and the imaginative writing on the whole, where often attacked on moral grounds by the rising Puritanism. Sidney defends then not just poetry but literature (*poesie*) in general.

The term "Puritan" was first applied to those who, starting with the second half of the sixteenth century, aimed at purifying the Church of England. The term eventually came to name a movement that was highly influential in the seventeenth century in both England and the New England colonies in America. Puritanism in England was an aftermath of Calvinism, an outgrowth of the Reformation, and later allied itself with the radical movement of Presbyterianism, objecting to certain forms of the Church of England, demanding certain reforms of the Church (as, for instance, by its 1603 "Millenary Petition"), and, in general, openly hating the Established Church of England (as, for instance, Thomas Cartwright, the first important exponent of Puritanism, did).

On the general social level, the Protestant concept of "actively serving God" developed in relation to the doctrine of individualism, the individual consciousness, and the right of the individual to religious and political independence. An extreme form of Reformation, Puritanism exaggerated some Protestant traits, aiming at a global restructuring of the religious institution, rejecting the religious ritual, opposing any kind of worship, instead advising the reading of the Bible and preaching fundamentals of the faith.

The beginnings of Puritanism go back to the middle of the sixteenth century, and the Elizabethan period and the first half of the seventeenth century saw its development as a movement involved first in religion but also in art and literature, among other fields, and later in social life on the whole as to finally acquire the political control over Parliament. A consequence of the conflict between the King and Parliament, between the followers of Charles I, who were called "Cavaliers", and the members of the Puritan or Parliamentary party, called "Roundheads", was the Civil War that lasted from 1642 to 1646.

Led by Oliver Cromwell who came to power during the war, the Puritans abolished the monarchy by executing Charles I in 1649 and established the Puritan "Commonwealth", also called the "Interregnum" period, or the period of "Commonwealth Interregnum", or "Protectorate", or simply the "Puritan period", which lasted until the restoration of monarchy in 1660 and during which the country was ruled by Oliver Cromwell, who proclaimed himself "Lord Protector" of England.

As far as the literature of the Puritan period is concerned, the "Golden Age" of Elizabethan drama and the flourishing of the metaphysical poetry early in the seventeenth century were followed by a total decline during the Puritan middle decade of the century. The decline concerned first of all drama and theatrical representation: during the reign of James I theatres were already placed under the direct control of the crown, and later, in 1642, the Parliament decided the abolition of all playhouses, which proved a major disadvantage for dramatic production. The prose productions of the period, which consisted mainly in political pamphlets, historical writings and philosophical speculations, developed a new style of language which came to represent concreteness, clarity and simplicity, and which would be functional rather than allegorical or persuasive.

The years of Commonwealth represented a poor literary period, but there were notable works produced during the period, among which John Milton's *Defence of the English People* (1651), Thomas Hobbes's *Leviathan* (1652), Abraham Cowley's *Poems, Davideis, Pindaric Odes* (1656), and some translations of French romances and novels.

The Protestant theology reached the literary level, started to be reflected in literary works, and became the source of a distinct tradition of religious poetry in the seventeenth century, in particular in the works of John Milton and in the poems of metaphysical writers Andrew Marvell, George Herbert, and John Donne. Actually, the spirit of Puritanism found its supreme spokesmen in poetry in the writings of John Milton and Andrew Marvell, and in prose fiction in the writing of John Bunyan, though by the chronology of their works the three writers belong to other periods. For instance, Milton's *L'Allegro, Il Penseroso*, and *Lycidas* came in the previous Caroline Age and his *Paradise Lost* in the next Restoration period. Similarly, Bunyan's *The Pilgrim's Progress*, perhaps the most famous English Christian allegory ever written, also came in the next period of Restoration.

Yet it is the poetic work of Milton, the most representative poet of Puritanism, and that of Marvell, an active supporter of the new government of Cromwell's England, as well as the prose work of John Bunyan, that require a special critical consideration in the study of the literary expression of the Puritan outlook in literature.

Cromwell died in 1658, being followed by his son Richard who, unlike his father, was an incompetent ruler. The political and social crisis of the country was solved by the return of Charles II to London and his restoration to the throne of England in 1660. The political death of Puritanism in 1660 and the subsequent persecution of the Puritans made many of them leave England for the American colonies, a consequence of which, in cultural terms, being the Puritan period in American literature and arts.

The beginnings of English literary criticism in the Renaissance is therefore to be viewed in relation to the fact that the Protestant doctrine in Western Europe, in general, and, in particular, in England Puritanism and Presbyterianism extended themselves outside religious circle of ideas, reaching general social, economic and cultural levels, and, in relation to criticism, the field of literary practice. Many of the Puritans were people of culture and education, like Stephen Gosson, some of them even patrons of art, but their persecution by the institution of monarchy made them turn religious and social reformers.

The Puritans attempted to establish a theocracy and to involve in all spheres of social life. They attempted to control politics and economy as well as literature and arts in relation to which they emphasised the ecclesiastical and the virtuous over the light-hearted, lyric, sensual and chivalric, as in the case of Gosson's work aimed at Sidney's literary activity.

Philip Sidney was one of the most prominent authors of the Elizabethan Age as a part of English Renaissance, famous not only for his critical treatise but also for his pastoral poetry and sonnets. There were these and other literary genres of the period that were attacked by the rising Puritanism, including by Stephen Gosson (1554-1624), a Puritan who was earlier a poet, a playwright, and probably also an actor, and who later took Holy Orders and became Rector of the Church of St. Botolph's in Bishopsgate, London. Concerning the form of Sidney's critical treatise, in constructing his *apologia* – Greek for a legal defence – Sidney addressed himself less to Gosson than to Plato, whose *Republic* provides most of the ammunition the Puritan divine expended against poetry. Sidney's *Apology* is structured according to the principles of medieval rhetoric like a good legal brief, with an introduction that draws the reader into the case while offering reassurance of the ethical rightness of the speaker, a central argumentative section, a set of answers to objections, and a glowing peroration. (Richter 131)

By answering the objections and attacks on ethical grounds against poetry and drama of the period, which were regarded by Gosson and other Puritans as vehicles for moral degradation, Sidney was successful in achieving his purpose to defend literature in the face of Puritanism. He also assigned much praise to poets and the poetic art, arguing about the superiority of poetry over history, philosophy and other disciplines, and about the prophetic and moral function of poetry, while examining its typology and imaginative essence. Among the historians, excessively concerned with particular facts, and the obscure and too abstract philosophers, Sidney claims that

> is our poet the Monarch. For he doth not only show the way, but giveth so sweet a prospect into the way as will entice any man to enter into it (…). He beginneth not with obscure definitions, which must blur the margent with interpretations, and load the memory with doubtfulness: but he cometh to you with words set in delightful proportion, either accompanied with, or prepared for the well enchanting skill of music; and with a tale forsooth he cometh unto you, with a tale which holdeth children from play, and old men from the chimney corner; and pretending no more, doth intend the winning of the mind from wickedness to virtue.

Because of the religious condemnation voiced by Puritans in England in the second half of the sixteenth century, Sidney's defence and evaluation of poetry are done on moral grounds, the central concept being "virtue". Unlike philosopher's or theologian's writings, which can teach virtue only in abstract terms, and since the writer is an "inventor" or "maker", poetry both teaches virtue and "moves" reader to it.

The idea is that poetry makes the reader virtuous by means of moral instruction based on *catharsis* and *mimesis*, here imitation of the ethical manner, meaning on creating examples of ideal characters and conduct. Thus, poetry is superior to other disciplines and kinds of writing. Besides teaching, Sidney emphasises the idea of literature giving pleasure, which is another aspect which differentiates literature from other forms of writing. Apart from defending imaginative writing, Sidney's second major achievement is to have distinguished literature from other types of writing and proved that without the element of pleasure, the didactic and moral aims of literature are futile endeavours.

Like many Renaissance theorists, Sidney makes his argument consistent by relying on ideas of some predecessors, his "humanistic defence" of literature being, "in its broadest interpretation, Ceceronian"; his "conception of the poetic "image" derives from the scholastic analysis of Christian psychology"; but his "most pervasive literary debts are to Aristotle and Horace" (Trimpi 187). Aware of the need to rely on a respectable theoretical tradition, Sidney appeals to Plato's metaphysics, Aristotle's *mimesis* – for instance, at the beginning, when defining poetry, Sidney calls it "an art of imitation, for so Aristotle termeth it in his word *mimesis*" – and Horace's aesthetic principles – for instance, Sidney concludes his essay with the famous Horatian statement on the purpose of poetry, which for Sidney is the same: a poem is "a speaking picture, with this end, to teach and delight", or, rather, given the moralistic perspective, to delight in order to teach.

Apart from these, Sidney uses in his argument on the mission of literature another famous ancient definition of poetry, which is *docere delictendo* ("to teach by entertaining") by Ovid (43 BC – AD 17). Like ancients, Sidney emphasises the pragmatic nature of creative writing; for example, when discussing tragedy, the critic states that "the high and excellent Tragedy" is the one

> that openeth the greatest woundes, and sheweth forth the Ulcers that are covered with Tissue, that maketh Kings feare to be Tyrants, and Tyrants manifest their tyrannicall humours, that with stirring the affects of Admiration and Comiseration, teacheth the uncertaintie of this world, and uppon how weak foundations guilden roofes are builded.

The most interesting part of the work is the one containing the answers to objections. In it, Sidney firstly states the three accusations of the poet haters, the Puritans, against poetry, and, using the techniques of the rhetorical argumentation, answers them.

The first accusation is that poetry offers useless knowledge: poetry teaches nothing, is not a "fruitful knowledge", and "there being many other more fruitful knowledges, a man might better spend his time in them than in this". To this accusation, Sidney's answer is that poetry gives the most complete knowledge, as compared to other disciplines, because, the critic claims, poetry both "teacheth and moveth to virtue". For Sidney, "fruitful knowledge" is the one that both teaches what virtue is and determines the reader to become a virtuous being.

In answering the accusation, Sidney develops an interesting and at the same time systemic approach: (1) they say poetry is useless knowledge; (2) it might be so, but what is actually a "fruitful knowledge"?, asks Sidney; (3) the best learning is that "which teaches and moves to virtue", is the critic's answer to his own question; (4) only poetry, claims Sidney, performs both actions and therefore poetry is the most "fruitful knowledge in existence. The other types of writing, argues Sidney, only teach virtue, but poetry is an art and, applying the classical views of art as *mimesis* and *catharsis*, Sidney implies that poetry, by means of these two attributes, teaches/reveals what virtue is (like other disciplines) and also makes the human virtuous (only poetry performs this action). To teach virtue is "good", all forms of writing, including poetry, do it, but "better is better", and only poetry is "better" than others, or rather superior to others, in its double action of teaching and moving mankind to virtue by means of *catharsis*.

The second accusation is that poetry does not tell the truth, being "the mother of lies". Sidney's answer to this allegation is paradoxical, the paradox challenging the validity of the accusation itself. Like with the previous accusation, and using again rhetorical devices and the same systemic approach, Sidney asks what is to lie, and answers that to lie is "to affirm that to be true which is false", as is the matter of history, medicine, and other disciplines.

Unlike these, Sidney argues, poetry "nothing affirmeth, and therefore never lieth". Poetry does not affirm anything for the simple reason of being the result of a "good invention", the "profitable" product of the poet's imagination, and allegorically and figuratively written. Hence Sidney's paradoxical answer to this accusation: poetry does not tell of true things, indeed, since it is pure "invention" and the product of the imaginative faculty, but, at the same time, does not lie because it affirms nothing. Since the answer is a paradox, the accusation has no validity in its meaning, Sidney argues. Poetry affirms nothing, therefore it never lies, because of its imaginative, allegorical and figurative essence, and poetry must be taken seriously, for it helps the mind to escape the boundaries of earth and reach eternity by inspiring and elevating it.

The third accusation is that poetry is sinful, "the nurse of abuse, infecting us with many pestilent desires, with a siren's sweetness drawing the mind to the serpent's tail of sinful fancies". The answer to this grave accusation that implies the sexual desire stimulated by poetry (in the symbolism of the "siren's sweetness "and the "serpent's tail") is found in the answer to the first accusation, where Sidney claims that poetry both "teacheth and moveth to virtue", which is one of the most important, especially to Puritans, ethical principles.

Poetry, in Sidney's opinion, might have its origin in the sinful experience of mankind, but it ultimately offers both a vision of freedom and the sense of strength, both a celebration of mortal love and the hope for spiritual immortality. Moreover, argues Sidney, not poetry "abuseth man's wit, but that man's wit abuseth Poetrie".

Based on the classical views and conceptions, Sidney emphasizes the importance of poetry for mankind, and states its superiority over other human activities. Sidney also emphasises the importance of poetry over other arts: poetry offers delight and teaches virtue, but also moves the man towards this moral category so dear to the Puritan mind. By both teaching and moving to virtue, which is by making the human being virtuous and morally strong by means of *mimesis* and *catharsis*, poetry becomes the most complete and useful human knowledge.

The conclusion which emerges from the analysis of this fragment, as well as from *The Defence of Poesie*, in general, is that Sidney was not intentionally writing literary criticism, but a defence of poetry against Puritan attacks. In this respect, Sidney's criticism is to be considered as defensive, but also dependent on the period (Renaissance) to which it belongs, expressing its mentality and values.

Being one of the first English works of literary criticism, Sidney's *The Defence of Poesie* has its origin not in the critical act conceived as a self-conscious endeavour, but results from within the literary context and as being determined by an extra-literary problem. However, the three major components of a critical discourse – concern with particular literary texts, the use of theory and method, and the development of personal opinions – are, to a certain degree, found in Sidney's critical text. Here the main concern is not represented by individual texts but is his own and his contemporary poetry in general.

The theory is not far removed from the main principles of imitation and purification (Aristotle), and of usefulness of poetry (Horace's *utile et dulce*) from the ancient classical doctrine. The method is borrowed from the rhetoric and classical argumentative reasoning; also, the abundance of personal, subjective considerations of the poetry's superior status is easily noticeable.

Sidney's critical treatise resulted as a need to answer the accusations made by Puritans, the poetry haters of the time, namely by Stephen Gosson in *The School of Abuse*, against the poets and poetry of the Elizabethan period. Sidney, himself a Renaissance writer of pastoral poetry and sonnets, was the person Stephen Gosson directly aimed at by addressing his article to Sidney.

Sidney's criticism is first of all defensive, and he came to defend not just his own poetic work, or even the poetry of the period, but the entire imaginative writing from the second half of the sixteenth century. While answering the accusations, Sidney expresses his own ideas on poetry, and thus emerge some genuine parts of literary criticism, a type of critical judgement based on the works of ancients as well as modern poets. Sidney also aims at defining the future ways of English poetry by offering prescriptive definitions, his criticism being, in this respect, also normative and prescriptive.

Siding with Aristotle against puritans who side with Plato, Philip Sidney's critical text clearly shows the influence of Horace's *Ars Poetica*, which, according to Gilbert Highet, "was a very important formative factor in Renaissance literary theory", being translated for the first time into Italian by Dolce in 1535, then "into French by Grandichan in 1541 and by Peletier du Mans in 1544; into Spanish in 1592 by Luis Zapata; and into English, along with the other *Letters* and the *Satires*, by T. Drant in 1567" (142). The rise of the literary criticism in England reveals through Sidney's text obvious moral and defensive features, where, as an answer to Puritanism, Sidney defends poetry as a discourse that makes man a virtuous being. Meanwhile, he gives the famous definition of poetry in clearly neo-Horatian terms as an art of imitation which teaches and delights: "Poesie therefore, is an Art of Imitation: for so Aristotle termeth it in the word *mimesis*, that is to say, a representing, counterfeiting, or figuring forth; to speak Metaphorically, a speaking Picture, with this end to teach and delight."

Sidney borrows the ancient theory and praises those contemporary authors who are "climbing to the height of Seneca's style", but his critical treatise is not a mere rewriting or imitation of the classical doctrines. Sidney the writer-critic takes theoretical support from the ancients, but he is also a true representative of his period in both creative and critical writing, and thus develops a critical tradition based on the works of both ancient and modern writers.

Moreover, the text shows that the purpose of defending the value of poetry and literature, imaginative writing, in general, against the accusations made by a Puritan mind, is remarkably complemented by the expression of Sidney's own observations and ideas on poetry. Indeed, Sidney's "treatise is shaped both by a need to reply to the case put by Plato and his fellow mysomousoi or Poet-haters, and by an evident pleasure in displaying his own enthusiasm and observations" (Sanders 108).

Like Sidney, another Elizabethan critic of poetry, George Puttenham (1529-1591), a nephew of the humanist scholar Sir Thomas Elyot, in *The Arte of English Poesie* (1589), attempts "to trace a poetic tradition which embraces the work of the ancient and of selected vernacular poets" and "to define a way forward by offering descriptive definitions" (Sanders 106). A stronger adherent to classical standards is William

Webbe (1568-1591) in *Discourse of English Poetry* (1586), in which, based on these standards, he aims to differentiate between good and bad critics and to impose the classical verse on English poetry. Webbe's ideas and arguments are much below those of Puttenham and Sidney. Like Sidney, Puttenham display wit, cleverness, and scholarship, and, like his uncle, believes in "the cultural centrality and proper eminence of the cultivated courtier", establishing codes of literary good manners and emphasising the "enhancement of the dignity of the modern gentleman poet by the values and social standing of a princely court" (Sanders 107). Puttenham's critical voice is accurate and sound, but it is Sidney's defence of poetry which makes Renaissance to be the period of the rise of a critical tradition in English and Philip Sidney to be the first important English literary critic. Sidney is the first prestigious name in the development of English critical writing about literature, acclaimed for his "intellectual energy and stylistic vitality", to use Blamires's words, who continues: "Ideas flow from his pen. Apt illustrations, imaginative turns of thought and neat dialectical thrusts crowd his pages. And the prose, largely free of arid modish turgidities and superfluous contrivances, carriers the reader eagerly forward" (55).

2.

THE PERIOD AND ITS LITERARY PRACTICE

The writers of Renaissance produced literary works following two directions. The first represents innovation, and it is truly a modern one, based on the rejection of the entire past tradition, including ancient classical models, as, for instance, Petrarch and his sonnet. The second represents tradition, and it is based on ancient classical views and reproduces the classical forms, as, for instance, Renaissance drama of Shakespeare and Jonson. The concept of *mimesis* became dominant and was understood from both the perspective of Plato (faithful imitation) and that of Aristotle (imitation starting from something).

Indeed, the first thing that comes to mind about the period from the fourteenth to the seventeenth century is the "rebirth", revival, rediscovery and imitation of ancient classical tradition, but there was also formal experiment and a continuation of the more recent, medieval past, all these three perspectives of writing being seen in all the major genres of the period, drama as well as poetry and prose.

2.1 Poetry

The poetry of Renaissance owns its significance to the impressive contribution to the genre coming first from John Skelton followed by Thomas Wyatt, Henry Howard, Edmund Spenser, and Sir Philip Sidney. Wyatt wrote *Sonnets*; Howard also wrote *Sonnets*; Spenser wrote a complex poem entitled *The Shepherd's Calendar* (1579) in a series of 12 keglogai (tales), one for each month, *Amoretti*, containing 88 love sonnets, and *The Fairie Queene* (1589-1596), his unfinished masterpiece, which experienced, and still deserves, a special attention and extensive discussion, and which contains six books, written in the by now famous Spenserian stanza, which consists of 8 five-foot iambic lines, followed by an iambic line of six feet, rhyming ababbcbcc; Sidney is the author of 108 sonnets, printed in 1591 as *Astrophel and Stella*, a pastoral novel *Arcadia* (1590), and *Apologie for Poetrie* (1580), a critical handbook, in which he praises *The Shepherd's Calendar*, except for its rustic language, and defends literature against Puritan accusations.

As with Renaissance art in general, the poetry of the period, despite some vivid attempts at innovation and experimentation, imbibes its thematic material and especially formal component from tradition, rhetoric, and genre theory: "Reading English Renaissance literature, certainly poetry, without an appreciation of the rhetorical training of the writers concerned, is an unsafe exercise, as all forms and styles used are indebted to the theories of writing developed from classical times onwards" (Hadfield 243). Another important aspect of Renaissance art and literature, and of poetry and drama in particular, as one of the "stock defences of literature", was that it "inculcated virtue, and one of the dominant instructive modes was satire, the scourge of vices and follies of the age. A particular feature of Renaissance satire was that it was often deliberately railing: unpolished, shaggy, savage and often erotic.

This was because the word "satire" was believed to derive from the Greek "*satyros*", the mythological half-man, half-goat, an emblem of all that was bestial" (Hattaway 98).

The first poet of English Renaissance is probably John Skelton (c.1460 – 1529) but more famous and popular at the beginning of the period was Sir Thomas Wyatt (1503 – 1542), credited for the introduction of the sonnet writing tradition into English literature. Wyatt did it particularly through adaptations and translations from Petrarch, from whom he borrowed emotional appeal and highly decorated imagery, for example that of galleys carrying forgetfulness and passing over seas of tears. Other sources for his poetry are some Roman poets – from whom Wyatt borrows not only certain thematic aspects but also words from Latin when his contemporary English seems deficient to render the meaning – as well as Dante, for the use of *terza rima*, and Chaucer, for the mastery to convey satire and wit. Combining literary tradition with innovation, Wyatt wrote in various genres on different subjects: sonnets and songs on love, lost and thwarted, and a source of grief and suffering; paraphrases of the Psalms on sin and redemption; verse satires on vices of the court; and ballads, rondeaux, carols, and other types on various other thematic concerns.

Less innovative and more classical is Henry Howard, Earl of Surrey (c. 1517 – 1547), whose major achievement is a translation of *The Aeneid* by Virgil. He is also a character in *Unfortunate Traveller* by Thomas Nashe, perhaps the first picaresque novel in English literature, which is narrated by Jack Wilton, an English el picaro. Skelton, Wyatt, and Howard represent the beginnings and progress of Renaissance poetry; its concluding manifestations include poets such as Samuel Daniel (1563 – 1619), the author of *Delia* and *The Complaint of Rosamond* (both 1592), and Sir Walter Raleigh (c. 1552 – 1618), once acclaimed for the poem *The Ocean to Scinthia*.

The flourishing of Renaissance and Tudor poetry is attributed to Edmund Spenser and Sir Philip Sidney, the dominant literary figures of the period combining innovation and tradition, excelling in various genres – Sidney is also viewed as the father of English literary theory and criticism – and institutionalising English, autochthonous views on love and other thematic concerns during Renaissance. Just like Chaucer striving before Renaissance to drive away the barbaric and uncultivated features of English culture by rediscovering the classics and especially looking at contemporary developments in continental literary practice, Sidney and Spenser assume the task of writing a literature which would rival that of ancient Greece and Rome as well as Italian Renaissance, but they still rely on ancient classical tradition, Sidney, in *Arcadia*, for instance, using *anagnorisis* ("recognition" or "understanding") and *peripeteia* ("reversal of circumstances"). When innovation is considered within the literary context of the period, it is sonnet, as a particular subgenre or species of the lyric genre, which emerges in a dominant position in Renaissance literary art.

2.1.1 Sonnet

The word sonnet comes from the Italian word *sonneto*, which means "little song". Both Dante and Petrarch perfected the form, but Petrarch's *Canzoniere*, consisting of 366 sonnets which present an idealized love for Laura, paved the way for what is known as the Petrarchan sonnet. After several hundred years, two young poets, Sir Thomas Wyatt and Henry Howard, Earl of Surrey, after residing and studying in Italy, found delight in Italian poetic literature, especially in Francesco Petrarch's works, and, upon their return to England, tried to adapt the new poetic form to meet the requirements of a new, English language. Unfortunately, their efforts of implementing this new poetic form met only with partial success, as their sonnets were much indebted to their Italian sources. The remarkable thing about the sonnets is that they all end in rhymed-couplets and this arrangement is very difficult to be met in another language. The best suited form to the English language is the three quatrains and the couplet, which can be concisely presented in the following formula: A—B—A—B C—D—C—D E—F—E—F G—G.

Edmund Spenser was the next poet who tried to meet the requirements of expression in the sonnet. But even though he was a great metricist and a genuine poet who revealed his power in strong and impressive verses, he did not achieve the full force of this new poetic vehicle, the importance and beauty of which he undoubtly recognized. Spenser attempted to reach the effect of the fourteen-line poem in a well-adjusted blank verse, but he got dissatisfied with the results, and the quatrains-and-couplet pattern of Wyatt and Surrey left him equally discontented. His incessant trial brought to the modification of both English and Italian forms, which resulted in the rhyme-iteration of the Italian, in addition to the couplet-ending of the English sonnet. This might be considered as the best chance for the sonnet in English, and he applied this structure to his famous love sonnets *Amoretti*.

The Spenserian sonnet is frequently referred to as the transitional stage in the development of English sonnet: his method was to interweave the quatrains by using the last rhyme-sound of each as the key-note of the next, best expressed through the formula A—B—A—B / B—C—B—C / C—D—C—D / E—E. Spenser's contemporaries and his successors did not particularly enjoy this form, as they failed to attain the rhythmical freedom or the amplitude in confinement which they reached in the former structures.

Following Spenser, the Elizabethan soneteering is greatly enriched by Shakespearea's sonnet heritage. Shakespearian sonnet is named in honour of the great poet who made use of it. It differs from the Italian form by not being divided into two systems. Rather than having an octave and a sestet, the Shakespearian sonnet is composed of three elegiac quatrains, tied up by a couplet with a new sound. The Shakespearian sonnet gains a swiftness of motion which prevails over the Spenserian one.

From the beginning of the sixteenth century to the middle of the seventeenth century, the short poem becomes gradually one of the most persistent and durable literary forms of English Renaissance, appealing to the minds of the most talented literary voices of the period and fascinating the readers through its presence. Though proving its resilience through an extent of time which lasted longer than a hundred years, English Renaissance poetry underwent various metamorphoses which changed its nature, style and function. John Williams, in his book entitled *English Renaissance Poetry* (1990), mentions three distinct phases through which English Renaissance short poem passes, each of them being distinct but all proved to be inseparable and revealing continuity which should be seriously considered. Following Williams's separation of Renaissance short poem into (1) Native tradition, (2) Petrarchan tradition and (3) Major tradition of English poetry, our purpose is to reveal the progression of Renaissance poetry from one style to another, from one set of principles to another, and from one thematic predilection to another. Different theories concerning the nature of poetry and the poet are also of great importance, especially those which coexisted in Renaissance but were embraced and approached differently in each of the three phases. The emphasis was laid on the function of poetry and its impact on the individual and society, since poetry was considered a civilising power and an educational factor, which could lead to change or secret knowledge.

2.1.2 The Native Tradition

The first phase in the development of English Renaissance poetry derives its name from the English poetic heritage of the fourteenth and fifteenth centuries, and it clearly relies on the native medieval tradition of grammar and rhetoric. This tradition is represented by such poetic voices of Tudor and early Elizabethan periods as Sir Thomas More, John Skelton, Sir Thomas Wyatt, George Gascoigne, Sir Walter Raleigh, and others. These poets continue the vernacular poetic tradition of the precedent century without any trace of the Italian influence which spread throughout the entire Europe. Though the poems written within the Native tradition belong to three different generations of poets who varied greatly in their treatment of forms and genres, in their bold adaptation of conventions, some general characteristics still can be detected.

Concerning the subject, the poets of the Native tradition employed broad, universal issues of perennial human significance. By using the chosen subject, the poet seeks to instruct or inform the readers on certain matters. John Williams explains that in most cases, "the Native poet speaks from his own intelligence, as if he knew it existed; he feels no compulsion to mask himself, to assume a persona, to work from cunning, or to live in exile. Speaking from his own intelligence, he speaks to another intelligence, as if he knew that that, too, existed; he is a reasonable man, addressing with his own voice other reasonable men; and the tone of the voice tells us that he is confident of the existence of reasonable men in his audience" (xiv). The discourse in the poem of the Native tradition is logical and coherently organized. Frequently, the poem of the Native tradition is a comment on an aphorism or proverb; at times, it presents a series of maxims which continue each other and are related to some communal truths.

Regarding the structure of the Native poem, its expository manner can be observed, a manner in which a concern is chosen and handled, different aspects of the concern are examined and some of its consequences are rationally presented. The speaker in a Native poem is direct and straightforward, and though his language is colloquial and unsophisticated, he delivers certain truths which have validity for the entire community. In an apparently blunt and familiar tone, the speaker conveys a surprising wisdom, which reminds of the bard from the epic tradition. The style of a Native poem might appear, at first glance, flat and barren of emotions, but if approached with care, the initially seeming lifelessness of the poem surprises its readers by the sincerity, depth and vitality of the conveyed message.

2.1.2.1 John Skelton

John Skelton is one of the most important representatives of the Native tradition. There is certainly some difficulty in approaching Skelton's poetic heritage, since it stands at the crossroad between medieval and Renaissance poetics. He is mostly remembered for his long and playful poem on an alewife, *Elynour Rummyng*, in which motifs of popular literature such as wantonness and lewdness are employed. However, he is mostly memorable for his bitter attacks on Cardinal Wolsey, depicted in *Speke Parrot, Colin Clout*, and *Why Come Yet Not to Court?*. The free treatment of the fifteenth-century literary forms and genres contributed to his popularity, and his poems, which range from courtly verse to low comedy, from conventional political affirmations to political satires, made him become "the first English writer whose works excited interest across a wide social spectrum during his own lifetimes" (Edwards 8).

Known as a poet laureate from both Oxford and Cambridge, Skelton made himself a name especially due to his plain style, without any decorum specific to his age. While rejecting the ornate rhetorical devices used by his contemporaries, his poetry gained popularity mostly through his ability to mix high and low modes, by which Skelton frequently attained totally unexpected effects. Skelton writes his satires in short rhymed lines, well-known to the readers from the medieval satire. The "Skeltonic doggerel" gained admiration for most part due to the virtue of Skelton's inalienable meter, which stretches from two to five beats, and the lines which go on rhyming until the exhaustion of the resources of the language. Many critics consider that this strange Skeltonic meter confers vigour and originality especially to his satires. It might be the case of *Elynour Rummyng*, in which Skelton depicts a shattering image of an amazingly disordered alewife, where the Skeltonic meter intensifies both the effect of disorder and the social satire. W. H. Auden, along with other twentieth-century poets who developed an interest in Skelton's poetry, expressed the admiration for this metrical technique and also for the breathless urgency which is rendered through the narrative voice in the satires. In *Speke Parrot* and *Colin Clout*, Skelton continues the established practice of medieval anticlerical satire when he reveals the duty of a poet and a satirist, which is to assert the abuses that he perceives in community, but he also infuses a fresh perspective by stressing out the substantial moral purpose of poetry.

In his lyrics, Skelton relies again on the medieval poetic heritage, to which he brings a fresh voice. The traditional ballad *Mannerly Margery* presents a clerk with his serving maid and surprises the reader by its unexpected ironic ending, whereas *Lullay, Lullay, Like a Child*, a conventional lullaby, is transformed into a salacious parody in which the child Christ is rocked by Virgin Mary in her lap. In such adaptations from traditional medieval modes, Skelton emerges clearly as an entertainer; however, one would not omit that beyond this comic surface, Skelton is always a serious artist, preoccupied with the status of the poet in the community. Frequently Skelton depicts some intrinsically funny scenes, or makes them deliberately amusing in order to sustain the readers' delight with his own energy or vision. This aspect of Skelton's writing made G. S. Fraser compare him to Rabelais, who employed similar devices. Moreover, beyond this hilarious aspect of some of Skelton verses, there is also

Skelton's view of a poet as an educator and advisor, with both moral and social status, which places him in line with More and Elyot. Jane Griffiths explains that "[the] very multiplicity of stances on which [Skelton] draws and the way in which he repeatedly names himself as poet, *vates*, and *poet laureate* suggests that none of the sources of authority that he is able to name is quite sufficient for him. It is as if the idea of the poet carries a weight and a charge far beyond that contained in any one of the titles, for which Skelton persistently seeks an acceptable (or even a possible) form of words" (5). Surprisingly, this view on poetry is continued in the next two phases of English Renaissance poetry with little variation on the subject.

2.1.3 The Petrarchan Tradition

The Petrarchan tradition is frequently referred to as an intermediate stage in the development of English Renaissance poetry due to (1) its strong reliance upon the very popular poetry of Francesco Petrarch, which found many admirers not only in Italy but also in France, and (2) its dependence on the Classical Latin, which in Renaissance becomes the normative poetic language. The main representatives of this second phase are Edmund Spenser, Sir Philip Sidney, Thomas Campion, English Madrigalists, and others.

Even though the Petrarchan tradition was brought from Italy by Thomas Wyatt in the third decade of the sixteenth century, the initial imitation of the Petrarchan sonnets became a poetic fashion not until nearly the last decade of the queen Elizabeth's reign, when soneteering became an imperious habit, a conventional recreation, a fashionable mode of expressing gallantry and compliment. Every aspirant poet between 1590 and 1600 would try his skill on this poetic device and this poetic endeavour definitely left a strong mark on English poetry.

The subject and the themes developed by the poets of the Petrarchan tradition departed enormously from the ones of the Native tradition. The new convention in Renaissance poetry is to address the Muses, the moon, or the sleep, but these explicit references often function as a device by which the lyric I personifies an aspect of himself, in his double hypostasis as a poet and lover. Respectively, two major themes dominate the poetic discourse of this phase: poetry and love. In a fragment from Sidney's *Astrophil and Stella*, the lyric I exclaims: ""Fool!" Said my Muse to me, "Look in thy heart and write"", this statement exemplifying the interlocked hypostasis in which the poet-lover seeks divine inspiration to express in the best possible way his love in his verses. This conventional reference can also reveal "a serious embodiment of the tension between the classical and Christian images and vocabularies, heroic inspiration by the Muses sometimes fusing and sometimes contrasting with prophetic inspiration by angels or apostolic inspiration by the Holy Ghost" (Rivers 150).

Most of the poems of this second phase attempt to give a definition of love in a suggestive and indirect manner, relying greatly on the Platonic concept of the universe. Platonism was very popular during Renaissance period; especially admired was his bipartite division into two worlds – of Ideas and of Phenomena – where the first is apprehended by the intellect and represents the perfect, unchangeable, eternal and immutable ideal or the full perfection of Being, whereas the second is apprehended by the senses and is only a copy of the ideal world, respectively a sphere of imperfection, of transition, of change, thus impermanent and subject to decay and Non-being. The human soul emerges in the first world but becomes entrapped in the human body which belongs to the second world; it oscillates between Being and Non-being, attempting to escape the unsatisfactory perishable world of the material things by striving toward perfection. The Platonist principle of the two worlds adjusted well to Christian set of values. The Neoplatonist doctrine, however, struggled to reconcile with Christian precepts and its impact reached great proportions only after the theological perspective presented by the Florentine Neoplatonists of the fifteenth century. The most appealing concept from Neoplatonists was the freedom of will, in which, according to Ficino's system which closely followed that of Plotinus, each order/Being (God, angelic mind, soul, body) in the universal hierarchy perpetually strives to a higher level of existence. Man always aspires to attain God, but due to the soul's intermediate position between upper and lower levels, it possessed the liberty to achieve the truth or ignore it altogether. This Neoplatonic emphasis on human choice and strife to rise fascinated the Renaissance minds and it is not surprising that these concerns become illustrated in the literature of the Petrarchan period.

Hence, the subject of the poems of the Petrarchan tradition becomes the ascent of the soul to the world of Forms or Ideas, but it is conveyed indirectly, through the medium of love (Eros). Rivers explains that "[love] of the beauty of one human being leads to love of love of physical beauty in general, then to moral beauty, then to intellectual beauty, until finally the Idea of Beauty is reached" (35). The platonic concept of love, which is employed by poets of the Petrarchan tradition, displays an impossibly idealized angelic lady, of an ethereal beauty, whose virtues are praised by the lyric I in his double hypostasis of lover and poet. The physical beauty of the angelic lady is hyperbolically celebrated in the poems which become endowed with philosophical and spiritual significance. The speaker-poet gains the knowledge and wisdom of a philosopher, and becomes a kind of prophet, a demiurge, with a sacred purpose of apprehending the other-worldly perfection, but he fails to control or transmit it. However, being divinely inspired, the poet does not seek to imitate nature as it is; instead, he becomes the creator of a second nature, which does not correspond to the existing nature, but emerges out of the poet's imagination and gains its worth due the poet's ability to create and express beauty, which is frequently suggested through the depicted image of the idealized lady and through the poet-lover's love for this ethereal being.

Surely, the poets of the Petrarchan tradition were acquainted with Horace's view on poetry – to delight and teach – or Lucretius's metaphor for verse as wormwood coated with honey, which reveals the function of poetry as essentially didactic. But while embarking on the "profitable pleasure" of introducing philosophical ideas which were concealed beneath the pleasures of meter, rhyme, and fable of love, the poets of this period slipped frequently into a mechanical Platonism which became conventional equipment for the Petrarchan poets. A great damage is done to poetry, since the Petrarchan version of the unfulfilled love led to an excessive use, even abuse, of the conventional Platonism, as poets became more preoccupied with complimenting the angelic lady to an extent that she is reduced only to an ornament of the poem, departing from the purpose of moral profit of poetry.

Unlike the poet of the Native tradition, who addresses an audience with a message of essential importance for the entire community, the poet of the Petrarchan tradition addresses the Muses, the sleep, the moon, the conventional ladies, who exhibit strikingly similar features of golden locks, light foot, coral lips, lily hands, and starry eyes, presented in guises that deny them any subjectivity or agency. The substance of the poem is reduced to a rhetoric which frequently prevents the transmission of a genuine feeling, since it is usually sustained only by conventional themes and subjects like love of the lady and the desire to immortalise this love in poetry. The poetry of this period "has given way to an airy elegance, which does not so much support the substance of the poem as it decorates it, to a style distinguished by the ingenuity of its figures, a rapid association of details, a wordplay meant to dazzle rather than to inform, a diction that was faintly archaic and "literary" even in its own time, by an elaborate syntax, and by the varied and subtle rhythms resulting from the play of the syntax against the poetic line" (Williams xviii). Obviously, the poetry of this period gains certain qualities, such as delicacy, minuteness, elegance and sensory richness, which are alien to the Native tradition, but this gain is achieved at the considerable loss of a genuine experience, which becomes trivialized by the sophisticated techniques and conventional subject matters and themes.

2.1.3.1 Philip Sidney

Sir Philip Sidney (1554 – 1586), born into the family of Elizabeth's Lord Deputy in Ireland, lived a hectic and turbulent but short life which is known to us chiefly through the efforts of Sir Fulke Greville, Sidney's life-long friend and future biographer with whom Sidney entered in the same day of 1564 the school in Shrewsbury. In 1568, Sidney entered Christ Church, Oxford, but left it without taking a degree to travel abroad to learn foreign languages in 1572. Before returning to England in 1575, Sidney visited or stayed for shorter or longer periods Paris, Frankfurt, Venice, Genoa, Vienna, Prague, and other cities. It is said that on his journeys he impressed everyone whom he met, being instantly "beloved and obeyed", according to Greville. In 1577, Sidney's public career begins, which was never fulfilled for his relations with the queen were below favour, his Protestantism too ardent, his suggestions on politics too unacceptable. Finally given the appointment as governor of Flushing, Sidney left England in 1585. In 1586, involved in a conflict, Sidney was wounded in the thigh and, the wound not healing, he was dead within 22 days, having not reached his thirty-second birthday. Sidney's premature death sparked a sense of loss and grief in England and Europe both profound and long-lasting.

Less than politics and public life, English literature is indebted to Sidney as a critic, poet, and author of prose fiction rather courtier, namely for his critical work *An Apology for Poetry*, sonnets of *Astrophel and Stella*, prose romance *Arcadia*, as well as other minor works such as the playlet *The Lady of May* or a metaphrase of the first 43 Psalms.

Arcadia, greatly popular in its times, exists in three different versions because Sidney wrote the bulk of it in 1580 and then started revising the text but never finished it. The first version is known as *Old Arcadia*; unfinished and unrevised, it was never published in the sixteenth century, its copies circulating in manuscript form. Devised as a tragicomedy in five acts, it unfolds an intrigued story with a double plot and a comic underplot involving in a complex sequence of events numerous characters and, though largely focusing on love and its various types and effects on humans, raising various other issues such as ethics and justice. *New Arcadia*, the second version, published in 1590, is a revised text with major changes, including a different opening and new added stories, and it is longer by 50,000 words. The third version, known as *Countess of Pembroke's Arcadia*, or simply *Arcadia*, was also published posthumously, in 1593, perhaps under the supervision of his sister, the Countess of Pembroke, to whom it is dedicated and in whose house Sidney wrote the bulk of this work. This book is a hybrid version uniting the first three revised books of the *New Arcadia* and the last two books of the unrevised *Old Arcadia*.

Sidney's most ambitious work, *Arcadia* represents a mixture of genres and types of texts, appealing to the reader as a prose romance, moral treatise, courtesy book, philosophical speculation, a debate on justice and equity, a discussion of love, and even an attempt at rhetorical handbook. Nonetheless, it is primarily a romance thematically exalting the pastoral in a unique way in which the Greek model of Heliodorus combined with pastoral elements support Renaissance idealisation of a shepherd's life, to which Sidney adds, following the Hellenistic model, narratives of kidnap, battle, rape, political treachery, and other stories which are interwoven in the whole of the narrative sequence.

Sidney's more original work, *Astrophel and Stella* (first printed in 1591 and later published in an authorised edition in 1598, but composed in the early 1580s, probably 1582, and circulating in manuscript for many years), is the first important of English sonnet sequences, containing 108 sonnets and 11 songs. Attempted as English versions of Italian model Petrarch, the poems deal with emotion and love, relationships between lovers, and prompt some philosophical speculations and reflections on the act of poetic creation. On the structural level, the poems succeed in freeing the English sonnet from the strict rules of the Italian form.

The texts representing the sonnet sequence render a kind of narrative movement disclosing the love affair of the two which leads to Astrophel's disappointment and Stella's finally liberating herself from him (sonnet 11) and her eventual disappearance (final sonnet 108). The narrative also renders the change occurring in Stella's status and personality, where from a silent and unapproachable lover she emerges as a woman of light, rational and independent, able to speak and express different opinions. Building his narrative on the contrastive imagery of male and female, light and darkness, white and black, freedom and entrapment, speech and silence, Sidney's work is essentially a conceit of binary opposition derived from the contrast between Astrophel, a figure of dark sealed in dark thought and night, and Stella, a figure of light associated with bright sun and day.

In literature, Sidney still relies on classical heritage while searching for new themes and experiments with new means of artistic expression, particularly new ways of metrical experimentation, his works revealing not only a variety of mixed genres and subgenres but also a diversity of metrical and stanzaic forms. In critical thinking presented in *An Apology for Poetry* (this critical treatise having a second edition bearing the title *The Defence of Poesy*), Sidney likewise employs vestiges of ancient theory while producing some original ideas, and exceeds Renaissance critical commonplace by his work's impressive rhetorical discourse, elegant style, careful delineation of ideas, and engaging argumentation and persuasion.

Among the major poets of the Tudor literature, Sidney was the closest to the ideal of a Renaissance courtier, where immediately after his premature death he became the perfect exponent of an idealized Renaissance age. Although often self-depreciating his literary status – for example, in *An Apology for Poetry*, claiming of "having slipped into the title of a poet" – and despite his short life, Sidney contributed enormously to English imaginative writing: *The Defence of Poesy* is the best critical treatise of his times and a founding text for the English critical tradition; *Astrophel and Stella* is the first English sonnet sequence; *Arcadia* is among the best prose romances of the period and a proto-novel. Sidney soon became a symbol of wit, virtue, and literary genius, and grew into a legend which continued into the romantic period and beyond; contributing to this, among others, are his contemporary fellow-writers Nashe, who mourned the passing of a "Maecenas of learning", and Spenser, who lamented the death of a "gentle shepherd" and poet.

2.1.3.2 Edmund Spenser

Edmund Spenser (c. 1952 – 1599) produced a bulk of literature impressive and aesthetically valid enough to give his name to an age of poetry in England, which is comparable with any of European poems, pastorals, and romances. Born in London, he first studied at Merchant Taylors' School and then Pembroke Hall, Cambridge, which he graduated BA in 1573 and MA in 1576. Spenser began his public career in 1578 as secretary to John Young, Bishop of Rochester, Later, in 1580, he became secretary to Lord Grey de Wilton, Lord Deputy of Ireland, and he moved to Ireland in that year to live there until his return to England at the end of 1598 following Tyrone's rebellion during which the castle of Kilcolman in Cork, in which he lived at that time, was burned. Spenser died at Westminster on 13 January 1599 to be buried in Westminster Abbey and mourned by his fellow-writers as "the Prince of Poets in his time".

Like with other authors of the period, during his life, most of Spenser's writings would circulate in manuscript copies or published anonymously, his collected works being first published in 1611. It took ten years for English literature, from his 1569 anonymous translations of sonnets by Petrarch and Du Bellay, to see in 1579 the anonymously published *The Shepheardes Calender*, Spenser's first important work. The first three books of *The Faerie Queene*, Spenser's major achievement, appeared in 1590, published again in 1596 together with the next three books. His other works include a volume of nine poems entitled *Complaints* (1591), the elegy *Daphnaida* (1591), the autobiographical pastoral *Colin Clout's Come Home Again* (1595), in the same year *Amoretti* and *Epithalamion* came out in a single volume, and so on.

A source of inspiration for future generations, Spenser left a poetic legacy which would receive great appreciation from both the eighteenth-century Augustans, who enjoyed the ornamented and pictorial qualities of his work, and the nineteenth-century romantics, who expressed delight in his appeal to beauty, instinct, dream, and sensuous experience, as well as from writers and critics of later periods in literary history, including W. B. Yeats, T. S. Eliot, and C. S. Lewis.

Apart from Spenser's thematic charm affecting later poets, Byron, in *Childe Harold's Pilgrimage*, and Keats, in *The Eve of St Agnes*, use the so-called "Spenserian stanza", first used in *The Faerie Queene*, which is a variety of *ottava rima* adding a final alexandrine to eight iambic pentameters to produce a stanza of nine lines rhyming ababbcbcc.

The Shepheardes Calender, dedicated to Sidney, represents a series of pastorals – more exactly, it consists of twelve poems, one for each month of the year beginning and ending in winter – expressing regret for lost purity in love, lost moral and religious values, lost significance of high poetry, and other aspects of a lost golden age. Following the models provided by Theocritus and Virgil, particularly the latter's *Eclogues*, Spenser delivers through Colin Clout's complaints and the dialogues between shepherds his own views on religion, love, and art, especially the destiny of poetry and the status and responsibility of the poet, which co-exist with a keen satirical response to contemporary faults and failings.

Spenser's greatest poem is *The Faerie Queene*, an unfinished heroic romance of whose 12 books only 6 are completed. Mixing the tradition of English verse allegory with Renaissance epic borrowed from contemporary Italy, Spenser prompts a strong national and political statement in which a young prince Arthur – representing old British line of kingship – seeks Gloriana – the virgin fairy princess representing Queen Elizabeth – in order to be wed to her and in this way Britons would be united with the fairies race, symbolising the unity with the inner world, the spiritual aspect of human existence, and live in a state of personal and national joy under a queen who in real life (Queen Elizabeth) rules a new and flourishing country of the Tudor dynasty based on revitalized senses, timeless youthful spirit, and, above all, justice, kindness, and other eternal values. One should also remember that in real life, by 1590, when Spenser's work was produced, Elizabeth was already a 60 years old spinster, hardly attractive with her yellow skin, lost teeth, bold forehead, and who is to be the last of the Tudors.

Far from reality, as artistically rendered in Spenser's romance, the Fairy princess waits to be espoused by a British prince and achieve nuptial joy in union with him but more importantly is her national status as a bringer of justice, reviver of moral virtues, and even redeemer of English nation, ultimately Christian, whom she returns to God. Gloriana is Elizabeth and Elizabeth-Gloriana is "Souerayne Goddesse" who symbolises justice and provides "righteous doome" as well as "awfull dread" to her British subjects.

More than Arthur, who is linked to a British mythological past, Gloriana expresses a sense of continuity, historical and cultural, rooted in the ancient, pagan reign of Saturn, whose virtues, particularly justice, are now lost, which makes Spenser to be second, after Thomas More, important promoter of Greek thought into English writing. Gloriana-Elizabeth is in contact with these virtues, represents and revives them, mainly the forgotten justice and goodness. She provides continuity by making possible the return of justice in a new, Christian context: God rules primarily through the sacred power of justice which He offers to Christian monarchs as his deputies to "rule his people right, as he doth recommend". Being justice personified, Gloriana-Elizabeth becomes an eternal, undying prince, mysterious and sacramental, chosen by divinity to act justly against the humans who rebelled and estranged from God.

Living outside time, Elizabeth is nonetheless in contact with all Tudor and earlier rulers of the country, her presence giving a sense of a historical and cultural past, reifying the continuity, as well as of mutability and transitory nature of all social and human endeavours.

The forests of fairy land is a chronotope suitable enough for the thematic treatment of the union between a young Arthur and a timeless Gloriana ultimately building up a romanticized history through unequivocal celebration – heavily relying on decorum – of the vitality of senses, female personality, erotic love, openly displayed sexual behaviour in various types ranging from the gentle one of Adonis and Venus to the savage one of Hellenore copulating nine times a night with men-goats. The literarisation of love also emerges into a thematic typology ranging from the atemporal but historically placed union of Arthur and Gloriana to the love of Serena and Sir Calepine, who saves her from the cannibals and their "lustful fantasyes" over her body. Actually, her body is one of the most intriguing literary expressions of carnareality in English literature, a "pattern of conceits" in the poem involving – since the cannibals wish to adore Serena and humiliate her at once – the miracle of the sacrament and the divine banquet which are confused with a cannibalistic feast and the mystery of sexual consuming as dreamt into being by Dante (Pitcher 86-87).

The tradition of the romance receives in Renaissance a new poetic of literary expression which suppresses from its literary system the elements of martial arts, war, combat, dragon slaying, male fraternity, trawthe, magicians, even knights, and, not the least, the moral didacticism of a medieval work such as *Sir Gawain and the Green Knight*. The new poetic aesthetics proclaims decorum, stylized diction, verse ornamentation, complexity of metaphorical expression, wit and conceit as well as imaginative flight, thematic exaltation of senses, Orphic experience, old traditions reconstructed and new views asserted in literary practice, particularly on love, which is now true and false, divine and fleshly, spiritual and sensual, tender and lustful, private and public.

Still, Spenser values an ethics of redemption and reveals at least the intention to suggest ways of regeneration of his contemporary, Tudor culture from within by his thematization of the allegorical union of Arthur and Gloriana. To Spenser, she is "a kind of dreadful goddess of Justice who can restore the golden world" (Pitcher 67), which renders the author's belief that by continuity and a restored link to the first human experiences of contacting with the gods, values can be restored and human spirit may regenerate.

Edmund Spenser within and beyond the Elizabethan Sonnet Vogue

Edmund Spenser's sonnet sequence was published in 1595, under the title *Amoretti and Epithalamion*, when he already was an established poet with a great reputation at the court of Queen Elizabeth. Philip Sidney's *Astrophel and Stella*, written in the early 1580s, proved the artful versatility of the sonnet, and the prestige gained by his poetic sequence led to the rise of sonnet in the hierarchy of genres within the literary system of the period. But while Sidney's sonnet sequence remains mostly within the code of the Petrarchan discourse, Spenser questions the traditional paradigm, creating instead what A. D. Cousins names as "meta-Petrarchan verse" which distances Spenserian sonnet from both much admired poets Petrarch and Sidney (98). Even though initially he seems to pay tribute to Dante's and Petrarch's achievements and follows Sidney's example in writing a structured sequence, Spenser goes beyond the paradigmatic model established by his predecessors and contemporaries.

The change is introduced by the ingenious order of his sonnets, which follows a calendrical structure, inspired by the liturgical calendar of the Church of England, a correspondence noticed first by Alexander Dunlop (1969) and later broadened by Kenneth Larsen (1997). The relationship which Spenser establishes between *Amoretti* and the liturgical calendar is not simply limited to the appropriation of the language and the motifs of the day's symbolism; it also uses the calendrical frame in order to question some theological dilemmas which were present during Elizabethan period: the reconciliation of the Platonic and Neoplatonic ideas of the Universe with the Christian, particularly Protestant, theology. It is well-known that Spenser writes *Amoretti* sonnet sequence during his courtship of Elizabeth Boyle, while *Epithalamium* celebrates the union of the two lovers in the sacred bond of marriage. While the stages of his courtship literally refer to a progress in time, suggested by the calendrical motion through seasons and festivals of the liturgical year, Spenser's portrayal of his courtship might also refer to a more symbolic significance of the passage of time, suggested through the major theme of mutability, which dominates his sonnet sequence. As the Elizabethan poets frequently placed themselves at the intersection of the self and convention, it does not come as a surprise that Spenser's images used in *Amoretti* evolve from some of his personal experiences, but they still are delivered within the literary conventionalism of his time. The speaker-lover that Spenser projects in his poem sequence desires a transformation from the unmarried status to the married one, based on love and mutual acceptance of both partners in marriage; but, simultaneously, the lover uses this passage through time in order to require his own and his lady's transformation, developing their interactive metamorphosis into a distinct theology of love. Myron Turner explains that "love for Spenser is a mode of self-realization, a form of self-transcendence by means of which the self perfects its identity. This being so, lovers must be prepared to accept and to suffer inward change" (284). The antagonistic feelings brought by the need for change and the fear of change/mutability confer vigour to *Amoretti*, as they are mostly expressed through the themes of love of the divine and the yearning for mutual human love. Spenser, following the chronology of courtship, "recounts an experience of love that traverses Lent and yet his speaker moves, albeit often with trouble, towards integrated selfhood and sacramental union with the beloved" (Cousins 99).

The movement through time is also sustained by the variations in the images of the speaker-lover and his beloved lady. At the beginning of his sonnet sequence, Spenser's clearly sets himself within the Petrarchan poetic tradition, presenting his lady as a *donna angelica*, who holds a position of absolute authority over the lover. Inspired by Neoplatonic theories of love, he exalts his lady to the level of a spiritual mediator between the transitory world and the ideal one, viewing her as the epitome of earthly paradise; concomitantly, the lady possesses the power to guide the lover towards paradise itself. Respectively, Spenserian speaker-lover is a man who, while pursuing his beloved, embarks on a quest for self-accomplishment both in this world and beyond it.

Amoretti 1 begins with a typically Petrarchan image of a submissive *amoretto*, who is also a poet, engaged in the writing of his poems which would acknowledge and celebrate the lady's exceptionality and beauty; his "leaves, lines and rhymes, seek her to please alone", since she represents his muse, the source of heavenly enlightenment, a celestial being who might confer grace if "those lamping eyes will design sometimes to look, / and read the sorrows of my dying spright / written with tears in heart's close bleeding look". The lover-poet's suffering and anxiety emerge as a result of his fear that in his poetic plight, he may be entrapped in the contemplation of his own passion and omit a transcendental perception, embodied in the beatitude of the angelic lady, thus remaining locked in the world of representation and appearances. Hence is his desire to change, to move from the realm of physical nature and mutability to a realm of permanent and constant, which might be achieved by his acknowledgement of the metaphysical truth. The repetition of the word "happy" in relation to "leaves", "lines", and "rhymes", which are dedicated to the lady, indicate his blessed, joyful, paradisiacal state which he may reach if she would see the devotion of his soul. The words "my soul's long-lacked food, my haven's bliss" suggest the speaker's hunger for transcendence, the food metaphor revealing the poet-lover's desperate desire to attain fulfilment "for which he hungers and which will complete the act of self-transcendence" (Turner 286). The manifestation of the poet-lover's transcendence is reflected in the lady's beauty expressed by such heavenly charms as "angel's blessed look", "starry light" of her "lamping eyes", and "lily hands". But this imagery of heavenly beauty is juxtaposed to the imagery of captivity, as "those lily hands / which hold my life in their dead-doing might / shall handle you and hold in love's soft bands, / like captives trembling at the victor's sight". Following the tradition of *fin'amor*, Spenser represents the lady as the embodiment of perfect beauty and, therefore, she exercises total authority over her ardent admirer. Much in Petrarchan style, the beloved lady holds absolute power over the life and death of the poet-lover, his trembling indicating his frenzy at the prospect of the lady reading his poems and also "enacts a ritual of submission, of conquest and imprisonment", revealing the desired change in the lover-speakers status, his entrapment in her soft hands clearly projecting his hope to be accepted for his worth (Cousins 101).

In *Amoretti 34*, the *topos* of mutability is continued by the representation of the dangerous waters which the lover must cross in his route to his "happy" shore. The lover must undertake a perilous journey, his concern and vulnerability are made visible in the lines: "Lyke as a ship that through the Ocean wyde, / by conduct of some star does make her way, / whenas a storm hath dimd her trusty guyde, / out of her course doth wonder far astray". The conventional Petrarchan imagery of a lover as a lost ship is easily recognized in this sonnet, but this sailing metaphor encourages the idea of movement in time and space, a movement which strengthens the speaker-lover's need and desire for change from his present status. The lover's separation from his lady is conveyed through his desolation, as he wanders "in darkness and dismay, / through hidden perils round about my plast". Cut apart from his lady, the lover experiences an extraordinary grief, which equals the pain of the one being in exile, where he is exposed to various dangers. The lady, represented in typically Petrarchan conceits, like a "star" or "my Helice the loadstar of my lyfe", is his only hope to guide him away from his precariousness and insecurity. Separated from her, he is unable to find order and harmony within his self or in the universe. As Turner explains, "In his helpless ship, man has no special status, but is only another object of collision and accident in the vortex of Fortune: a wanderer, the poet sought direction but, [...] he is found [only] "by chance"" (292). The randomness of the word "by chance" is disconcerting; however, the Neoplatonic idea of the natural and divine harmony might have a resonance here, since the natural forms in the physical world represent God's means of imposing an order on Nature, which reflects God's divine harmony. The speaker's star, which is now "with clouds overcast", suggests a possibility for change and that at any moment, his star may re-emerge and "shine again", and such change is typical in nature, saving him from this position of a lost wonderer in a chaotic universe. The influence of Neoplatonic theories of harmony is made visible by the suggestion of transformation, which is required from the lover who must control the chaos of his passion and attain the sweetness of the harmony of the universe, which is represented by his acceptance of the moderate and virtuous *donna angelica*.

Amoretti 5 introduces a typical Renaissance theatrical metaphor, where the beloved lady is the cruel spectator to the lover who disguises himself in various roles, in hope to attain the recognition of the self. "Of this worlds Theatre in which we stay" serves as a possible confession of pretence, as the lover rejoices "when glad occasion fits, / and mask in myrth lyke to a Comedy: / Soone after when my joy to sorrow flits, / I waile and make my woes a Tragedy". Besides the conventional representation of the lady as ruthless and indifferent, which directly confirms her role as a conqueror, the recurrent allusions to the performance of feelings is disconcerting, as it reveals the possibility that the expressed emotions in his art are some masks rather than the delivery of genuine feelings. Thus, the indifference of the lady may be provoked by the lack of the lover-artist true perception of authentic feelings and the metaphysical truth, and it suggests again a demand for the transformation of his self and his art. The lover's words sound full of anger at the lady's disdain: "But when I laugh she mocks, and when I cry / She laughs and hardens evermore her heart", his final outburst, "What then can move her? If nor merth nor mone, / She is no woman, but a senseless stone", creating an ambiguity, which leads towards the thought of the lover renouncing his battle to concur the angelic lady. However, despite his apparent abandonment of his desire to change from the conquered to conqueror through his love and art, a very new and surprising idea is introduced by the possibility of the lady's change. Even though the beloved lady is represented with a heart harder than iron, that she "hardens evermore her heart" suggests the possibility of her transformation. So far, her reluctance to change was accepted as her resistance to change, since the virtues she displays embody *constantia*, permanence, as it stands in opposition to temporariness and evanescence embodied by the lover. But now, there is a demand for the lady's change, and her progressive hardening of the heart delivers such a possibility, whereas her representation like a "senseless stone" reveals her hopeful conversion from the hardest marble to softness of life, a metamorphosis reminiscent of Pygmalion myth, where the authentic art combined with genuine feeling of love produce such permutation. The analogy to the sculptor Pygmalion who achieved the transformation of his marble statue into the life of a beautiful woman by his exquisite art and genuine love through the divine intervention parallels the speaker-artist's desire for the upward transformation, and who transcends his former self and emerges reformed, hoping to become worthy of the lady's love.

The poet's "horror of aimless wandering is not a fear of mutability alone, but of mutability without *form*. This form is a process of upward, sacred transformation, through which change becomes meaningful and, far from threatening human identity, becomes the means by which the self achieves perfection" (Turner 297). Therefore, in *Amoretti*, the speaker-lover's attitude towards love and the changes that the love entitles is not frightening, but rather welcome. The arduous journey towards his triumphant accomplishment of his purpose takes the lover to an earthly paradise, as represented in *Amoretti 64*: "Coming to kiss her lyps (such grace I found) / Me seemed I smelt a garden of seweet flowers / That dainty odours from them threw around, / For damsels fit to decke their lovers bowers." The Petrarchan convention of representing the natural world as a mirror of man's feelings is clear in this sonnet. This time, however, the lover's love does not create a cosmic cataclysm; instead, it produces a prospect of paradise, where the body of the lady becomes a kind of *locus amoenus*, an enclosed garden which is profusely delicious: "Her goodly bosome lyke a Strawberry bed, / Her neck lyke to a bounch of Cullumbines; / Her breasts lyke lillyes, ere theyr leaves be shed, / Her nipples lyke young blossomed Jassemynes". Rather that presenting the female beauty as an entrapment which causes man to deviate from his inner peace, the beauty of the lady mirrors the transcendent beauty of God. The correlation of beauty with God, as Joan Cubert claims, "leads to a re-reading of the beloved's physicality itself, which might be vindicated, and experienced without moral danger ... The body might be seen, in purely Neo-Platonic fashion, as the recipient of the highest good – the rational soul – and as a reality that has to be dignified as befits its role as such" (52). Moreover, the intertextual relations with the sensual gardens of *The Song of Solomon* confer biblical weight and spiritual meaning to the erotic, which clearly transpires from Spenserian verses. Turner specifies that in the exegetical tradition, the kiss embodies "the wedding of the flesh and spirit"; therefore, this "garden must encompass more than the individual soul; it must extend to embrace both lovers. Thus, it becomes a shared garden of both flesh and spirit in which the lovers are united" (293). The sexual desire which was conventionally viewed as opposite to love, gains a new connotation in Spenserian sonnet, as love and desire can be celebrated without offence, especially in the prospect of marriage.

In spite of the dread of mutability, the lady's gradual metamorphosis takes place, her resistance to alteration being diminished due to the pleasurable anticipation of the lovers' union. *Amoretti 67* marks the crucial moment of change which, after the lover's entrance into the garden, reveals the beloved one's willingness to accept the change, and, respectively, endorse the alteration of the self, which initially seemed so frightful. The transformation of the two lovers, which emerges as a result of the experience of love, is conveyed in the sonnet 67 through the imagery of hunting, where the roles of the beloved and the lover are completely inverted: "Lyke as a huntsman after weary chace, / Seeing the game from him escapt away, / Sits down to rest him in some shady place, / With panting hounds beguiled of their prey". The reversal of the lover from prey to huntsman suggests his humanisation, this essential progress to human dignity being vital for the speaker in order to find his place in the universe. However, the significant change of the beloved from the position of authority of the predator to prey/the deer might seem a bit unsettling. It should not be forgotten that Spenserian sonnet sequence is written in the dialogue with other traditions, especially the courtly love poetry, in which the deer corresponds to female body or serves as a metaphor for it. Surprising is the deer's docility, as

> There she, beholding me with mylder looke,
> Sought not to fly, but fearless still did bide:
> Till I in hand her yet half trembling took,
> And with her own goodwill hir fyrmely tyde.
> Strange thing me seemed to see a beast so wyld,
> So goodly wonne with her own will beguiled".

The imagery of the trembling dear creates juxtaposition with the trembling lover from *Amoretti 1*, revealing once again the striking transformation of both lovers by the power of love. The evolution of the lover from the position of a captive to an empowered huntsman who is capable of taming "a beast so wild", by extension, may indicate to his ardent desire to domesticate both human and external nature. His growing ability to tame his inner world intrinsically suggests his capacity to control the external world. The deer's submission to her hunter "with her own goodwill" is of crucial importance, as the "brooke" serves as a metaphor of love and fertility, and thus, the significance of the sonnet takes a Christian turn, with the depiction of human love which is sanctified by betrothal of the two lovers. In this respect, Cubert explains that "the history of Petrarchan poetry before Spenser had endowed love itself with such a strong spiritual force, it had blurred so much the barriers between it and religious devotion, that a radical alteration in that love – here a shift in the attitude of the beloved towards the poet – also had to be expressed through an allegory of God's love" (54).

Amoretti 67 can be considered as the moment of departure from Petrarchan tradition, but this break is made more visible in *Amoretti 68*. This sonnet, according to the church's liturgical calendar, corresponds to Easter, and it produces a theological inquiry concerning the concept of love. The opening of the sonnet resembles to a prayer: "Most glorious Lord of lyfe, that on this day, / Did make thy triumph over death and sin: / and having harrowd hell, didst bring away / Captivity thence captive us to win". These lines change completely the significance of captivity of the Petrarchan discourse. If in the earlier sonnets (1, 67) this metaphor was used to express the lover's dependence on the acceptance of the other counterpart, in sonnet 68, the lovers grow aware of the true significance of captivity through the reference to the biblical phrase of St Paul from the *Ephesians*, which delivers the example of Christ's love. Lord's liberation of the humans from Hell equals to the human's salvation from our own inner captivity. The newly gained awareness is that love is a form of imprisonment "in which captivity is captive, freeing the lovers to model themselves on their Lord, to give back to God and the world the gifts of their creativity" (Turner 290). Rather than asking for lady's guidance for the true meaning of divinity, this time the speaker seeks the assistance of Christ: "thy love we weighing worthily, / May likewise love thee for the same again: / and for thy sake that all lyke deare didst buy, / With love may one another entertain". The allusion to Christ's resurrection as the greatest example of love for humankind functions as a reference to the lovers' awakening to the transcendental truth. The invitation made to the lady is "So let us love, dear love, as we ought: / Love is the lesson which the Lord us taught", and beneath this invitation, there is the theological affirmation of the lovers' newly attained awareness.

Amoretti 79 confirms once again Spencer's departure from the Petrarchan tradition, as it strongly questions the conventions of the Petrarchan discourse: "Men call you fayre, and you do credit it, / For that your selfe ye dayly such doe see: / But the true fayre, that is the gentle wit, / And virtuous mind, is much more praised of me". The speaker-lover's transformations is made visible through his progress of the self, as he gains a new awareness that the true "fayre" is not the exceptional beauty of the lady. With the passage of time, "how ever fayre it be, / Shall turn to nought and loose that glorious hew". The decay even of such a beauty indicates the changes in nature, and, inevitably, the speaker's change is his awareness of this nature of this universe. The movement from the courtly wit to a mature acknowledgement that "He only fayre, and what he fayre hath made; / All other fayre, lyke flowers, untimely fade" confers a sobering truth of mutability. Spenser views love as a journey towards self-realization. As Turner aptly states, "[o]ne must have the courage to break forth out of the inward part, to voyage out on the sea of mutability whose dangers provide the only access to one's true self. That self is found waiting in the bosom of another human being, the "happy shore" on which the Divinity has planted the garden which will nourish and sustain this life" (298).

Even though the final sonnets of the sequence reveal again the anxiety of separation of the lovers, there is no uncertainty concerning this journey's end, as it only preludes the happiness displayed in the festive poem *Epithalamion*, which celebrates the union of lovers by the sacred bond of marriage. The sense of mutuality of love opens its way for the *Epithalamion*, which is gained as a result of a rigorous confrontation of the self, of the idea of beloved and, mostly, of the idea of true harmony attained through love. The calendrical structure of the sonnet sequence reveals the speaker-lover's evolving through the passage of time from a conventional courtly lover to a person who has gained moral and philosophical insights into the mutability of things as well as the true knowledge of love and transcendence.

In conclusion, it can be said that Spenser frees the male lover from the traps of the Petrarchan convention. Unlike the other sonneteers of the period, who respected strictly the Petrarchan paradigm, Spenser's *Amoretti* begins with the conventions of the Petrarchan discourse, but as the sequence evolves, he moves forward by seeking new identities for the lover and the beloved. Rather than presenting a speaker in a perpetual exile, spurned and rejected, Spenserian persona experiences love and desire as an accomplishment of his being, as a homecoming, where his identity and existence are at stake. Spenserian lover acquires a new identity which is "resonant with the heroic and the ideally marital, an identity that allows him to look homewards rather than to see himself trapped in exile" (Cousins 98). This possible marital status of the lover in the sonnet allows the change in the perception of the beloved lady from sacred and inaccessible object of desire to a more secularized vision of the beloved, as an earthly, but extremely beautiful partner, who, nevertheless, acquires the knowledge of mutuality in love. Emerging from his personal experience, Spenser produced one of the most highly developed sonnet sequences among all his contemporaries, his speaker-lover attaining a degree of elevation and depth which anticipates Shakespeare.

2.1.4 The Major Tradition

The third phase in the development of English Renaissance poetry assimilates and surpasses the poetic discourse of the preceding two phases, strengthening the virtues of the earlier practices and abandoning some of their vices to produce – as a result of conscious progression from one set of conventions to another – a body of great poetry which gained a resonance throughout the century and beyond it. Among the representatives of this phase are William Shakespeare, John Donne, and Ben Jonson. At first glance, some of Shakespearian sonnets might appear as endorsing the Petrarchism only to reveal how much Shakespeare's poetic discourse exceeds his model through the display of a perceptivity and complexity which are clearly superior to any of his contemporaries; on the other hand, the straightforward, abrupt and direct opening of some poems remind undoubtedly of the Native tradition.

2.1.4.1 William Shakespeare and the English Renaissance Sonnet

William Shakespeare's sequence of sonnets was published for the first time in 1609 by a London publisher, Thomas Thorpe, in a period when the Elizabethan sonnet vogue began to decline. Even though the sonnet tradition started to wane, Shakespeare's volume, which contains 154 sonnets, offered to the public some of the most beautiful and impressive poems in English literature. It should not be ignored that Shakespeare's *Sonnets* are the product of a doubting age, materialised in Martin Luther's theology and Francis Bacon's and Rene Descartes's philosophical discourses. Particularly, it is to be acknowledged the doubt towards the tradition, which felt strongly by the time of the publication of Shakespeare's volume. Though the writers of Shakespeare's period still are devoted to the classical tradition and believe in the wisdom of their predecessors, gradually, like in the case of Spenser's *Amoretti*, they attempt to break the familiar poetic conventions, doubting their validity and seeking a new truth which comes from the poet-lover's state of mind. Since the sonneteers delivered an apparent immediate access to the speaker's most intimate experiences, by which providing a deliberate construction of the poet's identity, great doubt concerning Shakespearian poet-lover's identity emerges, as his first 126 sonnets are addressed to a beloved young man, whereas the rest of his sonnets are concerned with a dark lady. The lyric I, projected in these sonnets, is torn between hope and despair, delight and misery, a variety of feelings which emerge as a result of the speaker's longing for different lovers and the acknowledgement of their multifariousness. The male-focused desire of the Shakespearean speaker "often indeterminately implicates the homosocial with the homoerotic, and each intermittently with what seems an aspiration to patronage" (Cousins 256). The female presence in Shakespeare's sonnets is also confusing, as "disingenuous reverence plays against carnal adulation or disgust, and problematic intimacy against misogyny" (Cousins 256).

Although the critical tradition has established a clear distinction between the sonnets addressed to an unnamed young man and the sonnets addressed to a promiscuous dark lady, nothing is certain in this most famous and unique collection of sonnets in European literature. The intimacy and the intensity of emotions transmitted in this sonnet sequence are unparalleled, but mostly striking is that the two unworthy and deeply flawed lovers frequently appear fundamentally anti-Petrarchan. Shakespeare interrogates the conventional paradigm of the angelic lady and, in his unusual mimesis of the Petrarchan model, he overturns all the expectations concerning the addressees. The first 126 sonnets portray an object of desire as an opposite image of the angelic lady, a transgendered male of aristocratic origin, who intensely embodies grace, measured at moral and aesthetic levels; the last sonnets reveal another object of desire, built again in stark contrast to the paradigmatic angelic lady, the so-called "Dark Lady", which desacralises the previous female model epitomizing a transcendent spirituality, presenting instead the profanation of grace through the experience of love. By creating unprecedented objects of desire, Shakespeare departs from the Petrarchan paradigm, but while he projects his hybridised lovers, he refigures the Petrarchan motifs through a new representation of grace, beauty, love and, quest for immortality.

|Sonnet 12| is considered to be one of the "procreation sonnets" in its depiction of the typically Renaissance preoccupation with the passage of time and its impact upon human beauty. Shakespeare obviously rewrites the Renaissance *topos* of mutability as his speaker acknowledges the lack of permanence and constancy in the physical nature. The beginning of the sonnet delivers the meditation upon the order of things in the natural world:

> When I do count the clock that tells the time
> And see the brave day sunk in hideous night,
> When I behold the violet past prime
> And sable curls all silvered o'er with white,
> When lofty trees I see barren of leaves,
> Which erst from heat did canopy the herd
> And summer's green all girded up in sheaves
> Born on the bier with white and bristly beard.

The complete absence of any reference to transcendence should be noted, as well as the lack of any implications that the beloved one might embody a transcendent spirituality. Shakespeare created a lyric I which is distinct from anything before him. Crucial in the sonnet is the motif of cruelty, which is exercised against the speaker-lover in order to accomplish an epiphanic moment of self-recognition. In this Shakespearean sonnet, the cruelty is not displayed by the angelic lady who spurns the insufficient lover. On the contrary, the only manifestation of cruelty is experienced by the speaker as a result of the ticking of the clock, which brutally indicates all nature's subdual and decay due to the passage of time. A rising anxiety is built by the imagery of the swinging of the pendulum of the clock through "When I do count the clock that tells the time", which is delivered in the astonishingly regular meter, without any variations, and the use of the exclusively single-syllable word, reinforces the idea that the ticking of the clock is in fact a motion of the "Time's scythe" which brutally but orderly destroys everything. The only constancy alluded to is the inescapable passage of time that devours "the brave day", "the violet past prime", and "the summer's green", and, regardless of the "bravery" displayed to prevent this orderly motion, everything ruthlessly sinks to the "hideous night". The speaker's anxiety increases by the juxtaposition between "brave day" and "hideous night", which is meant to emphasise the malignant and destructive force which allows the disappearance of beauty and its transformation into ugliness and barrenness. The rising despair of the speaker gives the recognition of the mutability of everything, the turning point of the sonnet being "Than of thy beauty do I question make", as the passage of time exposes the fallibility of all beauty. The speaker's state of mind divulges a ferocious emotion at the awareness that "though among the waste of time must go, / Since sweets and beauties do themselves forsake, / And die as fast as they see others grow". The intense metaphor of the "waste of time" strengthens the speaker's sense of uncertainty and vulnerability in a world without permanence and intelligibility. However, at the moment of unparalleled despair, the speaker discovers hope and belief in the "growth" existent in nature: "And nothing 'gainst Time's scythe can make defence / Save breed, to brave him when he takes thee hence". The earlier military imagery of defeat in any attempts to fight the passage of time is overturned by the nature's course itself, as the speaker acknowledges that at the individual level the human is mortal, but the "breed" of humankind is immortal due to procreation. "Breed" is the only way to prevent "the waste of time" for it possesses the power to preserve the youth and beauty in this world. Hence, the "brave" attitude exhibited by the speaker at the end of the sonnet, when he attains the epiphanic moment of truth that beautiful things should save the "breed", they have the duty to replicate themselves, achieving thus the immortality of beauty. Rather than remaining locked in the despair produced by mutability, the speaker discovers the salvation of the beauty in the cyclical view of nature.

Sonnet 18 leads to a new employment of the sonnet space, since in this poem, Shakespeare questions most of the Petrarchan metaphors delivered in a conventional sonnet discourse. It is quite common in a sonnet to have the mistress compared by the speaker-lover to the beauty of nature, where the heavenly beauty of the angelic lady surpasses clearly all beauties in nature. In this sonnet, however, rather that stating the heavenly charms of the perfect beauty of the lady, Shakespeare rewrites the discourse of love and beauty anew. The first line of the poem "Shall I compare thee to a summer's day?" reveals the spirit of a doubting age, particularly expressing the doubt in the "truth" of the conventional clichés. Shakespeare overturns the expectations of representing a typically Petrarchan lady as the object of the speaker's desire primarily by casting some ambiguity upon the figure of the addressee, referring to his beloved one by a "thee", so that the uncertainty concerning a female or male beloved is preserved throughout the entire poem. But mostly striking is the doubt infused in his speaker's hesitation to make such a comparison, especially after acknowledging the lack of permanence and fallibility of everything in this world. In an apparently Petrarchan paradigmatic fashion, Shakespeare continues with his speaker's assertion: "Thou art more lovely and more temperate: / Rough winds do shake the darling buds of May, / And summer's lease has all too short a date". The ambivalence of the first quatrain of the sonnet partially asserts the Petrarchan conventional claim of the beloved one's uniqueness, "Thou art more lovely and more temperate" confirming that the virtues of the lover transcend any other splendid presence in nature. it simultaneously dethrones all the Petrarchan conceits, bringing them into questions, especially after gaining the awareness that the conventional comparison of the beloved to "a summer's day" subverts the much desired constancy of beauty and youth, suggesting instead impermanence and decay. This ambivalence emerges from the knowledge that any ostentatious attempts to express the permanence of beauty within the mundane world inevitably "fail", and in order to combat the effects of time, poetry should capture the inalterability of the lover's beauty. But while employing the traditional modality of triumph over death, as Sean Keilen claims, "the poet-lover begins to notice his limitations as a writer and susceptibility of language to misunderstanding" (246). Therefore, the determination of the speaker-poet to immortalize the youth and beauty is expressed clearly: "But thy eternal summer shall not fade, / Nor lose possession of that fair thou ow'st; / Nor shall death brag thou wander'st in his shade, / When in eternal lines to time thou grow'st". The invocation of the word "eternal" celebrates the immortalizing powers of poetry, which, unlike the "decline" of the fair in this world, confers the epiphanic dream of permanence, possible to be achieved in the memory of the future generation. In this respect, it can be said that Shakespeare rewrites the conventional Renaissance association of poetry to divinity and consequently to eternity; instead, he confers a physical dimension to the poem, suggesting the idea that the eternity of a poem shall last "So long as men can breathe or eyes can see./ So long lives this, and this gives life to thee". Shakespeare presents a very secular and innovative concept of eternity of the poetry which is related to the existence of the readers, where ""this" is the poem embodied by readers, living through them as they live. [Here] readers emerge as the single most important factor in a poet's pursuit of poetic greatness" (Zukerman 636).

Sonnet 55 revives the polemics over the low cultural status of lyric poetry. Despite the enormous popularity produced by Petrarch's poetry in Continental Europe, the English writers were initially reluctant to embrace the lyric form, the English love poetry preserving a low status until the publication of Sydney's *Astrophil and Stella* (1591), which ignited the sonnet fascination. In this sonnet, Shakespeare clearly states the prevalence of poetry over any other forms of art: "Not marble, nor the gilded monuments / Of princes, shall outlive this powerful rhyme". The boastful tone in which the speaker makes this initial statement is impressive, a tone which challenges somehow the arrogance and egocentrism of all those powerful men who imagine the immortality they reached due to their representation in gilded monuments. The superiority of lyric poetry is stated by the witty display and control of alliteration between "not/nor" and "marble/monuments", with the playful use of consonance on internal "m/n" and consonance on "l/d" and "/r/" sounds, together with assonant "o/" and "e/" vowels, all introduced in one single line. By infusing power and control in the language of the first two lines of the poem, the poet does not allow any hesitation concerning the fact that poetry will "outlive" any "marble" and "gilded monuments".

It can be noticed that this Shakespearean sonnet engages deliberately into a dialogue with Horace's poetics. Horace conveys the immortality of his work through the imagery of a monument which confers static solidity and, though Horace clearly suggests that his poetry would outlast the old monuments, a static and physical dimension emerges out of this imagery. Shakespeare, however, goes against the traditional attitude towards poetry as static, producing instead the notion of poetry as a lived experience, particularly the fluidity of the experience of the reader as primary attribute in attaining immortality. Shakespeare creates the juxtaposition between the solid structures which exist in time and space and can be "overturned" by war or "sluttish time" and structures of poetry which provide "the living record of your memory". As Zukerman explains, "rather than arguing that his work will be stronger and better than those structures, he suggests that those seemingly permanent structures are subject to the buffets of time *because* of their very physicality" (637). Moreover, it seems that the battle for prominence of poetry over other forms of arts is taken at times in the most unpoetic and shocking manner, when the speaker claims: "But you shall shine more bright in these contents / Than unswept stone besmeared with sluttish time". This statement clearly explodes Sydney's claim of the poet as a prophet that should create by his poetic language a kind of transcendental experience, the derogatory and offensive language clearly departing from the poetic decorum of the time. However, this rejection of the poetic language functions in a very striking manner in Shakespeare's sonnet, as it transmits the entire fury and frustration of the speaker against the passage of the "sluttish time", by which granting power to his rhyme. Coming in a full circle, it seems that the low or high culture would not confer everlasting memory to Shakespearian sonnet, nor would any notion of transcendence. While continuing the exploration of the *topos* of poetic immortality, Shakespeare states that

'Gainst death and all oblivious enmity

Shall you pace forth; your praise shall still find room
Even in the eyes of all posterity
That wear this world out to the ending doom.
So, till the judgement that yourself arise,
You live in this, and dwell in lovers' eyes.

Again, Shakespeare produces a very secular notion of eternity, which lasts as long as the readers read these love poems. Moreover, a new dimension is added to it, particularly "the identificatory process of reading", since the beloved is not represented passively in the poem, but "is actively encountered by readers who then incorporate him into their own experience of love. In this way, the beloved and the poem never stay same; they are always changing in relation to the new readers and readerly experience" (Zukerman 638).

Sonnet 116 is one of the most famous Shakespearean sonnets. It comes as a surprise that the entire sonnet tradition dwells on the *topos* of love, but no one prior to Shakespeare had truly attempted to provide a definition of love. Shakespeare apparently tries to cover this deficiency in *Sonnet 116*. He starts with a very bold declaration: "Let me not to the marriage of true minds / Admit impediments, love is not love / Which alters when it alteration finds, / or bends with the remover to remove". This utterance has a clear purpose to persuade, either the beloved or the reader, or maybe both. The speaker-lover intensely creates a space in which he tries to convince his addressee and/or hearer that in a world of mutability, the only permanent thing is love, though there are clear "impediments" which might prevent this constancy. In a world of "alteration", love is presented as "an ever-fixed mark, / That looks on tempest and is never shaken; / It is the star to every wand'ring bark, / Whose worth's unknown, although his highths be taken". This statement simultaneously deconstructs and strengthens the Petrarchan discourse, because Shakespeare employs the most vivid Petrarchan conceits such as the North Star, "the tempest", and "star to wandering bark", but instead of using them in relation to an unattainable angelic lady, he engages this hyperbolic language in order to convey the feeling of love. Despite the un-Petrarchan attitude, the verses yet surprise by a very Petrarchan desire for something unchanging. The speaker-lover powerfully creates the image of love as an eternal ideal which is mostly unattainable in a world in which persons alter, bodies alter, and beauties are "removed". The speaker continues his meditation: "Love's not Time's fool, though rosy lips and cheeks / Within his bending sickle's compass come; / Love alters not with brief hours and weeks, / But bears it out even to the edge of doom". This idealistic definition of true love becomes somehow threatened by the ambiguous reiteration of the words "bending" and "alters", the two words gaining an enormous weight as they are reinscribed in the verses in relation to Time, who, like the grim reaper, devours the "rosy lips and cheeks" and, apparently, the only thing which remains free of alteration is love. The explicit reference to time and its destructive impact upon physical beauty "also exhibits an authorial pentimento, by which a love first described in transcendent vertical terms as a secular Petrarchan fixed star subsequently takes on the immanent horizontal Christian Pauline form of stoic fidelity in endurance" (Vendler 491). The endurance is necessary when the speaker acknowledges that the attempts to cross the barrier which separates perishable from eternal inevitably fail. In the face of these limitations, the speaker-lover tries to combat the mortality with the inscription of love in his poetry, striving to transmit his truth beyond the time's jurisdiction: "If this be error and upon me proved, / I never writ, nor no man ever loved". The last lines display the unique characteristic of Shakespeare to achieve ambiguity and intensify the resources of language in those moments which reveal mostly the insecurity of the speaker's own selfhood, expressed in love. Out of his own vulnerability, the speaker-lover creates a sense of endless time in which his love poetry achieves immortality, again through the agency of future readers.

Sonnet 130 contests once more various sonnets conventions while revealing concomitantly the poet's ingenuity and wit. The sonnet clearly divulges the artificiality of sonnet conventions: "My mistress' eye are nothing like the sun; / Coral is far more red than her lips' red; / If snow be white, why then her breasts are dun; / If hairs be wires, black wires grow on her head". The sonnet introduces a Dark Lady, constructed in a parodic reiteration of the angelic lady motif. But despite the caricature and parody of the Petrarchan lady, Shakespearean speaker is "preoccupied with a beloved whom he portrays as, in effect, emblematising its deformation, its violation. The speaker fashions an elaborately desacralised image of his mistress" (Cousins 271). Rather than depicting the conventional excess of the supernatural beauty of the angelic lady and the overwhelming effect of her beauty on all beholders, Shakespeare's speaker ingeniously contests the artificial depiction of the main elements of the angelic lady *topos*, exhibiting scepticism and doubt concerning the truth conveyed in art. Shakespeare's perception of the poetic truth was clearly influenced by the spirit of Reformation, in which the voices of Luther, Bacon and Descartes can be recognised. Instead of the conventional preoccupation of the poet-lover to depict the ideal truth, Shakespearean poet-lover is mostly concerned with the problem of misrepresentation in art: "I grant I never saw a goddess go: / My mistress when she walks treads on the ground. / And yet, by heaven, I think my love as rare / As any she belied with false compare". Although the image of the beloved is totally desacralised, in this sonnet, the speaker-lover celebrates his lover's everyday attractiveness, which gains worth exactly in the authenticity it displays, and it derives value especially in the genuine love which the speaker experiences vis-à-vis the object of his desire. The ironic reference to "heaven" stresses out the falsehood of the conventional love discourse and, in an age of misrepresentation, proclaims the superiority of the natural over the supernatural. Instead of following the traditional aesthetic standard for female beauty, Shakespeare seems to establish a new aesthetic, which is founded on the genuineness of appearance and authenticity of feelings.

In conclusion, it can be said that in his sonnets, Shakespeare rewrites the Petrarchan discourse concerning the angelic lady and love, each time revealing this genre as a site of contestation, both in poetic intertextual terms and as a space of a struggle over the constitution of an aesthetic and meaning. In a way, Shakespearian sonnet can be seen as a *locus* for the expression of the contemporary Renaissance anxieties about the mutability, lack of permanence and intelligibility of the world, and especially about the representation and/or misrepresentation in art.

2.2 Prose Fiction

The first novel in modern world literature is considered to be *Don Quixote*, but it would be more correct to say that the first type of modern fiction is represented by the picaresque narratives which emerged in the Renaissance, particularly in Spain. On the general literary level, the domains of drama and poetry were dominant, but along them, prose narratives were also much read in the period, where many were translations from the Iberian peninsula, novels as well as romances. Autochthonous prose works were primarily romances, which should not be confused with or equalled to novels:

Romances are not novels: their plots are episodic, their settings imaginary, noble characters are set against monsters and grotesques, and their morality is based on feudal idealization projected forward from medieval predecessors. Often, as with the case of Lyly's *Euphues* (1578) and Sidney's *Arcadia* which was published in 1590 after the author's death (although it had previously circulated in manuscript), they appeal as much for the savour of their prose style as for the adventures of their heroes: the subtitle of Lyly's work is *The Anatomy of Wit*. (Hattaway 101)

The literary system of the medieval romance of chivalry changes in the modern period, starting with the Renaissance, into the system termed by the noun "roman" (in English, "novel"), originally meaning any Romance vernacular, as opposed to Latin, and nowadays used in most European languages to denote a novel. During the metamorphosis, some elements are preserved (such as extended narration, setting, plot, themes, character representation, point of view, narrator, and others, which are enriched, diversified, and acquire a different typology), whereas others are replaced and become extinct. Thus, the main changes that occurred in the medieval romance and made possible the rise, in the Spanish Renaissance, of the novel writing tradition – of which the first type was the picaresque – concern the replacement of the verse form by the prose form and of the fantastic element by the realist element, respectively.

Verisimilitude, or the *vraisemblable* (Tzvetan Todorov's term), synonymous with realism and the realist element, is responsible for the development of the fictional form of writing which requires fidelity to actuality in its representation regarding both the social and cultural context and the character representation strategies. Responsible for the rise of the novel, the critics would also argue, is the Renaissance distrust of the high forms of culture and literature, the challenge of hegemony, the popular laughter and the carnivalesque with its various categories such as the grotesque and the picaresque. However, although traditionally the picaresque is viewed "as the antiromance par excellence, it is now also viewed as reflecting a pervasive longing for romance wish fulfilment" (Brownlee 28), as in the rogue's quest for a home (in the sense of a social position, social and material fulfilment), or in his spiritual betterment by acquiring moral values and a sense of union with God.

With respect to the rise and development of the novel as a new and distinct literary genre, the Renaissance represents, in its cultural and literary context, the moment of transition from the romance to the novel (*roman*, in most European languages) at the beginning of modernity. In the Renaissance, Spain was ahead of the rest of Europe in the development of the novelistic form. With his *Don Quixote de la Mancha* (1605 and 1615), extolled as the last romance and at the same time the first modern novel, Cervantes is credited with having made possible and consolidating the transition from medieval to modern times.

The father of the novelistic genre is Cervantes, critics would claim, for, the change from verse to prose form having already occurred, now verisimilitude (the realist element) substitutes for the fantastic element in the novelistic concern with human existence and the social background. The textual representation of this concern follows the principle of faithfulness to actual reality in its textualization. Cervantes starts what later will be called realism and defined, such as by Northrop Frye, as the art of verisimilitude and implicit simile. Terry Eagleton, however, claims that to call *Don Quixote* the first novel, or even a novel, is a mistake, because the picaresque prose fiction had also challenged the romance in this way, at least implicitly, at that time. Moreover, Cervantes's great work "is in fact less the origin of the genre than a novel about the origin of the novel," showing "how the novel comes about when Romantic idealism, here in the form of Quixote's chivalric fantasies, collides with the real world" (Eagleton 3).

The conflict, emerging in the Renaissance, between the literary tradition of the romance and that of the novel concerns the conflict between the fantastic element and the realist element, which is the conflict between romanticized imaginative flight and actual fact, idealism and realism, dream and reality, and, finally, the conflict between "the person having noble aspirations and the reality that is alien and hostile to these aspirations, that is to say, that type of conflict which will be typical of the later social novel and the realist literature on the whole" (Pavlicencu 112). A similar conflict would be found later, in the eighteenth and nineteenth centuries, between romantic novels, especially gothic, still called romances, and realist novels as anti-romances. The transition from romantic illusion to realist maturity can be sensed at work in Walter Scott's *Waverly*, Jane Austen's *Sense and Sensibility*, William Makepeace Thackeray's *Pendennis*, or in Charles Dickens's progress from *David Copperfield* to *Great Expectations*.

Both Cervantes and the picaresque authors that had started earlier in the sixteenth century to produce their narratives should be accredited with the rise of the modern novelistic genre based on the principle of verisimilitude. The rise of the fictional form of writing in the Renaissance is also indebted to the French François Rabelais, the author of *Gargantua et Pantagruel* (1532, 1534).

2.2.1 The Rise of the Picaresque Novel and Its Alternatives

Fundamental for the rise of the novel as a genre in the modern period is the production of picaresque fiction as standing against the romance, or, in Bakhtin's words, against the high chivalric novel of ordeal, the extra-literary rhetorical genres – such as biographical, confessional, and sermon genres – and the later Baroque novel. In his "Discourse in the Novel", a study on style and stylistics, Bakhtin defines the novel as "a diversity of social speech types (sometimes even diversity of languages) and a diversity of individual voices, artistically organized" (262). The combination of languages and styles, speech types and utterances into unities, as well as their links and interrelationships, represents the rise of the novel as well as the defining feature of the stylistics of the novel. In this way, *raznorecie* ("heteroglossia", or different speech types) is introduced in the novelistic text:

The novel orchestrates all its themes, the totality of the world of objects and ideas depicted and expressed in it, by means of the social diversity and speech types [*raznorecie*] and by the differing individual voices that flourish under such conditions.

Authorial speech, the speech of narrators, inserted genres, the speech of characters are merely those fundamental compositional unities with whose help heteroglossia [*raznorecie*] can enter the novel; each of them permits a multiplicity of social voices and a wide variety of their links and interrelationships (always more or less dialogized). (263)

Concerning the development of the novel and differentiating between the First Stylistic Line (rooted in the Sophistic novel with its single style and language, later changed into the Baroque novel, the adventure-heroic novel, and the sentimental psychological novel) and the Second Stylistic Line, Bakhtin argues that *raznorecie* enters the novel with the emergence of the second line, whose first great example is the picaresque novel. What made possible the appearance of *raznorecie* is the main character's status as an anti-hero with a distinct voice: he/she is a speaking person with a distinct discourse, striving for social significance, whose speech type is determined by personality as well as conditions; he/she is an ideologue and his or her perception of the world is an ideologeme.

In what he calls the "picaresque adventure novel", Bakhtin focuses on the image of *el picaro* (the rogue), the artistic representation of his or her discourse and action:

The hero of such novels, the agent of gay deception, is located on the far side of any pathos – heroic or Sentimental – and located there deliberately and emphatically; his contra-pathetic nature is everywhere in evidence, beginning with his comic self-introduction and self-recommendation to the public (providing the tone of the entire subsequent story) and ending with the finale. The hero is located beyond all these basically rhetorical categories that are at the heart of a hero's image in novels of trial: he is on the far side of any judgment, any defense or accusation, any self- justification or repentance. A radically new tone is given here to discourse about human beings, a tone alien to any pathos-charged seriousness. (406)

The picaresque novel (Sp. *picaro* meaning "rogue") originated in sixteenth-century Spain, an early example being the anonymous *Vida de Lazarillo de Tormes* (1554). Another example would also be *La Celestina* (1499). The most important Spanish authors of picaresque novels are Mateo Aleman, who wrote *Guzman de Alfarache* (1599, 1604), Francisco de Quevedo, who wrote *La Vida del Buscon don Pablos de Segovia* (1626), and Luis Velez de Guevara, the author of *El Diablo Cojuelo* (1644). These four works form the nucleus of the Spanish picaresque tradition and govern other major and minor writings which were produced between 1600 and 1646.

Along with picaresque fiction reified in a number of individual texts, the greatest of all Spanish novels, Cervantes's *Don Quixote*, written at the beginning of the seventeenth century, also contains a number of picaresque elements. It depicts the contemporary context while satirizing chivalry and, in Bakhtinian conception, parodying other earlier genres, in particular the romance as symptomatic of the medieval literary incorporation of chivalry. As parody and satire, it is unquestionably the principal work to expose the narrative and thematic discrepancy of the romance, and it does so by a comic outlook on the conventions of chivalry and by contrasting them with the realities of ordinary life, to concentrate on everyday routine.

Cervantes incorporates verisimilitude into his novel through play, parody, irony, ridiculous and other forms of the comic that focus on the romance and its main thematic components, and on other literary forms, especially on the protagonist and his relations with other characters, in particular Sancho. Don Quixote is tragic and humorous, ridiculous and comic, but always faithful to the assumed ideal; his values are always highly moral, his feelings true and profound, and in his madness he remains superior to all other people by his spirit and by the strong character of his ethics. Don Quixote's madness, actually, is at the core of the novel's treatment of actual reality. Madness transposes the protagonist from immediate reality into the realm of imaginary life; the comic effect and entertainment result from the various clashes between these two worlds. In fact, "from the numerous clashes between Don Quixote and reality, there never results any situation that would question the right of existence for this reality; it is always right against him, and after a few comic situations, it continues to flow as static and calm as before" (Auerbach 311). Don Quixote's adventures, consisting mainly of comic confusions, do not reveal much, do not point to any stringent issues of everyday existence, do not satirize or criticize much, do not disclose profound philosophical debates, but mainly form a pretext to present the writer's contemporary social and human life in all its complexity and diversity. Don Quixote's madness does not reveal much of the contemporary tragic and problematic aspects of existence, either, the "whole book being a game in which madness becomes ridiculous through its clash with a solidly built reality" (Auerbach 312). Don Quixote is not tragic or problematic; he is humorous rather than ridiculous, but above all he is dignified, superior, educative and formative, as Sancho becomes in his company wiser and morally bettered. Despite playing a role and playing with his master's madness, Sancho sincerely loves and respects Don Quixote. In employing madness in the treatment of his protagonist, Cervantes himself plays not only with various literary forms but also with reality, which yields to a never-ending and complex game that is prompted by Don Quixote's madness which "transforms the real, actual world into a funny play performed on stage" (Auerbach 316). But Don Quixote's madness also transforms the world into the way of spiritual and moral improvement, and in this respect his madness reveals wisdom which is "the reason, nobility, common sense and dignity of a wise and balanced man", humble, modest, and helpful (Auerbach 314). By these spiritual features, Don Quixote remains static, but the experience of his personality is assumed and assimilated in its totality by Sancho more than others, in that he transposes himself into Don Quixote's soul, whose madness and wisdom become productive in Sancho. Thus, the reader understands the protagonist better through Sancho's behaviour and attitudes. Sancho is Don Quixote's alter-ego, his adversary and consolation, his contrastive figure, but their spiritual connection is developed to such an extent that, in matters of the character formation principle, one would claim, as Auerbach does, that these two protagonists, "each for himself as well as their relationship, would form themselves gradually and without intention" (319).

More explicitly dealing with elements of development and growth is picaresque fiction; Cervantes's novel assimilates the picaresque narrative of adventure, its travel scheme, its motifs of trial and quest, but only in some of his *Novelas ejemplares* is Cervantes closer to the picaresque mode of writing.

The picaresque (or rogue) novel emerging in the Renaissance influenced the fiction writing of centuries to come, in its turn being influenced by and drawing on previous traditions. Thus, it uses elements reminiscent of the novel and epic in antiquity, and of the romance in the Middle Ages. But it also reveals some new aspects of the third-person strategies in terms of a protagonist's process of development and thus provides, in matters of both content and form, new steps towards the consolidation of the literary pattern of the Bildungsroman.

The rogue novel has its origins in an age of instability on different levels and of changing human values. A mixture of virtue and impudence, spirit of adventure and of revolt, the protagonist of the anonymous *Vida de Lazarillo de Tormes* or of Mateo Aleman's *Guzman de Alfarache* always changes his condition and social position; he is almost all the time a servant to different masters, a beggar, soldier, robber, merchant, actor, passing through different social levels and meeting in his wanderings all sorts and conditions of men. The narrator of the picaresque novel can reveal a pessimistic view on the human condition, as in *Lazarillo de Tormes*, but always with a mixture of understanding, humour and criticism. The author of the picaresque novel may fail to render characters with moral qualities, or does not mean to do that, as is the case of Mateo Aleman, but he would identify himself with the protagonist, providing long moral speculations and fusing the moral with the picaresque.

The picaresque novel of the Renaissance is viewed as the product of an age of crisis, of a period of transition, and is accredited with having contributed to the infiltration of innovative ideas in various realms (religious, political, economic, artistic, and so on) against the traditional mind-set. In this respect – and contrary to a chivalric social idealism still preserved in Cervantes – the picaresque narrative is devised as a "socio-critical genre" that displays at once a critique of traditional mores and values of an aristocracy typical of medieval Spain, and a support for the ascendance of the new, materialistic and capitalist mentality and ethical system. In other words, this type of fiction emerges in a period of transition from the conflict between the old, chivalric idealism and the newly emerging values of material basis and social ascension, where with regard to the literary character, the medieval pilgrim and knight are replaced with the rogue and the fool.

In connection with carnivalesque categories, picaresque writing is also viewed as a literary response to and rejection of the contemporary cultural hegemony. It is a form, at first, of popular culture concerned with disrespect for and challenge to authority, which is in dialogue with the form of high, aristocratic culture in the Renaissance as the embodiment of dominant ideology.

The picaresque fiction of the Renaissance continues, in terms of structure and theme, the ancient narratives of travel and ordeal, and those of biography or autobiography, whose elements now combine to construct a new type of protagonist (which implies the principle of development). The ordeal is committed to wandering and both types of character experience intermingle with many biographical or autobiographical elements. In the picaresque novel, which may be considered a type of the travel novel, or of the novel of ordeal, or a type of pseudo-autobiographical novel, depending on the predominance of certain elements, the status of the character may change sharply – from beggar to rich man, from homeless wanderer to nobleman – but he himself seems to remain unchanged as an individual. Gradually, however, the novel becomes more complex with regard to individual existence and provides the narrator's deeper insight into human psychology and inner existence. It reveals the concern with the character's physical and intellectual growth, with his gradual self-discovery amid the complexity of the external world.

The picaresque novel constitutes a remarkable sequence of Spanish and then general European literature from its beginnings in the Renaissance until late into the eighteenth century; while it remained influential in the nineteenth century, its elements can also be found in the twentieth century and even nowadays, in narrative texts of various stripes. The thematic pattern of picaresque fiction represents a syntagmatic and fixed structure of a series of definite elements rendering a rather normative fictional tradition, in other words, a system. In so far as it appeals to readers as a didactic form of entertainment, it has remained popular to this day and in various countries and cultural backgrounds, for it offers the possibility of laughter and playing, while verbalizing/textualizing the concern with individual experience and the social background, that is, verisimilitude in its twofold perspective.

The picaresque novel has dynamic thematic features and rejects literary conventions, while being open to innovations and influences of every kind and going through various mutations. However, many critical voices, such as Walter L. Reed, Harry Sieber, and Peter N. Dunn, point to the difficulty of conclusively defining the picaresque as a distinct subgenre of the novel genre as well as to the flaw in regarding it as a homogeneous whole, stable and with invariable elements. Nevertheless, a more formal and formalist approach would attempt a definition and classification capable of providing clarification, not of generating confusion. In pursuit of such a goal, Claudio Guillén (in "Toward a Definition of the Picaresque" 71-89) has identified eight main features of picaresque fiction, summarised as follows: (1) the picaro as the main focus of the novel; (2) pseudo-autobiography as the narrative form; (3) a subjective point of view; (4) a challenge to social norms and values while learning from personal experience; (5) the lack of money and a continuous struggle for survival; (6) detailed observation and account, and often satire, of various circumstances of human existence and social conditions; (7) travel and adventure as the main types of the picaro's experience; and (8) the episodic structure of the novel to depict a chaotic world of confusion and disorder.

As for the definition, a picaresque novel is a pseudo-autobiography narrated in the first person by the protagonist/autodiegetic narrator *el picaro* (or *picara*), a rogue, whose discourse constructs an individual, self-conscious subject in a continuous, omniscient dialogue with the reader in the form of what has been called a "spoken epistle". Concerning the thematic treatment of the relationship between the individual and his/her milieu, the natural goodness of the protagonist is supressed by external conditions that make him/her repudiate moral values such as decency and virtue, and thus transform him/her into an anti-hero/anti-heroine who has to deceive and pretend in order to survive and be accepted in a desired social group. Wit and irony, pragmatism and sentimentalism, deception and theft, and for the picara also prostitution, are means for survival and obtaining employment, money, marriage, and other forms of economic security. The picaro's changing of masters is equalled by the picara's changing of lovers and husbands; in the case of both, each experience is either a new beginning or a new step towards becoming a gentleman or gentlewoman.

With regard to this ethical component, a picaresque fictional narrative is a moral history of the self and society, a chronicle of a corrupt world whose false ideals imperil the spiritual innocence of a character in development. The literary system of picaresque fiction reveals that the novel as a new genre developed in its incipient stage from some previous literary traditions as well as from other discourses, in particular the legal one. Victim and at the same time exponent of a social order in a turbulent process of transition, the rogue occasionally displays naivety, more often wit, and sometimes a humorous, more often satirical attitude towards the human condition and especially society, in particular its corruption, which he or she exploits. In a society retaining a strong sense of social hierarchy, the picaro's experience is in most cases bound to lower levels of employment, especially as a servant. The position of servitude strengthens his valueless status in society, while it also grants the anti-hero the possibility to observe, tell, comment, evaluate, be a victim or take advantage of society, as well as wander and change his condition, and above all learn, strive, change the inner perspectives of existence, and acquire a philosophy of living and an identity.

The protagonist, at first a kind of social parasite, struggles and aspires to higher values and embarks on a process of social-climbing never explicitly deployed thematically but which emerges clearly at the moment of existential debate to highlight the drama of individual consciousness. The true picaro is forced to travel and change his condition in order to earn his living and learn life, and consequently, while acquiring knowledge, he "criticizes the corrupt society of whose disease he is a symptom" (Giddings 34). However, suggestive of social improvement and paralleling a personal betterment, and amid the general corruption and moral degeneration of a period of transition, a picaro may yet integrate into a milieu, whose evolving on genuine and ethical principles he would eventually come to accept and adopt.

Built around the chronotope of the road, the elements that construct the system of picaresque novels constitute a complex typology which covers a life-time sequence with the formula "from childhood to maturity or old age". In his wanderings, the character changes his condition, encounters various social levels and professional groups, various types of human and social existence, which are recounted and evaluated by him/her while displaying a comic, predominantly satirical, attitude and a particular philosophy of life.

From place to place, from master to master, from job to job, and from childhood to adolescence and so on, the panoramic picture of contemporary society unfolds in a narrative structure of an episodic plot seemingly deprived of unity; its only linking principle is the temporal and spatial movement of the picaro or, in other words, the chronotope of the road, which, according to Bakhtin, determines the plots of the picaresque novels of the sixteenth through eighteenth centuries. The picaresque novel as a series of episodes relies less on the cause and effect organization of events in a narrative sequence than on chronology; the picaro acts as bound by chance, or fortune, or providence, or accident, or personal choice or initiative, but always travelling on. In the chronotope of the road, time fuses with and flows in space, thus fashioning the road, in Bakhtin's words, as a place suitable for particularly random encounters, a place for events to find their denouement as well as a place for new departures, for new beginnings in the course of an individual's life. On the actual road, various adventures and various types of meetings occur. The asocial picaro's experience of life is also a kind of road that belongs to no one in particular but to human-kind in general, and on this road ("the high road") various encounters take place; also on this road, like on an actual one,

> the spatial and temporal paths of the most varied people – representatives of all social classes, estates, religions, nationalities, ages – intersect at one spatial and temporal point. People who are normally kept separate by social and spatial

distance can accidentally meet; any contrast may crop up, the most various fates may collide and interweave with one another. On the road the spatial and temporal series defining human fates and lives combine with one another in distinctive ways, even as they become more complex and more concrete by the collapse of social distances. (Bakhtin, "Forms of Time and of the Chronotope in the Novel" 243)

The thematic typology includes, first, the experience of the rogue as a child at home, usually in a provincial setting where he or she is dissatisfied with the present conditions, or future perspectives, and leaves or is driven from it to face a larger, disordered world and a chaotic, uncertain existence, just as their narrated form is, without much concern with causality on the part of the author. Except the protagonist, asocial but depicted with individual personality, the other characters lack unified and psychologically nuanced selves, representing instead social and moral types. The road of life becomes for the picaro a complex experience of changing conditions, backgrounds, jobs, masters, and meetings, where the events and adventures that the picaro encounters in the course of his real life determine his failings, wrong choices and mistakes, on which depend his turning into a cunning and shameless subject and his gravitating towards immoral and lawless behaviour. At first a warm-hearted and naïve person, the picaro loses his innocence in the encounter with the milieu and emerges as a ruthless opportunist who learns to turn every chance to his advantage in order to survive and overcome the difficulties of life. Nonetheless, some rogues break the pattern and preserve their innocence despite succumbing to vices and temptations.

In these two and other cases, however, as the universal principle of "crime and punishment" dictates, on reaching a particular moment in his stage of maturity, the narrative flow is in the phase of a moral and existential debate which dramatizes the drama of individual consciousness as the conflict between personal values and social ones. This conflict reaches its climax at a moment of inner, psychological and emotional tumult from which there is no escape and which can end in either success or failure. To overcome the painful moment generated by the opposition between self-assumed values and those that he should have adopted for social integration, the rogue has to reassess his earlier life course, largely immoral and lawless, and change his life philosophy accordingly. However, acquiring a social status and attaining happiness do not necessarily mean that they are definite assets and will last forever, as they indeed cannot be confirmed by or quarantined from the chaotic and changing world, but rather imply a sense of open ending.

The conflicting and painful episode in personal development becomes a thematic constant in fiction, as in *Tom Jones*, *Wilhelm Meisters*, *Sartor Resartus*, and, more importantly, in the Bildungsromane in which it represents an epiphanic experience and *a priori* condition for individual formation.

Indeed, one may see clearly in our exposition of the typical plot pattern of the picaresque narrative a great number of elements that are also aspects of a typical Bildungsroman thematic pattern. The picaresque elements survive in other novelistic types too; for example, in the twentieth-century fiction of the Angry Young Men, and our presentation of the picaresque narrative can be said to describe exhaustively a novel like *Room at the Top*.

By playing with and reshaping previous literary forms, and establishing verisimilitude, the picaresque novel that emerged in the Renaissance (and remained influential throughout the seventeenth and eighteenth centuries) marks the rise of the novel as a modern genre. By its manner of handling the realist element, it also prefigures the realist type of fiction.

More important in our study, however, is that the picaresque novel contains many of the central, system-forming elements of the Bildungsroman. In this respect, it marks the mid-way between the earlier ancient and medieval narrative tradition encapsulating such elements, on the one side, and the novel of formation (the Bildungsroman) which would flourish in the nineteenth century, on the other. Like the medieval romance, picaresque fiction blends entertainment with moral lesson: personal accomplishment in matters of love, money, law, and the acquiring of a social status signify that the protagonist has achieved a kind of success and has adapted to society; this is possible, however, only after having changed the personal and social perspectives of existence by reviving decency, embracing virtue, and on the whole abandoning immorality. It proves the contention that the picaresque literary form developed from "Spanish doctrinal-moralistic literature during the second half of the sixteenth century" and that "the organization of a modern state in Spain, beginning in the reign of the Catholic kings and the attendant growth of a patrimonial bureaucracy", created a literary "discourse dealing with criminals and common people that writers found compelling partly because it also pertained to them as subjects of the new polity" (Echevarría xiv).

In the literary system of picaresque fiction, the elements of both tradition and novelty in the establishment of the novelistic genre, in general, mark the different as well as specific features of the rise of the novel of formation. Such features include: the autobiographical form; didactic and moral values; character portrayal along the adventurous versus provincial dichotomy; the road as the axis of narrative structure; the adventurous aspect of the plot; ordeal and the trial of life; the quest as trial of the character's moral validity; childhood, youth, and maturity as biological steps of the character's development; change in the character's condition along with the change of his inner perspectives (which is, as a literary concern, in its incipient stage) while gaining life experience.

The last feature is particularly important in so far as the character is no longer shown as static and as moving through the narrative structure by means of time and space categories, with certain changes only in his condition, destiny, and social position. The aspect of change alongside the loss of the static feature provides the image of man in his development and progress with the rising problem of apprehending the moment of the character's real change of consciousness on both the level of concrete reality (the passing from one social stratum into other, meeting all facets of the human condition, and so on) and that of moral and philosophical speculations (suggested by the character's experience of life and consisting of an impressive theory of living).

These general aspects have their direct representation in the picaresque writings of the Renaissance and in the novel of François Rabelais. *La vie de Gargantua et de Pantagruel* ("The Life of Gargantua and of Pantagruel"), which has remained popular to this day, can be classified (besides being a novel which satirizes and parodies the romance) as a work of grotesque, philosophy, fantasy, and as mythopoetic. Rabelais's basic source is the folk legend of Gargantua; the novel demonstrates the writer's attempt to create a realist novel of character development within the framework of folk time, as, indeed, folklore provides a stable basis for the novel's narrative structure and organization of thematic elements. Other forms of the time category are adventurous time (due to its aspect of travel), the psychological time of the novel of ordeal, and the biographical time (Gargantua's birth, his childhood and deeds). A certain pedagogic strain is of primary importance in the novel, for it reveals the pedagogic process of character development. The external world is viewed in terms of schooling and education, through which the protagonist has to pass in order to develop, change, and acquire an identity. The progress of the character allows the exclusion of his static features; likewise, the world assumes a changing historical dimension and, at the same time, becomes subject to a wealth of contrasting aspects.

With regard to this thematic aspect, in "The Bildungsroman and Its Significance in the History of Realism", Bakhtin gives special credit to Rabelais. Rabelais is among the writers of novels of emergence (or Bildungsromane), while *Gargantua et Pantagruel* (along with *Simplicissimus* and *Wilhelm Meister*) represents the fifth and most significant type of novel of emergence, the realist one, which shows the emergence of a changing hero in relation not to a static and stable world, as in the previous four types of the Bildungsroman, but as inseparable from historical emergence. The protagonist emerges as a new type of human being along with the world, and actually reflects the historical emergence of the world itself. Rabelais's importance in the history of the Bildungsroman lies both in "the entire problem of the assimilation of time in the novel" and in "the problem of the image of emerging man" since his novel is, next to Goethe's and, to some degree, to Grimmelshausen's, "the greatest attempt at constructing an image of man growing in national-historical time" (Bakhtin, "The Bildungsroman" 25).

Bakhtin also discusses Rabelais in a special study entitled *Tvorchestvo Fransua Rable i narodnaia kultura srednevekovia i Renessansa* (1965, "Rabelais and His World"). Dealing with the issues of "carnival", "grotesque", and "laughter", Bakhtin shows that the related concepts of the carnivalesque and the grotesque are based on folk laughter as it emerged against the medieval official culture (which prohibited laughter except on feast days). Folk laughter started to give form to carnival rituals and paved the way for the Renaissance self-consciousness. The function of laughter in the historical development of culture, art, and literature is immense:

Laughter purifies from dogmatism, from the intolerant and the petrified; it liberates from fanaticism and pedantry, from fear and intimidation, from didacticism, naivete and illusion, from the single meaning, the single level, from sentimentality. Laughter does not permit seriousness to atrophy and to be torn away from the one being, forever incomplete. It restores this ambivalent wholeness. (Bakhtin, *Rabelais and His World* 123)

The way – in which laughter's victory over fear and its power of freeing people indicate that folk laughter and folk humour play an important role in grotesque imagery – is that people are playing with fear and are trying to laugh at it, and the result is that all "that was terrifying becomes grotesque" (*Rabelais and His World* 91). Two aspects emerge out of this experience. First, medieval laughter is not a subjective, individual and biological consciousness of the uninterrupted flow of time. It is the social consciousness of all the people. Man experiences this flow of time in the festive marketplace, in the carnival crowd, as he comes into contact with other bodies of varying age and social caste. He is aware of being a member of a continually growing and renewed people. This is why festive folk laughter presents an element of victory not only over supernatural awe, over the sacred, over death; it also means the defeat of power, of earthly kings, of the earthly upper classes, of all that oppresses and restricts. (*Rabelais and His World* 92)

Second, no less important, is that medieval laughter, "when it triumphed over the fear inspired by the mystery of the world and by power, boldly unveiled the truth about both. It resisted praise, flattery, hypocrisy. This laughing truth, expressed in curses and abusive words, degraded power" (*Rabelais and His World* 92-93).

According to Bakhtin, there are four features endemic to the carnivalesque chronotope, namely the open dialogue between the participants; free, classless environment and subversion of hierarchies; eccentricity; and mockery, subversion of attitudes.

The carnivalesque, as a form of popular culture concerned with disrespect, challenge and subversion of authority and hegemony, is therefore in dialogue with the forms of high, aristocratic culture in the Renaissance as the embodiment of dominant ideology. Also, the carnivalesque categories are not "*abstract thoughts* about equality and freedom", but "they were able to exercise such an immense *formal, genre-shaping* influence on literature"; this included "the organization of plot and plot situations, it determined that special familiarity of the author's position with regard to his characters (impossible in the higher genres)" (Bakhtin, *Problems of Dostoevsky's Poetics* 123-124).

Bakhtin idealizes the potential of popular culture to challenge the hegemonic culture, but he fails to see the implications of the historical substratum: the carnivalesque only occurs if the authority permits it. Moreover, the subversive aspect would often hesitate to attack authority and hegemony, focusing instead on some categories that were underprivileged and marginalized even more than the common people such as women, national minorities, etc., amounting to "displaced abjection".

Nonetheless, nowadays, magical realism, using defamiliarization, is linked to Bakhtin's concepts of "grotesque realism" and "carnivalesque spirit". The Russian scholar exemplifies the latter concept with Rabelais, the French writer who is, among other things, "the purest and the most consistent representative of the grotesque concept of the body" (Bakhtin, *Rabelais and His World* 30). Magical realism is a postmodern type of fiction, but its antecedents, apart from Rabelais, can be found earlier, even in antiquity, with Apuleius's *The Golden Ass*, and later with Swift's *Gulliver's Travels*, in which exaggeration of exaggeration provides both the grotesque and the substratum for the author's satirical endeavours.

In *Gargantua et Pantagruel*, the triad of the carnivalesque, the grotesque, and laughter furnished Rabelais's means of literary expression, his most characteristic manner of presentation, his distinctive way of textual arrangement of the narrated material, which covers all major episodes in the novel from the reflection of the feasts to the issues of philosophy and education. Certainly familiar with the carnival life existing in his time in the cities and in the countryside, Rabelais describes the "feast of cattle slaughter" at the very beginning of the novel; this cattle-slaughtering feast coincides with a merry banquet during which Gargantua's miraculous birth takes place.

In Rabelais, the grotesque, inseparable from the carnivalesque and laughter, is expressed primarily through the textualization of the dismembered body and its anatomization as if to construct a whole comedy of the body. Human life, the social, even nature itself, everything is compared to body and bodily life, as in Book 5, Chapter 5: "Those trees seemed to us terrestrial animals, in no wise so different from brute beasts as not to have skin, fat, flesh, veins, arteries, ligaments, nerves, cartilages, kernels, bones, marrow, humours, matrices, brains, and articulations".

In one of the most remarkable episodes at the beginning of the novel, an anatomical analysis concludes with the unexpected and completely carnivalesque birth of Gargantua through his mother's ear, which is also a grotesque image (of reversal) since the child does not go down, but up. Comic as well is Gargantua's first cry, calling for a drink, which alludes to, or rather develops, along with the images of cattle slaughtering and dismemberment, the theme of the feast. According to Bakhtin, the images "continue to unfold along the lines of a banquet: devouring of the dismembered body"; these images are later transferred to the anatomic description of the generating womb and thus they "create with great artistry an extremely dense atmosphere of the body as a whole in which all the dividing lines between man and beast, between the consuming and consumed bowels are intentionally erased" (*Rabelais and His World* 226). These "consuming and consumed organs are fused with the generating womb", which results in "a truly grotesque image of one single, superindividual bodily life, of the great bowels that devour and are devoured, generate and are generated"; but this is not an "animal" or "biological" bodily life, as we can see "the devoured and devouring womb of the earth and the ever-regenerated body of the people", signifying, as Rabelais's novel demonstrates, that "the merry, abundant and victorious bodily element opposes the serious medieval world of fear and oppression with all its intimidating and intimidated ideology" (*Rabelais and His World* 226).

The grotesque co-existing with laughter and the carnivalesque is the substance of another famous episode in the novel, which is that of Gargantua's drowning 260,418 people in his urine "exclusive of women and children". Bakhtin is again the best in summarizing the episode and pertinently interpreting it:

This scriptural formula is taken directly from the Gospel story of the crowd fed with 5 loaves of bread. (Rabelais quite often uses these formulas.) Thus the entire episode of the drenching in urine and the crowd's reaction is a travestied allusion. We shall see that this is not the only travesty of that kind in Rabelais's novel. Before performing his carnivalesque gesture, Gargantua declares that he will do this only *par ris,* for sport or laughter's sake. And the crowd concludes its volley of oaths by using the same expression, which, as the author tells us, is the origin of the word *Paris.* Thus, the entire episode is a gay carnivalesque travesty of the city's name. At the same time it is a parody of the local legends about the origin of names in general (serious and poetic forms of these legends were popular in France and were created by Jean Lemaire and the other poets of the school of rhetoricians). The name of Paris, the names of saints and martyrs, as well as the Gospel miracle, were all drawn into the game for laughter's sake. This was a game in which "exalted" and "sacred" things were combined with images of the lower stratum (urine, erotic images, and banquet travesties). Oaths, as the unofficial elements of speech and the profanation of the sacred, were organically woven into the game and were in tune with it. (*Rabelais and His World* 192)

In Rabelais, as can be seen in this episode, in that showing the hero's birth, and in many others, characteristic of the grotesque concept of the body and bodily life is the thematization of the elements of fertility, death, and renewal of life, that is, the theme of life and death, or birth and death, or killing and birth, which reveals the grotesque figures and images to be interwoven, apart from the carnivalesque and laughter, also with cosmic phenomena. For instance, Rabelais in Book 2, Chapter 2: "At the age of four hundred fourscore and forty-four years, Gargantua begat his son Pantagruel upon his wife named Badebec, daughter to the king of the dimly-seen Amaurotes in Utopia. She died in the throes of childbirth. Alas! Pantagruel was so extraordinarily large and heavy that he could not have possibly come to light without suffocating his mother". To Bakhtin, this theme is already familiar to the reader "from the Roman carnival of combined killing and childbirth", but in Rabelais "the killing is done by the newborn himself, in the very act of his birth", so that "birth and death are the gaping jaws of the earth and the mother's open womb"; further on, "gaping human and animal mouths will enter into the picture" (*Rabelais and His World* 329). In this connection, a terrible drought occurring at the time of Pantagruel's birth is described: "beasts were found dead in the fields, their mouths agape. As for the men, their state was very piteous. You should have seen them with their tongues dangling like a hound's after a run of six hours. Not a few threw themselves into the wells. Others lay under a cow's belly to enjoy the shade". The theme of death and birth is further developed by Gargantua, who does not know whether to weep over his wife's death or to laugh with joy at his son's birth: he moos "like a cow", as his wife gave birth and died, and laughs "like a calf", as his son has just been born.

Certainly, like his father Gargantua's birth, Pantagruel's also occurs in a grotesque atmosphere involving laughter and the carnivalesque. The novel presents Pantagruel's emergence, "shaggy as a bear", from his mother's womb, preceded, indeed triggered, by a caravan of wagons loaded with salted, thirst-arousing food.

Of the five books of *Gargantua et Pantagruel*, which can be seen as distinct novels dealing with the life experience of the protagonists, the father Gargantua and his son Pantagruel, the first two focus more or less explicitly on their respective birth, growth, schooling, social interaction, learning knowledge and philosophy, participating in human affairs, and others aspects of a process of development. But the *Bildung* of the protagonists is not the main authorial aim, since Rabelais himself in the prologue to the first book of his novel, *Gargantua,* points out the meaning of his work to be rather reader-oriented: "Here you will find a novel savor, a most obstruse doctrine; here you will learn the deepest mysteries, the most agonizing problems of our religion, our body politic, our economic life".

Indeed, in Rabelais the narrative and thematic movement which depicts the life and adventures of the characters involves a wealth of various "avant-garde positions", as Bakhtin calls them, in the fields of politics, culture, science, morals, and values. Rabelais articulates them in various parts of his novel, as in the episodes of Gargantua's education, Gargantua's letter to Pantagruel, Pantagruel's speech on medieval commentators of Roman law, and others. These episodes disclose their rhetorical nature and are expressed in scholarly and official language, in a highly serious speech. This new form of discourse is "a progressive speech, the last word of the epoch and at the same time Rabelais's completely sincere opinion" (*Rabelais and His World* 453). Fortunately, the novel also contains other episodes and is built on the triad of laughter, grotesque, and carnivalesque; otherwise, Rabelais, to Bakhtin, "would be merely one of the progressive but commonplace humanists of his time, perhaps one of the foremost" (*Rabelais and His World* 453).

In focusing on the life of his father and son protagonists, Rabelais, the master of grotesque and satire, prefigures in his double proto-novel of formation certain thematic elements of the Bildungsroman literary system, in particular that of fictional biography, and especially the concern with education and its role in subject formation from childhood to maturity, which offers some dynamism to the developmental process. Pedagogical sources and perspectives are multiple and reflect mainly Rabelais's own ideas on various aspects of existence as well as his biography. Gargantua's famous letter to Pantagruel in Book Two, Chapter 8, contains such ideas in their theoretical expression and is also a piece of self-confession, philosophy, and prescriptive-moralizing discourse. Another example comes from Book 1, Chapter 24. The narrator, depicting young Gargantua's studies under the guidance of Ponocrates, declares: "Instead of herborizing, they would inspect the shops of druggists, herbalists and apothecaries, studiously examining the sundry fruits, roots, leaves, gums, seeds and exotic unguents and learning how they could be diluted or adulterated. He viewed jugglers, mountebanks and medicasters ... carefully observing their tricks and gestures, their agile capers and smooth oratory. His favorites were those from Chauny in Picardy who are born jabberers". This episode of young Gargantua's education, according to Bakhtin, can be interpreted as autobiographical, since Rabelais himself

> studied all these aspects of popular life. Let us stress that popular spectacles and popular medicine, herbalists and druggists, hawkers of magic unguents and quacks, could be seen side by side. There was an ancient connection between the forms of medicine and folk art which explains the combination in one person of actor and druggist. This is why the images of the physician and the medical element are organically linked in the novel with the entire traditional system of images. In the previous quotation we see medicine and the theater displayed side by side in the marketplace. (*Rabelais and His World* 159)

A substantial part in a young person's education is also attributed to games, which Ponocrates does not exclude from young Gargantua's education: they devote themselves to painting and sculpture, the ancient custom of playing dice, and while playing, they would often recall the ancient authors who mentioned this game; therefore, games are not a part of ordinary life but instead recall knowledge and contain philosophical meanings. In Gargantua's education, an important role is played even by feasts and banquets, with their images of people eating and drinking; as we have seen, even Gargantua's grotesque birth takes place during a banquet and the feast of cattle slaughter.

At the beginning of modernity, Rabelais also prefigures Goethe's formula of identity formation for Wilhelm Meister as encapsulated in the principles of humanism that promote "an ideal image of the multilateral and harmoniously developed man" (Auerbach 275). This image, supported by the late medieval notions of the perfect courtier and ideal knight, is essential to the humanist ideal of universal man. Auerbach wonders whether Rabelais "believed that a perfect culture consists in the mastery of all sciences; that universality would be the sum of all the specialized types of knowledge; and perhaps he took seriously, in this sense, the supra-realist educative programme of Gargantua" (275).

The dynamic feature of the character textualized within a process of character development is, to us, perhaps even more vivid in the picaresque novel in which education and pedagogical principles are often superseded by the protagonist's larger, social interaction. The literary concern with the character's experience of life representing a developmental/formative process reveals here, as in Rabelais, its incipient stage: it has already become a matter of narrative and thematic organization, but there are still the adventurous time and the travel scheme that dominate the fictional perspective.

Travel suggests an experience of life as a temporal and spatial movement through different components of the social setting, which provides both a realist and a satirical outlook based on action, analysis and self-analysis of the main character. Travel is also governed by the picaro's need to support his living and by his spirit of adventure; the latter, actually, dominates the narration and suggests that for the particular kind of character development as expressed in picaresque fiction, action counts more than welfare. The picaresque discourse uses the autobiographical form as another premise or principle of the developmental process. A first-person narrative recounts and assesses the experience of life of a character from childhood through youth and maturity to old age, and sometimes along with various changes of his inner life; for instance, from idealism and indulging in wishful thinking in youth to reason and pragmatism in old age. The development of the character is thus linked to both biological growth and the progress of psychological and sentimental activities, the latter as a result of a great number of changing and often contrasting circumstances and events, stimuli and conditions from beyond the hero's inner existence.

The narrative organization of the picaresque novel consists of a succession of different events/adventures – such as encounter, arrest, separation, escape, sudden acquisition and waste, robbery, as well as institutionalized and/or self-education, professional initiation, love affairs, ordeal by love, and others – which are coloured with both pure humour and irony. Satire often reveals the more or less explicit critical outlook of the picaro (sometimes the same as the narrator's, but almost always identified with the author's) on his milieu and generally the external world.

The picaresque mode of writing originated in Spain and influenced a significant number of Renaissance writers who belong to different cultural backgrounds. In England, in particular, it influenced the fiction of Thomas Nashe, who adapted many features of the anonymous *Lazarillo* to write *The Unfortunate Traveller; or, The Life of Jack Wilton* (1594).

2.2.2 Thomas Nashe

Thomas Nashe (1567-1601) is among those university graduates of the period, such as Robert Greene and John Lyly, who embarked on a literary career to excel as a satirist, pamphleteer, playwright and author of prose fiction after completing his studies at St John's College, Cambridge, in 1586, and after a tour through France and

Italy to settle in London in 1588. As a playwright, Nashe was close to Robert Greene, whom he admired and defended in a pamphlet written after his friend's death (namely in *Four Letters Confuted*, 1593) but his name is also present as co-author with Marlowe on the title-page of *The Tragedy of Dido Queen of Carthage* (1594). He is probably also the author of *The Isle of Dogs*, a play performed in 1597 but soon lost after being suppressed by the Privy Council which searched Nashe's house and arrested several suspected authors, among whom Ben Jonson. Definitely Nashe's is *Summer's Last Will and Testament* (1592), a play written for private performance and rooted in classical motifs as well as those from folk drama, which, apart from *The Unfortunate Traveller*, is his most admired work.

Mixing the contemporary fashionable euphuism with personal bitter attack, Nashe produced satires focused on literature of the period, rising against either artificiality in romances (*The Anatomy of Absurdity*, 1589) or plagiarism from the ancients (preface to Greene's *Menaphon*, 1589). Some of Nashe's pamphlets are anti-Puritan (for instance, *An Almond for a Parrot*, 1590) but most of them represent replies in the pamphlet war between Nashe and the Harvey brothers, Richard and Gabriel, which could be brought to an end only in 1599 when their books were ordered to be confiscated by a special decree. Showing a distrust of foreigners and a dislike of Puritans, employing burlesque, fantasy and imaginative flight, portraying grotesque figures and mixing linguistic sophistication with colloquial diction, Nashe's prose, including in *The Unfortunate Traveller, or the Life of Jacke Wilton*, reveals the lack of structural coherence.

The fiction of Thomas Nashe, displaying violence in its thematic treatment and disconnection in its structural organization, was influenced by the picaresque mode of writing, originated in Spain, which marked the work of a significant number of writers of Renaissance belonging to different cultural backgrounds. *The Unfortunate Traveller* is a precursor of the picaresque novel with certain experiments in realism, where the protagonist's account of his adventures represents "a certain kind of an appendix or page belonging or appertaining in or unto the confines of the English court". The reader's view of manners and events is controlled by Jack's vigorous and various first-person narration and by his generally unflattering observation, and it is not just what Jack sees, but how he sees.

The Unfortunate Traveller, despite its unfixed picaresque structure, is credited as the first English picaresque novel. This novel or proto-novel is also acclaimed for its experiments in realism, but disliked for its loosely constructed frame of episodes. Faithful to the picaresque disconnection and fragmentariness, the episodic structure is assembled as a sequence of events, travels, adventures, misfortunes, and various narrative fragments, by the voice of an autodiegetic narrator who recounts them as recollections of past experiences with comic commentary and wit. Experimenting with style and bringing lexical novelty, Nashe allows his narrators to express themselves in ways that correspond to their social condition and the incoherent and disorienting circumstances in which their life experiences occur.

Proving the superiority of his wit, Nashe's nominal hero-narrator controls the reader's views on events, displays vigorous and unflattering observation, and is delighted by his tricks, which he regards as achievements, wishes that his actions could be "booked in order as they were begotten", while reflecting upon them: "This was one of my famous achievements, insomuch as I never light upon the like famous fool. But I have done a thousand better jests, if they had been booked in order as they were begotten. It is pity posterity should be deprived of such precious records; and yet there is no remedy; and yet there is too, for when all fails, well fare a good memory".

The events are fictive but credible and they owe their verisimilitude to the employment of several techniques. First, Nashe's hero Jack Wilton, an English page and indeed a rogue and hardly "a Gentleman at least", is aggressive, digressive, and drunk, allowing – contrary to the early Spanish picaresque tales – no repentance, regret or atonement in a world of crisis, chaos and violence, where drinking and defiance side with wit to become a means of escapism as well as of dealing with a horrible reality. In his immorality, he voyeuristically watches a rape "thorough a crannie of my upper chamber unseeled", and records two executions in Rome after claiming that "Ile make short worke, for I am sure I have wearyed all my readers".

Second, intermingled with the fictional material is the historical one of real historical people and events, which also grants the narrative a certain degree of veracity. The novel glances with nostalgia at the age of Henry VIII, "the onely true subject of Chronicles", the promoter of chivalry and martial arts, and refers to many contemporary social and historical realities. Accompanying Henry Howard, earl of Surrey, a real historical figure, in his sentimental endeavours for Geraldine, a beautiful Florentine woman, Jack Wilton, Howard's fictional travel companion and the novel's character-narrator in his journey, is involved in various adventures in Italy, Germany, and France, where Italy with its Venice and Florence is presented as the centre of European civilization, culture, and arts. In a typical picaresque mode of narration, the character's spatial movement is a pretext to provide a complex picture of the contemporary late sixteenth-century culture, mores, mentality, as well as social realities, history and politics, and to comment on these and other aspects. Jack witnesses the massacre of Baptists in Germany, meets Erasmus and More in Rotterdam, and along with these history-based experiences, Jack is involved in Howard's quest to defend the honour of his beloved lady in a tournament in Italy. Howard returns to England, and Jack continues his adventures, quests and ordeals, wanderings and sufferings, yet learning little and remaining essentially static, and pursuing his own sentimental experience with Diamante, whom he eventually marries. Although Italy is ahead of Europe, they finally escape "the Sodom of Italy", its immorality and political crisis, and as in a cyclical type of life experience, at the end they are back at the English military encampment in France where the story actually began.

Mixing genres and combining tradition and novelty, fantasy, often grotesque, and realism, sophisticated diction and colloquial inventiveness, the prose of the period slowly began to nuance clearly its two distinct and common types of which one is to be fiction or imaginative prose, for instance Nashe's picaresque novel or Lyly's prose romances, and another as non-fiction, excelling in philosophical works, essays, councils, critical treatises, historical writings, and so on. Apart from Thomas Nashe with his *The Unfortunate Traveller, or the Life of Jack Wilton*, the prose of the time includes Francis Bacon (1561-1626), the author of the famous *Essays or Counsels Civil and Moral* (1597, 1625), containing 58 counsels, and the unfinished philosophic and literary utopia *The New Atlantis* (1626); John Lyly (1554-1606), who wrote *Euphues, or the Anatomy of Wit* (1579) and *Euphues and his England* (1580) – the peculiar style of these works received the name "Euphuism"; and the so-called "realistic novels" of Robert

Greene (1558-1592 – *Mamilia* (1583), *Pandosto* (1588), *Menophon* (1589), Thomas Deloney (1543-1600) – *Jack of Newbury* (1597) and *Thomas of Reading* (1598).

2.3 The Elizabethan and Jacobean Drama

Apart from Humanism governing the intellectual background, drama, representing the literary field, is the crown of the Renaissance art in England and the name which is commonly associated with it is that of William Shakespeare.

The rise of drama in English literature occurred with the mysteries, moralities, and interludes in the fifteenth century; during Renaissance, it became the principal genre, its development going on throughout the first half of the sixteenth century as to flourish and dominate the literary scene during the Elizabethan Era, named after the Queen of this name, Elizabeth I (1558-1603), and Jacobean Era, named after James I (1603-1625).

Shakespeare's period overlaps largely with these two periods, but a more attentive diachronic consideration would name Greene, Peele, Kyd, Lyly, and Marlowe as representatives of the Elizabethan drama and include Chapman, Beaumont, Fletcher, and Jonson in Jacobean drama.

Some 250 plays were produced during Shakespeare's period, of which he wrote 38, which indicates that in his time, Shakespeare was one author among many others who knew each other, learned from each other, and worked both in collaboration and competition, sharing parts of a play, as well as themes and ideas, and even accommodation, like Kyd and Marlowe did. The most important writing partnership is perhaps that of Francis Beaumont and John Fletcher.

The dramatists would collaborate by actually dividing a play into scenes and writing it as a group; they would also imitate and borrow from each other and from their own text: for example, it is known that Shakespeare borrowed the line "set down the load" from the anonymous *King John* (c. 1588) in his *Richard III* and later in *As You Like It*. Since he also borrowed, it is a mistake to assume that Shakespeare's plays are original, this stereotype existing on the premises that he is the greatest of all and his works are more familiar.

2.3.1 Origins, Features, and Typology

To revert to the discussion of the Renaissance drama and theatre, in general, the main point is that apart from its aesthetic dimension, undoubtedly of high value and standard, the Elizabethan and Jacobean drama, covering largely the historical period between the 1550s and 1630s, represents an important artistic industry, consumerist and urban, involving smaller or larger groups of writers and actors writing and performing plays for a commercial theatre located in a particular city.

This commercial sector of the drama production flourished due to various opportunities for the poets and other authors to write for the stage. First, the years between 1575 and 1577 saw the foundation of commercial theatre in London by the appearance of permanent, purpose-built playhouses, namely the Theatre in 1576 and the Curtain in 1577. Second, the need for plays, since the new playhouses would require to perform a different play each day during a year, where, according to a written record from the 1590s, some 30 plays, not all of them new, were presented in rotation. Third, theatre started to represent a major investment of capital, which gave drama a stable institutional and economic infrastructure. Fourth, actors changed from strolling, travelling persons into businessmen and professional players related to a company. Fifth, related to the institutional stability of the professional theatre, is the phenomenon of patronage, which was made a legal requirement by the 1572 Act; before, actors were assembled in groups of players by aristocrats for their private, household entertainment or for the royal court, whereas now, the actors belong to a legal entity established as an officially recognized institution in the social structure. Also, particularly London theatre companies would tend towards patronage of the crown – the queen herself became the patron of a band of actors in 1583 – and senior courtiers for both higher financial reward and security in the face of puritans and other antagonists. Sixth, this growing connection to authority, however, led to censorship, where by the 1590s, there was a Master of the Revels responsible for selecting the plays to be performed at the court. In spite of rigid censorship and control from the court and the church, and the city authorities that firstly opposed theatre on grounds of morality and order, theatre developed and flourished as a new public professional theatre to become the crown of English Renaissance art and achieve a popularity equal to romance in medieval period or novel nowadays.

Apart from this commercial theatre (or playhouse drama), representing the commercial aspect of the drama industry, there are other kinds of theatre, for instance those which began as part of an educational movement and which can be generically called **academic theatre** (or university drama).

Unlike the commercial stage – more money-oriented as well as more professional, and, at the same time, a part of the "capital's entertainment scene" – the academic stage would provide rather amateur performances and, although, like commercial drama, displaying its own aspects of financial enrichment and entertainment or recreation, academic drama focuses primarily on educational and pedagogic tasks. Related to (1) university or academic drama are (2) school drama and (3) choirboy theatre. The amateur performances of the choirboy theatre would be done by choirboys or choirboy actors, a kind of boy companies performing in public under the supervision and for the financial gain of masters (a recorded name is that of Sebastian Westcott, the master of the choir school attached to St Paul's Cathedral). The university drama and school drama, also on an amateur level, would be performed by school and especially university students as part of the university curriculum. For this, there would be a return to the ancients, endeavours to revive the ancient cultural tradition, first the works of Terence and Seneca, and then of other classics, followed by attempts at originality to produce new plays by the university proctors and students, or schoolmasters, who turned dramatists. The amateur performances of the university, school, and choir types of drama display clear purposes: (1) be a part of the course of study, (2) develop rhetorical skills of the students, (3) a means of entertainment, and (4) financial profit for the school or university officials.

The academic theatre and commercial theatre, although in competition, were interrelated, but neither academic or university drama nor school and choirboy drama could achieve the success, in matters of both economic benefit and aesthetic validity, of the professional commercial theatre. The academic, school and choirboy theatre, with its erratic history, saw the interest of the public lost, or its being suppressed for political satire and sexual expression, or some of its authors having no real writing talent or theatrical inclination, or its entering under the authority of the Master of the Revels and becoming part of the commercial theatre. For instance, Marlowe and Greene were university graduate to become professional dramatists; other university men or university-wits turning dramatists were Lyly and Nashe; Stephen Gosson moved from study at Oxford to play-writing in London; Chapman and Jonson had professional experience with the adults but also moved to boy companies when they reopened. Non-university dramatists were Kyd and Shakespeare, but their contribution to the aesthetic as well as commercial value of Elizabethan and Jacobean drama is immeasurable.

The emergence of the commercial theatre of the playhouse, the rise of the academic stage, the foundation of dramatic companies, the legal establishment of patronage, and the establishment of permanent playhouses are among the contemporary cultural circumstances which constitute the primary origin of Elizabethan drama. Other origins would be various social institutions or economic entities supporting writing and production to fulfil their desires and needs. Others, of more artistic and literary types, would be ancient traditions, ideas and themes influencing the rising modern creativity in drama; also, the continuation of its earlier autochthonous development, particularly interludes and allegorical moralities; and, not the least, contemporary Italian sources.

Indeed, concerning the last origin, early Elizabethan prose was dominated by translations from Italian literary sources and the Elizabethan playwrights would reshape thematically and transform structurally prose fiction into plays. This piece of information, which is rather correct, comes to us in 1582 from Stephen Gosson, a former professional playwright who embraced puritanism and embarked on a successful ecclesiastical career but remained in the literary field and turned a skilled prose writer disclosing a coherent style, a clear sense of narrative, and a patterned way of exhibiting and arguing on the ideas. He is mostly known in the history of critical thinking rather than in literary history and this is in relation to both his status as a critic and the first modern text of literary criticism in England, which is *An Apology for Poetry* (or *The Defence of Poesy*) by Philip Sidney. Previously a successful scriptwriter for theatre, Gosson raises now a rather anti-drama and anti-theatre voice and declares drama to have emerged indirectly from English Reformation – in particular, the Elizabethan Settlement of 1559 – where the conversion from Catholicism to Protestantism gave a boost to the spiritual health of England, but, argues, Gosson, the "shows" were on the evil's side which "inspired men devices to set them out, the better thereby to enlarge his dominion and pull us from God". The end of drama, according to the puritan Gosson siding with Plato, is extreme melancholy, idle hedonism, useless knowledge, lies, and, especially, "sinful delight"; these accusations would be gracefully and argumentatively answered by Sidney siding with Aristotle and Horace and relying on the principles of *catharsis* and *utile et dulce*.

In the last decade of the sixteenth century, English theatre was in a very experimental phase, as most theatrical companies struggled to capture the attention of the audience and, even though the fascination with the classical writers and genres continued, many playwrights took great liberty with the boundaries of different forms of drama, using the space of the stage in order to explore all sorts of dramatic possibilities. The mark of experimentation is vivid in the plays of John Lyly, Thomas Kyd, Christopher Marlowe, and William Shakespeare; the playwrights of the period, though extremely alert to the demands of classical genres, chose to explore various opportunities which emerged with the fusion of modes and different sorts of rhetoric, a fact which led inevitably to the formation of some hybrids rather than the much desired generic purity of the classics. This tendency to seek a suitable style in drama is captured very well in Shakespeare's play *Hamlet*, when Polonius remarks that "The best actor in the world for tragedy, comedy, history, pastoral, pastoral comic, historical pastoral, scene individable, or poem unlimited. Seneca cannot be too heavy or Plautus too light..." (*Hamlet*, Act II, scene 2, 400).

But the awareness and joy experienced by the dramatists of the period as a result of hybridisation of genres is not shared by the critics of the period. Philip Sidney expressed clearly his complaint regarding this lack of respect for the principles of drama, claiming that the Elizabethan playwrights produce works which are "neither right tragedies, nor right comedies (...) but [they] thrust in clowns by head and shoulders, to play a part in majestical matters, with neither decency nor discretion, so as neither the admiration and commiseration, nor the right sportfulness, is by their mongrel tragic-comedy o btained".

Ignoring this criticism, the English playwrights continued to deliberately mingle different genres, and even though they found a predilection in the mixed modes in their dramaturgies, three broad types were mostly cultivated in the period: **tragedy**, **comedy**, and **history play**.

Tragedy

The traditional distinction between **tragedy** and **comedy** was well established already in Greek and Roman drama and, with the import of the ancient models in Renaissance, this clear distinction seemed to be well known by the Renaissance dramatists too.

Tragedy is centred on the dramatic portrayal of *suffering* of a great man, capable of displaying his excellence to an entire community (*arête*), who experiences the fall from fortune as a consequence of his pride (*hybris*) or a fatal flaw or error in judgement (*hamartia*). The reversal in fortune (*peripeteia*) is followed by the recognition or self-awareness (*anagnoris*), a crucial moment in the protagonist's development, as he acquires substantial insight through suffering and comes to acknowledge the things in life as "they are". Almost invariably, the tragic hero's understanding of his own potential and limits as well as his position in the universe is followed by the protagonist's death, a moment which, according to Aristotle, is expected to produce a **cathartic effect** in audiences, triggered by **fear** and **pity** towards the protagonist's experience of immense suffering. In his *Poetics*, Aristotle insisted that tragedy must focus on an individual of a special social prominence whose fall is terrible, yet unquestionably just, as the moment of the protagonist's fall or death is used for **moral reflections** upon virtue, justice and order, and the suffering or punishment of the protagonist confers opportunity to explore some ultimate questions about men and divinity, about the moral framework of human life in the face of such fundamental issues as free will versus destiny or the confrontation with limits of human condition. Hence, the punishments for arrogance, excessive pride, or overreaching were emblematic for the re-establishment of the lost equilibrium and always conferred hope in justice for the future of the entire community.

Tragedy inevitably delivers a message, which is "moralistic rather than moral" (Moseley 61), resulting from the larger than life protagonists' confrontations with major questions of human existence, such as motivation, choice, human dignity, self-knowledge, and human condition. Robert N. Watson explains that

> Tragedy characteristically reminds its spectators of something they share and commonly struggle to forget: the progress from aspiration to death, from moments that promise glory (even if they are only the infantile fantasies of omnipotence) to eventual surrender (even if it is only the banal fact of mortality). Tragedy also attunes itself to the sharings of primal guilt, in the practice of ritual sacrifice it essentially re-enacts, as well as in durable parables like that of Oedipus. (294)

Elizabethan playwrights were not much familiar with the Greek dramatists, but they knew the classical principles of Aristotle's poetics and they tried to implement the classical principles of drama in their tragedies, especially the principles dramatized in the tragedies of the Roman poet Seneca. The fascination with Seneca's tragedies in England led to their frequent performance in schools and universities, which resulted in the creation of a vogue imitated by the English dramatists in their plays. It implied high rhetoric, grand manner of display of the English dramatic utterance, with plots typically concerned with revenge, the inclusion of supernatural phenomena and a display of bloody violence.

Even though the Elizabethan playwrights were aware of the Greek tragic models mostly through the prism of Seneca's plays, it would be wrong to assume that they worked on a certain blueprint of what tragedy should be like. Living in a period of transition, the Renaissance playwrights experienced first-hand the changing concept of tragedy and the set of values which it implied. Definitely, the Elizabethan and Jacobean drama evolved not only from the classical models, some of its roots deriving also from local and immediate influences.

First, recent scholarship emphasises the influence of Christian cycles of mystery plays and later morality plays, such as *Everyman* (c. 1500) and *Mankind* (c. 1465), which were very popular in the Middle Ages in northern Europe. The easily recognizable parables of temptation, vice versus virtue, sin and redemption, which were central to medieval drama, become strong metaphors in Marlowe's and Shakespeare's plays, through which the ethical or didactic messages are conveyed.

Second comes the impact of the popular stories of revenge and usurpation, blended with the highly rising vogue of Seneca's paradigm, which led to the creation of a sub-genre known as **revenge tragedy**. This type of tragedy reveals an acute moral dilemma, which presents the concern with justice and, inevitably, the demand for the punishment of the offender, but it also offers an opportunity for reflection upon the degree of culpability of the avenger as a result of committing the vindictive act. From Shakespearean repertory, *King Lear* and *Macbeth* bear significant elements of revenge and usurpation, but most powerfully they are illustrated in *Hamlet*, where the dilemma confronted by the protagonist represents best the moment of transition of values and sense of morality, since the justice performed by an individual is considered to be a sacred act in antiquity, but it clashes completely with the Christian demand for mercy and patience and the principles of Humanism which were widespread in Renaissance.

Third, Elizabethan and Jacobean tragedy evolved from its own cultural peculiarities, its own distinctive religious and political concerns. Most of the tragedies written in this period are not simply some stories about outstanding individuals whose tragic flaws lead them to their fall; they emerge from and respond to the shifting constitutional and ideological principles, combined with the anxieties of their own age. The increasing scepticism concerning the natural and supernatural order in the universe merged with the preoccupations about a social and political order, and it brought to the reconsideration of overreaching and hierarchical design. Indeed, the medieval concept of the "Great Chain of Being", according to which every existing thing in the universe has its "place" in a divinely prescribed hierarchical order, still held validity, as humans were expected to act rationally, without going beyound one's proper place. Well aware of his "place" between angels and beasts, human being is fascinated by the thought of going beyond the boundaries set by the chain of being. The Italian philosopher Pico della Mirandola, in a work entitled *On the Dignity of Man*, explains that through philosophical contemplation human being is capable of rising towards the angelic state. However, regardless of the fascinating premise of going beyond one's place, there was always the awareness of "disorder" which this act would presuppose, most worrying being the political ramifications which this possibility would present, and, for the political rulers, it was convenient to reinforce the belief in one's place. But in this period of crisis, such widely accepted traditional concepts as the "Great Chain of Being" and the theory of "correspondences", which maintained the authority and validity of the order between all living things, become questioned, the new changes assuming now different values, like man's abilities and achievements and his role in society. As Stephen Regan explains, the tragedy of Shakespearean period "has important social origins and social repercussions; it emerges not from the failings of solitary individuals, but from the interactions of those individuals with prevailing structures of power" (82-83). Christopher Marlowe's *Dr Faustus* is an example of a character who tests his boundaries especially because he is a man proving exceptional abilities and achievements.

Fourth, the idea of guaranteed salvation through the performance of good deeds is challenged by the Reformation spirit, and also questioned becomes the concept of God's mercy. Rather than relying on the promise of divine mercy, the exploration of one's conscience is encouraged, assisted by the certainty that only in this manner can an individual clear his conscience and his own guilt. The more the human conscience is explored, the clearer the fluctuations from the dignity of man to the wickedness of man are acknowledged. In *Tamburlaine*, Marlowe brings about a very appealing and refreshing attitude regarding the boundless potential of human being, as his hero creates himself and his own destiny contrary to all social and divine opposition. Martin Wiggins clarifies that in the drama of this period, the hero fails "to realize his full human potential, either because of the kind of the world he lives in or the kind of self he makes through his own actions" (49). Thus, exploring human conscience and human potential in the light of the humanistic view of man gave rise to some mostly tragic characters who acknowledge the great disappointment in human being. Among

Shakespeare's tragic heroes, this disillusionment is explicitly expressed by Hamlet: "What a piece of work is a man! How noble in reason, how infinite in faculty, in form and moving how express and admirable, in action how like and angel, in apprehension how like a god – the beauty of the world, the paragon of animals!" (Act 2, scene 2, 305-9). The exploration of the human potential together with the human conscience led to the awareness that the man could rise in the cosmic hierarchy of the Great Chain of Being to the perfection of divinity, but, as a result of overreaching, excessive ambition, jealousy or desire for power, man can easily degenerate to the ranks of the beasts. As Hamlet observes, the man could be a Hyperion or a satyr, the choice being always of the individual. Such deep reflections on human nature as well as on the sense of guilt confer a specific peculiarity and unprecedented complexity to Renaissance tragedy.

It would be wise to consider that the Elizabethan and Jacobean dramatists, especially Shakespeare, "used the stage as a 'laboratory' in which the question of man's identity could be tried out in an experimental manner" (Fisher-Lichte 54). The tragic poets of Renaissance focused mostly on the conflict of values rather than on the character's personality and, while exploring new situations and new questions, it frequently brought about a tragic conflict which is generated mostly by their culture. As Robert N. Watson explains, "the chief consolation at the end of many Renaissance tragedies is the recognition that the hero has reasserted his or her personal will and identity in the very face of death" (300).

History

As most of the plays of the late sixteenth and early seventeenth centuries were primarily designed as commercial ventures, it signified that the playwrights had the task of dramatizing the stories which would appeal to varied tastes in order to draw the crowds to theatre. Historical characters and events fascinated Renaissance men, with their constant focus on politics and rule, and although Roman, Eastern or Western European historical events appealed to the mind of Elizabethans, the subjects related to Medieval English history proved mostly captivating to them. Certainly, Edward Hall's *The Union of the Two Noble and Illustre Families of Lancaster and York* (1547) and Raphael Holinshed's *Chronicles of England, Scotland, and Ireland* (1577) served as great sources of inspiration for the Renaissance playwrights, bringing to the creation of a vogue in theatre at the end of the sixteenth century. Christopher Marlowe contributed to the popularisation of this genre in the professional theatre, but Shakespeare is the playwright who established the trend of dramatizing history on stage.

The rise of the interest in recording history in all ways possible corresponded to the historical event of 1588, when the English fleet defeated the Spanish Invincible Armada, which contributed to the formation of a national awareness, accompanied by a strong sense of national pride. Therefore, "the dramatists recognized the signs and times: the history play seemed excellently suited to satisfy the growing need to see England's national greatness celebrated and, equally, to warn impressively of the dangers which could grow out of national ignorance and complacency" (Fischer-Lichte 55). But while the representation of English history confirmed and encouraged the spectator's feelings of national awareness, it was difficult for the playwrights of the period to choose what event in history and how to represent it on stage, given that possible parallels could be drawn between their current sovereign and a historical character. Such parallel was visible between the events of Richard II's last years of life and the aging queen Elizabeth, whereas in the rebellion of Bolingbroke, Essex's betrayal was echoed.

History frequently presents irreconcilable paradoxes, and there were some challenges met by the playwrights concerning the representation of the past. Two main models of past were available to Renaissance men: the Classical model of cyclical time and the Jewish linear model of time.

The first model views history as perpetually cyclic, revealing one's beginning, growth, decay, collapse, and then new beginning. Such a mode of past saw kings, lords and statesmen emerging to power in order to meet later their downfall. The ancient concept of the "Wheel of Fortune" stresses out the impermanence and mutability in a world where everything and everyone is in a transition from delusive prosperity to misfortune and inevitable death. This model of history presents the world as constantly untrustworthy, questioning the limits of motivation, free will, human dignity, and self-knowledge.

The second, linear paradigm, views time against this permanent premise of an end, and is developed mostly by the Church, which sees time in the passage from Eden to Apocalypse, where all things perish to allow the emergence of new heaven and new earth. This teleological (Greek *telos* meaning "end") view of time, in which only the ending makes sense, is frequently emulated in the Renaissance plays, where God punishes in the end all acts of injustice. The plays which depict this model of time stress out the taking away of agency from human being and his subjection to a divine order, depriving one completely of free will and choice and questioning every merit of the worldly eminence.

However, instead of simply dramatizing the great men who appear insignificant, guilty and temporary, the playwrights of the period reveal how one transcends mortality through fame. This attitude presents how history matters because it perpetrates fame. By representing history on stage, an educative message was conveyed: "Morally famous actions are to inspire emulation, infamous ones aversion" (Womack 69).

The representation of the two models of history in the plays of Elizabethan and Jacobean drama shaped history plays into a mould similar to that of tragedies, as these hybrids also presented insights into human condition, exploring frequently the ironies of choice in Fortune in a world of randomness and mutability. Moreover, the uncertainties and anxieties concerning their future, triggered by the heirless aging queen Elizabeth I or the rise to the English throne of James VI of Scotland, produced histories and tragedies with an atmosphere of the "end-of-the-world", in which apocalypse might be the only "promised end" to confer hope in a disintegrated world.

Renaissance history plays, though stylistically varied, explore some common concerns which reveal the problematic essence of early modern kingship. All these plays reflect on the preoccupation with succession and the historical causation. Some historical events are represented in terms of divine providence, whereas others as the result of human actions.

First, especially in Shakespeare's histories, the identity of the king is explored, bringing once again to the centre of everyone's attention the widespread concept of the "King's Two Bodies", which was formulated by the Elizabethan scholar Edmund Plowden in 1588. Plowden explains that the king incorporates two bodies: a Body natural and a Body politic. The Body natural represents the mortal Body, which is subject to frailty, human or natural; the Body politic consists of Policy and Government and, since it was constituted for the Direction of the People and the Management of public welfare, it is immune to frailty brought by age, accident, or imbecilities. Whatever choices are made or acts taken in the hypostasis of the Body politic, it cannot be invalidated by any insufficiency of the natural Body. Respectively, there is never the Death of the King, the only possibility is the Demise of the King, where the Body politic becomes transferred and conveyed over from the now dead Body natural to another Body natural. This concept of the two bodies of the king creates some ambiguities, since in the situation of succession, the body politic is legitimately transferred to another member of the royal family due to the frailty of Body natural, but, concomitantly, this situation allows another Body natural, which is a member of the royal family, to fulfil the duties of the king, therefore illegitimately making claim upon Body politic. It is not surprising that the plays of the period abound in such themes as usurpation and betrayal, each time loaded with uncertainties concerning the position of the king, whether resulting from human effort or divine providence. Especially in Shakespearean history plays, the role of the king is explored vastly, and such historical characters as Henry VI or Richard II are viewed in their status of usurpers or legitimate kings, demystifying monarchical rule in quite a radical manner.

The **second** concern, which is much considered in the drama of the period, is the "Politics of Machiavellianism", a concept which derives its name from the popular work of Machiavelli, *The Prince* (1513). The Renaissance men were both fascinated and scandalized by the treatment of power which Machiavelli encourages, since, according to the Italian thinker, all means are justified for a Prince in order to stay as a Prince or achieve whatever purpose is set by him. Drawing upon multiple examples from ancient history, Machiavellian politics ignores altogether any grand philosophical or theological design, disregards the teleological significance, and "simply concentrates on people, on what people do, and on the minutiae of what motivates people to behave as they did" (Moseley 59). This model of politics encourages duplicity, and, in order to secure the power in the kingdom, the ruler relies on totally amoral political actions. The Machiavellian ruler instils fear upon his subjects, and in a twisted quest for knowledge, encourages eavesdropping, deception, and betrayal. Distorting completely the concept of "free will", the Machiavellian ruler deliberately sets his own course of action, self-determining his position in the state as a result of deceptive practices. This spirit is best exemplified in Shakespeare's Polonius, but certainly Claudius is a more successful operator of this kind of politics.

The **third** concern in the plays of the period represents the opposition between appearance and reality, much stimulated by the deceptive nature of life at the court and also by the growing awareness of the relativity of human perception. Respectively, it divulges the tension between the individual as an authentic being and actor and the role he/she plays in order to construct a duplicitous reality. The history plays portray the king in his "role", capable of wearing the costume and the props designed for a king, but unaware of how to be a genuine king. It is in this discrepancy that some historical figures are viewed as usurpers, since they are only capable of playing the role of the king rather than genuinely being one.

Comedy

In Shakespearean times, the Aristotelian principles of comedy were mostly known through the elaborations of medieval and Renaissance writers. Comedy was mostly viewed as a genre set to represent lower types of characters, to ridicule the deformities and misconducts of men and women, and to deliver an example of virtue to the audience by providing a negative illustration of behaviour. But even though the Renaissance dramatists knew the generic norms of comedy, regarding structure, plot, and moral input, they mostly ignored those norms, bending the generic boundaries in order to fit their agenda. Since there was a fierce competition between rival companies seeking to win over audiences, the dramatic principles of comedy used by the playwrights were quite flexible, frequently incorporating the most popular modes which brought exceptional innovation and variety.

G. K. Hunter stresses out the fused matrices and paradigms of the Elizabethan and Jacobean comedy, defining it as "a spectrum of comic forms running from the dynamic at one end to the static at the other" (31). Hunter continues to explain comedy as an interaction between plot and character, with the plot dominating in farce, whereas character dominating in romance. Rather than providing an explanation of Renaissance comedy, this description stresses out mostly the miscellaneous nature of the plays of the period. True, the emergence of new genres out of the fusion of old ones is not a complete novelty, Plautus and Ovid providing good examples of this phenomenon. The writers of Renaissance comedy indulge completely in the generic metamorphoses, blending some ingredients of most popular comic modes in order to satisfy the horizon of expectations of the audience.

Clearly, Renaissance comedy relies much upon Roman models, Plautus and Terence being unquestionable sources of inspiration for the English playwrights. The type of comedy developed by these Roman dramatists is known as "New Comedy", or "comedy of manners". New Comedy is primarily domestic in its focus and its major concerns centring around the issues of money, property, family squabbles, and so on. Some stock characters created by the Greeks and then Romans include adulterous husband, the clever servant, the nagging wife, the squanderer mistress, the concupiscent son, the boastful soldier, and others. As New Comedy incorporated easily some elements of satire, it became a convenient vehicle for the dramatists to disseminate some moral lessons on virtue or proper conduct and to ridicule the wrong one. This type of comedy was appealing to those Renaissance dramatists who were interested on the imitation of the classical models. They also found this form attractive because of the degree of naturalism which it displayed, providing a world of recognizable characters, settings, and situations. The setting of a street, a market square or a facade of a mansion presented an opportunity for the emergence of a conflict bound to domestic spectrum, which, though unexpected, would always be resolvable. Coincidences occurred frequently, but they never broke the credibility of the event.

Opposite to the conventions of New Comedy stands another comic type, known as "Popular Comedy". Being loosely scripted, it allowed a great deal of improvisation, which emerged from the interaction with the audience, local allusions, singing, dancing, joke-telling, and so on. Since it never followed any particular conventions, it tended to be more spontaneous, colloquial and physical, and a degree of vulgarity, which would not be accepted by the New Comedy, is now embraced by Popular Comedy. From professional wrestling to extravagant display of costumes, the stage had no space for moralising messages, its enjoyment deriving mostly from variety, physical vigour, and spontaneity. The Renaissance playwrights were quick to hold on to some elements of Popular comedy, since women rubbing their buttocks or men's muscles being displayed in a wrestling match fascinated the audience. One would remember Rosalind being swayed off her feet when she sees Orlando in his wrestling combat at the beginning of *As You Like It* pointing to the public standards of decency being abandoned altogether when this type of physical attraction is enjoyed by the spectators. Crude and unexpected, this kind of action provided a good entertainment and attracted spectators to theatre.

Apart from these two types of comedy, highly appealing to the Renaissance tastes is "pastoral drama". Like pastoral literature in general, this type of drama provides an idealized mode of country life, where shepherds and shepherdess meet in nature to discuss happily about love. An important convention of the pastoral drama is the representation of country life from an urban perspective, a standpoint which allows the dramatist to oppose countryside to court, and from this opposition the idealization of country life and the criticism of the urban life and values emerge. Love becomes the major concern of the pastoral drama, where the elements of romance are blended into its structure. Since pastoral drama is set in a non-urban environment, it provides an opportunity for the characters to detach themselves from their customary social roles and temporarily experiment with the opportunities of an alternative life. Hence, the social and political responsibilities are abandoned and, instead of being preoccupied with the restrictions of the city, the characters are only anxious with the demands of the clock. The pastoral setting revitalises the presence of fairies, woodland spirits, enchantment, outstanding coincidences, and so on. Never preoccupied with verisimilitude, pastoral drama encourages an action where anything can occur.

An important theme of pastoral comedy is the exploration of the nature of love. Even though colloquial language of the country folk is present, the play displays a degree of sophistication when love is explored through poetry, music, and song. The elements of pastoral drama are clear visible in *As You Like It*, and Orlando's attempt to write sonnets in order to express his love for Rosalind is a reminiscent of this dramatic mode.

Certainly, all these forms of comedy were available to the Elizabethan playwrights, but in their strife for fame and prominence, they frequently disagreed upon what a "proper" comedy should look like. The rivalry between the dramatists was vehement, some insisting on the moral purpose of comedy, whereas others were adamant concerning its primarily entertaining purpose. Regardless of their aim, the dramatists of the period continued to fuse genres, subgenres, and modes, which brought to an unprecedented plasticity which acquired a protean quality. As Jill Levenson explains, "[many] generic elements mingled within the host form, the myriad configurations producing a remarkable variety of individual comedies" (256).

These myriad configurations are recognizable especially in Shakespeare's comedies, where in some romantic comedies, a powerful dark undercurrent is scattered *(The Merchant of Venice)*, or the spell of magic cast upon lovers and a dream soften the edges of betrayal *(A Midsummer Night's Dream)*, the tragic intensity of lovers is spoilt by the ineptitude of the actors *(A Midsummer Night's Dream)*, and so on. Defying the expectations of the spectators, Shakespeare stripped romantic comedy of some of its conventions, infusing at times some moments of cruelty which both shocked and fascinated the audience. His capacity of infusing into the frame of fairy tale excessive hatred and some cultural tensions increased radically the plays appeal.

It is almost impossible to consider a certain paradigm for Renaissance comedy. However, when it comes to Shakespearean comedy, a pattern could be envisaged. The mostly detected pattern, as Michael Mangan explains, is set by the opposition between "authoritative (even authoritarian) structure and […] something subversive, something which will reject or oppose and potentially undermine that authority" (153). Usually this opposition is represented by the conflict between law and love. A conventional binary opposition discovered in some of Shakespeare's plays is the one between court and country. Such opposition is visible in *As You Like It, A Midsummer Night's Dream,* and *The Winter's Tale*. The court is represented as a punitive and hostile environment, whereas the country is viewed as a place of escape, in which the temporary edenic space is still allowing some possible threats for the itinerants. Another opposition which emerges in the plays is the one between reason and madness. The reason is associated with the law, the state, the power, and, consequently, is frequently viewed as repressive and authoritarian. Due to brutal authority of the court and law, a refuge to country or woods is sought, which is an act equalled to madness, because the traversed space is chaotic and full of perils, but, paradoxically, is liberating and healing for the characters who cross this space. After all, the healing of the itinerants might be the ultimate objective in comedy, since, after traversing through so many perils of court and country, the lovers emerge transformed, as they gain an inner insight which changes their worldview. They eventually return home safely and go back to the identities and roles which they possessed prior to their itinerary, but with a new awareness of the world. Wiggins explains that in a way "it is a process of restoration: the characters' displacement creates a complicated knot of error, disorder, and delusion which is finally unravelled when they regain their true identities" (62). Moreover, the itinerants' return to the court signifies the end of their ordeal and political repression, thus presenting the ultimate harmony not only as a result of love and marriage, but also as a result of healing of a greater error in the state and, respectively, in law.

2.3.2 The Pre-Shakespearean Dramatists

The Elizabethan drama and pre-Shakespearean dramatists represent the next landmark in the English history of literature and are largely identified with the national greatness of the Elizabethan Era or the Age of Spenser (1579-1600), when the entire English nation experienced a sense of supreme confidence and supremacy never experienced before or since in the history of England. The greatness and primacy of the monarch were unchallenged and constituted a fundamental Elizabethan concept, for to Spenser's age the ruler was quite literally the country itself (one may notice how freely Shakespeare designates the King of Denmark as "Denmark", the King of France as "France", or Cleopatra telling Anthony "*I'm dying Egypt*"). Thus, the Elizabethan age saw a nation deriving its spirit and tone from the ruler, hence Spenser's England is glorious because Gloriana (Elizabeth) is its head: the stability of the realm, assured by an able ruler, was an earthly reflection of the essential harmony of the universe.

In their "pioneering period", a critic would distinguish the following kinds of plays: (a) Moralities, represented by John Skelton, who wrote *Magnyfycence*, 1515), John Bedford (*Wyt and Science*, 1530), and an anonymous play *The Four Elements* (1519); (b) Interludes: Henry Medwall (c. 1462-1502), who wrote *Nature* (printed in 1530) and *Fulgens and Lucrece* (1497), and John Heywood (1497-1580), the author of *The Play of the Wether* (1533) and *A Play of Love* (1534), but he later moved nearer to true stage comedy, writing, among others, *The Playe Called the Foure PP* (1544); (c) Comedies: Nicholas Udall (1506-1556), the author of *Ralph Roister Doister* (1553-54), and William Stevenson, who wrote *Gammer Gurton's Needle*; (d) Tragedies, represented by Thomas Sackville's and Thomas Norton's *Gorboduc, or Ferrex and Porrex*, and Thomas Preston's *Life of Cambises* (1569); and (e) Historical plays, represented by John Bole (1495-1563), for example, who wrote *King John* (1561).

There was also a number of other dramatic forms: (a) Revenge Play, which, largely an adaptation of Senecan tragedy to the English stage, seems to have begun with Thomas Kyd's *Spanish Tragedy*, its pattern consisting of an act of revenge coloured with physical violence (it also includes the so-called "Fall of Princes" tragedy, which apparently began with Marlowe's *Tamburlaine*, and the material and scheme of which follows the familiar "Wheel of Fortune" concept in medieval times: the great of the world rise to an apogee through ruthless ambition, and then descend to misery and destruction); (b) Chronicle Play, which probably began with Marlowe's *Edward II* and which is a rather free dramatization of history with the primary purpose of praising the nation's past (frequently the dramatist works his subject into the pattern of Revenge Tragedy or "Fall of Princes" tragedy); (c) Romantic Comedy, where central motif is a love affair, appears to begin with Peele's *Old Wife's Tale* and Greene's *Friar Bacon and Friar Bungay*; and (d) the Masque, a form of dramatic entertainment which combined verse, music, dancing, and scenic effect in about equal proportions. The Masque flourished in England between 1580 and 1630, and represented a special type of drama because it was essentially an aristocratic style of entertainment, especially popular at the royal court. The performers were commonly professional actors, while the masquers themselves, who remained silent, were played by ladies and gentlemen of the court; the subject was often symbolic – the conflict between virtue and vice – or ceremonial, celebrating an important person. The Masque was often preceded by an anti-masque, the content of which was comic and often satirical; and the anti-masque was always performed by professionals.

Pre-Shakespearian drama, apart from a number of anonymous plays (*Woodstock*, 1591-95, *Arden of Feversham*, 1592, and *Edward III*, 1596), includes the great authors Christopher Marlowe, Thomas Kyd, John Lyly, Robert Greene, and Thomas Nashe,

Thomas Lodge, George Peele, and others, of whom Marlowe and Kyd, excelling in writing tragedy, and Lyly, in comedy, exerted considerable influence on Shakespeare.

2.3.2.1 Thomas Kyd

Thomas Kyd (1558-1594) is to the present famous and greatly acclaimed for his *The Spanish Tragedy* (c.1589), one of the first and among the greatest samples of Elizabethan revenge tragedy, modelled largely upon Senecan dramas, although our certainty of Kyd's authorship rests on a short reference in Thomas Heywood's *Apology for Actors* (1612). Critics also believe Kyd to be the author of another play, *Cornelia* (1594), also imitative of Seneca but less original than *The Spanish Tragedy*. Even less is known about Kyd's life, except that, after being born in London and educated at the Merchant Taylors' School, he worked as a scrivener and then in the service of some lord; associated with Marlowe, Kyd's arrest for heresy followed in 1593, which resulted in being tortured and the premature death soon after his release.

Kyd is often compared to Marlowe in matters of the thematic perspectives in their tragedies, where, though both are satirical and ironic, Kyd promotes a *vanitas vanitatum* view on human existence in a world dominated by irrational and capricious forces in which everything has been predestined and the struggle of the characters is in vain; for Marlowe, characters may build their own paths in life through obstacles and discover new foundations for existence, but both paths and foundations ultimately fail; the characters in play by both Kyd and Marlowe are trapped in their life, where Kyd's individual hero is predetermined, whereas Marlowe's is unable to find a proper way. The shepherd Tamburlaine, for example, makes his way in life by the strength of his individual personality, but spiritual dignity turns disagreeable.

2.3.2.2 Christopher Marlowe

Christopher Marlowe (1564-1593), son of a shoemaker in Canterbury, studied by scholarship at Corpus Christi College, Cambridge, to receive his BA in 1584 and MA in 1587. Records of his private life, short as it were, supported by the thematic implications of his works, suggest a rebellious personality, radical and free-thinking, indiscreet and openly defying contemporary social, religious, and moral values, starting his career as an agent in the secret service of the queen and throughout a chaotic existence coloured with blasphemy, atheism, and homosexuality to end prematurely his life in plaque-affected London murdered in a tavern.

Might Marlowe have gone on to write, critics often speculate, English literature had known another dramatist equal to Shakespeare. The beginnings of his dramatic career, at least, looked extremely promising when, in 1587, both parts of *Tamburlaine the Great* delivered on London theatrical scene were an instant success, secured by uncommon character representation strategies, eloquent craftsmanship, and high rhetoric, as well as the great scenic performance of Edward Alleyn, leading actor of the Lord Admiral's Men. The chronological order of his other works and even the authorship of some are difficult to establish.

Apart from *Tamburlaine the Great* (published 1590), Marlowe's other works presumably include tragedies *The Tragedy of Dido, Queen of Carthage* (published 1594 and revealing a return to the classics, its subject being drawn from Virgil's *Aeneid*), *The Famous Tragedy of the Rich Jew of Malta* (c. 1591, viewed more as a grotesque comedy than tragedy), *Massacre at Paris* (c. 1589, survived in a heavily corrupt text), *Edward II* (c.1592, acclaimed for its taking the rough chronicle play into its aesthetic maturation as history play of Shakespeare), *Doctor Faustus* (survived in two corrupt texts of 1604 and 1616), and a long poem – *Hero and Leander* (published 1598) – of some 800 lines written by Marlowe and finished by Chapman.

His scandalous biography aside, Marlowe's great dramatic achievements were (a) "Marlowe's mighty line", as Ben Jonson termed it, and Marlowe's expressive force, elegance, and greatness were to be passed on to Shakespeare; and (b) "The Muses' darling", as Peele termed him. No previous English dramatist had such a sense of theatre, dramatic construction, and stage maneuver, stiring the audience by its true theatricality. Nor since Chaucer had an English literary voice sounded the challenges and glories of living, and Marlowe senses the tragic glory of life, his character being a figure of greatness, endlessly desiring to fight with his own experience of life (not even Shakespeare pictured such a superman, driven by such a desire, or "just as well", say some critics).

Marlowe's greatest dramatic achievement is considered to be *The Tragical Historie of Doctor Faustus* (1592), a "Fall of Princes" tragedy, claimed by scholars to be the last of Marlovian plays. Being the first to see the poetry in the Faust theme (later to reach its highest expression in Goethe's *Faust*, 1790-1833), Marlowe transformed the old German folk-tale, probably known to him after the translation of *Historia von Dr. Johann Fausten* (1587), into a "Fall of Princes" tragedy for the Renaissance intellectual in terms of aspiration, achievement, and inevitable failure, for his central character is consumed with the ambition for complete intellectual power. Dissatisfied with barren philosophy, Dr. Faustus, an aged German scholar, rejects the values of society and suffers for doing so. He receives superhuman powers and his youth from Mephistophilis, who agrees to be his slave for 24 years in return for Faustus's soul. He roams the world in search of all knowledge and experience, performing supernatural deeds, including summoning of spirits, and finally, when the years of the contract expire, the hero tries to appeal to Christ and God, but he has lost his right to pray, and, at the stroke of twelve, Lucifer bears the soul of Dr. Faustus away to perdition. Although Marlowe was reputed by his contemporaries to be heretical, the play is completely orthodox in its Protestant Christianity as well as didactic and moralizing by pointing at ambition as the driving force of human nature representing a mixture of intellectual aspiration and personal flaws such as greed and the untamed desire to go beyond the limits of human existence as prompted by divine order and common sense. The surviving texts from 1604 and 1616 seem modified by some intervening scenes which do not match the superb opening and conclusion, showing signs of playhouse adaptation, and we know that two minor playwrights were paid in 1602 for revisions (they are probably to blame for the banal comic bits and prose passages, and the presentation of Good and Bad Angels as coming straight out of the medieval Moralities). Despite having survived in two corrupt and unsatisfactory texts, apparently modified and adapted, the character of Faust and his relationship with Mephistopheles display magnificent dramatic appeal and apparently survived unaffected.

The only reliable text of Marlowe's plays is *The Troublesome Reign and Lamentable Death of Edward the Second*, published during his lifetime, in 1592, certainly the best constructed of his dramas. Here, Marlowe's problem is that of Shakespeare's *Richard II*: how can the audience sympathizes with a weak wrongheaded king? Marlowe's solution is to show the selfish court and powerful barons tormenting a homosexual king, and to bring to a pathetic climax (much admired by Charles Lamb) in the slaying of Edward II. Further sympathy arises from the belated loyalty of Duke of Kent (king's brother) and the love of the prince. Edward possesses a great psychological strength, but the sense of guilt, raised from his passion for Gaveston and later for Spencer, paralyses his will. His defeat and eventual murder would be the appropriate resolution which, despite attentive personality delineation on the part of the author dedicated to the king's lover Gaveston, to Isabella, to her lover Mortimer, and to others, keeps Edward again at the centre of attention making the play a great Renaissance character tragedy.

In his drama, Marlowe points to the absurdity of conventional beliefs and values and suggests the impossibility of improving or replacing them, as in *Doctor Faustus*. His plays are also full of violent action, murderous excess; his heroes aspire boldly to accomplish themselves usually unscrupulously and assume wrong-doing and become villain-heroes, like Barabas and the Duke of Guise, receiving central position and often best lines, admired rather than disapproved.

These and other features of his work prompt Marlowe's singularity and make him the greatest pre-Shakespearian dramatist, equally well-regarded and condemned, in matters of private and public life, whereas in matters of literary activity, certainly appreciated and imitated.

2.3.2.3 Robert Greene

Robert Greene (1558-1592) was the first dramatist who imitated Marlowe, particularly in *Alphonsus, King of Aragon* (c. 1587), but he himself was greatly annoyed by Shakespeare's more or less famous habit of "stealing" themes and plots from his contemporaries, calling him an "upstart crow, beautified with our feathers, that with his tiger's heart wrapped in a player's hide ... is in his own conceit the only Shake-scene in a country". Although, like Shakespeare, Greene came from a provincial background, he resented Shakespeare for coming into writing plays from the ranks of the actors and lacking an academic education, whereas Greene was a university man with degrees from both Cambridge and Oxford. Having deserted his wife soon after marriage, Greene self-assumedly embarked on a life of pleasure in London associating himself with the university wits. To be able to lead financially such a life, Greene wrote prolifically in various genres from pamphlets and prose romances to plays, among which *George-a-Greene the Pinner of Wakefield* (1588), *The History of Orlando Furioso* (1591), *The Scottish History of James IV* (1591), but he is mostly known for *The Honourable History of Friar Bacon and Friar Bungay* (c. 1589, first printed in 1594), a comedy combining prose with verse in its form, and, on its thematic level, events involving the thirteenth-century Franciscans of Oxford, Roger Bacon and Thomas Bungay, with a subplot telling of the love of Lord Lacy and the Prince of Wales for the beautiful Margaret.

2.3.2.4 John Lyly

John Lyly (c. 1554-1606) excelled as both playwright and author of prose romances. Lyly was brought up in Canterbury and probably was Marlowe's colleague at King's School there. In his public life, Lyly struggled unsuccessfully to become Master of the Revels, though for a period he served as MP. Another university graduate of his times entering literary field, from Magdalen College, Oxford in 1575, Lyly built up his dramatic works on thematic patterns borrowed from Terence and Plautus and combined them with contemporary Italian pastoral intrigues. Gaining control over Blackfriars Theatre through his marriage to Beatrice Browne, Lyly embarked on extensive comedy writing for boys' companies and aiming at a court audience. Lyly is often identified as the first English writer of what is essentially high comedy for which he adopted prose as a medium for its expression, his only play in prose being *The Woman in the Moon* (?1594). Lyly's best plays are *Alexander and Campaspe* (1584), *Sapho and Phao* (1584), *Endymion* (1591), *Midas* (1592), and *Mother Bombie* (1594).

Lyly's name is also included among the writers of prose fiction of the period, particularly as the author of *Euphues: or, The Anatomy of Wit* (first published in 1578), a prose romance famous enough in its period to give its name – "euphuism" – to an exaggeratedly flamboyant and elegant style as well as to determine Greene, for instance, to attempt a continuation in *Euphues, His Censure of Philautus* (1587). Lyly himself wrote a continuation in *Euphues and His England* (1580) which only added popularity to the story of the young Athenian Euphues and his friend Philautus.

Mixing in *The Anatomy of Wit* the story of the Prodigal Son with a Boccaccio narrative, Lyly manages to employ the trivial subject of a love triangle involving Euphues, Philautus, and Lucilla as the foundation for building up discussions on friendship, love, art, wit, education, religion, and morality. More centred on love is the sequel *Euphues and His England*, in which Lyly also focuses more on England, English virtues of both sexes regarding love-affair and marriage, ending the story by making Euphues return to Greece and enter a monastery, while Philautus gets happily married.

As a playwright, Lyly used prose but achieved a high level of ornamentation and artifice, and a keen insight into character which influenced some of Shakespeare's comedies such as *Much Ado About Nothing*.

2.3.3 William Shakespeare

William Shakespeare (1564-1616) is the major representative of the Elizabethan drama, poet, dramatist, and man of the theatre, whose contributions to the development of modern English literature and language are immeasurable. His great monument of literary work is the folio collection of his *Comedies, Histories, and Tragedies*, collected by his fellow in the King's Men and published in 1623.

The eldest son of John Shakespeare, a glover and dealer who played a prominent part in local affairs, but whose fortunes later declined, William was baptized in Holy Trinity Church, Stratford-upon-Avon, on 26 April 1564. His birth is traditionally celebrated on 23 April, which is also known to have been the date of his death. His mother, Mary Arden, who came from a family of higher social standing, married John Shakespeare in 1557; of their eight children, four sons and one daughter survived childhood. William might have received his early education at the local grammar school, whose records for the period are lost. On 28 November, 1582, he married Anne Hathaway of Shottery, a village close to Stratford; she was eight years his senior. A daughter, Susanna, was baptized on 26 May, 1583, and twins, Hamnet and Judith, on 2 February, 1585. We do not know how Shakespeare was employed in early manhood, and nothing is known of his beginnings as a writer, nor when or in what capacity he entered the theatre.

The death of an actor of the Queen's Men in 1587 through manslaughter shortly before the company visited Stratford suggests that Shakespeare may have filled the vacancy. However, later printed allusions to him starting from 1592, among which Greene's attack on him, show that very soon he was established on the London literary scene: Shakespeare became a leading member of the Lord Chamberlain's Men soon after their refoundation in 1594; with them, he worked and grew prosperous for the rest of his career as they developed into London's leading company, occupying the Globe Theatre from 1599, becoming the King's Men on James I's accession in 1603, and taking over the Blackfriars as a winter house in 1608 (Shakespeare is actually the only important playwright of his time to have had so stable a relationship with a single company).

Theatrical life centred on London, which became Shakespeare's professional base, as various records testify, but his family remained in Stratford. Also, from different records, we find out that in August, 1596, his son Hamnet died; in October, Shakespeare was housed in Bishopsgate, London; in May of the next year, he bought a substantial Stratford house, New Place; his father died in 1601; in 1604, he lived in London with the Mounjoy family; in June 1607, his daughter Susanna married a physician, John Hall; in 1608, his mother died and was buried, as his son and father, in Holy Trinity; in February 1616, his second daughter, Judith, married Thomas Quiney. Evidence of Shakespeare's life at this time suggests that he was withdrawing to New Place, but his name continues to appear in London's records. Shakespeare died, according to the inscription on his monument, on 23 April, and was buried in holy Trinity. His widow died in 1623 and his last surviving descendant, Elizabeth Hall, in 1670.

Shakespeare's literary activity includes a number of writings for the press (the narrative poems *Venus and Adonis* and *The Rape of Lucrece*, published in 1593 and 1594, respectively, each with the author's dedication to Henry Wriothesley, earl of Southampton, and the short poem *The Phoenix and the Turtle*, published in 1601), the *Sonnets*, and the plays. Shakespeare's plays were published by being performed, scripts of only half of them appeared in print in his lifetime, some in reported texts; also, the records of performance are scanty: as a result, dates and order of composition, especially of the earlier plays, are often difficult to establish. His literary activity, however, is often described as falling in three periods with uncertain dates of composition of the dramatic works.

The first period includes King *Henry VI, Part I* (1589-1590), *King Henry VI, Part II* and *King Henry VI, Part III* (1590-1591), 1592-1593 – *King Richard III, Titus Andronicus*, and *Venus and Adonis, Sonnets* (1592-1598), 1593-1594 – *The Comedy of Errors, The Taming of the Shrew*, and *The Rape of Lucrece*, 1594-1595 – *The Two Gentlemen of Verona* and *Love's Labour's Lost*, 1595-1596 – *Romeo and Juliet, King Richard II*, and *A Midsummer Night's Dream*, 1596-1597 – *King John, The Merchant of Venice, King Henry IV, Part I* and *King Henry IV, Part II* (1597-1598), 1598-1599 – *Much Ado about Nothing, King Henry V, The Merry Wives of Windsor*, 1599-1600 – *Julius Caesar, As You Like It, Twelfth Night*.

Second period includes *Hamlet* (1600-1601), *Troilus and Cressida* (1601-1602), *All's Well That Ends Well* and *Othello* (1602-1603), *Measure for Measure* (1603-1604), *Timon of Athens* (1604-1605), *King Lear* and *Macbeth* (1605-1606), *Antony and Cleopatra* (1606-1607), and *Coriolanus* (1607-1608).

The third period saw the production of *Pericles* (1608-1609), *Cymbeline* (1609-1610), *The Winter's Tale* (1610-1611), *The Tempest* (1611-1612), and *King Henry VIII* (1612-1613).

The richness of Shakespeare's literary activity, in Dryden's words from *An Essay of Dramatic Poesy*, is due to his "the largest and most comprehensive soul", all the "Images of Nature were still present to him", he was "naturally learned; he needed not the spectacles of Books to read Nature; he looked inwards, and found her there". Also, by the early 1590s, the death of Kyd, Greene, and Marlowe opened a gap in the playwriting field which allowed Shakespeare to occupy it. Indeed, in 1594, together with Richard Burbage and William Kempe, Shakespeare is settled as a leading man of a new company of actors under the patronage of Henry Carey, first Lord Hunsdon, who took office as Lord Chamberlain. On his death in 1596, his son, George Carey, second Lord Hunsdon, became the company's new patron, who also became Lord Chamberlain in 1597. The company is therefore first known as "Hunsdon's Men", afterwards as "Lord Chamberlain's Men", and then again "Hunsdon's Men", then once more it was known as the "Lord Chamberlain's Men" until the accession of James I in March, 1603.

The new king brought all main acting companies under the protection of the members of the royal family, and the company – by now the most important and prosperous company in the country – became the "King's Men". William Shakespeare wrote only for them, becoming their best dramatist, and they also had the best actors and, since 1599, their own building, which is the famous "Globe Theatre".

Over 200 years after Shakespeare died, doubts were raised about the authenticity of his works (for instance, Baconian theory), probably because of the reluctance to believe that a man of humble origins wrote many of the world's greatest dramatic masterpieces, or because of the desire for self-advertisement; however, without any solid proof, these doubts do not resist the highest evaluation given to Shakespeare by his contemporaries and later generations.

2.3.3.1 The Poet

Shakespeare adopted the sonnet writing in a different from original Italian form. Sonnet (ital. *Suonetto*) is an Italian verse form that first appeared in the thirteenth century, and was first imitated in England by Wyatt and Surrey in the early sixteenth century. The English sonnet owed less to the original Italian form than to the contemporary French development of it. A sonnet is a poem of 14 lines (of 11 syllables in Italian, 12 in French, and 10 in English), sometimes with a pause after the octave or first 8 lines (a break in the thought of the poem in the traditional Italian form, which is not always observed by English imitators), with rhymes arranged according to one or other of certain definite schemes, of which the Petrarchan and the Elizabethan are the principal. The Petrarchan sonnet never became generally popular, probably because of the difficulty of its rhyme scheme (abbaabba for the octave or octet, followed by six lines, sestet, rhyming usually cdcdcd or cdecde), though Milton, Keats, Wordsworth used it. The arrangement which became the standard English form of the sonnet, and made famous by Shakespeare, contains 14 iambic pentameters representing three quatrains with cross rhymes followed by a couplet: ababcdcdefefgg. The last couplet, in its traditional Elizabethan form, serves either to summarize or in epigrammatic form to serve as an antithesis to the rest of the sonnet

Shakespeare's 154 *Sonnets*, regarded first and foremost as love poems with a remarkable range of feelings expressed in them, appeared in 1609, but were probably written earlier; they bear a dedication to the mysterious "Mr W. H." (probably they are addressed to William Lord Herbert or Henry Wriothesley) over the initials of the publisher, Thomas Thorpe. Most of them, indeed, trace the growth of writer's affection for a young man of rank and beauty, becoming the main subject of the sequence from the beginning to sonnet 126, a sonnet in which a break occurs and which is incomplete.

The sonnet 127 begins the group concerning the Dark Lady – she occupies the sequence 127-152 and the cycle closes with two sonnets on conventional themes. Other characters, who played a real part in the poet's life, are a stolen mistress, sonnets 40-42, and a rival poet, sonnets 83-86.

Shakespeare's sonnets dwell primarily on the themes of love, art, and time, which may be found as interrelated in one single text. His sonnets follow and respect tradition, specifically the Platonic model, but also ironize it; similarly, concerning the Petrarchan and Renaissance pattern, in general, Shakespeare rejects ornamentation and artificiality and promotes genuine experience.

Shakespeare's sonnets are essentially about love but this seemingly unilateral thematic perspective is actually very diverse and emerges from particular subjective experiences , not only from following a pattern.

Sonnet 12, for instance, discusses love in relation to the transitory essence of existence, the passage of time and its destructive effects which nothing can resist except "breed".

The first line of the Sonnet 18 – "Shall I compare thee to a summer's day?" – also points to the passage of time, the transitory nature of beauty but here the protection is eternity provided by art: "So long as men can breathe, or eyes can see, / So long lives this, and this gives life to thee".

The proclamation of the self-sufficiency of love, its strong, eternal condition can be seen in the Sonnet 116, in which, after declaring "Let me not to the marriage of true minds / Admit impediments", the lyric I declares that love is "it is an ever-fixed mark, / That looks on tempests and is never shaken", which is emphasized at the end by an argument of combined personal writing experience and general human ability to love: "If this be error and upon me proved, / I never writ, nor no man ever loved".

Unusually drastic and unilateral is the view on love in Sonnet 129, which is lust, acknowledged as a constant of human existence, impossible to overcome: "All this the world well knows; yet none knows well / To shun the heaven that leads men to this hell".

One of the most famous and enjoyed with the reader poems, Sonnet 130, after stating that "My mistress' eyes are nothing like the sun" or "Coral is far more red than her lips' red", and so on, proclaims that love has value in itself and genuine love is for what a person represents spiritually, as rare and unique, and not for the way in which she looks, her physical beauty: "And yet, by heaven, I think my love as rare / As any she belied with false compare". Shakespeare's sonnets, on the whole, reveal a poetic voice standing against artificiality and ornamentation, false and pretentious, and pleading for genuine feeling against the established pattern in Renaissance poetry, its stereotypes. The reader will find a "dark lady" and "golden boy" instead of a "fair lady", Shakespeare rejecting, just as Donne will do it in his work, the motif of a beautiful lady who, lacking spiritual essence, is placed on a pedestal rejecting the poet whose frustration is his source of inspiration.

2.3.3.2 The Playwright

Shakespeare's dramatic works include both tragedy and comedy, as well as history play, both tradition and novelty, and, where tradition is involved, his plays are not within a single tradition, as is the case of his early **comedies**. Their sources are ancient Roman comedy, such as the Comedy of Errors, and contemporary Italian novels and plays, particularly *commedia dell'arte*, as well as English interludes and court comedies produced by Lyly and others.

The main theme of Shakespeare's comedies is love, which is interrelated with a focus on art and life or rather on the relationship between art and life, where art is art since it is not life but an image of life. Not separating them may lead to confusion and failure; consequently, claims such as Jaques's "All the world's a stage, / And all the men and women merely players" from *As You Like It* – reminiscent of Macbeth's "Life's but a walking shadow" – appear as self-mockery of Shakespeare.

With love as their main theme, the typical plot of Shakespeare's comedies contains a setting in Italy with a duke, a clown, a heroine disguised as a boy, adventures in a woodland, and an ending with young love awarded (Edwards 118). The intrusion of the supernatural makes these plays light-hearted fantasies, witty and lyric, ironic or satirical, but always comic, their purpose being to achieve comic relief and provoke laughter as a healing power, to take the viewers "out of themselves" and "this working day world" into "holiday foolery" (*As You Like It*).

The therapeutic power of laughter is generated also within the action, which moves the characters from a state of unhappiness, or misery, or lack of communication (as between two towns in *The Comedy of Errors*), or forced decision (for instance, Hermia obliged to marry a man whom she hates in *A Midsummer Night's*

Dream), or rivalry (as between the brothers in *As You Like It*) to a state of happiness, unity, fulfilment, and peace.

Intermediary between misery and happiness is the state of confusion, which is induced by various forces beyond or the condition of the heroes and heroines rather than by the actions of the characters themselves; for example, Viola disguised as a man and her resemblance to her twin brother in *Twelfth Night*, or two sets of identical twins in *The Comedy of Errors*. The forces determining the movement from misery through confusion to happiness are ambiguous and beyond rational explanation; they could be represented by the king and queen of fairies in *A Midsummer Night's Dream* or by such semi-divine figures as Prospero in *The Tempest*. Confusion is often connected to or determined by a change of identity occurring by characters attempting to alter the lives of others without having control over their own lives and destinies.

In order to transcend pain and attain pleasure, characters rely on their virtue and determinism, and the plays end with the celebration of the victory of true love, which is experienced as pleasure, happiness, and fulfilment of the self. The movement from misery to happiness is ultimately a pursuit of love which is thematized by various literary motives such as disguise (women into men and vice-versa)), transformation (for example, Bottom transformed by the power of love in *A Midsummer Night's Dream*), acquiring of new identities (Bottom again, by the spell of Pick), imposition of new identities (Bottom degraded to a beast in order to be risen to become the consort of a goddess), and recognition (usually a mistake which leads to a change of identity).

True love is first concerned with love between sexes, not necessarily and exclusively platonic, since sexual relationship is also a source of completeness and happiness. Also, Rosalind, in *As You Like It*, declares "Love is merely a madness", where men are less true and constant in their love pursuing instead passion and desire, whereas women are more stable and even rational in their affections. True love can be also between friends of the same sex or members of a family: Valentine, for instance, in *The Two Gentlemen of Verona*, values his friendship and feelings for Proteus above the love of women. Whatever its nature, in comedies, true love is attained especially by those characters that are distinct individuals possessing clearly defined personalities and speaking in *propria persona*; such distinct voices are particularly found in *A Midsummer Night's Dream*, a play designated to possess a polyphonic construction.

Shakespeare's comedies and tragedies combine innovation with tradition, but the real originality of the Elizabethans is the history play, perhaps the most important contribution of English Renaissance writers to world literature and, at the same time, signifying the creation of a national literature. Thematically rooted in the history of England, Shakespeare's histories display the influence of Peele, Munday, and especially Greene and Marlowe (who wrote on Tamburlaine). Unlike the other dramatists, Shakespeare saw and presented history not as narrative or description but as drama, dramatic conflict, dressed in the aesthetically highest form and thematic content of tragedy.

Shakespeare's major plays dealing with historical figures and events are grouped into two sequences, the so-called "first tetralogy" (containing *Henry VI* part 1, *Henry VI* part 2, *Henry VI* part 3, and *Richard III*), written in the early 1590s, and "second tetralogy" (*Richard II*, *Henry IV* part 1, *Henry IV* part 2, and *Henry V*), also called "Henriod", finished in 1599.

The three parts of *Henry VI* exhibit violent action and political wrestling involving, in first part, the figure of Joan of Arc and events about the loss of Henry V's empire, and, in second and third parts, more brutal events full of murder and killings, struggle for power and the civil War of the Roses, which end in the stabling of Henry VI in the Tower by Richard of Gloucester, the protagonist of the last and the mostly discussed as well as performed play in the tetralogy, *Richard III*. Richard is ugly both spiritually and physically, a hunchback with a limp and a withered arm, where, according to the views of the period, physical deformities reveal a deformed mind, destructive wit and evil intentions.

Shakespeare adheres to these views and thematically reflects Richard's deformity as a symbol of social deformity and develops for the audience an image of a king-actor, who sees history as a shapeless mass to be given shape by duplicity and pretence and contempt for the others (Edwards 128), the resulting meaning being that Richard creates history in his own image: an ugly spectacle of horror. The wounded and suffering country receives hope for peace and regeneration when Richard III – shouting his famous words "A horse, a horse, my kingdom for a horse!" – receives his justice by being killed at the Battle of Bosworth Field by Henry, Earl of Richmond, who is to succeed as Henry VII. With the new king, the Tudor dynasty is inaugurated to the throne of England, symbolically proclaiming the end of Middle Ages and the beginning of Renaissance. To come closer to its thematic context, this play, like all histories, ends in a military victory which proclaims the end of a bloody, brutal period and the beginning of a new one of peace.

The plays of the second tetralogy contain less violent events and build up an image of kingship which is less brutal. Focusing on three reigns preceding the War of the Roses, Shakespeare asks questions, embarks on philosophizing, looks at the nature of the regal office, and attempts to reveal the cause and effects of the chosen action. Richard II, for example, is apparently an exemplary figure for a medieval autocratic monarch, a true king possessing real power, but his mistake, reminiscent of the tragic *hamartia*, is his view of the sanctity or holiness of his position as a king, which in turn leads to another mistake, that of believing in his invulnerability.

Gradually, however, he becomes aware of himself and the reality of his political situation, the truth concerning political power, which challenges his belief in the sanctity of kingship. This sense of invulnerability added to his somehow irresponsible ways of leadership, which alienate the great nobles, plus the discovery that his office is actual vulnerable, given the army built up by the Duke of Lancaster against him, lead to tragic consequences – Richard's dethronement and death – and make this play one of the greatest political tragedies.

The two parts of *Henry IV* disclose Shakespeare's view of the possibility of personal betterment by the example of Prince Hal – the name is used to refer to Henry V, also known as Henry of Monmouth, son of Henry of Bolingbroke (Henry IV), before his accession to the throne of England – who, eventually rejecting the immoral Falstaff, turns from a depraved and immoral young person into a mature, successful and efficient ruler, like his father, a hero-king who has assumed the values of political commitment, caution, self-control, and protection for himself and others.

Henry VIII and *King John* are dramatic works which belong to no sequence of history plays. The latter, in particular, is liked with the public for its character Bastard Faulconbridge, celebrated for being a personality more than a character type and, like Prince Hal, for his ability of self-improvement to rise from an irresponsible person to a saviour of the country from French invasion as well as its own nobles.

In his histories, Shakespeare cannot avoid representing various aspects of human condition both as personal life and that of the community, but his main focus is on England's past and his drama becomes a form of national self-discovery through a critical scrutiny of this past. In his history plays, historical accuracy is intermingled with the author's imaginative flight which prompts a particular view on kingship as a chain of violent struggles for power. Seemingly pessimistic and even horrifying, a play usually begins with events and states displaying brutal action, murder, betrayal, cruelty, and violence, and ends with a sense of hope and reconciliation, which is abandoned by the next play in the sequence showing again violence and cruelty in a kind of cyclical movement (Edwards 127-135).

Shakespeare, nonetheless, exhibits pride in his England, its power to regenerate and progress; there is pride along hope also in the existence in English turbulent historical past of certain kings such as Richard III and Henry V, who, although essentially tragic, were genuine leaders of the nation; and Shakespeare apparently believes in the authority and potential of the Tudors to lead the country out of wilderness into a brighter future, a great imperial one.

For this reason, many of Shakespeare's historical plays represent an alternation between recollection of the past miseries and promise of a better future pointing to the playwright's optimistic belief and hope in that there will always be a quest for peace, stability, and welfare, and an expected true leader would eventually emerge.

Another common feature of his histories is the tragic element that may dominate or not the thematic movement but it is always present revealing the link between tragedy and history, the intrusion into tragedy of a strong political element. The same link is exposed in many of his tragedies as well, where the issue of political stability in the country is debated upon in *King Lear*; the historical issues of rebellion, power usurpation, and civil war are dwelt with in *Macbeth*; *Hamlet* raises the question of a personality's recesses but it is also about Denmark; on more general level, the relationship between individual and society is discussed in *Othello* and *Romeo and Juliet*.

Shakespeare's great cycle of tragedies extends for some eight years, significantly beginning and ending with two Roman subject-matters: *Julies Caesar* (1599) and *Antony and Cleopatra* (1607). In the history of criticism, attempts have been made to provide thematic groupings of the tragedies, the most common one promoting the three headings of revenge, love, and political action.

The difficulty of including his tragedies in particular groups result from the co-existence of the three thematic concerns in one play. Explicitly dealing with revenge is *Titus Andronicus*, whereas in *Hamlet*, by an act reminiscent of the narrative line of Atreus family, Hamlet – like Orestes – is alienated from Danish society, which is about political action; love is also an important and persistent element in the plot of the play.

But revenge is the main theme of *Hamlet*, its main issue forming the essence of choice and action – being asked for by the voice of the Ghost – and patterning a typology: (1) revenge gives meaning to life; (2) revenge concerns the problem of justice and the responsibility of the individual in achieving it; (3) revenge is a complex mission including killing Claudius, moral rescue of his mother, and cleansing of Denmark.

Concerning the first point, doubts emerge about the value of any act, which is expressed through Hamlet's famous soliloquy "To be or not to be". Choosing to act, Hamlet – as if preceding at the beginning of modernity the existentialist precept from the end of modernity that "existence precedes essence" – materializes the revenge making the play end in both victory and failure: Hamlet understands that it is right and just to kill Claudius who is conceived as a problem in society rather than the murderer of his father and his replacement on throne and in bed, on personal level, which is victory of the fulfilled revenge.

Hamlet, however, is wounded and dies, and the country passes into the hands of a foreigner, Fortinbras, which can be viewed as a failure of the achieved revenge. Prompted on social basis more than on personal one, revenge expresses itself to be a victory on personal level and a failure on the social one.

Concerning the second point, a dichotomy emerges – society condemns the act versus divine authority permits it – to which family issues are added, including the Oedipal relationship between a son and his mother. Sigmund Freud actually declared once that if Oedipus character would have not existed in mythology, he might have called his complex the complex of Hamlet.

Concerning the third point, Hamlet also becomes subject of a counter-revenge since he is to be killed by Laertes for the murder of his father Polinius, wrongly killed by Hamlet.

Another thematic concern is love, dominating the thematic level of plays such as *Romeo and Juliet*, *Troilus and Cressida*, *Othello*, *Anthony and Cleopatra*. Unlike in his comedies, in which love is liberating and a source of happiness, in tragedies, it is liberation at first but soon enough, due to various reasons, mostly social, fails to sustain its strength and value and ends disastrously.

In *Romeo and Juliet*, for instance, love, which is happy and joyful at the beginning, becomes undesirable to society and lovers turn victims. Family prejudices and conflicts rather than fate determine the course of life and the elders of the protagonists shape their tragic destiny while disturbing the balance of a harmonious existence. The two lovers become victims; they are sacrificed in order to re-establish the universal harmony as well as a higher scale of values of their worldly society. *Catharsis* implies here that lovers are safe and they complete their union only in death, which symbolises their sacrifice for a higher cause.

Unpalatable to society is also love as textualized in *Othello*. Particularly, Othello's love is undesirable or it can be said that it is viewed as not normal for the civilized citizens of Venice, namely Desdemona's father Brabantio. Likewise, it is against "all rules of nature" for Desdemona to fall in love with a black man. For her, love is genuine and she assumes her love courageously; for Othello, love is a miracle, a happiness which he is shy and cautious, and somehow afraid, to assume.

Othello, epitomising, in postcolonial terms, the subjected and marginalized person, is placed in binary opposition to Iago, epitomising the malevolent colonizer as well as the destructive nature of the human being and a damaging social response on individual endeavours to achieve happiness and fulfilment. Since Iago cannot influence and corrupt Desdemona, he works on Othello's complex of inferiority rooted in his sense of blackness, of being different and marginalized, ignored by a cultivated society.

This results in Othello losing faith in Desdemona's fidelity, which leads to murdering an innocent woman. Desdemona, in turn, is disowned by her family to be rejected and killed by Othello. Desdemona's and Othello's love is undesirable just as Romeo's and Juliet's is; Desdemona's and Othello's love is also an offence to the elders and society, and they become, like Romeo and Juliet, tragic figures in their postures as victims.

Tragic figures, whose love is impossible to survive, prosper or be happily consumed, are also Antony and Cleopatra. Again, the social determinism dictates the nature of the relationship between lovers, raising the issue of choice between love and honour, namely concerning the inappropriateness and shame for a great leader such as Antony to neglect the empire and duty for the seductive sensuality of Cleopatra. Moral or immoral, true or deceptive, noble or fallen, Cleopatra reveals a complex personality which remains concealed – "Not knowe me yet?" is her famous question addressed to Antony – and he fails to discern her mystery.

The tragic end in the play is prompted by confusion: Antony believes that Cleopatra has betrayed him, whereas she sends word that she is dead; Antony attempts to kill himself and he dies in her arms with his Roman greatness rather than love in his mind; Cleopatra dies as well not before contemplating their love and her adoration of the dead Antony indeed represents one of the greatest hymns to love.

Love transcending spiritual realm into the sphere of the sensual is vivid in *Troilus and Cressida*, which is more about sex than love and which, based of Trojan war, thematically renders the interconnectedness of the motif of lust (in the seizure of Helen) and that of aggression (in the war which followed).

The third thematic perspective of Shakespeare's tragedies – political action – can be better seen in *Julius Caesar* and *Macbeth*, and, to a certain extent, in *King Lear* which may be also assigned as dealing with love. *King Lear* is Shakespeare's only play which is difficult to categorise precisely. Though not a historical play, it is frequently compared to *Richard II* for its concern with the painful process of the collapse of the hero's world and self, and a likewise painful process of learning a new identity (Edwards 146). The starting point is Lear committing unjust act of banishing Cordelia, followed by insanity and, eventually, after being reunited with her when both are defeated in war and although both imprisoned, he feels liberated and happy for spending the remaining time with Cordelia.

The prison is a symbol of social and political pressure, a means by which the external world thwarts individual aspirations. Against imprisonment is love with its liberating and transfiguring power, but the world in its societal structuring destroys its spark immortal inflicting cruel vengeance for the flourishing of love: Cordelia is hanged and Lear experiences the depth of suffering holding her body in his arms and repeating five times the famous "Never".

In *Julius Caesar* and *Macbeth*, the political action is clear in the hero's aim to change the existing *status quo* of the society by assassinating its ruler. Macbeth, like Richard III, performs this act not as being impelled by lust for power but rather as driven into a world of imaginings and dreams, sharing with his wife a guilty indulgence into wishful thinking of becoming King and Queen of Scotland. At first, royalty is a vague dream for him but soon enough he becomes a prey of strange fantasy and hence the life of his mental, imaginary world is real to him and as real as the real world around him. The three witches speaking to him only aggravate the condition and Macbeth indulges into "horrible imaginings"; also, "a dagger of the mind" is "in form as palpable" as the dragger which he uses.

Thus, tempted by the witches, who call him the future king, as well as his wife, Macbeth turns his dream into reality by undertaking the sinful act of assassinating the king Duncan, which results in a state of horror and in acquiring, instead of glory, an acute awareness of the committed murder.

Likewise, the Byronic hero Cain, unable to discern between reality and non-reality, strikes his brother to death and only then his confused mind returns to self-consciousness in order to acquire the tormenting knowledge of what he has done. Like Byron's Cain, Shakespeare's Macbeth understands that he is also dead, dead inside, which he realizes when hearing the "cry of women within". For Lady Macbeth, the outcome of the killing is madness, occurring when the reality created out of their fantasy and dream reinvades her dreams and mind, and eventually death. When Macbeth hears that his wife is dead, he proclaims the meaninglessness of existence by the famous metaphor that life "It is a tale / Told by an idiot, full of sound and fury, / Signifying nothing". Macbeth himself dies, being killed by Macdaf, and he dies with dignity showing his personality to emerge, personality of a man who is not evil but is brought or brings himself into evil-doing.

One of the Aristotelian principles of tragedy is that the hero's downfall is caused by a moral weakness or flaw which inexorably leads him to his tragic destiny. In this respect, *Macbeth* can be seen as an Aristotelian tragedy, since Macbeth displays some basic human flaws or weaknesses which contribute to his downfall, but a modern reader cannot escape questioning the presumption that at the end of the play, Macduff kills Macbeth in a scene easily read as the victory of Good over Evil, asking instead whether this is an accurate characterization, or is Macbeth *wholly* evil and Macduff *wholly* good.

The character performing political action in *Julius Caesar*, Brutus, unlike the individualistic Macbeth, acts with the aim to restore moral values and social harmony, which links him to Hamlet.

Both Macbeth and Brutus, like Hamlet, aim in their attempts at the existing social order by killing the ruler of the state, but their motives as well as repercussions are quite different. Macbeth acts by a personal, selfish ambition in killing Duncan; Brutus, like Hamlet, goes beyond the narrow boundaries of individual existence and looks socially, acting for principle rather than personal advantage. This is possible, like for Hamlet, only because Brutus, perhaps the best in Rome, is a philosopher, an intellectual being, thoughtful as well as altruistic and gentle, performing an act of violence against the leader of the state in order to restore society or, more precisely, to restore old republicanism, which is actually Brutus's hubris (spiritual blindness) or error of judgement. Nonetheless, as called by Antony, who takes the initiative and emerges victorious, Brutus remains in the mind of the receiver of dramatic discourse to be "the noblest Roman of them all" who tries to act for "common good to all" and by which entering the line of the most admired literary figures.

Shakespeare's later comedies are called "tragicomedies", the term being used to differentiate them from his early comedies. These later comedies are divided into two groups as (1) problem comedies of 1602 – 1605 (*All's Well That Ends Well* and *Measure for Measure*) and (2) romances of 1608 – 1613 (*Pericles Prince of Tyre*, *The Winter's Tale*, *Cymbeline*, and *The Tempest*).

Both *All's Well That Ends Well* and *Measure for Measure* contain the folk motif of "bed-trick", where Helena from the former play displays passionate love for Bertram and, substituting herself for another girl, succeeds in making herself his wife, whereas Isabella from the latter work shows passionate asceticism in refusing sex with Angelo in exchange of her brother's life. Also, both plays explore moral problems by means of individuals placed in passionate conflicts, where women save men from sin by valuing them more than the audience does.

The Winter's Tale uses the motif of reunion of husband and wife to knit a narrative movement comprising three impressive scenes, namely that of King Leontes's jealousy, the sheep-shearing scene, and the statue scene. Of all the romances representing Shakespeare's later comedies, *The Tempest* has earned the status of the most popular play with the reader and audience, standing in matters of aesthetic validity above *The Winter's Tale* (with its far-fetched romantic story) and *Cymbeline* (with its disorganized structure mixing the genres of comedy, tragedy, and history play) due to its more tightly joined elements of the plot, its more organized action and unity of tone.

The Tempest, nevertheless, reveals itself within its structure a mixture of genres – tragicomedy, romance, courtly masque, and commedia *dell'arte* – but, at the same time, it displays a neoclassical rigour in its style as well as character representation strategies, as, for instance, Prospero can be viewed as a rational magician.

Prefiguring neoclassicism, *The Tempest* also shows a romantic spirit but more importantly, *The Tempest* is acclaimed for its metatheatrical techniques disclosing its own process of becoming raising the issue of the relationship between art and reality. As metadrama, the play deals with its own nature as a play, where the whole sequence of events is the stratagem of a magician, Prospero, who tries to bring happy conclusion from the deeds of men just like dramatist tries to create a play. This allows the play to destroy the reality it creates. By his art, Prospero – the textual expression of Shakespeare – produces a play within play and brings his enemies to island, but his idea of future is not punishment but to unite Naples with Milan through the marriage of his daughter Miranda with Ferdinand, the son of the King of Naples. Prior to this, Prospero, as if involved in a Cain and Abel scenario, was usurped as duke of Milan by his brother Antonio, while Prospero himself usurped the island from Caliban. Now, Prospero, in his speech, tells Miranda and Ferdinand that what they have been watching is only a play and that its end is to keep with the fleeting and transient nature of everything in this world: "(...) We are such staff / As dreams are made on, and our little life / Is rounded with a sleep".

Enriching the thematic context formed by revenge, love, and political action there are various other issues and concerns such as rebelliousness, defeat, loss, death, failure, disappointment, betrayal, hate, and so on.

In his tragedies and histories, the tragic depiction of human existence is extended beyond the limits of tragedy, and the first tragic model he inherited was the medieval concept of the turn of the Wheel of Fortune. To the medieval mind, the tragedy was the fall of a great man, whose greatness and decline were alike measured in purely material terms. Also, the medieval tragedy was not much concerned with moral values, but Shakespeare adds depth to the tragic pattern by the use of moral colour: the hero's fall may be a turn of Fortune's wheel, but there are also other factors which bring him down, usually a combination between objective (external) and subjective (internal) forces. Shakespeare introduces an evil external agent acting upon the hero and the forces of good, causing them to make wrong decisions (Lady Macbeth, for example, Iago, or the three witches), and, at the same time, the author makes the character reveal his own moral weakness which combines with external circumstances to ensure that his position becomes fallen (Othello's jealousy, Macbeth's ambition, Lear's vanity).

Shakespeare's tragic account of humanity is mingled with superhuman elements, it prevails over human feelings, especially love between hero and heroine (sometimes platonic and innocent as in *Romeo and Juliet*, sometimes experienced and uncontrollable as in *Antony and Cleopatra*, but in both cases passionate), and is extended in the case of his comedies. In the general background of the Elizabethan era, Shakespeare's tragic concept suggests that a universe essentially of harmony and benevolence sometimes deviates from its proper structure when man's evil disturbs it. The sacrifice of Hamlet, for instance, may be needed to right the wrong, but the concluding note is confident of a return to the initial order and justice of the universe.

Such a perfect universe, to which spiritual nature is attributed, is reflected in the stability of the realm assured by Elizabeth, but, given the viewpoint of the time as a variety of Platonism, the physical world is just a faint imitation of the spiritual universe of truth, and in this dualism of matter and spirit, the ideal was a synthesis of both worlds, the ideal which is postulated by Shakespeare (Mark Antony eulogizing the fallen Brutus in *Julius Caesar*): "His life was gentle, and the elements / So mix'd in him that Nature might stand up / And ney to all the world, "This was a man!"".

2.3.3.2.1 *A Midsummer Night's Dream*

It is considered that Shakespeare's comedy *A Midsummer Night's Dream* was produced for a noble wedding in 1595. Despite many uncertainties regarding the recipients of this play, it is obvious that this play combines a princely wedding with a popular seasonal rite. Even though the frame of the play is set by Theseus's and Hippolyta's wedding, the rites of May are clearly hinted at in the title, by the words "Midsummer's Night", a night deeply enrooted into the traditional customs of England.

During Elizabethan period, May Day celebrations carried the significance of erotic licence and magic, because this popular tradition allowed people a day of self-indulgence prior to Lent, which is a period of abstinence. François Laroque explains the Midsummer celebrations:

> In England, as in most countries of mainland Europe, the advent of summer and the triumph of light over darkness was greeted with a show of bonfires. These bonfires were the focus of all kinds of revelries which perpetuated the memory of superstitions and quite a few magic rites, all of which were associated in popular culture with the particular powers of this, the shortest night of the year. The magical fascination of fire was supplemented by the burning of certain herbs to the accompaniment of incantations.
>
> In London and other large towns, the Midsummer festival was also an occasion for grand parades (…) [including such figures as] giants who were no doubt the equivalent of those who paraded at Carnival time on the Continent. As many of these figures also appeared in the May game, a certain confusion arose between the rites of May and those of Midsummer's Eve (…). At all events, Midsummer was a season which became synonymous with confusion and even mental aberration. Midsummer's Eve was traditionally a night of mistakes and wandering wits. (141)

It is not surprising that the Puritans expressed their vehement accusations of the Midsummer's Eve's celebrations, considering them as "heathen customs", and Philip Stubbs made his allegations in his *Anatomy of Abuses* (1583), going so far as calling the "pleasant pastimes" as "repulsive" rites. But the rejection of these customs by the Puritans did not prevent their popularity. Partially, the fascination with these celebrations is related to the carnival spirit they exhibit, an atmosphere which was inherent in the medieval Catholic culture. Penny Rixon claims that

> the carnival spirit is subversive in the fullest sense of the word, temporarily turning the world upside down, giving servants authority over master and mistress, and children authority over schoolteachers: in short, inverting hierarchy and thus dethroning deference and respect for ranks. In carnival, the urges of the body dominate and people are allowed to stuff themselves, get drunk and, although this form of licence is more controversial, indulge freely in sex. So carnival mocks refinement and restraint, implying that, since life is for the most part harsh and full of privations, you should grab what you can when you can and forget about consequences. And in its preoccupation with the body's needs it carries a reminder that we are all equal: whether we play the role of king, courtly lover or peasant in our normal lives, we are all the same when the costumes come off, all subjects to the demands and indignities of flesh. (20)

The changes brought by the Protestantism diminished clearly the significance of these rituals in the new culture, but the spirit of carnival remained preserved in the commercial theatre which sought entertainment. This might be one of the reasons for the Puritan vehement opposition to theatre. Moreover, the brief suspension of hierarchy, which the carnival spirit encouraged, partially invigorated the power of the existent authority and partially picked at privilege and hierarchy, hoping for some social change.

One may say that in *A Midsummer Night's Dream*, Shakespeare incorporates these attitudes in the texture of the play, when he playfully blends the spatial and temporal elements of the Midsummer's Day festivities with the carnival spirit. The structure of the play reverberates with the order of things during the May celebrations. The events in the play start in Athens, during the day; then the lovers and the mechanicals retreat to the woods, and eventually return to the city in the morning after exhilarating experiences. Erika Ficher-Lichte considers that the structure of the play

> creates a complex net of analogies and oppositions between characters and groups of characters. Thus, the young lovers and the mechanicals share the experience of the same spacial and temporal stations. In this respect, the princely couple (Theseus and Hippolyta) and the fairies provide an opposing group. The princely pair is accorded the city and day-time (they only step beyond the borders of the city and forest in daylight), while the fairies are accorded the forest and night-time (they only step between forest and city during the night). (64)

Most of these visible oppositions emphasize a subversive spirit, which is brought about at the beginning of the play by the ambiguity of the wedding preparations for Duke Theseus and Hippolyta, Queen of the Amazons. The apparent gallantry and passionate love of the impatient groom Duke Theseus – "Now, fair Hippolyta, our nuptial hour / Draws on apace. Four happy days bring in / Another moon – but O, methinks how slow/ This old moon wanes!" (1.1. 1-5) – is thwarted by the very confusing feelings exhibited by the reluctant bride – "Four days will quickly steep themselves in night, / Four nights will quickly dream away the time" (1.1. 9-8) – and, especially, by the Duke's display of his enforced love: "Hippolyta, I wooed thee with my sword, / And won thy love doing thee injuries. / But I will wed thee in another key – / With pomp, with triumph, and with revelling" (1.1. 16-9).

The Duke's words cast an ambiguity upon the experienced love of the royal lovers, since, though apparently an impassionate lover, Theseus knows to win love only by subduing and imposing, and if love is won at the expense of injuries, one questions love to be a possibility at all. Considering that the bride is the Queen of Amazons, a very proud and powerful sovereign, she becomes dethroned, enthroned, and then dethroned again concomitantly in a very evocative manner. Primarily, she is dethroned as a Queen when she becomes Theseus's conquered vassal, then she is enthroned to become the Queen of Duke Theseus's court, but this regal position equals to her dethroning, because, even as a queen, she loses the power of decision which she once possessed as an Amazon, and now, though a royal, her status is reduced to that of a wife, who is voiceless in matters of state.

Ironically, this female monarch is silenced in the matters of justice in a time when England is ruled by Queen Elizabeth I, thus mischievously casting doubts concerning the ability of a Queen, regardless of her strength and ingenuity, to hold authority and power in a patriarchal state.

However, though some allusions to their present state are made, the spectators remember that the events in the play unfold in Athens, where women and children were rendered powerless. It is their ruler who is capable of enforcing love and even the merry spirit into the state when he exclaims:

Go, Philostrate,
Stir up the Athenian youth to merriments.

Awake the pert and nimble spirit of mirth.
Turn melancholy forth to funerals –
The pale companion is not for our pomp. (1.1. 11-5)

At first glance, Theseus's words suggest the enthusiasm of a passionate lover who is willing to share his joy and love with the entire state, but, given that he has subdued Hippolyta in war and he would mostly impose whatever dispositions he considers fit, his words have a resonance of despotism which contradicts the democratic spirit of Athens altogether. Shakespeare builds this moment of power for Theseus partially to legitimize his position of authority in the state and partially to raise the awareness to the harshness and brutality of the legitimate system which is masked skilfully in the state. The summoning of the mirth for the royal wedding draws spectators' attention to the existent pretence in a state of civilization.

It is not surprising that in a world where those in power legitimise their position through menace and abuse, we witness Egeus, Hermia's father, who comes to Duke Theseus in order to impose his paternal force upon his daughter's choice in love. Egeus justifies his demand to have Hermia marry Demetrius with the ancient custom, according to which the child must obey the authority of the father. This custom is a commonplace in Elizabethan period, and, although the state is ruled by a Queen, nobody questions the hierarchical concept of society which views the father as an absolute authority of the household. Therefore, Egeus's words "As she is mine I may dispose of her" (1.1. 42) may seem initially shocking, as Hermia is treated as a commodity by her own father, who is incapable to sympathise with his daughter's love for Lysander, but in a world where the father's authority parallels the one of the ruler in the state, the obedience in this societal hierarchy is not even challenged. Theseus confirms Egeus's demand, telling Hermia that

To you your father should be as a god:
One that compos'd your beauties, yea, and one
To whom you are but as form in wax
By him imprinted, and within his power
To leave the figure, or disfigure it. (1.1. 47-51)

One would expect the lover Theseus, who is preparing for his own nuptials, to be more considerate to lovers Hermia and Lysander, but, as the voice of court and law, Theseus choses to implement this cruel law even on his own wedding day.

Such a situation renders court as harsh, brutal and uncompromising to the young lovers who simply want to exert their own will, to express their own choice, and to confirm their right to self-determination. But when a father easily agrees to his daughter's loss of the right to life in case of disobedience, such concepts as reason, clarity, and justice, which are usually associated with the state and authority, become blurred in the circumstances of so much an abuse. Since in a state of civilization lovers meet such oppressive norms, they attempt to exert their right to love and choice by eloping to Lysander's aunt, where they hope to find a more tolerant and compassionate environment.

In their willingness to validate their own authority over the parental one, the lovers choose to escape from Athens, but their itinerary passes through woods during the Eve of May Day. Mangan claims that "'wood' [is] the place of liberating 'madness', of healing chaos" and when the lovers are denied freedom to love, they intuitively strive for "the magic of the wood, and of the creative order-in-chaos of nature which they encounter there, [which] acts to heal the wounds of a society in which parental authority seeks to trample over the desires of young lovers" (155).

Shakespeare creates a paradigmatic journey for his characters, during which they change literally and metaphorically. At the heart of the experience of a journey is the moment of crossing a threshold, which in this case separates the city from fairylands, but it implies the traversing from a known zone to an unknown one. The stepping into the unknown territory supposes the exposure to perils and threats, which would be confronted by the itinerants in order to accomplish their purpose. These perils determine, in a way, the future identity of those performing the journey.

Needless to say that the lovers decide to escape from the menace of Athens on Eve of May Day, a night of wandering wits and confusions, thus exposing themselves to other possible dangers. However, since this action occurs in a comedy, it becomes softened a bit by the power of magic. Hermia and Lysander elope into the woods to seek a space for the freedom of their love. But Demetrius follows them to get Hermia for himself, while Helena follows them because she wants Demetrius. Even though the crossing of the woods implies danger for the lovers, the threat becomes diminished as a result of the love potion made by Puck, a situation which escalates into mistaken identities, which is frequently at the heart of many comedies.

Typical to comedies is the creation of comic situations. But when Hermia enters the woods, nothing hilarious occurs. On the contrary, she is alert to the rules of propriety, and even if she distances herself from the norms of the court, she does not forget that she is a young lady who must preserve a distance from Lysander while sleeping. But her conformity to the requirements of the city leads to Puck's mistaken magic spell which allows the beginning of her tormenting experience. Prior to entering the woods, Hermia is courted by two noblemen, Lysander and Demetrius, both competing for Hermia's heart. Upon her awaking after a nightmare, Hermia is alone, unloved and spurned by both young men. The panic Hermia experiences bears nothing funny either:

> Help me, Lysander, help me! Do thy best
> To pluck this crawling serpent from my breast!
> Ay me, for pity. What a dream was here?
> Lysander, look how I do quake with fear.
> Methought a serpent ate my heart away,
> And you sat smiling at his cruel prey.
> Lysander – what, removed? (2.2. 151-7)

Hermia's dream reveals the fears enrooted in her subconscious regarding her elopement with Lysander. Mangan points out the "dual way in which Lysander is represented in Hermia's subconscious: on the one hand he is the phallic serpent, emblem of a threatening sexuality which attacks and harms her (just as Lysander had wanted to lie closer to her than she had been comfortable with); on the other, there is cold, removed aspect, sitting smiling by while she is tortured" (158). Hermia's dream transmits her insecurity towards Lysander's feelings, given that once she will be married, he might become the repetition of the ruthless patriarchal figure embodied by Egeus, the sinister figure that holds power over her life or death and also can control her sexuality.

The reiterated motif of the dream in the play strengthens the awareness that it might be an unknown reality, especially when the audience shares a superior knowledge of Lysander's betrayal of his love as a result of the magic potion. So far, the play seems to present only a nightmarish experience which has nothing in common with the genre of comedy.

The shift in the atmosphere of the play is made only when Helena, who is in love with Demetrius, after her entering the woods, dares to cast off all the restrictions of the courtly conventions. Working upon the widespread motif of the spurned lover, Shakespeare attains comic effect by inverting the roles between the unreachable lady and the pleading lover, bringing about an outstanding comic situation. Demetrius becomes now the cruel one, who rejects the lady when he says: "I love thee not, therefore pursue me not" (2.1. 188). Helena is reduced to a comic character with her supplications for the man: "You draw me, you hard-hearted adamant, / But yet you draw not iron; for my heart / Is true as steel. Leave you your power to draw. / And I shall have no power to follow you" (2.1. 195-8).

In the conventional language of love poetry, the lady is empowered by her angelic perfection, leaving the lover-man to subdue to her will, regardless of her cruelty. Here, the comic effect emerges when Helena becomes a complete submissive and abandons altogether all restraints of courtly life:

I am your spaniel, and, Demetrius,
The more you beat me I will fawn on you.
Use me but as your spaniel: spurn me, strike me,
Neglect me, lose me; only give me leave,
Unworthy as I am, to follow you. (2.1. 203-7)

Even though the spaniel might be the symbol of loyalty, it is not ignored that it is still a dog, an animal, and, in the Renaissance understanding, it represents a decrease in the hierarchy of the Great Chain of Being, especially when in the conventional language of love, the lady already is considered to belong to the angelic sphere. The decay into the position of a beast in this instance injects a note of eroticism, which is enjoyed greatly in relation to words such as "spurn me, strike me". Moreover, this situation blends some Ovidian elements of the myth of Apollo chasing Daphne, with Shakespeare hilariously reversing the roles between the passionate Apollo and the virtuous Daphne. Instead of the supplicant Daphne, who seeks to protect her virtue from the pursuing lover Apollo, Helena is the one preoccupied with Demetrius' virtue: "Your virtue is my privilege, for that / It is not night when I do see your face; / Therefore I think I am not in the night, / Nor does this wood lack worlds of company" (2.1. 220-3).

This moment definitely creates a comic situation, with Helena breaking all the norms of propriety and literally offering herself to Demetrius, but for the audience that follows the lines of several love plots in the play, it serves as a reminder that love might be fickle, inconstant, similar to a dream, and may drive many to madness. This is exactly Hermia's situation when she wakes up after her horrible dream and discovers that Lysander, who swore to love her eternally, no longer cares for her but has eyes only for Helena. And it is not only Lysander, but also Demetrius struck by love for Helena, both men adoring her enormously, upgrading her from the position of a "beast" to a "goddess". Definitely, this reversal of fortune is extremely hilarious and becomes extended with the two ladies losing completely their tempers and fighting for their love with all their strengths. When the four lovers are confronted, they quickly abandon all conventional behaviour and reveal their faces as they are driven by animal passions:

> HELENA: O, when she is angry she is keen and shrewd.
> She was a vixen when she went to school,
> And though she be but little, she is fierce.
> HERMIA: Little again? Nothing but "low" and "little"? –
> Why will you suffer her to flout me thus?
> Let me come to her. (3.2. 324-8)

The existent friendship between Hermia and Helena dissipates completely after they enter the woods, as these two delicate maidens abandon all courtly pretence and throw insults at each other. Laughter emerges inevitably because of the reversed roles again, as contrary to the expected calmness of women who should keep down male aggression, the young women betray their loyalty to each other and undergo such disturbing experiences due to the rivalry in their love. In a humorous manner, in a time when the cult of love is so much elevated, Shakespeare presents the metamorphosis which takes place in the young lovers, which occurs not necessarily as a result of a magic potion but as a result of escalating feelings and blinding passions which bring one to abandon reason and decay to foulest positions.

Luckily, in comedy, all ends well, and, as the night of wandering wits falls, Hermia, Helena, Lysander, and Demetrius fall asleep near to each other and awake next day to discover that their love is just as where it should be and, after meeting Theseus and Hippolyta, they all return to the city as three couples which "shall eternally be knit" in a temple (4.1. 178).

The transformation of characters from childish and passionate lovers to mature social identities, who are constant in their love and in their social roles, takes place in the forest, a space of the fairyland, which is, *par excellence*, a place of magic transformations. This world of fairyland, though believed to be radically different from the world of Athens, bears some unexpected similarities. Primarily, both worlds are based upon some strict social hierarchies, ruled by a sovereign whose authority is undisputable. If a battle of wills ever occurs, certainly the ruler wins it. Theseus wins his love in war, subduing his consort by a sword, whereas Oberon fights Titania over a changeling boy in a more tricking manner, by the help of enchantment, which still asserts his will upon Titania's. In both worlds, the Queen must submit to the will of the king eventually, confirming once again the patriarchal authority.

The differences between the Athenian world and the fairyland are numerous. Contrary to the way in which in Athens the child is perceived, namely as a commodity for a parent, in fairyland, there is an expression of affection and compassion for a child, visible in Titania's stepping into the role of a caregiver for the changeling boy after his mother died, her fondness for the child being expressed when she "crowns him with flowers, and makes him all her joy" (2.1. 27). She eventually submits to Oberon's will, giving up the boy, but only after she is tricked by the magic spell. In the world of enchantment, love and desire justify the union of lovers, whereas in Athens, love is accepted only if it corresponds to all hierarchical demands of society.

Moreover, Titania, as a Queen of fairyland, possesses her own court, in parallel to that of her husband, Oberon, and calls for equality next to her king. However, regardless of Titania's demands for independence and sovereignty, when it is important for Oberon, he knows to subdue her to his own will even by the power of enchantment.

There is a striking difference concerning women's sexual behaviour, since in Athens, as well as in Elizabethan London, women's sexuality is strictly controlled by the patriarchal conventional morality, whereas the land of fairies seems to create a space for sexual liberation, where the Queen Titania can "aggressively" pursue Bottom, leaping upon Bottom with her legs, which places Oberon in the position of a cuckolded husband, of which he does not seem to mind. Definitely, the greatest difference comes from the affinity of the world of fairies to that of subconscious mind, of illusions and random desires which are brutally prevented in the rational world of Athens.

In this world of profound transformations reins the spirit of carnival, as it tries to mock most of the forms and emblems of authority. Carnival spirit is present in a world turned upside-down, where the widespread ideas and the absolute truths are tested and contested, all demanding concomitantly equal dialogic status. The carnival mode subverts and liberates the authoritarian style or atmosphere through humour and chaos. According to Mikhail Bakhtin, laughter is essential to the concept of carnival. Bakhtin considers that carnival laughter is "the laughter of all people (…) universal in scope and directed at all and everyone, including the carnival's participants" (101).

Therefore, plenty of carnival laughter emerges in fairyland, from the very fact that a queen expresses her reverence to a mechanical and makes him her lover; or young ladies drop their courtly façade to pursue a lover and even engage in a fight for a lover; Bottom's metamorphoses and his unrestricted indulgence in eating and sex with Titania, and so on. Shakespeare presents the carnivalesque atmosphere without any expectations of criticism of certain facets of life, with all their regulatory norms. Since the carnival experience is participatory, it is something in which all become involved, thus producing an ambivalent laughter, concomitantly celebrating and mocking, sympathizing and insulting and referring to all conventional hierarchies, ranks, and norms of the everyday community. Rixon explains that the values of carnival and the everyday life are

> complementary facets of human experience, operating cyclically, just as the moon alternates with the sun (…) the carnival spirit is a levelling force, subtly undermining claims to elite status, whether based on birth, morality or education, and asserting the validity of the demands of the body against more rarefied notions of the superiority of the spiritual. And, perhaps most important of all, the carnival spirit pokes fun at those who take life, and themselves, too seriously. (25)

Due to the Puritan pressure, in Elizabethan London, the licensed carnival is experienced only as a part of theatre, as it stood outside the city's jurisdiction and allowed sometimes the display of an oppositional or even subversive perspective of social reality. This aspect of life led to the creation of the vision of Elizabethan theatre-as-carnival, since it permitted the exploration of more unorthodox cultural norms, "to debate moral and social definitions, and to enact imagined possibilities which could range from the frivolous to the deadly serious and from the conventional to the subversive" (Mangan 162). Concomitantly, it permitted the exploration of the theatrical experience and to observe what happens when the costumes come off and some roles are shifted.

The carnival spirit is interwoven in the sub-plot, which presents a group of amateur actors who attempt to put on a show the story about lovers Pyramus and Thisbe, especially when the main plot of the play is primarily concerned with the nature of love. Mostly due to the mechanicals' ineptitude, love is celebrated and mocked, tested and contested. This sub-plot allows also the opportunity to examine the nature of theatre and the relationship between stage and the audience.

First, one observes the danger to which the mechanicals expose themselves by putting on a play for those in power. Bottom and his crew are trying to rehearse for a play which they intend to be staged for the Duke Theseus's wedding and this makes them extra-cautious about what and how it should be represented. Of course, their play entitled *The Most Lamentable Comedy and Most Cruel Death of Pyramus and Thisbe* is a parody on the theatrical contract between the actors and the audience, but it also delivers uncertainties concerning genres and the basic principles of dramaturgy. The fact that the mechanicals rehearse in the woods rather than in the city reveals their constant preoccupation about being misunderstood by those who hold the authority.

Thus, they are preoccupied with the staging of violence: "BOTTOM: Let me play the lion too. I will roar that I will do any man's heart good to hear me. I will roar that I will make the Duke say 'Let him roar again; let him roar again'. QUINCE: An you should do it too terribly you would fright the Duchess and the ladies that they would shriek, and that were enough to hang us all" (1.2. 65-72). The threat of those in power being so palpable leads the mechanicals to reconsider the presence of a sward on the stage, or the brutal enactment of suicide, which again may frighten the ladies and displease the powerful, so that they think of abandoning their presence in the play altogether. The laughter emerges especially from the audience's knowledge of the story of Pyramus and Thisbe, and the absence of any of its parts would suggest the actor's lack of skill, and this moment becomes even more hilarious because the audience is already witnessing the mechanicals' ineptitude when they try to stage the moonlight or a wall. Like all theatrical companies of the period, these actors must prove to be creative while staging something in order to be convincing for the audience. Therefore, powerful laughter emerges as the spectators witness the actors' challenge of staging the moonlight, having the alternative of a literal representation of the light during a night when a moon shines or, in a more symbolic manner, having a man to stand and present "the person of Moonshine" (3.1. 55).

This ridiculous solution of turning the moon into a character continues with another similarly absurd solution of begetting the character "The Wall". In the story, the lovers Pyramus and Thisbe are separated by a wall, and this wall becomes the source of the lovers' strength, as they can rely on it to share their innermost secrets of their hearts. The situation becomes ludicrous when the object which separates the lovers becomes a man upon whom the lovers lean: "BOTTOM (as Pyramus) And thou, O wall, O sweet O lovely wall, That stand'st between her father's ground and mine, Thou wall, O wall, O sweet lovely wall, Show me thy chink, to blink through with mine eyne" (5. 1. 171-4). These amateurs seem to imagine that the spectators might believe in the conventional representation of the reality on the stage, tacitly agreeing that the wall will become invisible, but the laughter surely proceeds when Flute, performing as Thisbe, exclaims: "O wall, full often has thou heard my moans / For parting my fair Pyramus and me" (5.1. 87-8). In this moment, it becomes impossible for the audience to suspend the disbelief and accept "The Wall" as invisible, and the incapacity of these amateur actors to suggest a barrier between two lovers changes into a "manage a trois", because the lovers express their affection to the wall, which culminates with Flute's words as Thisbe: "I kiss the wall's hole, not your lips at all" (5.1. 200). The eroticism suggested by this moment is outstanding, but beyond this hilarious situation, the spectators grow aware of the challenges in theatre, especially when a failed attempt to stage love leads to the mockery and the distortion of it, and, consequently, the truth becomes lost in the representation.

Shakespeare's play *A Midsummer Night's Dream* reveals not only the problematic of the representation of elevated feelings of idealized love for courtly lovers when such a rhetoric was in vogue at the Elizabethan court, but it also states the difficulties of theatrical representation in general, especially when the reality which should be staged is not convincing enough in theatre and a new sign system should be improvised in order to transmit the wanted message to the audience. One would say that the only magic expected to take place in Elizabethan theatre was the solving of the mystery of the nature of the theatrical experience.

2.3.3.2.2 *Macbeth*

The forty-five years of rule on the English throne by Queen Elizabeth I ended up in 1603 and, since the death of the queen almost coincided with the turn of the century, this was viewed by many as a moment for great changes. The anxieties of the England's last decades over the absence of an heir to the crown increased even more with the rise to the English throne of James VI of Scotland, from the house of Stuart. The worries in the state escalated to a great extent, since James Stuart, who became James I, was the son of Mary Stuart, the Queen of Scots, whose execution was sanctioned by Elizabeth I, and the new ruler signalled many uncertainties for his subjects.

This crucial moment in the history of England signifies a time of great changes, and James I delivers upon the expectations with his authorization of uniting the three kingdoms of England, Scotland, and Wales under one single crown as the Kingdom of Great Britain. The extraordinary transformations, which took place at the English court, brought about some intellectual and political issues as well, which held a profound significance for the subjects. Especially uncomfortable were the concerns about the rights and privileges of kings, the prospect of treason, the possibility of the royal execution, the complexities of succession and hereditary rights, and, above all, the question concerning legitimate power. The rise of these uncomfortable issues corresponds to the turn of the century, a time labelled by many as apocalyptic, triggered by the decay of human nature and civilization.

The apocalyptic atmosphere was connected to the rise of James I to the English throne, but some considered his coronation as the first resurrection of a promising future because there certainly would be benefits for the nation in having a man as the head of the state.

Theatre also passes through radical changes after the coronation of James I. Even though the new king shows his support to the acting companies, in his struggle against the depravity of the theatre, he gathers the best actors under the royal protection, whereas other theatres' licences are declared invalid. Shakespeare's company, known as "Lord Chamberlain's Men" under the new royal patronage becomes well-known as "King's Men". Since there was a strong emphasis between James I and the apocalypse due to the multiple prophesies which circulated in the period, in the theatre, under the king's patronage, the apocalypse becomes a dominant motif and its presence on the royal stage served as a proof of loyalty to the king.

Shakespeare's play *Macbeth* (1606) is created exactly in this apocalyptic atmosphere and the dramatist sets as his purpose to honour James I with a new play, which would focus on the history of Scotland, and to emphasise in the play the king's royal lineage as a descendant of noble Banquo and the king's prospects for the future. Moreover, in the times of the growing national awareness, theatre allowed an opportunity for the spectators to familiarise with Scottish history and acknowledge the ancestry of some legendary Scotsmen.

The tragedy of *Macbeth* is written after Shakespeare's major tragedies *Hamlet*, *Othello*, *King Lear*, and others, and the stress upon "end-of-the-world" with motifs from *Revelations* are not surprising. Along with the general preoccupation with the wickedness of man, which brings about the destruction of the world, the play's major concern centres upon the identity of the king and the possibility of regicide. In Renaissance, Pico della Mirandola's speech *On the Dignity of Man* (1494) brought to the formation of the idea that man can create himself. But the beautiful and enthusiastic prototype of man produced by the Italian Humanist, of one who can model and work on himself until becoming whoever he chooses to be, is twisted and misused by the opportunists who believe in the power of self-determination, convenient especially in cases of usurpation.

In parallel to this attitude on man, there was the belief in Providence and divine will which renders human as part of a divinely ordained scenario; others believed that destiny can be flexed or bended by the help of witchcraft. Particularly, in both English and Scottish histories, there were multiple examples of prophets and sorcerers held accountant for some interference into the affairs of the government, and, even though the witchcraft was severely persecuted during the reign of James I, people widely believed and feared the power and influence of witches.

The witches' presence at the beginning of the play sets an apocalyptic atmosphere with the thunder, chaos, and confusion which they create. Act 1, scene 1 is extremely brief and intense; nevertheless, it provides an opportunity to introduce the witches to the stage, and their ritualized and stylized speech manners, combined with the thunder, lightning, and rain, contribute to the creation of confusion and ambiguity regarding the future events: "FIRST WITCH: When shall we three meet again? / In thunder, lighting, or in rain? / SECOND WITCH: When the hurly-burly's done, / When the battle's lost an won" (1.1. 1-4).

The reference to a battle which might be "lost" or "won", when coming from the witches, delivers the impression that there are some mighty and inscrutable forces which determine human life, and the way the witches speak in a ritualized manner three times, and then refer to the time and place they establish to meet Macbeth after the end of the battle, bring about powerful fears and ambiguities concerning man's ability to create himself as well as strong uncertainties concerning the future. The choric couplet of the three witches produces an overwhelming sense of their presence: "ALL: Fair is foul, and foul is fair, / Hover through the fog and filthy air" (1.1. 9-10).

The last words spoken at the three witches' colloquy intensify the atmosphere of ambiguity and paradox which will dominate the entire action in the play. When the difference between fair and foul collapses, and the beautiful can stand for ugly or malicious, then strong doubts concerning any moral values emerge. But the greatest query stated is, in fact, whether the moral decay occurs as a result of human free will or as a consequence of some inscrutable forces which lead one towards transgression rather than virtue.

Shakespeare juxtaposes the prospect of having a fate as a result of the intervention of some supernatural forces into human lives with the view of a man who can create himself, delivered in the second opening of the play. The ambiance of doubt and obscurity established in the first scene of the play is sustained in the second scene, and the words "What bloody man is that?" (1.2. 1), though literally referring to the bleeding Captain who comes as a messenger from the uprising, symbolically create a reference to the main protagonist, Macbeth, who is introduced immediately by the Captain when he gives the account of Macdonald's rebellion to the King Duncan:

> For brave Macbeth – well he deserves that name! –
> Disdaining fortune, with his brandished steel
> Which smoked with bloody execution,
> Like valour's minion
> Carved out his passage till he faced the slave,
> Which ne'er shook hands nor bade farewell to him
> Till he unseamed him from the nave to th' chops,
> And fixed his head upon our battlements. (1.2. 16-23)

This gruesome introduction of the main character, though shocking, seems to be in concordance with the expectations of manliness of the milieu, as this bloody story is greeted by King Duncan with an admiring "O valiant cousin, worthy gentleman" (1.2. 24). Primarily, this brutal outset tries to emphasise Macbeth as an honourable man who possesses sufficient valour and courage to fight for his king, and he "carved out his passage" by being loyal to his lord. Ames Berquist points out that "Macbeth is presented to the viewer almost in the visage of a Homeric hero insofar as he strives mightily to make his own fortune as he carves his own way. One must note that there is a true excellence and goodness here" (110). In a true Aristotelian manner, Shakespeare presents his protagonist's distinction, especially by praising his warlike virtues, but also his capacity to be honourable while making his own name and place in the world.

However, the ambiguous reference to the "bloody man" makes one wonder whether such brutality is necessary in order to be viewed as a "gentleman". Harold Goddard suggests that there is a powerful irony which emerges from Duncan's praise of Macbeth as a "worthy gentleman" and his final view by Malcom as "this dead butcher and his fiend-like queen" (5.11. 35) in the last speech of the play (109). Therefore, even though a self-created man is an admirable example for the

Renaissance spectator, doubtfully such a slaughterer is commendable from the Humanist and Christian perspectives. The witches' choral repetition of "Fair is foul, and foul is fair" from the previous episode creates a powerful resonance, referring to the moral ambiguities and confusion created by the main protagonist.

The uncertainties concerning the moral boundaries of the tragic protagonist suggested in the opening of the play has led to the consideration of Macbeth's depravity, and the very structure of the play as a tragedy comes under scrutiny, since, according to Aristotle's principles, a tragic hero should be good, appropriate, admirable and consistent, whereas a monstrous being would prevent the evocation of the tragic emotions of pity and fear, necessary for the emergence of *catharsis*. However, it should not be forgotten that the Elizabethan spectators recognized in the depiction of Macbeth some aspects of Norse mythology regarding the ideal of masculinity, which were related to the cult of Odin.

The concept of a battle-god who brings his worthiest warriors to Valhalla in order to be ready to fight in the final battle of Ragnarok was still familiar to and admired by the audience. Shakespeare counts on this familiarization when he depicts his protagonist in such brutal colours, since in this model spectators would immediately identify the animal battle frenzy which was a hallmark of an Odinic warrior. The fury in battle displayed by the warrior was expected to parallel the one seen in wolves, bears, and birds of prey's fight, beasts which were frequently associated with god Odin. The battle-lust of Macbeth might have thus appealed very much to the heroic ideal which still stirred the spectators' imagination.

The ambiguity concerning Macbeth's heroic status emerges from the clash between this still admired Odinic ideal of manhood and the model of man created as based on Humanistic and Christian values. The ferocious warrior could still be accepted as an admired heroic model as long as he preserved some moral values, and Macbeth, by proving his loyalty and service to Duncan, and by revealing an example of self-determination, creates a much esteemed profile of his own self.

But this shrewd depiction of the self-created tragic hero is blurred immediately in Act 1, scene 3, when the witches re-appear, with their typical occult atmosphere, strengthened by thunder, and prompt again confusion:

THIRD WITCH: A drum, a drum –
Macbeth doth come.
ALL (dancing in a ring)
The weird sisters hand in hand,
Posters of the sea and land,
Thus do go about, about,
Thrice to thine and thrice to mine,
And thrice again to make up nine.
Peace! The charms wound up. (1.3. 27-35)

The charms recited by the witches during thunder in such a ritualistic manner, with the frequent use of the mystical number three, create a rich polysemy, alluding to the Three Fates from classical mythology possessing the ability to shape human lives. Moreover, the vagueness of the depiction of the "weird sisters" in Banquo's description of the witches as "withered, and so wild in their attire, / That look not like th'inhabitants o'th'earth" (1.3. 38-9), completed with "choppy finger laying / Upon her skinny lips" (1.3. 42-3), adds to the excessive confusion which these creatures represent, including by their physical description and gender uncertainty which produce an uncanny effect: "You should be women, / And yet your beards forbid me to interpret / that you are so" (1.3. 43-5).

The uncanny ambiance is also sustained by the doubts concerning Macbeth's presence in this place and time, since one wonders whether he came here upon the witches' summon or as a result of his own will. This disconcerting atmosphere is elevated to a greater extent by the witches' prophesies which give "royal hope" (54) to Macbeth and then "vanish" like "bubbles" (77).

Stephen Regan comments that

> the witches are associated with disorder in nature, including stormy weather; they are accompanied by 'familiars' or demon followers; they can transform themselves into animals; they have a fondness for charms and curses; they invert accepted moral values; they have the physical features of old women and yet look *not* like the inhabitants of the earth. If the appearances of the witches are ambiguous, so too is the strange prophetic language they speak. Macbeth twice bids the witches to speak (45, 76) and calls them 'imperfect speakers' (68) – not because they are inarticulate, but because their speech is incomplete and offers only glimpses of what might be to come. (93)

Macbeth's meditation upon the witches vanishing act "into the air, and what seemed corporal / Melted as breath into the wind" (1.3. 79-80) apparently alludes to the witches' ghostly abilities to disappear, but they also suggest the ability of an entity to transform, to change its shape. This law of physics would be otherwise inoffensive, but in relation to the most frequent interpretation of the witches as the psychological projections of one's repressed fears, temptations, and anxieties, there arise concerns about the transformation of human nature and the changes in one's moral values in case if the repressed elements are stirred. The vagueness regarding the witches' gender or their physical description may symbolically refer to the twisted or distorted conscience of an individual when dominated by desires, anxieties, and fears.

This can be one of the reasons that Shakespeare allows the audience to witness the transformations which take place in Macbeth's conscience, and in parallel to a very witty suggestion of Macbeth's moral transgression as a result of magic spells, the dramatist delivers the internalization of Macbeth's troubled mind, together with the consequences of his gruesome deeds. An example is presented at the beginning of the play in the account of Macdonald's rebelliousness, whose "multiplying villainess of nature" (1.2. 11) suggests the transformation from the noble Thane of Cawdor to a beast which is chopped and beheaded as a result of his moral deterioration, and this event functions as a foreshadowing of Macbeth's later degeneration.

The metamorphosis which takes place in a human as a result of moral corruption is stated by Duncan, who, upon the execution of Macdonald, meditates on possibilities of loyalty and trust:

> There is no art
> To find the mind's construction in the face.
> He was a gentleman on whom I built
> An absolute trust. (1.4. 11-4)

Duncan's words suggest the fluctuations in human values as a result of some perverted desires, but they also raise some doubts concerning his ability as a king to judge human nature, since in Renaissance, a "virtuous" prince was expected to be capable of observing and judging correctly his subjects. Duncan's failure to detect treachery in a man whom he absolutely trusted calls into question his royal "goodness". Shakespeare creates a moment of dramatic irony from the juxtaposition between Duncan's lavish praising of Macbeth as a "valiant cousin, worthy gentleman" and his "absolute trust" in the rebellious Macdonald. The irony increases even more after Macbeth's entrance and the king exclaims:

> O worthiest cousin,
> The sin of my ingratitude even now
> Was heavy on me! Thou art so far before
> That swiftness wing of recompense is slow
> To overtake thee. (1.4. 14-8)

His admiring exclamation concerning Macbeth's military prowess may stem out of his deliberate desire to parade his royal appreciation of any worthy and loyal subject, but instead of exhibiting his "princely virtues", Duncan unwittily exposes his own vulnerability as a prince, because he seems to be mostly an observer rather than a participant in the troublesome events in his state. Moreover, his reliance upon "brave Macbeth" (1.2. 16) rather than upon his own strength divulges his precarious sovereignty. King Duncan's immediate comment "More is thy due than more than all can pay" (1.4. 21) ironically justifies somehow Macbeth's secret desire for "more", especially since Duncan as a ruler seems to fail to express his gratitude as a recompense for a subject's service and loyalty and it may trigger one's desire to compensate himself, or, as a part of the pre-monarchic order, any worthy thane capable of exhibiting leadership qualities and princely virtues may have a legitimate claim on the throne.

Therefore, Macbeth's desire to take Duncan's throne might be considered legitimate, since he has proved his worth, whereas Duncan fails in many respects and the consequences of the vulnerability in his authority are visible in the uprisings which exist in the state. However, Macbeth's possible claim to the throne of Scotland is brutally curbed by the announcement of Malcom, Prince of Cumberland, Duncan's son, as a successor to the throne, and this signifies the annulment of earlier possible feudal claims for a thane to be elected as king and the installation of the present king's absolute power and his divine right. Macbeth's surprise and disappointment is expressed in an aside:

> The Prince of Cumberland – that is a step
> On which I must fall down or else o'erleap,
> For in my way it lies. Stars, hide your fires,
> Let not light see my black and deep desires;
> The eye wink at the hand; yet let that be
> Which the eye fears, when is done, to see. (1. 4. 48-53)

Shakespeare uses *aside* as a device to reveal the character's inner world and stress out the character's alienation, as well as his inability to rely on anybody. It also provides an opportunity to deliver the internalization of the protagonist's mind; in Macbeth's case, his troubled consciousness, bothered with his "deep" and dark desires, is shared with the audience.

The "step" which Macbeth mentions refers to Duncan's strategic movement to strengthen his authority in the kingdom, but it also refers to his overstepping in the social and political sense and also to the act of crossing over the boundaries of certain virtues valued by him.

Macbeth's mental chaos and moral confusion are stimulated powerfully by Lady Macbeth who perverts completely the code of manly virtues. Jarold Ramsey observes that

> [dwelling] hardly at all on the desirability of Duncan's throne, she instead cunningly premises her arguments on doubts about Macbeth's manly virtue. All of his previous military conquests and honors in the service of Duncan will be meaningless unless he now seizes the chance to crown that career by killing the king. And striking more ruthlessly at him, she scornfully implies that his very sexuality will be called into question in her eyes if he refuses the regicide. (288).

She dares her husband to assert his manhood through murder when Macbeth shows some hesitations:

When you durst do it, then you were a man;
And to be more than what you were, you would
Be so much more the man. Nor time nor place
Did then adhere, and yet you would make both. (1.7. 49-51)

The archetype of *femme fatale* is delivered through the Biblical motif of satanic temptation which brought to the loss of paradise. Shakespeare skilfully depicts Lady Macbeth as the temptress who lures her husband by his lust for power. The extremely erotic vocabulary suggests an irresistible lust, which is revealed in Lady Macbeth's speech:

Hie thee hither,
That I may pour my spirits in thine ear
And chastise with the valour of my tongue
All that impedes you from the golden round
Which fate and metaphysical aid doth seem
To have thee crowned withal. (1.5. 24-8)

The biblical motif of temptation signals the moral corruption and suggests further transgressions. The blatant allusion to sexuality by which Lady Macbeth tries to manipulate her husband reminds of the Whore of the Babylon, the mythical harlot which is associated with the Beast of Revelation that brings the apocalyptic downfall. In a way, Lady Macbeth triggers Macbeth's degeneration into the lower order of animals, but, unlike the initial association of Macbeth to the beasts of Odin, which indicates his battle frenzy, this time the reference to the beast reveals his progressive disjunction from the humane order. Lady Macbeth's goading and manipulation of Macbeth's desire of Duncan's throne affect deeply Macbeth's flawed conscience, who, though fights courageously on the battlefield, is reduced to someone who is "too full o'th' milk of human kindness" (1.5. 16) unless he commits the crime and becomes a "man". The perverted understanding of manliness infused upon him by Lady Macbeth makes him detach from the set of male virtues or from human nature to the extent of threatening his own self.

Ironically, this strong and virtuous self-made man produces his own self-destruction as a result of ethical confusion and the mental chaos which he experiences. Macbeth's gradual dislocation from the humane values begins with his very rational understanding of his offence, delivered in his soliloquy:

> If it were done when 'tis done, then 'twere well
> It were done quickly. If th' assassination
> Could trammel up the consequence, and catch
> With his surcease success: that but this blow
> Might be the be-all and end-all, here,
> But here upon this bank and shoal of time,
> We'd jump the life to come. But in these cases
> We still have judgement here (1.7. 1-8)

Usually, a tragic hero's *hamartia* refers to an error in judgement which triggers the hero's downfall. The flaw of the protagonist should be one common to all humans in order to allow the audience's identification with the character's situation and consequently attain *catharsis* at the end of the play. According to Aristotle, the purpose of tragedy is to achieve a state of pity and fear so that the final cleansing is attained. When it comes to Macbeth, it becomes difficult at times to view him as a tragic hero, since his *hamartia* is not a simple error in judgement but an outrageous crime, committed as a result of violation of natural feelings of kindred, hospitality and gratitude.

Robert Watson argues against the consideration of Macbeth as a tragic hero claiming that "the portrayal of Macbeth's fate as poetic justice fall far short of tragic complexity. He is not caught between conflicting imperatives: all he has to do is ignore some obviously sinister advice and he will be able to settle into the sociable contented old age he envisions" (177). It is easy to agree with Watson, as Macbeth's error implies a very conscious harm of friends, connected to him through various bonds. However, one may not forget that a tragedy is centred primarily on *suffering* of the hero, and, in this respect, Shakespeare brought much variety and innovation.

The above soliloquy is an example of a very conscious understanding of the protagonist's "great error". He is much aware of the moral values which should be violated with the act of regicide. His guilty conscience is constantly preoccupied with the judgement which awaits for him during his lifetime. The words "judgement here" indicate the self-inflicted shame, "upon this bank and shoal of time", produced by the brutal severing of the bond with other humans. The speaking voice delivers a privileged access to his distorted conscious to a degree of allowing the spectator witness the innermost depths of his reasons.

The spectators may not associate with Macbeth's "vaulting ambition" (1.7. 27), since such cruelty is not typical to the human being, but the urging frenzy, which he experiences when he fights his temptation with the "if", "when", and "then", allows spectators to experience empathy with this troubled character, because it is common to all to be tempted by some desires. The words "trammel up the consequence" produce a very powerful fishing imagery which suggests entrapment of the victim, necessary to diminish the damage of his deed, but this imagery allows the spectators to sympathise with the ignorance of the tragic hero who imagines that the bloody deed committed "here" will entrap someone else and make his own way free.

He is blind to the possible repercussions of this deed "here", as he ensnares himself in his suffering and guilt to an extent of dragging hell upon himself with his bloody deed which, as he acknowledges, will "return / To plague the inventor" (1.7. 10).

The strong torment is also produced by the possibility of the arrival of the Last Judgement. Reflecting upon the cosmic repercussions of Duncan's murder, Macbeth projects the image of Apocalypse:

> So clear in his great office, that his virtues
> Will plead like angels, trumpet-tongued against
> The deep damnation of his taking-off,
> And pity, like a naked new-born babe,
> Striding the blast, or heaven's cherubin, horsed
> Upon the sightless courier of the air,
> Shall blow the horrid deed in every eye
> That tears shall drown the wind. (1.7. 18-25)

Macbeth's soliloquy is saturated with images of Christian retribution, with angels blowing trumpets and deep damnation, the heaven's cherubin, whereas the new-born babe indicates Christ who should stand as a judge during the Apocalypse. This imagery evokes Macbeth as standing in front of a divine trial, revealing his deep embarrassment which emerges as a result of the dissipation of the worthy image of himself after his transgression, and this self-shame is aggravated by his acknowledgement that his brutal "deed" will be juxtaposed to Duncan's "virtues", "in his great office", so that the experienced anxiety places him into position of almost begging for "pity".

Regan explains that "many puzzling ambiguities and complexities in Macbeth's soliloquy are entirely in keeping with the idea of an insecure, unstable identity, and also with the idea of an unstable order in which legal, ethical and theological discourses clamour for recognition" (103).

The fluctuations between opposing concepts of manhood and the ambiguities concerning worth generate Macbeth's state of fundamental instability which leads him to an error in judgement. Macbeth's hubristic desire, triggered by the witches' prophecy and then manipulated by Lady Macbeth, is accomplished with Duncan's murder, which is his *hamartia*, but instead of expected gratification and delight, this deed condemns him to an unprecedented torment. The horror which he experiences from Duncan's blood and the extreme self-repulsion which he feels are reflected in his frantic talk: "Methought I heard a voice cry 'sleep no more, / Macbeth does murder sleep' – the innocent sleep" (2.1. 33-4).

Macbeth's troubled consciousness is revealed in his own damnation, as he exclaims that "Macbeth shall sleep no more" (2.1. 41). The voice of his conscience resembles the Furies from the classical mythology, the underworld goddesses who punish the assailant. But unlike the ancient tragic hero, who is severely punished by an external force, Macbeth internalises his torment by inflicting self-punishment for his atrocious murder:

> What hands are here! Ha, they pluck out mine eyes.
> Will all great Neptune's ocean wash this blood

Clean from my hand? No, this my hand will rather
The multitudinous seas incarnadine,
Making the green one red. (2.1. 57-61)

The agony which Macbeth experiences is delivered through his own psychic dislocation and in his extreme form of suffering, he visualises the various methods for his punishment. The imagery of Furies plucking out his eyes or the imagery of the flood incapable of cleansing his sin transmit the despair of the awareness of his guilt. Since he understands that he has violated the moral and divine laws by a deed which he carried out in full awareness, he loses the human values through his failure to correspond to divine virtues and begins a process of self-mutilation which is visualised in a sea of blood. This blood signifies his severed bond with humaneness, as his inhuman crime transforms him into a beast, which places him beyond atonement.

Ironically, his expected social prominence and elevation, through Macbeth's fatal error, turns into his "downfall". In his rise to power, he employs Machiavellian politics, imagining that as a result of his free will he may plan and achieve whatever he desires; however, ironically, his choices lead him eventually to his self-destruction.

From a man of virtues, Macbeth becomes a treacherous being, who separates himself from God and humans, greedy for power, egotistic and scheming, a tyrant who is capable of multiple ruthless killings. The murder of Banquo, his loyal friend, and Lady Macduff and her children, among other atrocities which he commits, produce a temporary alienation of the spectators from the tragic protagonist, jeopardising the identification with the character, necessary for the cathartic experience. But the inner struggles of Macbeth, along with the state of complete numbness which he attains as a result of his detachment from humanness, reinvigorates the audiences' sympathy for Macbeth. The chilling speech which he delivers upon his wife's death – "She should have died hereafter. / There would have been a time for such a word" (5.5. 18-9) – indicates the degree of his dislocation of the self and dehumanization, especially after observing that the intimacy, which they initially share by addressing each other as "my dearest partner in greatness", or as "love" and "chuck", is now reduced to a simple "word" which signifies nothing. Barren now of any humane feelings, Macbeth reveals his profound deception:

Life's but a walking shadow, a poor player
That struts and frets his hour upon the stage,
And then is heard no more. It is a tale
Told by an idiot, full of sound and fury,
Signifying nothing. (5.5. 23-7)

The biblical reference to the human life as a shadow is echoed in Macbeth's words which deliver the emptiness of any lofty ambitions. His flawed understanding of manliness attained through the distorted images of a self-created, self-determined and autonomous individual becomes a pure self-deception when he acknowledges that this is a "tale told by an idiot (…) signifying nothing". Macbeth understands that the carving out of his fortune with martial virtues in the detriment of humane virtues reduces him to a beast, a "butcher" alienated from the community of men. The entire essence of the play seems to be enveloped in this speech.

Shakespeare revitalises the audiences' sympathy towards Macbeth by making his hero understand that the degree of his violation of human and divine laws has reached a point in depravity which is beyond atonement or absolution. But this protagonist, who has abandoned everything humane and feels himself entrapped and reduced to the condition of a solitary animal, makes spectators "pity" and "fear" for his personal descent into hell, as he becomes a tragic guilt-bearer who cannot be absolved of his guilt. In a surprising turn, Macbeth manages to attract the audiences' admiration, because, instead of falling further into a pathetic self-lamentation, even in the most desperate moment of his awareness of the impossibility of his absolution from human or Christian perspectives, he finds a way to rise to his greatness again.

The imagery of Macbeth's final entrapment by Malcom and Macduff leads to his final decision: "I cannot fly, / But bear-like I must fight the course" (5.7. 1-2). These words indicate Macbeth's determination to narrate his own "story" of his final battle which enacts the Odinic warrior's mystical sacrifice of himself into himself, where he fights his opponents with battle frenzy in his ultimate hope to be accepted to Valhalla and be ready for Ragnarok. The association of himself with a bear reveals his quest for redemption in pagan terms through *kleos*, which would provide him with eternal glory, since his temptations and acts destroy his worth and deny him the possibility of facing God during Apocalypse from the Christian perspective.

The final performance of a mortal man bravely facing his death is juxtaposed with Macduff's reappearance with Macbeth's head, whom Malcom triumphantly proclaims as a "dead butcher", which creates a sense of moral ambiguity. In his brave hope for redemption, Macbeth throws himself into his final fight, and even though he has degenerated greatly, the audience never suspends the empathy with him due to his ultimate quest for honour. But when Macbeth is considered the wicked man in the play, Malcom's rise to throne though the act of severing of the "usurper's cursed head" (5.11. 20) creates a disconcerting imbalance in the claims of justice and the spectator questions the rightful heir's virtues and legitimacy to throne after "butchering" an anointed king.

The conclusion of the play is still read as a victory of good over evil and the triumph of virtue over transgression, vivid through the agricultural imagery of trees "which would be planted newly with the time" (5.11. 30), suggesting the new reign in Scotland and evoking a promise of a better future after the apocalyptic cleansing. But the goodness and virtues suggested at the end at the play are not completely stainless, nor is the evil totally tarred due to the ethical ambiguities and unstable concepts regarding the king's legitimate power.

2.3.3.2.3 *Richard II*

Richard II (1595) is commonly considered to be a history play, a distinct dramatic subgenre adjusted to accommodate some stringent political concerns. The editors of the 1623 Folio edition separated ten of Shakespeare's plays from the widespread comedies and tragedies, classifying them as "histories", but this ambiguous dramatic genre continued to generate confusion. Since most of Shakespearean plays were designed primarily as commercial enterprises, the playwright did not hesitate to modify some of the conventional dramatic boundaries to appeal to the diverse tastes and interests of the heterogeneous theatregoers of the period. In order to raise the popularity of some plots, Shakespeare fused various generic modes, and his play *Richard II* represents such a hybrid, the generic confusion generated by the play being visible in its publication in 1597 in Quarto format as *The Tragedy of King Richard the Second*, and this title is preserved in the 1598 edition. Moreover, from romantics to modernists, Shakespeare's play *Richard II* was viewed as a tragedy, since it represents the fall of its protagonist and elicits the emotions of pity and fear, which are peculiar to tragedy. Especially appealing is the "universal moral and aesthetic significance of Richard's tragic fate" (Elliot 256).

Despite the created generic confusions, Shakespeare frequently made use of historical material and he often highlighted some of the current political controversies in many of his plays, but *Richard II* was based more on a very popular historical myth which continued to fascinate the Elizabethans to a great extent. Particularly, it delivers the episode in history about Edward III's grandson, Richard II, who became a king in his early childhood, precisely in 1377, and was overthrown by one of his cousins, Henry Bolingbroke, who staged a forced abdication of Richard in a *coup d'état* in 1399.

Bolingbroke, Duke of Lancaster, becomes King Henry IV, and the ambiguities and controversies set around this royal succession led to a long lasting period of unrest and civil wars, known as the Wars of Roses. The war between the houses of Lancaster and York ends only after Henry VII of the house of Lancaster, defeating Richard III at the Battle of Bosworth Field, rises to the throne and unites the battling houses in his marriage to Elizabeth of York, inaugurating Tudor dynasty. Partially, the popularity of this historical episode is explained by the strengthening of the *status quo* of the Tudor monarchy, because it reveals how the rise of this dynasty to throne ended up anarchy and bloodshed, bringing instead peace, order, and stability to the state. Queen Elizabeth I, of the House of Tudor, enjoyed and indulged in this displayed model of harmony and prosperity, and it is not surprising to have such a historical account in Shakespeare's play.

Besides the provided explanation for how things came into order in England, this historical myth delivers a "paradigm of misgovernment" (Womack 144). A common feature of history play is the focus on political issues, which is conveyed through historical examples. Since it is very dangerous to criticize or comment on the present government, the historical parallels offer an opportunity to refer to stringent contemporary political concerns.

Richard II addresses the sensitive issues of a just sovereign and of legitimate succession to the throne; therefore, the political implications of an unwise ruler who behaves recklessly by promoting upstarts over noblemen, setting his own will above the law, introducing irregular taxations, or appropriating the wealth and titles of noblemen, and so on, are references extremely appealing to the audience, especially in the context of an aging Queen.

The dramatists of the sixteenth-century history play would not assume the purpose of attaining historical accuracy; the playwrights mostly attempted to create some persuasive models in order to reveal the ethical and political challenges of a sovereign. Margaret Healy explains that "playgoers in Shakespeare's day went to a tragical history like *Richard II* expecting to see, not a pale reflection of times past, but a more stimulating vision, one pertinent to the conduct of government in their own times" (52).

By presenting this historical fable in his play, Shakespeare consulted some historical authorities of his days, such as Raphael Holinshed's *Chronicles* (1577), Edward Hall's *The Union of the Two Noble and Illustre Families of Lancaster and York* (1548), Samuel Daniel's *Civil Wars* (1595), Jean Froissart's Chronicle (1525), William Baldwin's *Mirror for Magistrates* (1559), and others. Shakespeare seems to have approached all this various sources with care, especially as these sources present contradictory views on Bolingbroke's succession on Richard's throne.

Talbert (232-233) suggests three principal attitudes towards Bolingbroke's usurpation. First, the "Lancastrian" view presents Richard as an incompetent and corrupt ruler, and, consequently, Bolingbroke as a capable, righteous, and trustworthy successor. Second, the "Yorkist" view, even though aware of Richard's shortcomings, views Bolingbroke as a devious manipulative man who usurps the throne for selfish reasons rather than for public welfare. Third, the "Richardian" view presents Richard as a martyr, intimidated and deposed by a ruthless and unscrupulous politician who later murdered the legitimate king. These opposing views reveal the conflicting political loyalties of the chroniclers during Richard's reign, and their contradictory attitudes were transmitted to the sixteenth-century historians. Shakespeare juxtaposes some aspects of these attitudes in his play in order to emphasize the full complexity of the political controversies of Richard's reign and he did not hesitate to invent some episodes which have no historical accuracy in order to fit his purpose.

The opening scene of the play presents not only Richard, but also Bolingbroke, in a combat of honour, but this battle is guised as a confrontation between two feudal lords who accuse each other of "treason". The two sparring knights, Mowbray and Bolingbroke, throw hot-blooded assaults at each other, and, like in Holinshed account, Bolingbroke is presented as a loyal subject who is concerned with Mowbray's extortion of money from the royal treasury, and this conflict culminates with the accusations of the murder of the Duke of Gloucester, who is king's uncle. The long-winded words of Mowbray are very defensive and even though the allegations against him are very incriminating, the king steps in, like an impartial judge to bring peace and order:

> Wrath-kindled gentlemen, be ruled by me.
> Let's purge this choler without letting blood.
> This we prescribe, though no physician:
> Deep malice makes too deep incision;
> Forget, forgive, conclude, and be agreed;
> Our doctors say this is no time to bleed.
> Good uncle, let this end where it begun.
> We'll calm the Duke of Norflok, you your son. (1.1. 152-8)

The initial impression is of a splendid king who takes the model of divine order and applies it at his Court, and Richard, as the God's vice-gerent, must convey judgement and justice at his assembled court. At first glance, Richard's words "Forget, forgive, conclude, and be agreed" produce the impression of an impartial royal peace-maker, who exerts his sovereign authority to prevent any bloodshed and to reveal his laudable concern with the welfare of all his subjects. Even though Bolingbroke is his cousin who apparently commits the sacrilege of fighting against God's substitute, Richard, in an example of ideal majesty, exhibits his intention to prevent any conflict, but all kingly intentions seem to be only a sham which covers Richard's involvement in the political assassination of Gloucester. Richard's earlier pacifying words "Our doctors say this is no time to bleed", which suggest his reluctance to let his subjects bleed in useless conflicts, are juxtaposed to the image of Gloucester's blood, whose "precious liquor spilt; / Is hacked down, and his summer leaves all faded / By envy's hand and murderer's bloody axe" (1.2. 19-21), both allusions referring to medicinal practice of blood-letting, which may heal or kill someone conveniently.

Richard's weakness of command is obvious, as all his attempts to attain reconciliation between the opponents fail, and the decision to have a trial by combat between the knights is cancelled by the king, who offends both combatants by denying their right to defend their honour and to display their military prowess. Moreover, his verdict of banishing the opponents is an example of clear injustice and inequity, given the serious nature of the charges against Mowbray.

However, as Moseley explains, "we may see Richard's difficulty – that to allow the issue to come to a fight necessarily involves himself and his guilt – this is no kingly behaviour; in ignoring the claims of the combatants' honour it strikes at the very roots of feudal loyalty" (137). The initial deceptive image of the ideal majesty displayed by Richard collapses by the allegations to his complicity in the murder of Gloucester, and by exiling the appellants Bolingbroke and Mowbray without an opportunity to vindicate their honour, Richard fails to give justice in their conflict.

Moreover, Richard's violation of the traditional legal right of a nobleman to defend his honour reveals his insecurity as a ruler. Envious of the bond between Bolingbroke and the people in the state, Richard reflects upon Bolingbroke's "courtship of common people, / How he did seem to dive into their hearts / With humble and familiar courtesy" (1.4. 23-5).

Richard's meditation upon his cousin's popularity among common people places him to a pathetic level of a jealous sibling who wishes to annihilate his rival double by banishment or murder. This instance of the king who shares honestly his thoughts about his cousin reveals the discrepancy between the image of the public king and the person who bears the crown, respectively, the Body politic and the Body natural. Shakespeare deliberately opposes the image of the public role of the majestic ruler, which Richard assumes when he is expected to deliver a public performance, to the true, honest depiction of an envious, insecure and conniving person who uses his position in order to assert his political authority. Speaking of the uprising in Ireland, Richard says:

> We will ourselves in person to this war,
> And for our coffers with too great a court
> And liberal largess are grown somewhat light,
> We are enforced to farm our royal realm,
> The revenue whereof shall furnish us
> For our affairs in hand. If that come short,
> Our substitutes at home shall have blank charters,
> Whereto, when they shall know what men are rich,
> They shall subscribe them for large sums of gold,
> And send them after to supply our wants; (1.4. 41-51)

The way in which Richard commits such abuse of power by using his role of a king reveals him in the light of a feeble actor who wears the costume of a king, handles the props of sceptre and crown, but is incapable of grasping the significance of this role. Shakespeare uses the distinction between the actor and his role in order to provide a theatrical representation of the tragedy of the King's Two Bodies, but he uses this opportunity to reveal the reality beneath the mask of power, developing it into a metaphor for kingship. And when the mask of justice and impartiality slips away, Richard exhibits a deceitful and empty face of himself, which is that of a man who does not hesitate to employ Machiavellian politics in order to secure his authority on the throne. Greedy for power, Richard decides to "help" the fortune of the old John of Gaunt: "Now, put it, God, in his physician's mind / To help him to his grave immediately" (1.4. 58-9).

Richard's mistaken understanding of his role as a king who deliberately plans the course of his action does not result into an image of himself as a self-created, self-determined and autonomous individual, but produces instead a ruthless king in a process of self-destruction. In this respect, Klinck explains that "Richard, who is in his body natural is the occupant or tenant of the king's body politic, by farming out his "royalties", his prerogatives and responsibilities, effectively changes the relationship of King to subject and relinquishes incidents of the "Dignity royal" to base men. By subverting the essential nature of the king's body politic, he debases it or commits waste upon it" (29).

John of Gaunt, Bolingbroke's father and Richard's uncle, is a lord who truly understands the significance and responsibilities of a monarch. In Shakespeare's improvised episode in which the Duchess of Gloucester tries to persuade Gaunt to avenge Gloucester's death, even though Gaunt grows aware of Richard's shameful abuse of power, he struggles with such a perspective, because he says:

God's is the quarrel; for God's substitute;
His deputy anointed in his sight,
Has caused his death; in which if wrongfully,
Let heaven revenge, for I may never lift
An angry arm against his minister. (1.2. 36-41)

Gaunt is usually portrayed in chronicles as a covetous and avaricious lord, much feared by people, but Shakespeare works upon this historical model, creating instead an extremely intelligent, loyal and wise lord who is truly capable of understanding the responsibilities of the crown. Gaunt views the king as the "anointed" minister of God who is above the earthly law and is held accountable only to God. His devotion to the king is shattered only when he understands that Richard's uncontrolled appetites and fiscal abuses destroy his country. Gaunt's venerable patriotism emerges as he witnesses the increase of Richard's injustices and his earlier adamant belief in the sacredness of king's authority dissipates, making him contest the immunity of the king in front of law: "Landlord of England art though now, not king. / Thy state of law is bondslave to the law" (2.1. 113-4).

Gaunt implies that Richard is the "landlord" of England and not the king, and this suggests his anger and disappointment, as his ruler is like a tenant of body politic who has abused the state and "wastes" the land itself, bringing only devastation to "this other Eden, demi-paradise", "this blessed plot, this earth, this realm, this England, / This nurse, this teeming womb of royal kings" (2.1. 50-1). Gaunt's dilemma originates in the confusion that an anointed sovereign is capable of ruining England, this earthly paradise, that his penchant for excess destroys the heavenly ordained justice, and in his capacity of a king, he fails to produce a heir to the throne, symbolically suggesting his incapacity to fruitfully "farm the royal realm", leaving behind only a pathos of nothingness.

The legitimate monarch, Richard, has become a tyrant who does not hesitate to "help" the noble Gaunt to death, to appropriate immediately Gaunt's property, to instil self-will and fear upon his subjects, thus becoming fundamentally inadequate for the office. The consequences of his tyrannical misdeeds are conveyed in the garden scene, an episode which resonates with Gaunt's reference to the "waste" of land:

> and Bolingbroke
> Has seized the wasteful King, O, what pity is it
> That he had not so trimmed and dressed his land
> As we this garden! We at time of year
> Do wound the bark, the skin of our fruit trees,
> Lest, being over-proud in sap and blood,
> With too much riches it confound itself.
> Had he done so to great and growing men,
> They might have lived to bear, and he to taste,
> Their fruits of duty. Superfluous branches
> We lop away, that bearing boughs may live.
> Had he done so, himself had borne the crown,
> Which waste of idle hours hath quite thrown down. (3.4. 55-67)

The gardener, even though not prone to the idea of rebellion in the state, questions the actions of the greatest gardener of England, the king, who neglects his land and allows its ruin.

The England-garden metonymy is used to refer to the form of governance when the leading cultivator of the land, the king, fails to set a good example and the greatest danger of this failure will be seen in "superfluous branches" in the kingdom, the rebels that the king "himself had borne [to] the crown". The consequences of the commission of waste are suggested in the future choice of some boughs of royal blood that may come to power because the garden is full of weeds and to stop this negligence, a cleansing is required. In other words, if Richard is only a careless tenant who wastes the sacred land, Bolingbroke, of the royal branch, is in expectancy to trim away any disorder and substitute this tenant for the crown.

Shakespeare creates a careful opposition between Richard and Bolingbroke. Richard is ruthless, unsympathetic, tyrannical and unmerciful, and deserves to be punished; Bolingbroke is loyal, wise, courteous and considerate, and is worthy of crown. However, Shakespeare "highlights the theatre as an emergent space of political uptake and public deliberation" (192). In the light of the earlier example of Richard's elaborate showcase of ideal kingship, doubts may arise in the spectator's mind concerning the image which Bolingbroke displays for people. So far, Bolingbroke has represented a model of noble behaviour and the spectators sympathize with the injustice committed against him by Richard, especially as the king breaks the law of inheritance, the very same law which placed him on the throne.

Bolingbroke's actions may be justified by the illegality of king's actions, but Shakespeare places a seed of suspicion regarding Bolingbroke's behaviour prior to his banishment, in particular, his "courtship of the common people" (1.4. 23). These words earlier suggested Richard's jealousy at his cousin's popularity and his envy that Bolingbroke "dives" easily into their hearts, but Shakespeare's audience was accustomed to some noblemen's "courtship" for sympathy, as it was the case of Earl of Essex, who entertained the possibility of becoming Queen Elizabeth's successor. Doty observes that

> Richard censures Bolingboke's behaviour, whose gestures are objectionable because they reverse the customs of decorum, giving the people "reverence" instead of demanding it from them. Hat-doffing, bowing, and warm assertions of fraternity relax protocols of social hierarchy, and they communicate to the people that Bolingbroke, despite his rank, is really one of them. For Richard, "wooing poor craftsmen with the craft of smiles" is an act of debasement, since in doing so Bolingbroke acts like a player whose job it is to tease smiles from his audience. "Craft" links Bolingbroke with "craftsmen" and with playing; it also associates him with Machiavellian guile and cunning. (193)

Richard, even though "plays" in public performances the role of an ideal ruler, finds security in the divine right of the king. He imagines that though his behaviour increases in recklessness, as a monarch, he has the power of an absolute law, regardless of its injustice, and, therefore, he is above all people, above the entire humanity. He claims that:

> Not all water in the rough rude sea
> Can wash the balm off from an anointed king
> The breath of worldly men cannot depose
> The deputy elected by the Lord. (3.2. 54-7)

This false security ignores the arrangements and changing values of a society, for even though Richard is an anointed king, no divine "balm" would protect him when his army abandons him on the battlefield, because a more sympathetic candidate to throne emerges. In harmony with his peers, with his realm and with expected understanding of justice, Bolingbroke seems to be an appealing and reasonable contender to throne.

Bolingbroke, concerned with public opinion, has revealed until now an example of loyalty, obedience, and care for his monarch, but after the exile, he dares to break this carefully constructed image of the self, locating his political identity and loyalty in "mother England" rather than in the person of the king. Like in the case of his father, his loyalty shifts when the love for England prevails over the subject's love for the monarch. His choice is completely justifiable, but upon his arrival to England, an ambiguity concerning his true objectives emerges. His initial purpose is the restitution of his dukedom, but his intentions shift quickly from dukedom to throne when the opportunity appears. When he must judge Bushy and Green, he assumes a calculated stance, acting already like a monarch, condemning the assailants to death, even though he has no right to do it.

This quick indulgement in a princely attitude divulges the possibility that he "acted" all along and he was always aiming for the throne. Moreover, the initially constructed heroic attitude dissipates gradually as he is incapable of being impartial during the trial, when he judges the offenders from the perspective of a private vengeance:

> Myself – a prince by fortune of my birth,
> Near to the king in blood, and near in love
> Till you did make him misinterpret me –
> Have stooped my neck under your injuries,
> And sighed my English breath in foreign clouds,
> Eating the bitter bread of banishment,
> Whilst you have fed upon my signories,
> Disparked my parks and felled my forest woods (3.1. 16-23)

Bolingbroke's embittered language discloses his different face, one which was hidden so far beneath the mask of honour and patriotism. It appears that Shakespeare creates on purpose such scenes and invites his spectators to judge both Richard and Bolingbroke, especially as it appears that none of them is purely heroic or villainous. When Richard fails in his office, Bolingbroke may seem at first to be a perfect candidate for the throne, but his meteoritic rise to power is observed by the audience who in the process hesitates about his ambiguous code of honour and respectively about his perfect suitability for the throne.

Shakespeare skilfully orchestrates the reversal of sympathy from Bolingbroke to Richard in the deposition scene, clearly depicting both of them as the fortune's fools rather than defendants of national interests:

> Here, cousin, seize the crown.
> Here, cousin. On this side my hand, on that side thine.
> Now is this golden crown like a deep well
> That owes two buckets filling one another,
> The emptier ever dancing in the air,
> The other down, unseen, and full of water.
> That bucket down and full of tears am I,
> Drinking my griefs, whilst you mount up on high. (4.1. 171-8)

Ironically, Richard seems to acknowledge the significance of the crown and the responsibilities which come with it only when he no longer holds it. To this point, he has appeared completely unappealing to the spectators due to his weaknesses, but now he gains an insight regarding the divinely sanctioned role, which changes the emotive response of the audience towards him. He challenges all men present at his deposition, all who have abandoned him, betrayed him, destabilizing completely the concept of justice by his question: "And who sits here that is not Richard's subject?" (4. 1. 113). The reference to the biblical parable of Judas who betrays Christ confers legitimacy to his claim, and if he failed in his obligations, so did each of them, who deserted their king, leaving him alone and vulnerable. Bolingbroke is now politically strong, but Richard holds the audiences' sympathy, for he acknowledges the ultimate fragility of the human condition and with that he admits the vulnerability of kings. His earlier reference to "golden crown like a deep well / That owes two buckets filling one another" leads to the well-known concept of the Wheel of Fortune, which indicates the random rise to and fall from power, and the visual symbol of the round crow that turns around like a wheel reveals the temporariness of the power which it implies.

Even though the one holding the crown indulges in the belief of his invulnerability as a divinely protected Body politic, it quickly becomes clear that this position is not impenetrable, as it is inhabited by a Body natural, which is subject to frailty and passage of time. At the same time, the reference to the wheel of fortune suggests the temporariness of Bolingbroke as King Henry, whose triumphant progress due to his popularity might have a short span of life, especially when the audience knows from history that this king will also be overthrown.

In his play *Richard II*, William Shakespeare demystifies the supposition of the invulnerability of the royal figure. Instead, he produces a strong impression that the monarch is a frail being, since, as the Body natural, the king is only an actor or a tenant whereas the true ruler is only death. The sole true adversary to all kings and humans is time itself and, in this context, all ambitions, temptations, and desires become as transitory as human "breath".

2.3.4 The Post-Shakespearean Dramatists

The two periods in the first half of the seventeenth century are called "Jacobean Age" (1603-1625) and "Caroline Age" (1625-1649). In the first period, during his reign, James became more and more autocratic as a king trying to limit the role of Parliament and, in arts, to control literary and theatrical production. Accordingly, "many writers became disillusioned with James's reign. Numerous Jacobean tragedies represent corrupt Italian courts ruled by a vile despot, undoubtedly a reflection, however obscure or hyperbolic, on the rule of James", such as *The Maid's Tragedy*, which "reflects more directly on tyranny and the right of the abused subject to resist injustice" (Hadfield 22).

Both "Jacobean Age" and "Caroline Age" display more than before – which is during the sixteenth-century Renaissance – the co-existence of both traditional and innovative elements in literature, the former being displayed in the writings by Ben Jonson and his followers and the latter maintained and strengthened by the late Renaissance cultural extravaganza of Baroque which manifested in English literature as the metaphysical poetry of John Donne and his followers.

Jonson's name, fame, and literary credentials were strong enough to determine literary historians to call those authors, rather inexactly, actually, who, like Jonson, produced literary works reflecting classical models and therefore extending the Renaissance revival of and emphasis on ancient classical tradition, "Sons of Ben", and to call others, again inappropriately, who attempted to achieve originality and experiment as exponents of metaphysical trend in poetry, "School of Donne".

Far-fetched or inappropriate as it might be, this classification prompts, nonetheless, Ben Jonson, with his drama and poetry modelled after classical tradition, among the dominant literary figures of the first half of the seventeenth century, even having his own disciples such as Robert Herrick (1591-1674), a devoted and true member of the "Sons of Ben". A student in English literature may find them also referred to as "Cavalier Poets", a group of poets attached to Court, who admired and imitated the works of Ben Jonson. Apart from Herrick, other cavalier poets, active mainly before the Civil War, are Thomas Carew (1595-1640), Sir John Suckling (1609-1642), Colonel Richard Lovelace (1618-1659), George Wither (1588-1667), and others who follow in their poems the classical principles of Jonson combining them with motifs and poetic strategies borrowed from metaphysical poets.

Other more or less devoted to classicism, so-called disciples of Ben Jonson, are the Jacobean playwrights John Fletcher and Francis Beaumont. The literary qualities of Jonson's drama and non-dramatic writings – reliance on the revived ancient classical spirit, intellectual insight, emphasis on mind and reason, and promotion of the classical values of order, measure, common sense, clearness, and proportion – indeed appear in the plays of Fletcher, who collaborated with Beaumont until Beaumont's retirement and early death in 1616.

2.3.4.1 John Fletcher

John Fletcher (1579-1625) met Francis Beaumont and became his friend probably after having joined Ben Jonson's circle in London. Until then, even less is known about his life, except that he was the son of a bishop of London and studied at Cambridge. It is certain, nonetheless, that Fletcher throughout his creative life mainly collaborated with other dramatists, particularly his friend Beaumont. Together as partners, Fletcher and Beaumont contributed to their contemporary commercial theatre extensively first for the fashionable boys' companies and then almost exclusively as chief dramatists for the King's Men, seemingly having replaced Shakespeare and after the company began to perform indoors at the Blackfriars Theatre. Although considered to be the authors of more than 50 plays, modern researchers ascribe to them with certainty no more than seven or eight plays, among which the most successful in their times being *The Maid's Tragedy* (c. 1610), *A King and No King* (1611), *Cupid's Revenge* (c. 1611), and *The Coxcomb* (1612). After the partnership with Beaumont had ended, Fletcher actively and willingly collaborated with other playwrights, among whom with Shakespeare in *Henry VIII* (1613) and *The Two Noble Kinsmen* (1613), with Field in *The Knight of Malta* (c.1618) and other plays, and especially with Massinger in more than twenty plays. It is also accepted that Fletcher is the single author of various other plays such as *The Faithful Shepherdess* (c. 1609), *Monsieur Thomas* (1610), *The Chances* (c.1617), *The Island Princess* (c. 1620), *Rule a Wife and Have a Wife* (1624), and other plays.

Fletcher, apparently committed to the theatre and profession of playwright more than his friend Beaumont and other contemporary dramatists, continued working throughout his entire life, both solely and in collaboration with other writers, producing until his death about fifty plays which, by the middle of the 1610s, secured him a popularity equal to that of Shakespeare, and which influenced the tragicomic writings of his contemporaries and remained a major part of the King's Men's repertory until the closing of the theatres in 1642. On the reopening of the theatres and amid the attempts to revive the great English dramatic tradition during the Restoration period in the second half of the seventeenth century, Fletcher's influence emerges again to provide the characteristic for the period type of drama – comedy of manners – with a realistic insight into a changing world, careful character delineation, emphatic language, well-packed composition of individual scenes, and elevated handling of the subgenre of tragicomedy. Among those influenced is John Dryden, himself an author of Restoration drama; also, as a literary critic, in *Essay of Dramatic Poesy*, evaluating, promoting and defending English drama in opposition to contemporary French as well as ancient and modern ones, Dryden provides Fletcher, along with Beaumont, Shakespeare, and Jonson, with a respectable place in the history of English dramatic genre.

2.3.4.2 Francis Beaumont

Francis Beaumont (1584-1616), whose private and public life is almost unknown to us (probably born into rural aristocracy, perhaps left Oxford without a degree, presumably studied law at Inner Temple without practicing it, but certainly married to a heiress in 1613, which determined him to abandon the theatre), built up his reputation as a playwright first imitating the work of Jonson but received fame and popularity as Fletcher's friend and co-author. Indeed, culminating as a leading dramatist of the King's Men, Beaumont's dramatic career is largely indebted to his collaboration with Fletcher, infusing the partnership with poetic appeal and a keen sense of comic relief.

Written for the boys' company of St Paul's, Beaumont's first play, *The Woman Hater* (1605), is a prose comedy written in imitation of Jonson, whose company he enjoyed and where he probably met Fletcher. Mocking the unstable and mediocre taste of an unsophisticated theatrical audience in *The Knight of the Burning Pestle* (1607), of which he is believed to be sole author, Beaumont, nevertheless, moves towards falling eventually under the influence of public taste, particularly after beginning his friendship and writing partnership with Fletcher, where both writers, especially as chief dramatists of the King's Men, seem to have sacrificed the depth of thought and linguistic sophistication of Shakespeare's dramatic discourse to superficial sentimental appeal, unpretentious intrigue, and almost direct utterance in language use.

Despite sacrificing whatever highest standards of Renaissance drama to the shifts in popular taste, the playwrights Fletcher and Beaumont emerge aesthetically finer in some of their plays – such as *The Maid's Tragedy, A King and No King, The Scornful Lady*, and *The Captain* – and became leaders of public sensitivity in their times with an well-deserved reputation which was increased and sustained by their impressive collaborative work, but the most important dramatist of the post-Shakespearean period is Ben Jonson (1572-1637).

2.3.4.3 Ben Jonson

Of Jonson's life is known with certainty, through references in the papers of Philip Henslowe, an important theatre manager of those times, that in 1597, Jonson is already established as a dramatist and actor; according to these and other written references, Jonson exhibited a violent and combative temperament, killing, in 1598, a fellow actor in a duel but escaping execution by pleading benefit of clergy, and fearless speaking of his opinions, being most likely one of the actors imprisoned after the performance of *The Isle of Dogs* in 1597. Bringing further trouble to his emerging dramatic career as well as his threatening of his emerging as a court poet and masque writer are the writing of *Sejanus, His Fall* (1603) and contribution to *Eastward Ho* (1604).

The former brought Jonson before the Privy Council on charges of "popery and treason" since, having converted to Roman Catholicism in 1598, it would have been inappropriate for such a play by a Catholic to be staged during the first winter season of the King's Men under the new patron, James I. The latter led Jonson to be briefly imprisoned once again.

Subject to speculation is his place of birth, probably Westminster, and that of education, probably Westminster School. Also, before embarking on a career as playwright and poet, Jonson might have worked with his stepfather, a master bricklayer, and served as a soldier in Flanders, being already married and father to the first of his several children.

The reputation for openly speaking of his mind is supported by his literary activity in which the revived ancient classical tradition joins ethical principles which are involved in the thematic context of his plays to emerge textualized throughout much of Jonson's dramatic work which also promotes the comic genre as the mode of its expression.

From short-lived "humorous" comedy in *Every Main in His Humour* (1598) to satirical comedy in *Every Man out of His Humour* (1599) and *Cynthia's Revels* (1600) and finally to the best period of his literary activity – which is between 1605 and 1614, containing *Volpone* (1605), *Epicoene* (1609), *The Alchemist* (1610), and *Bartholomew Fair* (1614) – Jonson became a celebrity of his times and built up a solid reputation, enduring and well-deserved for his display of classical scholarship while embarking on formal and thematic experiment, artful control of the episodes and incidents while allowing scenic spontaneity, characters created to incorporate vices and follies while permitted to freely command the stage.

Nonetheless, contemporary audience and that of later periods may have blamed Jonson for quickly taking offence, immediately assuming adversaries, involving in the war of the theatres as well as for his belief in his own superiority of talent, his self-assumed arrogance as a playwright and provider of theoretical precepts for writing drama, which can be seen, for instance, in his decision to portray himself in *The Poetaster* (1601) as Horace whose *Art of Poetry* Jonson translated. Also, the publication in folio in 1616 of his dramatic and poetic *Works* renders further his sense of his own outstanding status.

But his ingenious stagecraft and secured stature as a writer of dramatic, poetic and prose works would be rewarded by his appointment as Poet Laureate and a royal pension, and his knowledge of London life was rewarded with appointment as City Chronologer in 1628.

Also, his drama and prose but especially his poems and songs exerted an influence on various younger poets of his period which was strong enough to establish a trend and determine them to call themselves "sons" or "tribe" of Ben. Advancing tradition through literary works rooted in ancient antecedents, these writers are contrasted to others representing the contemporary metaphysical trend in poetry, self-styled "school" of Donne. Jonson, however, as part of Christopher Brooke's circle of literary associates, was seen among Donne's friends, where Donne himself was Brooke's friend and his chamber-fellow at Lincoln's Inn.

Unlike Donne promoting poetic experimentation and innovation of content and form, Jonson relies in his work, in general, on classical models. In matters of dramatic production, unlike for Shakespeare, Jonson's comedies are rooted in satire rather than romance, and Jonson's satire is indispensable from moral principles and values, the playwright involving thematically his comic attitude through satirical effects and ethical didacticism on both private and public levels. In the Prologue to the revised *Every Man out of His Humour* of 1616, Jonson promises an "image of the times". This image, a rather uncomfortable one for its compulsive depiction of moral decay and folly, persists throughout most of his dramatic works providing dupes and deceivers with a huge part to play, whereas the virtuous are left with limited scenic representation.

Epicoene: or, The Silent Woman, first produced in 1609 and published in 1616, is a comedy dealing with private life, with family and marital themes, and focusing on human faults and frailties consisting of individual arrogance, deception, embarrassment, and ridiculousness. Morose the protagonist, an self-centred bachelor, who hates noise, would marry only a quiet woman while intending to remove his nephew, Sir Dauphine Eugenie, from his will. Cutbeard, Morose's barber, recommends Epicoene, who hardly utters a few words, but immediately after marriage, shows herself far from being a silent woman. In order to get rid of the talkative and quarrelsome Epicoene, Morose agrees to a bargain with his nephew promising to restore him to inheritance in return for his help. Sir Dauphine reveals Epicoene to be a young man by removing "her" wig, which strengthens the sense of satire and the ridiculous. The comic effect also results from the involvement in the plot of two more characters, Sir Jack Daw and Sir Amorous LaFoole, who, having earlier claimed to have enjoyed Epicoene's favours in the past, try hard to somehow cover their embarrassment.

Involving in thematic context a concern with public and social issues is Jonson's masterpiece and, to the present, most frequently performed play entitled *Volpone: or, The Fox*, published in 1607, but put on stage by the King's Men one or two years earlier.

One of his finest comedies, it creates a witty intrigue of a rather complex plot in which the social interacts with the personal, immorality is opposed by virtue, comedy co-exists with moral didacticism, since the immoral characters – Volpone himself, along Mosca, Voltore, Corbaccio, and Corvino – are punished, and only the virtuous ones, here Corbaccio's son and Corvino's wife, are rewarded. Acclaimed for its "merciless moral scrutiny" (Ousby 982), the play directs its satire on Jacobean London with its rising merchant class and aims to disclose the values and customs of a society which is on its way of losing the genuine ones. Formally, however, the comedy is set in Venice and peopled with characters strictly defined by their names: the rich Venetian man named Volpone (fox) and his witty servant Mosca (fly) plot to dupe fortune-hunters, for which spreading the news of Volpone's imminent death. Having no heirs, Volpone is apparently an easy prey for Voltore, Corbaccio, and Corvino, three local leading citizens revealing their real, corrupted and immoral, selves.

The promise of acquiring unearned wealth eradicates the last stances of morality and virtue in these people: Voltore (vulture) is a lawyer who will go against the laws he has vowed to protect; Corbaccio (crow) will disinherit his own son; and Corvino (raven) is prepared to send Celia, his virtuous wife, to Volpone's bed. Overreaching himself, Volpone wills his property to Mosca and pretends to be dead, which infuriates everyone, especially Voltore who takes the matter to court, which precipices the events and allows resolution to occur and truth be revealed. Eventually, both the deceivers and the deceived are punished to stress once again the author's interest in delivering a moral message and his confidence in the victory of true moral values over vileness, duplicity, avaricious intent, corruption, dilapidation, depravity, and egocentrism.

The devious humans in their moral decay surpass in wrong-doings Pug, a junior devil allowed a day of malpractice on earth in *The Devil is an Ass* (1616). The failure of this play, actually, seems to have discouraged Jonson to continue writing drama and it was not before nine years that *The Staple of News* (1625), his next comedy, was staged, followed by *The New Inn* (1629), and his dramatic career completed by *A Tale of a Tub* (1633).

Apart from comedies, Jonson is a prolific author of masques, with which he continuously provided the court, as well as poetry and prose which, like drama, are founded on classical precedent.

The Masque of Blackness (1605) is the first of many written in collaboration with Inigo Jones, a collaboration which, however, would be eventually destroyed by rivalry. His poems and songs emerge in the masques and are also collected in the verse volumes of *Epigrams* (1616), *The Forest* (1616), and *Underwoods* (1640). His prose is represented by the published notes of William Drummond of Hawthornden (1623) and the posthumously published *Timber* (1640).

In Britain, Renaissance element of tradition is best represented by Ben Jonson, whose drama reflects the revival of and reliance on ancient classical values that emphasize rational and satirical approach, reliance on rules and norms of writing, as well as order, reason, and good sense, by which Jonson came to influence and remain a model for those writers whose work constitutes the masterpieces of neoclassicism for more than one hundred years between 1660 and the 1780s. For instance, the first comedy of manners is regarded Shakespeare's *Much Ado about Nothing*, but it was Jonson's comedy of humours that directly influenced the genre of the Restoration comedy.

Jonson's dramatic work is equalled by his critical endeavours in the prologues written to his many plays and in the book *Timber, or Discoveries* (1640). Like his literary practice, they reassure the Renaissance revival of ancient classical tradition and emphasise rules and decorum while speculating on various writers. Concerning Shakespeare, Jonson acknowledges his literary achievement, praises him but is reluctant to accept abundant originality and unbounded imaginative flight entering polemics on behalf of the newly emerging neoclassical perspectives of order, measure, and common sense: "He [Shakespeare] was (indeed) honest, and of an open, and free nature: had an excellent Phantasy; brave notions, and gentle expressions: wherein he flow'd with that facility, that sometime it was necessary he should be stopp'd".

Ben Jonson, who continued writing drama and non-dramatic poetry at the beginning of the seventeenth century, shows in both genres the revival of the classical spirit. His lyric poetry is less emotional then intellectual, emphasising the strength of the mind in the manner of the epistles and satires of Horace, as well as the classical virtues of reason, common sense, clearness, brevity, proportion, and rejection of all excess.

These features were remarkably observed and critically displayed by John Dryden during Restoration in his seminal work in the history of English literary criticism, *Of Dramatic Poesie, An Essay*, in which, apart from Jonson, Dryden focuses on Shakespeare, Fletcher and Beaumont.

Through the voice of Neander, his alter-ego in this critical treatise, Dryden speaks on behalf of an English dramatic tradition against recent French dramatic practice, represented by Lisideus, another dichotomy being ancient dramatic tradition, represented by Crites, versus modern drama, represented by Eugenius, each of the four fictional characters defending and arguing about the aesthetic values of a particular type of drama.

It is interesting to see how Neander shifts his focus from general literary issues concerning drama to a less general discussion and defence of English drama and eventually to a critical, and, at certain moments, comparative appreciation of Renaissance playwrights, namely Shakespeare, Jonson, Fletcher, and Beaumont. Here, after briefly but pertinently discussing Fletcher and Beaumont, Dryden turns to Shakespeare and Jonson, who receive enhanced critical attention, and, with regard to Jonson, apparently a more thorough one.

For Dryden, Shakespeare has "the largest and most comprehensive soul"; he is naturally gifted, the greatest of all writers, following in general but also breaking some of the Aristotelian and Horatian "rules", by which combining in his works both the innovative spirit of Renaissance and the revival of ancient classical models.

When compared to Shakespeare, Jonson is "the most learned and judicious writer" that any theatre ever had, as well as "saturnine" and satirical, and being "deeply conversant in the Ancients, both Greek and Latin", Jonson borrows boldly from the ancient writers and faithfully follows the classical doctrine.

Finally, when comparing the two playwrights, Dryden concludes that Jonson is "the more correct Poet, but Shakespeare the greater wit. Shakespeare was the Homer or father of our dramatic poets; Jonson was the Virgil, the pattern of elaborate writing; I admire him, but I love Shakespeare".

The reader of the critical treatise still cannot escape the impression that through Neander, Dryden is a true defender of English drama arguing in favour of a national, English literary tradition: for instance, when asked by Eugenius, Neander states, at the beginning of his discussion on English playwrights Shakespeare, Beaumont, Fletcher, and Jonson, that in doing so "I shall draw a little envy upon my self", and, after arguing in favour of their value, he claims that "we have as many and profitable Rules for perfecting the Stage as any wherewith the French can furnish us".

In the differences between Shakespeare and Jonson as expressed by Dryden, one may easily notice that the art and literature of Renaissance reveal the emergence of two contradictory but co-existing aspects of "innovation" based on the freedom of artistic expression and "tradition" based on the revival and imitation of ancient classical models.

The manifestation of the innovative spirit in arts continues after Renaissance as Baroque, or metaphysical poetry in British literature, which – together with the literary activity of John Milton – is considered by some critics to be the last manifestation of English Renaissance. The Baroque/metaphysical cultural extravaganza is rejected and suppressed by the much stronger and dominant traditional element which, based on the revival of ancient classical artistic doctrine and practice, becomes itself a period and dominates as Classicism (neoclassicism, in England) the entire social as well as cultural and literary background of Europe for more than one hundred years starting with the middle of the seventeenth century until the last decades of the eighteenth century.

The beginnings and consolidation of neoclassicism in England – during some four decades called the "Restoration Period" in English literature and arts which took place from the restoration of monarchy in 1660 until the end of the century – together with the prior to it Puritan Commonwealth Interregnum, metaphysical trend in poetry, and the literary activity of John Milton, among others, represent the main aspects of the diachronic advancement of British literature in the seventeenth century, but this is to be the concern of our next book in the series.

CONCLUSION

THE "PROFITABLE PLEASURE" OF THE LITERATURE OF ENGLISH RENAISSANCE

The period called "Renaissance" in the history of English literature covers largely the sixteenth century encompassing, first, the advancement of thought, a new learning, particularly the humanist philosophy, which would be immediately followed by and co-exist with a remarkable sequence of literary practice covering all major genres.

With regard to the relationship between humanism as philosophy and the literary field, the greatest achievement in the practice of writing is the genre of "utopia", as in Sir Thomas More's assertion and promotion of humanism via his *Utopia*, which can be named a "speculative political essay" concerned with the search for the best possible form of government.

More provided a Renaissance description of a fictional realm, but his Utopia is less an "imagined land where fantasies can become realities (as in fairy stories)" than serious "reforming visions of the "best state of a commonwealth"" (Hattaway 130).

The students of English would consider the persistence of the genre during the periods following Renaissance to the very present day with developments, related and sharing similarities to utopia, such as dystopia, anti-utopia, the gothic, science-fiction, and so on.

Meanwhile in Renaissance, by means of his *Utopia*, More expresses the dissatisfaction with the contemporary background and offers an alternative which is better and in the present. Here, the "opinions of Hythloday (the name means "expert in nonsense") need not to be the opinions of the author, and Book 1 of the work (written it would seem after the description of Utopia in Book 2) is a rhetorical dialogue where Hythloday's opinions are sceptically challenged – after the manner of Plato's dialogues" (Hattaway 130).

Nevertheless, throughout his work, More advances the principles of humanism making it the first phase in the rise and consolidation of a modern type of thinking – emphasising principles such as learning, knowledge, progressive emancipation of humanity, rationalism, observation, experiment, reality, system, foundation, essence, and so on – whose crown would be the Enlightenment.

Actually, students might consider the modern thought as a developing line, a process throughout the whole modernity keeping these principles but having various manifestations: modern period begins with Renaissance and ends with after WWII, it begins with humanism, then Bacon, then the seventeenth-century Rationalism and Empiricism, followed by idealism and Kant, culminating in Enlightenment in the eighteenth century, positivism in the nineteenth century, and, in the first half of the twentieth century, Phenomenology, which attempts to bring a note of certainty and coherence in the last part of modernity representing a period of crisis in the history of modernity reified in art by modernism.

To revert to Renaissance, in matters of literary practice, in sixteenth-century England, drama is the greatest achievement. There was (1) formal experiment and (2) a revival and imitation of the ancients, but there would not be a radical break with the recent, (3) medieval past, since

> [m]any conventions of the period – the mingling of jest and earnest in the theatre, for example – are features of medieval dramaturgy, and traditions of allegorical thinking, which for centuries had imbued so much art and biblical interpretation, did not disappear with the reconfiguration of tragedy in Senecan moulds, the writing of historical epics for the stage (witness Shakespeare's history plays), or the writing of new kinds of verse, like that of John Donne, seemingly written to the moment and rooted in experience. (Hattaway 68)

In matters of philosophical thought, humanism remains the governing philosophy of this period, influencing its type of thought and set of beliefs, its theory and criticism in art and literature, and its artistic and literary practice from Wyatt, Sidney and Shakespeare to Jonson and later Donne.

Following the English Renaissance literature – largely overlapping with what is termed "Tudor literature" between 1485 and 1603 – Ben Jonson appears to prolong into the seventeenth century the humanist attitude that a good poet must be a good man, a guide and guardian of morality, while prefiguring the neoclassical precepts of reason, order, measure, common sense, and imitation of the classics as some of the central principles which would come to be theoretically institutionalized and creatively asserted later by John Dryden, Alexander Pope, and Dr Samuel Johnson.

Shakespeare's comedy is rooted in romance aiming at comic relief; whereas Jonson's comedy is rooted in satire – his plays, for example *Volpone* (1606), being directed towards the exposure of vice and folly – and emphasises the need for ordered, restrained, rational, civilized living.

Again, this need and the satire represent other central elements of the neoclassical literary system which, in the seventeenth century, will be in the process of becoming and, in the eighteenth century, will flourish and eventually weaken and decay.

William Shakespeare, the complete Renaissance man, whose literary activity comprises both innovation and tradition, would embrace the contemporary artistic experimentation and originality but also remain faithful to the ancients allowing us to detect in his dramatic work, particularly tragedy, the elements of *arête* ("excellence"), *hamartia* ("tragic flaw"), *hubris* ("spiritual blindness"), *hybris* ("excessive pride"), as well as *anagnorisis* ("recognition"), *peripeteia* ("reversal of circumstances"), and many others.

Unlike Shakespeare, who embraced innovation and tradition, and developed complex genre and theme typologies, Jonson would be a faithful follower of the revived in Renaissance ancient classical tradition, which he harmoniously mingles with a comic, particularly satirical, mode of expression and a message of moral didacticism in one dramatic discourse.

As such, in literary history, Jonson is contrasted actually not with Shakespeare but with Donne, both representing, in the first decades of the seventeenth century preceding the Puritan Commonwealth Interregnum, two aspects of literature: "sons of Ben" standing for tradition and the imitation of the classics versus "school of Donne" or metaphysical poetry standing for innovation.

To revert to Elizabethan and Tudor drama, William Shakespeare along with Marlowe, Greene, Lyly, Kyd, Fletcher, Jonson and others represented the so-called "commercial theatre" or playhouse drama, which is the first type of drama of the period requiring investment of capital and permanent, purpose-built playhouses, involving professional writers and players, being subjected to censorship, and depending on patronage.

This sector of drama – representing an artistic industry of the period, professional, consumerist and urban – coexisted and was interrelated with the so-called "academic theatre" or university drama, which is the second type of Renaissance drama, also profit oriented but more educational as well as more amateur and, in this respect, being related to various other types, such as school drama and choirboy theatre.

Professional theatre developed with the opening of many metropolitan playhouses (such as the Curtain, the Red Bull, the Rose, the Globe, and so on); it flourished with the patronage and protection of important people, particularly the queen and her Privy Council; and it was impossible without the talent and hard work of various writers and players.

The literary history remembers names such as Shakespeare, Marlowe, and Jonson, but of equal importance was the contribution of James Burbage, for instance, an actor of the period, first a member of a strolling group of players under the patronage of the earl of Leicester, where, in 1574, Leicester's men was the first company of actors to receive a royal patent by which they could act throughout the country. In 1576, James Burbage built the "Theatre", the first purpose-built theatre in England, and his son Richard became the leading actor in Shakespeare's plays.

Touching various areas of human experience, Shakespeare's tragedies, nonetheless, can be grouped according to their thematic focus on love, revenge, and political action. The critical cliché of "tragedy extended beyond the limits of tragedy" in Shakespeare's plays answers to the explanation about "objective correlative" as postulated by T. S. Eliot during the age of modernism.

The tragic account of human condition is textualized in Shakespeare's dramatic works with diverse thematic implications just as there are various reasons responsible for the emergence of the tragedy into the world.

Among these, evil, inherent in human nature, is portrayed in different characters such as Iago or presented as a supernatural force, beyond and below the level of human life, but ready to intervene and enter unexpectedly the human world or society and disturb it leading to tragic consequences in its action through the hero's once loyal friend, or general, or brother, or spouse, tragic consequences which ultimately result in death. Sparking off tragedy is also the conflict between generations.

Tragedy can be also triggered by the binary opposition of the present (competent and efficient) versus past (simpler, older, more humane, but incompetent). Another conflict prompting tragic existence of the character is between personal ambition or advantage and the need for social order to be institutionalized or restored.

The hero or heroine, whose tragic account represents the essence of dramatic expression, follows the ancient "tragic flaw", or displays weakness of character, particularly moral weakness, or is subjected by his or her own error of judgement, or has taken a wrong decision.

The hero or heroine, however, only directs or accompanies the tragic impetus, because he or she in his or her commitment to love, or revenge, or political action, achieves a tragic commitment, since, by this, he or she defies society, the things as they are, the status quo, and seeks freedom by which he or she disturbs – assertion of freedom by their act leads to disturbance – and ends in failure: the act of liberation has its cost, which is the essence of a tragic existence.

In the first half of the seventeenth century, most of the Elizabethan dramatists, many of them contemporary to Shakespeare, began to fall into oblivion. The dramatic production of his time and, on the whole, of the golden age, the great period of Renaissance literature, still alive through Fletcher (who succeeded Shakespeare as chief dramatist), Beaumont and especially Jonson, is now sharing the literary field with metaphysical poetry; drama is apparently almost extinct in the mid seventeenth century during and due to the puritan Commonwealth Interregnum; and the attempts are made, in the second half of the century during the Restoration period, by Dryden and others, to revive it and, albeit unsuccessful, to restore it to the previous status and value.

In short, in the Elizabethan and Jacobean periods, Shakespeare was an author among others, though distinguishable in his creative complexity of genre and theme.

In the Restoration period, Dryden, particularly in *An Essay of Dramatic Poesy*, promotes a trinity of Shakespeare, Jonson, and Fletcher, and asserts Shakespeare's "most comprehensive soul", inborn personal genius, and unbound creativity;

For Dryden, Shakespeare is truly the complete Renaissance man, borrowing from ancient predecessors but also promoting innovation, originality, and experimentation, whereas regarding Jonson, his characteristics are among the main principles of neoclassicism. During Restoration, the first phase of neoclassicism, Dryden's adherence to classical inheritance is revealed through his admiration for Jonson and his more detailed as well as comprehensive critical appreciation of Jonson, as compared to the more general and superficial one of Shakespeare, which shows that for Dryden, Jonson is a kind of prototype found in late Renaissance period of a complete neoclassical man, whose plays should be taken as models of dramatic writing.

It seems likely that Dryden during Restoration – which represents the period of the rise of neoclassicism in English literature – promotes Jonson as a model for stagecraft in English literature and, while prescribing to his fellow writers the classical and contemporary, in particular French, doctrines to be followed in thought and theory, he certainly emphasises the Elizabethan and Jacobean drama of Shakespeare and Jonson to be revived and the contemporary European models to be imitated in literary practice.

Ever since the eighteenth century, Shakespeare became more widely accessible with the theatre public; romantic critical thought proclaimed him a genius, where Coleridge, among others, made him a solitary romantic archetypal poet; the Victorians made him also a best-seller; and throughout the twentieth century to the present, we live, as advanced by cultural and literary history, with the idea of being "Shakespearean" and the myth of his superiority and originality.

We have to break this critical cliché along binaries such as "Shakespearean" and "non-Shakespearean", or "pre-Shakespearean" and "post-Shakespearean", and objectively recognize him as a Renaissance theatre professional collaborating closely with his colleagues, influencing and being influenced, and combining originality and tradition, innovation and imitation.

We might participate in the efforts made nowadays to restore a continuum of dramatic experience and revive the value of Lyly, Kyd, Greene, Marlowe, and others who, along Shakespeare, created and promoted aesthetic values by means of scholarship, observation, influence as well as literary experiment, formal and thematic reconstruction, and imaginative flight.

At least, we ought to admit "the extent to which they enabled one another's work" while it can be also meaningful "to differentiate between him and his great contemporaries" (Wiggins 5).

Lyly, Kyd, Greene, Marlowe, Nashe and others during Elizabethan Age are Shakespeare's predecessors or contemporaries, and Jonson, Fletcher and Beaumont, representing Jacobean drama, are his successors, while Shakespeare himself covers both periods.

According to exact historical periodization as well as strictly chronologically, the literary activities of Ben Jonson, John Fletcher, and Francis Beaumont belong to the seventeenth century, but culturally and with regard to their literary implications, the works of these writers correspond to the "family resemblances" of Renaissance literary system, which is also supported by those who are inclined to include in Renaissance the first two parts of the seventeenth century: "Jacobean Age", between 1603 and 1625, and "Caroline Age", between 1625 and 1649.

These first two periods of the seventeenth century include also Francis Bacon's works, King James's translation of the Bible, Chapman's translation of the *Odyssey*, some of John Milton's major works, and especially Donne's, Herbert's and Marvell's metaphysical poems.

The first half of the seventeenth century, which saw the closing of the theatres in 1642, the Civil War, and the execution of Charles I in 1649, is literary dominated by Ben Jonson, promoter of the revived ancient classical tradition, and John Donne, promoter of metaphysical innovation and originality, making literary scholars to classify the writers of the period, somehow inappropriately, as the "Sons of Ben" and the "School of Donne".

The seventeenth century is commonly divided into four parts, the other two being the Puritan period of "Commonwealth Interregnum", between 1649 and 1660, a rather humble literary period except the works, literary and not only, by Milton, Hobbes, Bunyan, and Cowley, and its last part, called "Restoration Age", between

1660 and 1700, which saw the restoration of the Stuarts to the throne of England as well as the restoration of arts and literature, and being dominated by the literary and critical figure of John Dryden.

But the condition of English literature in the seventeenth century, a rather turbulent age, is to be the concern of our next book in this series on the historical advancement of literary practice and critical thinking in England.

REFERENCES AND SUGGESTIONS FOR FURTHER READING

References

Abrams, M. H. *The Mirror and the Lamp: Romantic Theory and the Critical Tradition.* Oxford: Oxford University Press, 1953.
Abrams, M. H., and G. G. Harpham. *A Glossary of Literary Terms* (9th Ed.). Belmont: Wadsworth Publishing Company, 2009.
Auerbach, E. *Mimesis: The Representation of Reality in Western Literature.* New York: Anchor Doubleday, 1957.
Auerbach, Erich. *Mimesis: Reprezentarea realitatii in literatura occidentala.* Iasi: Polirom, 2000.
Bakhtin, M. M. "Epic and Novel: Toward a Methodology for the Study of the Novel". *The Dialogic Imagination: Four Essays.* Ed. Michael Holquist. Austin: University of Texas Press, 1981. 1-40.
—. "Forms of Time and of the Chronotope in the Novel". *The Dialogic Imagination: Four Essays.* Ed. Michael Holquist. Austin: University of Texas Press, 1981. 84-258.
—. "Discourse in the Novel". *The Dialogic Imagination: Four Essays.* Ed. Michael Holquist. Austin: University of Texas Press, 1981. 259-422.
—. "The Bildungsroman and Its Significance in the History of Realism: Toward a Historical Typology of the Novel". *Speech Genres and Other Late Essays.* Ed. Caryl Emerson and Michael Holquist. Austin: University of Texas Press, 1986. 10-59.
—. *Rabelais and His World.* Bloomington: Indiana University Press, 1984.
—. *Problems of Dostoevsky's Poetics.* Minneapolis: University of Minnesota Press, 1984.
Baldick, C. *The Oxford English Literary History, Volume 10. 1910-1940: The Modern Movement.* Oxford: Oxford University Press, 2005.
Barry, P. *Beginning Theory: An Introduction to Literary and Cultural Theory.* Manchester: Manchester University Press, 2009.
Barthes, R. *Mythologies.* New York: The Noonday Press, 1970.
Berquist, James. "Macbeth as Tragic Hero: A Defence and Explanation of Macbeth's Tragic Character". *Ramify*, 5 (1). 2015. 105-118.
Blamires, Harry. *A History of Literary Criticism.* London: Macmillan, 1991.
Bomher, N. *Initieri in teoria literaturii.* Iasi: Editura Fundatiei Chemarea, 1994.
Bressler, C. E. *Literary Criticism: An Introduction to Theory and Practice.* Englewood Cliffs: Prentice-Hall Inc., 2007.
Brownlee, Marina S. "Discursive Parameters of the Picaresque". *The Picaresque: A Symposium on the Rogue's Tale.* Ed. Carmen Benito-Vessels and Michael Zappala. Newark: University of Delaware Press, 1994. 25-35.
Cartianu, A. and I. A. Preda. *Dicționar al literaturii engleze.* Bucuresti: Editura Stiintifica, 1970.
Castle, G. *The Blackwell Guide to Literary Theory.* Oxford: Blackwell Publishing, 2007.
Ceuca, J. *Evoluția formelor dramatice.* Cluj-Napoca: Dacia, 2002.
Christensen, E. O. *A Pictorial History of Western Art.* New York: The New American Library, 1964.

Cioranescu, A. *Principii de literatură comparată*. București: Cartea Românească, 1997.
Cole, David. *The Theatrical Event*. Middletown: Wesleyan University Press, 1975.
Collini, S. "Introduction: Interpretation terminable and interminable". *Interpretation and Overinterpretation: Umberto Eco with Richard Rorty, Jonathan Culler, Christine Brooke-Rose*. Ed. S. Collini. Cambridge: Cambridge University Press, 1992. 1-21.
Cook, Guy. *Discourse and Literature: The Interplay of Form and Mind*. Oxford: Oxford University Press, 1995.
Cousins, A. D. "The Mythology and Theology of Love in Spenser's *Amoretti*". *English Studies*. 98: 2, 2017. 97-119.
Cousins, A.D. "Refiguring the Donna Angelica and Rewriting Petrarch in Shakespeare's Sonnets". *English Studies*, 99: 3, 2018. 255-279.
Cubert, Joan. "Edmund Spenser's Bestiary in the "Amoretti". *Atlantis*, Vol. 24, No. 2, 2002. 41-58.
Cuddon, J. A. *The Penguin Dictionary of Literary Terms and Literary Theory*. London: Penguin Books Ltd, 1992.
Culler, J. *Structuralist Poetics: Structuralism, Linguistics and the Study of Literature*. London: Routledge and Kegan Paul, 1980.
Culler, J. *Literary Theory*. New York: Sterling Publishing Co., Inc., 2009.
Daiches, D. *Critical Approach to Literature*. London: Longman, 1982.
Davis, J. C. "Thomas More's *Utopia*: sources, legacy and interpretation". *The Cambridge Companion to Utopian Literature*. Ed. Gregory Claeys. Cambridge: Cambridge University Press, 2010.
Doty, Jeffrey S. "Shakespeare's Richard II, "Popularity" and the Early Modern Public Sphere". *Shakespeare Quarterly*, Vol. 61, No. 2, 2010. 183-205.
Ducrot, O., and J.-M. Schaeffer. *Noul dictionar enciclopedic al stiintelor limbajului*. Bucuresti: Editura Babel, 1996.
Dunlop, Alexander. "Calendar Symbolism in the Amoretti". *Notes and Queries* 214, 1969. 24-26.
Eagleton, T. *The English Novel: An Introduction*. Oxford: Blackwell Publishing, 2005.
Eagleton, T. *Literary Theory: An Introduction*. Oxford: Blackwell Publishing, 2008.
Echevarría, Roberto González. *Love and the Law in Cervantes*. New Haven: Yale University Press, 2005.
Eco, U. "Overinterpreting texts". *Interpretation and Overinterpretation: Umberto Eco with Richard Rorty, Jonathan Culler, Christine Brooke-Rose*. Ed. S. Collini. Cambridge: Cambridge University Press, 1992. 45-66.
Eco, U. "Between author and text". *Interpretation and Overinterpretation: Umberto Eco with Richard Rorty, Jonathan Culler, Christine Brooke-Rose*. Ed. S. Collini. Cambridge: Cambridge University Press, 1992. 67-88.
Eco, U. "Interpretation and History". *Interpretation and Overinterpretation: Umberto Eco with Richard Rorty, Jonathan Culler, Christine Brooke-Rose*. Ed. S. Collini. Cambridge: Cambridge University Press, 1992. 23-43
Eco, U. *Apocalypse Postponed*. London: Flamingo, 1995.
Edward, Anthony. *John Skelton: The Critical Heritage*. London: Taylor and Francis Group, 1996.
Edwards, Philip. "William Shakespeare". *The Oxford Illustrated History of English Literature*. Ed. P. Rogers. Oxford: Oxford University Press, 1996. 112 – 159.
Eliot, T. S. *The Sacred Wood: Essays on Poetry and Criticism*. New York: Alfred A. Knopf, 1921.
Elliot, Jr. John. R. "History and Tragedy in Richard II". *Studies in English Literature,*

1500-1900. Vol. 8, No. 2, 1968. 253-271.
Fairley, I. R. "The reader's need for conventions". *The Taming of the Text: Explorations in Language, Literature and Culture.* Ed. W. Van Peer. London: Routledge, 1988. 292-316.
Ficher-Lichte, Erika. *History of European Drama.* Florence: Routledge, 2001.
Fokkema, D., and E. Ibsch. *Theories of Literature in the Twentieth Century: Structuralism, Marxism, Aesthetics of Reception, Semiotics.* New York: St Martin's Press, 1995.
Fowler, R. "Literature". *Encyclopedia of Literature and Criticism.* Eds. M. Coyle, P. Garside, M. Kelsall, and J. Peck. London: Routledge, 2000. 3-26.
Frye, Northrop. *Anatomy of Criticism: Four Essays.* London: Penguin Books, 1990.
Gardner, H. *The Business of Criticism.* Oxford: Oxford University Press, 1970.
Gengembre, G. *Marile curente ale criticii literare,* Iasi: Institutul European, 2000.
Giddens, Anthony. *Modernity and Self-Identity: Self and Society in the Late Modern Age.* Cambridge: Polity Press, 1991.
Goddard, Harold C. *Meaning of Shakespeare.* Chicago: Chicago University Press, 1960.
Griffiths, Jane. *John Skelton and Poetic Authority: Defining Liberty to Speak.* Oxford: Oxford University Press, 2006.
Guillén, Claudio. "Toward a Definition of the Picaresque". *Literature as System: Essays Toward the Theory of Literary History.* Princeton: Princeton University Press, 1971. 71-110.
Hadfield, Andrew. *The English Renaissance 1500-1620.* London: Wiley-Blackwell, 2000.
Hampshire, S. *The Age of Reason: The 17th Century Philosophers.* New York: The New American Library, 1956.
Harland, Richard. *Literary Theory from Plato to Barthes: An Introductory History.* New York: Palgrave Macmillan, 1999.
Hattaway, Michael. *Renaissance and Reformations: An Introduction to Early Modern English Literature.* Oxford: Blackwell Publishing, 2007.
Healy, Margaret. "Richard II". *Shakespeare: Text and Performance.* Ed. Kiernan Ryan. London: Macmillan Press, 2000.
Heidegger, M. *Poetry, Language, Thought.* New York: Harper and Row, 1971.
Highet, Gilbert. *The Classical Tradition: Greek and Roman Influences on Western Literature.* Oxford: Oxford University Press, 1976.
Hunter, G.K. "Comedy, farce, romance". *Comedy from Shakespeare to Sheridan.* Eds. A. R. Braunmuller and J. C. Bulman. London: Associated University Press, 1986.
Hutcheon, Linda. *A Poetics of Postmodernism: History, Theory, Fiction.* London, Routledge, 1988.
Jakobson, R. "Linguistics and Poetics". *Modern Criticism and Theory.* Ed. D. Lodge. London: Longman, 2000. 30-55.
Jauss, H. R. "Literary History as a Challenge to Literary Theory". *New Directions in Literary History.* Ed. R. Cohen. Baltimore: The Johns Hopkins University Press, 1974. 11-41.
Jauss, H. R. *Toward an Aesthetic of Reception.* Minneapolis: University of Minnesota Press, 1982.
Keilen, Sean. "The Tradition of Shakespeare's Sonnets". *Shakespeare,* 5: 3, 2009. 235-252.
Kennedy, W. J. "Humanist classifications of poetry among the arts and sciences". *The Cambridge History of Literary Criticism, Volume 3: The Renaissance.* Ed. G. P. Norton. Cambridge: Cambridge University Press, 2001. 91-97.
Klinck, Dennis R. "Shakespeare's Richard II as Landlord and Wasting Tenant". *College*

Literature. Vol. 25, No. 1, 1998. 21-34.

Laroque, François. *Shakespeare's Festive World: Elizabethan Seasonal Entertainment and the Professional Stage.* Cambridge: Cambridge University Press, 1991.

Larsen, Kenneth J. *Edmund Spenser's Amoretti and Epithalamion: A Critical Edition.* Tempe: Arizona State University, 1997.

Leech, C. *Tragedy.* London: Methuen, 1969.

Leech, G. N. *A Linguistic Guide to English Poetry.* London: Longman, 1979.

Levenson, Jill. "Comedy". *The Cambridge Companion to English Renaissance Drama.* Eds. A. R. Braunmuller and M. Hattaway. Cambridge: Cambridge University Press, 2003. 254-291.

Lodge, David. *The Novelist at the Crossroads and Other Essays on Fiction and Criticism.* Ithaca: Cornell University Press, 1971.

Machor, J. L., and P. Goldstein. *Reception Study: From Literary Theory to Cultural Studies.* London: Routledge, 2001.

Mangan, Michael. *A Preface to Shakespeare's Comedies: 1594-1603.* London: Longman, 1996.

McKeon, Michael. (2002). *The Origins of the English Novel, 1600-1740.* John Hopkins University Press.

Moseley, C.W.R.D. *English Renaissance Drama: An Introduction to Theatre and Theatres in Shakespeare's Time.* London: Humanities-Ebooks, LLP, 2007.

Moseley, C.W.R.D. *Shakespeare's History Plays: Richard II to Henry V, the Making of a King.* Penrith: Humanities – Ebooks, LLP, 2009.

Munteanu, R. *Metamorfozele criticii europene.* Bucuresti: Univers, 1988.

Munteanu, R. *Introducere in literatura europeana moderna.* Bucuresti: ALLFA, 1996.

Nicol, Bran. *The Cambridge Introduction to Postmodern Fiction.* Cambridge: Cambridge University Press, 2009.

Ousby, Ian. *The Cambridge Guide to Literature in English.* Cambridge: Cambridge University Press, 1993.

Pavis, Patrice. *Dictionary of the Theatre: Terms, Concepts, and Analysis.* Toronto: University of Toronto Press, 1998.

Pavlicencu, S. *Caiet de studiu la Istoria literaturii universale: Epoca Renasterii.* Chisinau: Litera Educational, 2004.

Peck, J., and M. Coyle. *Literary Terms and Criticism* (3rd Ed.). New York: Palgrave Macmillan, 2002.

Perkins, D. "Literary history and historicism". *The Cambridge History of Literary Criticism, Volume 5: Romanticism.* Ed. M. Brown. Cambridge: Cambridge University Press, 2000. 338-361.

Pitcher, John. "Tudor Literature". *The Oxford Illustrated History of English Literature.* Ed. P. Rogers. Oxford: Oxford University Press, 1996. 59 – 111.

Ramsey. Jarold. "The Perversion of Manliness in Macbeth". *Studies in English Literature, 1500-1900.* Vol. 13, No. 2. 1973. 285-300.

Regan, Stephen. "Macbeth". *Shakespeare: Text and Performance.* Ed. Ryan Kiernan. London: Macmillan Press, 2000.

Richter, David H. *The Critical Tradition: Classic Texts and Contemporary Trends.* New York: St Martin's Press, 1989.

Ricoeur, P. *Eseuri de hermeneutica.* Bucuresti: Humanitas, 1995.

Rivers, Isabel. *Classical and Christian Ideas in English Renaissance Poetry.* London: Taylor and Francis Group, 1994.

Rixon, Penny. "A Midsummer Night's Dream". *Shakespeare: Text and Performance.* Ed.

Ryan Kiernan. London: Macmillan Press, 2000.

Sanders, A. *The Short Oxford History of English Literature*. Oxford: Clarendon Press, 1994.

Schechner, Richard. "Drama, Script, Theatre and Performance". *The Drama Review*. Vol. 17, 1973.

Scholes, R. *Semiotics and Interpretation*. New Haven: Yale University Press, 1982.

Selden, R. *A Reader's Guide to Contemporary Literary Theory*. New York: Harvester Wheatsheaf, 1989.

Selden, R. "Introduction". *The Cambridge History of Literary Criticism, Volume 8: From Formalism to Poststructuralism*. Ed. R. Selden. Cambridge: Cambridge University Press, 1995. 1-10.

Shklovsky, V. "Art as Technique". *The Critical Tradition: Classic Texts and Contemporary Trends*. Ed. David H. Richter. New York: Bedford/St. Martin's, 1997. 774-784.

Shusterman, R. *The Object of Literary Criticism*. Amsterdam: Rodopi, 1984.

Stevenson, R. *The Oxford English Literary History, Volume 12. 1960-2000: The Last of England?*. Oxford: Oxford University Press. 2004.

Talbert, Ernest William. *The Problem of Order: Elizabethan Political Commonplaces and an Example of Shakespeare's Art*. Chapel Hill: University of North Carolina Press, 1962.

Trimpi, W. "Sir Philip Sidney's *An apology for Poetry*". *The Cambridge History of Literary Criticism, Volume 3: The Renaissance*. Ed. G. P. Norton. Cambridge: Cambridge University Press, 2001. 187-198.

Turner, Myron. "The Imagery of Spenser's Amoretti". *Neophilologus* 72, 1988. 284-299.

Tynyanov, Y. N. "Literaturnyi fakt". *Poetika. Istoria literaturi. Kino*. Moscva: Nauka, 1977. 255-270.

Tynyanov, Y. N. "O literaturnoi evolutii". *Poetika. Istoria literaturi. Kino*. Moscva: Nauka, 1977. 270-281.

Ubersfeld, Anne. *Reading Theatre*. Toronto: University of Toronto Press, 1999.

Vendler, Helen. *The Art of Shakespeare's Sonnets*. London: Harvard University Press, 1997.

Vickers, B. "The Seventeenth Century". *The Oxford Illustrated History of English Literature*. Ed. P. Rogers. Oxford: Oxford University Press, 1996. 160 – 213.

Vieira, Fatima. "The Concept of Utopia". *The Cambridge Companion to Utopian Literature*. Ed. Gregory Claeys. Cambridge: Cambridge University Press, 2010.

Watson, Robert N. "Tragedies of Revenge and Ambition". *The Cambridge Companion to Shakespearean Tragedy*. Cambridge: Cambridge University Press, 2003. 160-181.

Watson, Robert N. "Tragedy". *The Cambridge Companion to English Renaissance Drama*. Eds. A. R. Braunmuller and M. Hattaway. Cambridge: Cambridge University Press, 2003. 292-343.

Webster, R. *Studying Literary Theory: An Introduction*. London: Edward Arnold. 1993.

Wellek, R., and A. Warren. *Theory of Literature*. New York: Harcourt, 1962.

Wiggins, Martin. *Shakespeare and the Drama of His Time*. Oxford: Oxford University Press, 2000.

Williams, John. *English Renaissance Poetry*. London: The University of Arkansas Press, 1990.

Womack, Peter. *English Renaissance Drama*. London: Wiley-Blackwell, 2006.

Zukerman, Cordelia. "A Multitude of Eyes, Tongues, and Mouths: Readerly Agency in Shakespeare's Sonnets". *History of European Ideas*, 42: 5, 2016. 629-639.

Suggestions for Further Reading

General Literary History and Criticism

Abrams, M. H. (Ed.). *The Norton Anthology of English Literature*. New York: Norton, 1986.
Allen, W. *The English Novel: A Short Critical History*, London: Penguin Books Ltd., 1954.
Baker, E. A. *The History of the English Novel*, London: Witherby, 1969.
Bakhtin, M. M. *The Dialogic Imagination: Four Essays*. Austin: University of Texas Press, 1981.
Bakhtin, M. M. *Rabelais and His World*. Bloomington: Indiana University Press, 1984.
Bakhtin, M. M. *Problems of Dostoevsky's Poetics*. Minneapolis: University of Minnesota Press, 1984.
Bakhtin, M. M. *Speech Genres and Other Late Essays*. Austin: University of Texas Press, 1986.
Bateson, F. W., and H. T. Meserole. *A Guide to English and American Literature*. London: Longman, 1976.
Beachcroft, T. O. *The English Short Story*, London: Longman, 1964.
Belsey, C. *Critical Practice*. London: Routledge, 1980.
Bernard, R. *A Short History of English Literature*. Oxford: Blackwell Publishing, 1995.
Bjornson, Richard. *The Picaresque Hero in European Fiction*. Wisconsin: The University of Wisconsin Press, 1977.
Blamires, H. *A Short History of English Literature*. London: Routledge, 1984.
Blamires, H. *A History of Literary Criticism*. London: Macmillan, 1991.
Bressler, C. E. *Literary Criticism: An Introduction to Theory and Practice*. Englewood Cliffs: Prentice-Hall Inc, 2007.
Cartianu, A., and I. A. Preda. *Dictionar al literaturii engleze*. Bucuresti: Editura Stiintifica, 1970.
Ceuca, J. *Evoluția formelor dramatice*. Cluj-Napoca: Dacia, 2002.
Clement, B. *Tragedia clasică*. Iași: Institutul European, 2000.
Conrad, P. *The Everyman History of English Literature*. London: J. M. Dent and Sons Ltd., 1985.
Cuddon, J. A. *The Penguin Dictionary of Literary Terms and Literary Theory*. London: Penguin Books Ltd, 1992.
Cusset, C. *Tragedia greaca*. Iasi: Institutul European, 1999.
Daiches, D. *English Literature*. Englewood Cliffs: Prentice-Hall Inc., 1964.
Daiches, D. *A Critical History of English Literature*. New York: The Ronald Press Company, 1970.
Daiches, D. *The Penguin Companion to English Literature*. New York: McGraw-Hill, 1971.
Day, G. *Literary Criticism: A New History*. Edinburgh: Edinburgh University Press, 2008.
Day, M. S. *History of English Literature to Sixteen Sixty*. New York: Doubleday Books, 1963.
Drabble, M. (Ed.). *The Oxford Companion to English Literature*. Oxford: Oxford University Press, 2000.
Dunn, Peter N. *Spanish Picaresque Fiction: A New Literary History*. Ithaca: Cornell University Press, 1993.

Dutton, R. *An Introduction to Literary Criticism*. London: Longman, 1984.
Eagle, D. *The Concise Oxford Dictionary of English Literature*. Oxford: Oxford University Press, 1987.
Eagleton, T. *The English Novel: An Introduction*, Oxford: Blackwell Publishing, 2005.
Eliade, M. *Images et Symboles*. Gallimard, 1952.
Eliade, M. *Aspecte ale mitului*. București: Editura Univers, 1978.
Ford, B. (Ed.). *The New Pelican Guide to English Literature*. London: Penguin Books Ltd., 1982.
Fowler, A. *Kinds of Literature: An Introduction to the Theory of Genres and Modes*. Oxford: Clarendon Press, 1987.
Fowler, A. *A History of English Literature*. Cambridge: Harvard University Press, 1991.
Frank, M. *Gender, Theatre, and the Origins of Criticism: From Dryden to Manley*. Port Chester: Cambridge University Press, 2002.
Freidenberg, O. *Image and Concept: Mythopoetic Roots of Literature*, Amsterdam: Harwood Academic Publishers, 1997.
Frevert, U., and H.-G. Haupt. *Omul secolului al XIX-lea*. Bucuresti: Polirom, 2002.
Frye, N. *Anatomy of Criticism: Four Essays*. London: Penguin Books, 1990.
Galperin, I. R. *Stylistics*. Moscow: Higher School Publishing House, 1971.
Graf, A. *Marile curente ale filosofiei moderne*. Iasi: Institutul European, 1997.
Hall, V. *A Short History of Literary Criticism*. London: The Merlin Press, 1964.
Heidegger, M. *Poetry, Language, Thought*. New York: Harper and Row, 1971.
Highet, G. *The Classical Tradition: Greek and Roman Influences on Western Literature*. Oxford: Oxford University Press, 1976.
Holman, C. H., and W. A. Harmon. *A Handbook to Literature*. New York: Macmillan, 1992.
Jauss, H. R. *Aesthetic Experience and Literary Hermeneutics*. Minneapolis: University of Minnesota Press, 1982.
Jauss, H. R. *Question and Answer: Forms of Dialogic Understanding*. Minneapolis: University of Minnesota Press, 1989.
Kirkpatrick, D. L. (Ed.). *Reference Guide to English Literature*. London: St James Press, 1991.
Knellwolf, C., and C. Norris. (Eds.). *The Cambridge History of Literary Criticism, Volume 9: Twentieth Century Historical, Philosophical and Psychological Perspectives*. Cambridge: Cambridge University Press, 2001.
Lawrence, K. *The McGraw-Hill Guide to English Literature*. New York: McGraw-Hill, 1985.
Leech, C. *Tragedy*. London: Methuen, 1969.
Leech, G. N. *A Linguistic Guide to English Poetry*. London: Longman, 1979.
Legonis, E., and L. Cazamian. *History of English Literature*. London: J. M. Dent and Sons Ltd., 1971.
Lotman, Y. M. "Lektsii po strukturalinoi poetike". *Y. M. Lotman i tartusko-moskovskaya semioticeskaia shkola*. Moskva: Gnozis, 1994. 10-257.
Magill, F. N. (Ed.). *Cyclopedia of Literary Characters*. New York: Harper and Row, 1963.
Minnis, A., and I. Johnson. (Eds.). *The Cambridge History of Literary Criticism, Volume 2: The Middle Ages*. Cambridge: Cambridge University Press, 2005.
Munteanu, R. *Farsa tragica*. București: Univers, 1989.
Nisbet, H. B., and C. Rawson. (Eds.). *The Cambridge History of Literary Criticism, Volume 4: The Eighteenth Century*. Cambridge: Cambridge University Press, 2005.
Norton, G. P. (Ed.). *The Cambridge History of Literary Criticism, Volume 3: The Renaissance*.

Cambridge: Cambridge University Press, 2001.
Ousby, I. (Ed.). *The Cambridge Guide to English Literature*. Cambridge: Cambridge University Press, 1993.
Parrinder, P. *Nation and Novel: The English Novel from its Origins to the Present Day*. Oxford: Oxford University Press, 2006.
Richter, D. H. *The Critical Tradition: Classic Texts and Contemporary Trends*. New York: St Martin's Press. 1989
Ricoeur, Paul. *Eseuri de hermeneutica*. Bucuresti: Humanitas, 1995.
Robert, M. *Romanul inceputurilor si inceputurile romanului*. Bucuresti: Editura Univers, 1983.
Rogers, P. (Ed.). *The Oxford Illustrated History of English Literature*. Oxford: Oxford University Press, 1990.
Sampson, G. *The Concise Cambridge History of English Literature*. Cambridge: Cambridge University Press, 1970.
Sanders, A. *The Short Oxford History of English Literature*. Oxford: Oxford University Press, 1994.
Shklovsky, Viktor. *O teorii prozy*. Moskva: Federatia, 1929.
Stapleton, M. *The Cambridge Guide to English Literature*. Cambridge: Cambridge University Press, 1983.
Stephen, M. *An Introductory Guide to English Literature*. London: Longman, 1984.
Thornley, G. C., and G. Roberts. *An Outline of English Literature*. London: Longman, 1995.
Ubersfeld, A. *Termenii cheie ai analizei teatrului*. Iasi: Institutul European, 1999.
Urnov, D. M. (Ed.). *The Idea of Literature: The Foundations of English Criticism*. Moscow: Progress Publishers, 1979.
Van Boheemen-Saaf, C. *Between Sacred and Profane: Narrative Design and the Logic of Myth from Chaucer to Coover*, Amsterdam: Rodopi, 1987.
Ward, A. C. *Illustrated History of English Literature*. London: Longman, 1960.
Ward, A. W., and A. R. Waller. *The Cambridge History of English Literature*. Cambridge: Cambridge University Press, 1953.
Waugh, P. (Ed.). *Literary Theory and Criticism: An Oxford Guide*. Oxford: Oxford University Press, 2006.
Wynne-Davis, M. (Ed.). *The Bloomsbury Guide to English Literature*. London: Bloomsburg Publishing Ltd., 1960.

English Renaissance Literature

Barton, A. *Ben Jonson: Dramatist*, Cambridge: Cambridge University Press, 1984.
Belsey, C. *The Subject of Tragedy: Identity and Difference in Renaissance Drama*, London: Routledge, 1985.
Buxton, J. *Elizabethan Taste*, London: Macmillan, 1963.
Champion, L. S. *The Evolution of Shakespeare's Comedy: A Study in Dramatic Perspective*, Cambridge: Harvard University Press, 1970.
Chapman, G. W. *Essays on Shakespeare*, Princeton: Princeton University Press, 1965.
Dash, I. G. *Wooing, Wedding and Power: Women in Shakespeare's Plays*, New York: Columbia University Press, 1981.
Dollimore, J. *Radical Tragedy: Religion, Ideology and Power in the Drama of Shakespeare and*

His Contemporaries, Brighton: The Harvester Press, 1984.
Eagleton, T. *William Shakespeare*, Oxford: Basil Blackwell, 1986.
Edwards, P. *Shakespeare: A Writer's Progress*, Oxford: Oxford University Press, 1986.
Elam, K. *Shakespeare's Universe of Discourse: Language-Games in the Comedies*, Cambridge: Cambridge University Press, 1984.
Ghose, Z. *Shakespeare's Mortal Knowledge: A Reading of the Tragedies*, New York: St Martin's Press, 1993.
Goldman, M. *Acting and Action in Shakespearean Tragedy*, Princeton: Princeton University Press, 1985.
Greenblatt, S. J. *Renaissance Self-Fashioning: from More to Shakespeare*, Chicago: University of Chicago Press, 1984.
Gurr, A. J. *The Shakespearean Stage 1574-1642*, Cambridge: Cambridge University Press, 1992.
Hamilton, D. B. (ed.) *A Concise Companion to English Renaissance Literature*, Oxford: Blackwell Publishing Ltd, 2006.
Hattaway, M. *Elizabethan Popular Theatre: Plays in Performance*, London: Routledge, 1982.
Heale, E. *Autobiography and Authorship in Renaissance Verse: Chronicles of the Self*, Gordonsville: Palgrave Macmillan, 2003.
Hillman, R. *Intertextuality and Romance in Renaissance Drama: The Staging of Nostalgia*, New York: St Martin's Press, 1992.
Hollander, J. *Vision and Resonance: Two Senses of Poetic Form*, Oxford: Oxford University Press, 1975.
King, J. N. *English Reformation Literature: The Tudor Origins of the Protestant Tradition*, Princeton: Princeton University Press, 1982.
Leggatt, A. *English Drama: Shakespeare to Restoration 1590-1660*, London: Longman, 1988.
Levin, H. *Christopher Marlowe: The Over-Reacher*, Cambridge: Cambridge University Press, 1952.
Lewis, C. S. *The Discarded Image: An Introduction to Medieval and Renaissance Literature*, Cambridge: Cambridge University Press, 1994.
Lotspeich, H. *Classical Mythology in the Poetry of Edmund Spenser*, Princeton: Princeton University Press, 1932.
Matz, R. *Defending Literature in Early Modern England: Renaissance Literary Theory in Social Context*, Cambridge: Cambridge University Press, 2000.
Muir, K. *The Sources of Shakespeare's Plays*, New Haven: Yale University Press, 1978.
Pomeroy, E. W. *The Elizabethan Miscellanies*, Berkeley: University of California Press, 1973.
Righter A. *Shakespeare and the Idea of the Play*, London: Penguin Books, 1967.
Root, R. K. *Classical Mythology in Shakespeare*, New York: Gordian Press, 1965.
Rowse, A. L. *Shakespeare the Man*, New York: Harper and Row, 1973.
Ryan, K. (ed.) *Shakespeare: Texts and Contexts*, London: Macmillan, 2000.
Schoenbaum, S. *William Shakespeare: A Documentary Life*, Oxford: Oxford University Press, 1975.
Simpson, P. *Studies in Elizabethan Drama*, Oxford: Clarendon Press, 1955.
Southall, R. *The Courtly Maker: An Essay on the Poetry of Wyatt and his Contemporaries*, New York: Barnes and Noble, 1964.
Stanley, W. (ed.) *The Cambridge Companion to Shakespeare Studies*, Cambridge: Cambridge University Press, 1986.
Stephens, D. *The Limits of Eroticism in Post-Petrarchan Narrative: Conditional Pleasure from*

Spenser to Marvell, Cambridge: Cambridge University Press, 1999.
Thomson, P. *Shakespeare's Theatre*, London: Routledge, 1983.
Wells, S. (ed.) *The Cambridge Companion to Shakespeare Studies*, Cambridge: Cambridge University Press, 1986.
Wheeler, C. F. *Classical Mythology in the Plays, Masques, and Poems of Ben Jonson*, Port Washington: Kennikat Press, 1970.

INDEX

Abrams, M. H., 22, 23
Ackroyd, Peter, 35, 38
Aleman, Mateo, 125, 127
Ali, Monica, 35
Amis, K., 35
Apollinaire, G., 35
Aragon, L., 35
Ariosto, Ludovico, 88
Aristotle, 22, 23, 66, 67, 76, 83, 86, 87, 88, 89, 90, 94, 95, 96, 97, 99, 142, 143, 144, 180, 184
Arnold, Matthew, 2, 11, 14, 34, 38
Auerbach, Erich, 18, 126, 136
Augustine, St, 79, 81
Austen, Jane, 1, 33, 124

Bacon, Francis, 12, 32, 74, 76, 87, 91, 117, 122, 139, 203
Bacon, Roger, 155
Bakhtin, Mikhail, 1, 4, 10, 24, 41, 42, 45, 46, 50, 53, 56, 124, 125, 129, 132, 133, 134, 135, 136, 175
Barca, Calderon de, 87
Barnes, Julian, 35, 41, 59, 60
Barrett Browning, Elizabeth, 9
Barthes, Roland, 20, 21
Beardsley, M. C., 51
Beaumont, Francis, 140, 196, 197, 201, 206, 207
Beckett, Samuel, 35, 37
Bedford, John, 152
Bellay, Joachim du, 89, 90, 108
Bhabha, Homi, 55
Blake, William, 33, 37, 41
Bloom, Harold, 46
Boccaccio, G., 156
Bole, John, 152
Braine, John, 35
Brontë, Charlotte, 34, 37
Brontë, Emily, 34, 37
Brooke, Christopher, 198
Browning, Robert, 34, 37
Bunyan, John, 93, 207
Burns, Robert, 34

Byron, George Gordon, Lord, 33, 34, 37, 89, 108, 166

Caedmon, 32
Calinescu, George, 19
Campanela, Tomaso, 79,
Campion, Thomas, 91, 104
Carew, Thomas, 195,
Carroll, Lewis, 37
Carlyle, Thomas, 34
Carter, Angela, 35, 54
Castelvetro, Lodovico, 89, 90
Caxton, William, 72, 90
Cazamian, Louis, 37
Cervantes, Miguel de, 1, 123, 124, 125, 126, 127
Chapman, George, 140, 142, 154, 207
Chateaubriand, 12
Chaucer, Geoffrey, 31, 32, 37, 73, 100, 154
Churchill, Caryl, 35
Cicero, 75, 76, 77, 83
Cinthio, 88, 89
Coelho, P., 54
Coleridge, S. T., 2, 28, 33, 34, 37, 41, 44, 207
Colet, John, 75
Comte, A., 34
Conrad, Joseph, 34
Cook, Guy, 10, 23, 24, 42, 57
Corneille, Pierre, 87, 91
Cox, Leonard, 90
Curtius, E. R., 18
Cynewulf, 32

Daiches, David, 51
Daniel, Samuel, 91, 100, 189
Dante, Alighieri, 1, 34, 89, 100, 110
Darwin, Charles, 34
Defoe, Daniel, 33, 37
Derrida, Jacques, 12
Descartes, Rene, 74, 91, 117, 122
Dickens, Charles, 1, 7, 34, 37, 124
Dionysius of Halicarnassus, 77
Donne, John, 1, 33, 37, 72, 93, 116,

160, 195, 198, 204, 205, 207
Doolittle, Hilda, 35
Dostoyevsky, F., 1
Doyle, A. C., 34
Drabble, M., 35
Dryden, John, 2, 33, 37, 39, 64, 91, 158, 196, 201, 204, 206, 208

Eagleton, T., 39, 124
Eco, Umberto, 12, 20
Eliade, Mircea, 54, 64
Eliot, George, 34, 37
Eliot, T. S., 1, 2, 13, 14, 35, 38, 41, 42, 45, 46, 47, 64, 108, 205
Elyot, Thomas, 90, 97, 104
Erasmus, D., 75, 76, 77, 78, 79, 81, 82, 86, 139
Euripides, 1, 87
Even-Zohar, I., 55

Faulkner, W., 35
Fielding, Henry, 2, 33, 37, 39
Fish, Stanley, 13
Fletcher, John, 140, 196-197, 201, 205, 206, 207
Fowles, John, 35, 38
Freud, Sigmund, 3, 34, 164
Frye, Northrop, 14, 20, 124

Galsworthy, John, 14, 35
Gascoigne, George, 90, 102
Goethe, J. W., 44, 45, 47, 56, 132, 136, 154
Golding, William, 35, 38
Gosson, Stephen, 91, 93, 94, 97, 142
Gower, John, 32, 37
Gray, Thomas, 33, 54
Greene, Robert, 137, 140, 142, 155, 161
Guevara, Luis Velez de, 125

Heaney, S., 35
Hegel, G. W. F., 66, 74
Heidegger, Martin, 85, 86
Herbert, George, 93, 207
Herder, G. H., 1, 12
Herrick, Robert, 195
Heywood, John, 152, 153
Hobbes, Thomas, 93, 207

Hoccleve, Thomas, 32
Homer, 1, 90, 179, 201
Hopkins, G. M., 34, 37
Howard, Henry, 32, 74, 99, 100, 101, 139
Horace, 22, 34, 74, 77, 82, 87, 88, 89, 94, 95, 96, 97, 105, 120, 142, 198, 200
Hughes, Ted, 35, 38
Hutcheon, Linda, 4, 54, 55
Huxley, Aldous, 35, 79

Ionesco, E., 54

Jakobson, Roman, 9, 10, 14, 23, 25, 42, 55
James, Henry, 2, 47
Jauss, Hans Robert, 18, 19, 20
Johnson, Samuel, 1, 2, 31, 33, 204
Jonson, Ben, 2, 33, 39, 54, 89, 91, 99, 116, 138, 140, 142, 154, 195, 196, 197-201, 204, 205, 206, 207
Joyce, James, 1, 28, 29, 35, 37, 38, 64

Kafka, Franz, 35
Kant, Immanuel, 74, 86, 203
Keats, John, 34, 37, 108, 159
Kipling, R., 34
Kis, Danilo, 54
Kristeva, Julia, 46, 55
Kundera, Milan, 54
Kyd, Thomas, 32, 140, 142, 143, 152, 153, 158, 205, 207

Langland, William, 32
Larkin, Philip, 35, 38
Lawrence, D. H., 14, 35, 37, 38
Legouis, Emile, 37
Lessing, G. E., 1
Leavis, F. R., 13, 18
Locke, John, 74
Lodge, David, 2, 15, 17, 35, 38. 64
Lodge, Thomas, 153
Longinus, 89
Lorca, Garcia, 35
Lotman, Yuri, 42
Lovelace, Richard, 195
Lowth, Robert, 12
Lubbock, Percy, 1

Lucian, 77, 81, 82
Lydgate, John, 32
Lyly, John, 32, 33, 123

Macpherson, James, 33
Malory, Thomas, 32, 72
Mandeville, Sir John, 32
Marlowe, Christopher, 33, 37, 89, 138, 140, 142, 143, 144, 145, 146, 152, 153-155, 156, 158, 161, 205, 207
The Tragical Historie of Doctor Faustus, 32, 154
Marquez, G. G., 54
Marvell, Andrew, 33, 37, 93, 207
Marx, Carl, 38
Maugham, W. S., 35
McEwan, Ian, 35, 38, 54
Medwall, Henry, 152
Milton, John, 33, 37, 71, 76, 93, 159, 202, 207
Minturno, Antonio, 90
Mirandola, Pico della, 75, 77, 145, 178
Mitchell, Margaret, 38
Monmouth, Geoffrey of, 162
More, Thomas, 75, 77-85, 86, 102, 109, 203
Utopia, 77-85
Morris, William, 34
Munteanu, Romul, 19
Murdoch, Iris, 35, 38

Nashe, Thomas, 32, 100, 108, 137-139, 142, 152, 207
Nicol, Bran, 4, 54, 55
Newton, Isaac, 34

Orwell, George, 35, 79
Osborne, John, 35
Ovid, 95, 149, 173

Pater, Walter, 1, 2, 28, 38, 47, 71
Peele, George, 140, 152, 153, 154, 161
Percy, Thomas, 12
Petrarch, 87, 99, 100, 101, 102, 104, 105, 107, 108, 110, 111, 112, 114, 115, 116, 117, 119, 120, 121, 122, 159, 210
Pindar, 88
Pinter, Harold, 35, 38, 66

Plato, 22, 76, 77, 78, 79, 81, 82, 83, 94, 97, 99, 104, 105, 111, 142
Plautus, 149, 156
Pope, Alexander, 2, 33, 37, 54, 73, 204
Pound, Ezra, 35
Preston, Thomas, 152
Proust, Marcel, 1, 29, 35
Puttenham, George, 97, 98

Quevedo, Francisco de, 125

Rabelais, Francois, 79, 103, 124, 131, 132, 133, 134, 135, 136, 137
Racine, Jean, 87
Radcliffe, Ann, 34
Raleigh, Walter, 100, 102
Reeve, Clara, 34
Richards, I. A., 13, 18
Richardson, Samuel, 33, 37
Ricoeur, Paul, 58
Robortelli, Francesco, 89, 90
Ronsard, Pierre de, 90
Rossetti, D. G., 34
Rushdie, Salman, 35
Ruskin, John, 2, 38, 71

Sackville, Thomas, 152
Safak, Elif, 54
Salisbury, John of, 72, 87
Sanders, Andrew, 31
Saussure, Ferdinand de, 9, 12
Scaliger, J. J., 90
Schlegel, Friedrich, 14, 20
Schleiermacher, Friedrich, 12
Scholes, R., 25
Scott, Walter, 34, 44, 124
Selden, R., 14, 25
Seneca, 83, 87, 88, 97, 141, 143, 144, 152, 153, 204
Shakespeare, William, 1, 32, 33, 37, 39, 41, 54, 64, 71, 77, 79, 87, 89, 99, 101, 116, 117-122, 140, 141, 142, 143, 144, 145, 146, 148, 149, 151, 152, 153, 154, 155, 156-195, 196, 197, 198, 200, 201, 204, 205, 206, 207
A Midsummer Night's Dream, 168-177
Macbeth, 177-187
Richard II, 187-195

Shaw, George Bernard, 35, 38, 89
Shelley, Percy Bysshe, 2, 33, 34, 37, 47, 89
Sheridan, R. B., 89
Shklovsky, V., 1, 41, 42, 45, 46, 47, 50
Sibilet, Thomas, 90
Sidney, Sir Philip, 2, 32, 37, 38, 74, 91-98, 99, 100, 104, 106-108, 109, 110, 123, 142, 143, 204
Sillitoe, Alan, 35
Skelton, John, 99, 100, 102, 103-104, 152
Snow, C. P., 35
Socrates, 78, 82
Southey, Robert, 34
Spark, Muriel, 35, 38
Spenser, Edmund, 32, 37, 72, 77, 88, 99, 101, 104, 108-116, 117, 151, 152
Sterne, Laurence, 33, 37, 64
Stevenson, R. L., 34
Stevenson, William, 152
Stoppard, Tom, 35
Suckling, John, 195
Surrey, Henry Howard, 100, 101, 139, 158
Swift, Graham, 35
Swift, Jonathan, 28, 33, 37, 133
Swinburne, C. A., 34, 38

Taine, H., 1, 20, 34
Tasso, Torquato, 88
Tennyson, Alfred, 34, 38
Terence, 141, 149, 156
Thackeray, W. M., 34, 124
Tynyanov, Yuri, 4, 6, 18, 41, 42, 43, 44, 46, 47, 48, 49, 50, 51, 53, 54

Tzara, T., 35

Udall, Nicholas, 152

Valery, Paul, 35
Vega, Lope de, 87
Vida, M. G., 90, 125, 127
Virgil, 90, 100, 109, 154, 201
Vonnegut, Kurt, 79

Wain, John, 35
Walpole, Horace, 34
Warren, Austen, 14, 18, 52
Warton, Thomas, 12
Waugh, Evelyn, 35
Webbe, William, 98
Wellek, Rene, 14, 18, 52
Wells, H. G., 34
Wieland, C. M., 44
Wilde, Oscar, 2, 14, 34, 38, 89, 163
Williams, W. C., 35
Wilson, Thomas, 90
Wimsatt, W. K., 51
Wither, George, 195
Woolf, Virginia, 2, 13, 28, 35, 38
Wordsworth, William, 2, 28, 33, 37, 41, 46, 47, 159
Wyatt, Thomas, 32, 74, 99, 100, 101, 102, 104, 158, 204, 217

Yeats, W. B., 35, 108

www.ingramcontent.com/pod-product-compliance
Lightning Source LLC
Chambersburg PA
CBHW051050230426
43666CB00012B/2642